JAMMIN' AT THE MARGINS

Krin Gabbard

JAMMIN' at the MARGINS

Jazz
and the
American
Cinema

The University of Chicago Press
Chicago and London

Krin Gabbard is associate professor of comparative literature at the State University of New York, Stony Brook,
and author of *Psychiatry and the Cinema,* published by
the University of Chicago Press.

The University of Chicago Press, Chicago 60637
The University of Chicago Press, Ltd., London
© 1996 by The University of Chicago
All rights reserved. Published 1996
Printed in the United States of America

05 04 03 02 01 00 99 98 97 96   1 2 3 4 5

ISBN: 0-226-27788-7 (cloth)
      0-226-27789-5 (paper)

"Straighten Up and Fly Right," words and music by Nat
King Cole and Irving Mills
© 1944 (Renewed) EMI Mills Music, Inc.
All rights reserved. Used by permission
Warner Bros. Publications U.S., Inc., Miami, FL 33014

Library of Congress Cataloging-in-Publication Data

Gabbard, Krin.
    Jammin' at the margins : jazz and the American cinema   / Krin
Gabbard.
        p.   cm.
    Includes bibliographical references and index.
    1. Motion pictures and music. 2. Jazz—History and criticism.
    3. Musical films—History. I. Title.
    ML2075.G33 1996
    791.43′657—dc20   95-25337
                                             CIP
                                             MN

⊗ The paper in this publication meets the minimum
requirements of the American National Standard for
Information Sciences—Permanence of Paper for Printed
Library Materials, ANSI Z39.48-1984.

For Paula

CONTENTS

First a few things this book is not. It is not a list of all the American films in which jazz musicians have appeared. That work has already been exhaustively undertaken by David Meeker (1981), whose alphabetical, international list of films that feature jazz artists has been invaluable to me throughout this project. Meeker's research has been continued approximately bimonthly in the "Jazz on the Screen" column in the British periodical *Jazz Journal International*. Originally undertaken by Reg Cooper and Liam Keating, the work carries on through the efforts of Peter Vacher. Although Meeker and his colleagues have made my research much easier, they concentrate entirely on films in which canonized jazz musicians appear. They are justified in omitting *Jailhouse Rock*, *The Jolson Story*, and many such films that feature no established jazz artists. I will, however, discuss these films because they are crucial to my interest in the representation of jazz in American movies.

This book is also not an attempt to write a complete history of jazz in the American cinema. I have instead singled out a few issues that I feel ought to be confronted in any serious account of how the movies have dealt with jazz. If a film like *The Benny Goodman Story* seems to pop up repeatedly, the reason is that I am convinced that it speaks to many of the most fundamental obsessions that American culture has brought to jazz. If important jazz films are left out of *Jammin' at the Margins*, it is seldom because I am unaware of them. Even some films with substantial jazz presences do not lend themselves to the types of analysis I have undertaken. I readily admit that another book could be written around entirely different themes, using an entirely different set of films.

At the outset I wish to acknowledge my debt to the extraordinary research undertaken by Klaus Stratemann for his *Ellington Day by Day and Film by Film* (1992) and by Thomas Cripps for *Slow Fade to Black* (1977) and *Making Movies Black* (1993). In addition, much of my thinking about jazz in this book has been influenced by the work of Bernard Gendron, Scott DeVeaux, and Eric Lott. They each have left a substantial mark on my work, but all judgments and misjudgments in these pages are entirely my own.

I have been extremely fortunate that several colleagues and friends have offered commentary on earlier drafts of this book. Louise O. Vasvari, Bob Mirandon, Steven B. Elworth, Michael Jarrett, Ilsa J. Bick, Kevin Whitehead, Robert Eberwein, Loren Schoenberg, Garth Jowett, Malcolm Lynn Baker, and Walter van de Leur all generously devoted time to reading through an entire manuscript and then told me what was wrong and what could be fixed. I hope that my revisions are worthy of their efforts. I was also fortunate to have criticisms and suggestions from William Luhr, Stanley Crouch, Mark Tucker, Lewis Porter, Robert T. Self, Michael Rogin, Ronald M. Radano, Dan Morgenstern, David Hajdu, Gary Carner, Christine Holmlund, Theodore R. Hudson, Tom Harris, Morris Hodara, Jerry Valburn, and James McCalla, all of whom read individual chapters. In addition, I am grateful for advice and encouragement from Kaye Laud, Lynne Mueller, Peter Lehman, Rob Walser, Richard Leskofsky, Elizabeth Weis, Maureen Turim, Eric Smoodin, Shawn Levy, Scott Bukatman, Brooks Kerr, John Edward Hasse, Jack Bradley, Kathleen M. Vernon, Mona Narain, Frederick Garber, Christopher Harlos, John L. Fell, and Paul Wiener. Prof. Sandy Petrey, the chair of the Department of Comparative Literature at the State University of New York at Stony Brook, deserves special thanks for protecting me from departmental duties while I was on sabbatical so that I could write the last half of this book. Valuable assistance also was granted me by Bruce Ricker of Rhapsody Films, Madeline Matz of the Library of Congress, Anne Kuebler and Tom Wiener of the Smithsonian Institution, Charles Silver, Terry Geesken, and Mary Corliss of the Museum of Modern Art, Michael Cogswell of the Louis Armstrong Archive, and Ed Berger and the staff of the Institute for Jazz Studies in Newark, New Jersey. I am especially grateful to T. David Brent and the staff at the University of Chicago Press for their simultaneous professionalism and good humor.

Finally, I thank my wife Paula for staying home with me on all those nights when she could have gone out to the movies as we once did before this book took over my life. I also thank her for making home such a wonderful place to stay.

Whose Jazz, Whose Cinema?

ost jazz films aren't really about jazz. But then, most jazz isn't really about jazz, at least not in terms of how it is actually consumed. Jazz is usually about race, sexuality, and spectacle. Since the 1980s, perhaps even since the 1950s, it has also been about art. The carefully culti-vated atmosphere in nightclubs, the photographs on album covers, the insider patter of jazz disc jockeys, the colored lights that play on musicians in concert halls, the studied aloofness of the performers—what Walter Benjamin (1969) would call the "aura" of jazz—are difficult if not impossible to separate from the music. In fact, it may be more accurate to think about jazz as *inseparable* from its aura and from displays of race, sexuality, and art. But doing so would mean setting aside some forty years of jazz criticism that have characterized the music as an autonomous art form which, like all autonomous art forms, can be pursued outside its historical and cultural moment.[1] I would suggest that the myth of jazz's autonomy has served its purpose and that new myths ought to be pro-posed. The old myths—as well as the new ones—ought to be seen as products of particular cultural moments and ideologies.

This book on jazz and American film is devoted in part to the ways in which large groups of moviegoers actually perceived the music. As jazz and narrative film—two areas in which Americans can claim some

1

unique achievements—grew up together during the twentieth century, a jazz mythology developed to meet the needs of the paying audience. Although much jazz criticism has been devoted to unraveling that mythology and to taking political stances both acknowledged and unacknowledged, the unravelers have created their own myths. As almost everyone knows by now, the classical Hollywood cinema has regularly trivialized the lives of blacks, women, and ethnic minorities, often to the point of caricature. As Roland Barthes (1972) has argued, the film industry is one of the many institutions that create mythology by transforming *history into nature,* by presenting culturally determined situations as the inevitable product of natural law. According to 1950s Hollywood, for example, blacks may play jazz more "naturally," but it is in the "nature" of white musicians to surpass them by learning to play a music that people really want to hear. In this book, my goal is not simply to condemn Hollywood mythology but to examine its transformations more closely in hopes of learning something about jazz, the movies, and the American obsessions to which they answer.

In a sense, I will be writing the "other history" of jazz, the history that jazz criticism has been scrupulously devoted to correcting. I would strenuously agree that correcting this history is an admirable pursuit since it is shot through with bigotry, sexism, cynical manipulation, and popular misconception. This other view of jazz has been created by the movies but also by those novelists, photographers, and journalists who have looked to jazz for Otherness as well as for reassurance that they themselves belong to the healthy, normal Same. As David Meltzer (1993) argues, even those white writers who support jazz have engaged in "permissible racism" by idealizing a black other as spontaneous, transgressive, and ecstatically free of bourgeois restraints. By concentrating on jazz myths and their development, however, a writing of the other history can also reveal a great deal about the dialogic relationship between jazz criticism and popular representations of the music. The other history has even provided a metalanguage for critics who are devoted to writing the more official histories. Thanks to Dorothy Baker's 1938 novel, *Young Man with a Horn,* the esteemed critic Gary Giddins can indicate the depth of his disappointment with a late recording of Miles Davis by writing, "Worst of all, [Davis] recorded a narcissistic sop to the airwaves with a title, 'The Man with a Horn,' that is scarifyingly close to Dorothy Baker's daydreams about trumpet players" (Giddins 1985, 80). Such statements suggest that a critical look at the old daydreams may be in order.

1. Kirk Douglas in a publicity photograph for *Young Man with a Horn* (1950, Warner Bros.). Museum of Modern Art Film Stills Archive.

The Myth of Jazz Purity

The daydreams, after all, often speak to very real needs. (I take up Dorothy Baker's *Young Man with a Horn* and the 1950 film of the same name in chapter 2.) Almost from its beginnings jazz has provoked daydreams and associations. Like all music in the twentieth century, jazz has been heavily dependent on the technologies that make it available to the vast majority of its listeners. Jazz has always been heard primarily through mechanical reproduction, beginning with the national craze set off by the first records of the Original Dixieland Jazz Band in 1917. A condition of the music's existence on record, and later on radio, was the missing bodies of the musicians, who could be dreamed of in forms as romantic as anything in Dorothy Baker's novel. The myth of the music's autonomy is dependent upon forgetting what the technology lacks and also upon overlooking what it actually has. John Corbett has compared the conventional study of music to a massive act of denial: students listening to a work of Beethoven with a record, a turntable, and a set of headphones are asked to understand the music as if the technology staring them in the face did not exist: "This is disavowal, as in the Land of Oz: 'Pay no attention to that man behind the curtain'" (Corbett 1994, 36).

In theorizing the nature of recorded music, Corbett relies upon the feminist/psychoanalytic film theories of Laura Mulvey (1975) to suggest that recorded music allows for an erotic fetishization of sounds as complete and pleasureful within themselves—they lack nothing. The fear of castration, or at least the fear of a gaping absence, is submerged in erotic fascination with an imagined unity, just as when Mulvey theorizes that the male spectator can deny the threat of castration presented by the woman's body by letting her fetishized body stand in for the missing phallus.[2] As with the voyeuristic spectator at the movies gazing at actors who cannot look back (Metz 1982), the listener is in a sense "eavesdropping" on the music playing on the radio or the phonograph. As part of what Corbett calls "fetishistic audophilia," listeners have devised a number of strategies for filling the gap left by the mechanical reproduction of music. One has been the claim of music's autonomy linked to an obsession with technology. The triumph of the compact disc is crucial to this claim: with proper equipment, the listener is promised an experience of the music in all its purity, free from snap, crackle, and pop as well as from the sound of the stylus scraping on vinyl. Appropriately, the CD player conceals the disc during playback in contrast to the old turntables that allowed a full view of the tone arm working its way across the record. The new technology literally disappears.

Corbett also sees a range of visual accompaniments to the music as equally important to "the scramble to negotiate the menacing void" of the recorded performance (38). The album cover has been especially important in bringing back the missing visual elements. Photographers such as William Claxton, William Gottlieb, Herman Leonard, Lee Friedlander, and Francis Wolff have provided stunning images that reintegrate the man and the occasional woman on the cover with the music inside. In an ingenious reading of Claxton's portrait of Sonny Rollins as a cowboy on the cover of the saxophonist's *Way Out West* (1957), Michael

Jarrett suggests that the photographer's metaphors—the tenor sax as six-gun, jazz as a westward movement toward unexplored territory—combine jazz myths with movie myths (Jarrett 1995). Even nonrepresentational cover art anchors the music in a visual language that dovetails with jazz myth. Ornette Coleman gave his music the same problematic cachet as Abstract Expressionism when he included a reproduction of Jackson Pollock's *White Light* on his 1960 LP, *Free Jazz*. For me, much of the disembodied music will always look like Francis Wolff's photographs of outrageously cool black musicians with their cigarettes and dark glasses as they appeared on the many Blue Note albums that I began collecting in the 1960s.

For Corbett, MTV represents a curious play upon the fetishization of pop music. Because most rock videos make no attempt at creating the illusion of a transparent reproduction of an actual performance—instead laying musical tracks over unrelated images or presenting performers who are obviously lip-synching—the viewer is invited to adopt the classic position of the fetishist: "I know (that the sound is coming from a speaker and not the character's mouth), but I don't know (because they belong together)" (Corbett 39). By effectively combining radio with the album cover photo and avoiding any real integration of the two, MTV has kept alive the erotic, fetishistic potential in the disarticulation of sound and image.

The CD won its first great victory with the classical music industry. Consumers of European art music, deeply invested in the notion of music's purity and autonomy, quickly succumbed to the promise of a technology that allegedly produced a transparent rendering of the music. Consumers of rock and pop, who are more overtly involved with the erotics of music, have made the music video industry essential to their experience of the music. If these two groups represent opposite poles along the continuum of how music can be experienced, then jazz today surely has more in common with classical music. In spite of the usual Luddites who will never renounce their LPs (or 78s, or cylinders), and in spite of the recent return of high-quality, twelve-inch vinyl discs for the prestige end of the market (significantly, as reissues of Blue Note records, their covers restored to full size), the compact disc is now the accepted medium for jazz recordings. Jazz videos modeled on the tradition of rock videos are as rare as classical music videos. Cover art for classical music and album photography for jazz may soon merge as the art discourse for jazz gains more currency and as jazz musicians continue to resemble the tuxedoed musicians of the symphony and the recital hall (and as classical musicians allow themselves to be photographed in less ceremonious poses).

Movies about jazz, however, are not videos. Because they are usually designed to render the music complete and whole, they deprive fetishists of the pleasure in the disarticulation of sound and image. Most fetishists would unhesitatingly embrace the photos of Claxton and Wolff over the vast majority of jazz films. So would any self-respecting jazz fan, not all of whom must necessarily be fetishists. For many fans, whatever is gained by the reintegration of sound and image is lost in the subordination of jazz to narrative and the attendant ideologies of the American cinema. As both psychoanalytic and structuralist film theorists have pointed out, musical numbers bring the film's story to an abrupt halt (Mulvey 1975; Altman 1989). Since narrative is indisputably what most audiences crave, then a film about jazz or a film with jazz cannot dwell on the music for too long. The music gets shoved aside to make way for the action, or worse, the music continues, barely audible in the background while the actors talk. Still worse, performances by some of the most revered jazz artists are the least likely to appear on film. For many years black artists were simply left out or confined to short performance scenes that could be excised by nervous exhibitors.

Even when blacks were not entirely excluded, they faced the same reality as all jazz artists. On the one hand, those performers who play to the crowd—"Clap your hands! We love you! You're a beautiful audience!"—seldom win the respect of the true believers, who prefer that performers devote their energies exclusively to the music. The devout fan who insists upon the music's autonomous value can choose to ignore the stage shenanigans of a Louis Armstrong or a Dizzy Gillespie and simply collect their records. The shenanigans might even be tolerated as a sop to the less sophisticated members of the audience, an interlude between the moments of improvisatory art. On the other hand, such interludes are what matter most to filmmakers. Consider Charlie Parker. At least in terms of what is known to exist, Parker was filmed for fewer than ten minutes during his fourteen years as a recording artist. Bebop was almost entirely ignored by Hollywood during Parker's life, so we can scarcely expect to see him popping up in movies. But when Clint Eastwood made *Bird* (1988), the first fiction film explicitly about Parker's life, the key moments were not the performance scenes but the spectacles that surrounded them. The most legendary of the visualizable moments in the Parker legend is the flying cymbal with which Jo Jones allegedly put an end to a young Parker's solo during a Kansas City jam session. In *Bird*, the cymbal flies repeatedly as Parker recalls the humiliation. At the end it becomes an omen of death.

Director Eastwood and writer Joel Oliansky invented an even more striking spectacle when they filmed their version of Parker's extraordinary "Lover Man" recording session of 1946. Gulping wine to stave off the effects of heroin withdrawal, Parker (Forest Whitaker) staggers his way through the tortuously beautiful performance. Told by the engineer that the recording is "very nice," Parker throws his saxophone through the glass of the recording booth. There is nothing in the Parker biographies to suggest that he threw anything during this particular session. *Bird*, however, protects itself against the charge that it has relegated music to spectacle by staging a climactic scene toward the end in which Parker walks in on a performance of Buster Franklin, a fictional alto saxophonist who had mocked the youthful Parker at the legendary Kansas City jam session. In the middle of the film, after Franklin has been driven to despair by hearing the mature Parker at a club date with Dizzy Gillespie, he unceremoniously drops his horn into a river. Now wearing a zebra-striped tuxedo and playing what a member of his entourage calls "rock and roll," Franklin works his rhinestone-encrusted horn into an elaborately choreographed stage show while a large crowd cheers him on. Parker is of course appalled, chastising Franklin for only knowing how to play in B-flat and for never playing "more than one note at a time." But the real charge against Franklin is that he has subordinated his music to mere display. Much the same can be said of *Bird*.

As I argue in chapter 4, display in jazz is much more important than devotees like to admit. Especially for male jazz artists, the music provides a unique opportunity for sex and gender display. Part of what has made jazz so intriguing is the number of alternatives it has offered to conventional notions of masculinity and male sexuality. For me, struggling through adolescence in Middle America with no real interest in sports, jazz offered appealingly unconventional paradigms of masculinity that did not necessarily involve the brute simplicity of high school athletics. I found role models in artists such as Miles Davis, Art Farmer, and Bill Evans, all of whom could express elegance, vulnerability, and romance alongside the more conventional desiderata for young men such as power, technical mastery, and cool strutting. With varying degrees of consciousness, most jazz artists cultivate these qualities in their performance demeanor even if only within purely musical gestures. And, of course, the articulation of maleness and sexuality takes different forms as the age, social class, and historical moments of the artists change. Much the same can be said for the differences in performance practice among female artists, who have experienced even greater changes in sex and gender role-playing over the past several decades.[3] The current ideology of jazz writing tends to repress the artist's display, but this will undoubtedly change as poststructuralist discourses of the body make their way into jazz studies.

Policing Definitions: *The King of Jazz* and *The Jazz Singer*

In writing a book about jazz and film I am excruciatingly aware of the problems raised by the term jazz. Many artists with permanent places in the jazz canon have rejected the term. Duke Ellington, Max Roach, and Anthony Braxton are only three of the most prominent. Before the modern era, jazz probably had a sexual reference, perhaps even evolving from an African word for sexual intercourse (Major 1994, 255). Early in the twentieth century it became associated with a specific music produced primarily by blacks in New Orleans. In the 1920s, after "hot" music had caught on with a national audience, the word came to mean nightlife and good times. The casual racism of the twenties simply repressed the African American component of the music. After all, the first jazz records that caused such a stir in 1917 were recorded entirely by white musicians. In 1926, Henry Osgood could write a book about jazz without mentioning a single black artist. One year later, the film of *The Jazz Singer* at least acknowledged black participation in jazz, but a white man in blackface was still "the jazz singer." The first talkie was not the first film, however, that attracted audiences with the term jazz while neglecting to include black actors and musicians. In his essay in *The New Grove Dictionary of Jazz*, Ernie Smith (1988) lists several movies with titles such as *The Jazz Bandits* (1920) and *Children of Jazz* (1923) in which the only goal of the consistently white characters seems to be "the pursuit of pleasure" (376).

Nevertheless, I am reluctant, on the one hand, to jettison the word jazz or, on the other, to redefine it in the more contemporary fashion that centers canonical geniuses but excludes some black premodernists and many white imitators. I will use the term broadly throughout this study if only to preserve the meanings that jazz has carried for filmmakers and audiences during this century. Jazz is the music that large groups of people have called jazz at particular moments in history. This broader sense of the term also acknowledges the extensive influence that jazz has had throughout cinema history, especially in terms of narrative conventions that were established early on. As I argue in chapter 1, the 1927 *Jazz Singer* was a founding moment for a basic American myth of generational revolt and successful assimilation by second-generation immigrants. The myth was forged in the lopsided interracial romance of the Jazz Age (lopsided because the desire went mostly one way), but it was still alive sixty years later in *La Bamba*, the biopic about the Mexican-American rock star Ritchie Valens who found success with a large Anglo-American audience but never completely abandoned his own culture. In *La Bamba*, Ritchie even has Donna, a wholesome blonde trophy of his crossover success, at the same time that his musical desire takes him in another direction, toward African American male performers.

As the case of *La Bamba* makes clear, rock and roll long ago replaced jazz as the music of circumscribed rebellion and social change. In the 1920s, Bix Beiderbecke scandalized his bourgeois midwestern parents by playing music associated with the brothels of New Orleans. By the 1950s, however, the records of Bix Beiderbecke were unceremoniously trashed by young men in black leather jackets in *Blackboard Jungle* (1955). Although audiences were supposed to feel sympathy for the balding, bespectacled high school teacher (Richard Kiley) whose records were being smashed, the film itself became a recruiting poster for a new urban youth culture. "Rock Around the Clock" had been a minor hit for a little-known band called Bill Haley and the Comets, but when *Blackboard Jungle's* director Richard Brooks chose the tune—perhaps ironically—to play behind the opening credits of his film, the record became a million-copy seller (Doherty 1988, 76). Kiley's character, who preferred Beiderbecke and Stan Kenton, seemed out of touch, stuffy, and elitist. A defiant youth culture built around the rockabilly sounds of Bill Haley was much more attractive for a significant portion of the audience.

Although the early meaning of jazz is forgotten in *La Bamba* and reversed in *Blackboard Jungle*, current notions of the music ought not to obstruct an understanding of how the music functioned during the first decades of the American cinema. As I hope to show in chapter 3, our current sense of jazz as art is less than fifty years old, and even younger in its institutionalized forms such as the new repertory orchestras and the jazz division at Lincoln Center. I believe that these contemporary understandings of jazz ought not to be read into interpretations of cultural artifacts from an earlier moment.

A revealing, though not entirely innocent example of how many Americans once perceived jazz is offered by the 1930 vehicle for Paul

Whiteman, *The King of Jazz*. A more elaborate, more thorough denial of the African American role in jazz is difficult to imagine. Not surprisingly, the repression of blackness leaves its mark all over the film: there are constant allusions to African Americans, and much of the film explicitly evokes minstrelsy, the film's grand predecessor in the ambivalent appropriation of blackness by whites. Directed and "devised" by John Murray Anderson, the film is a gaudy, two-color Technicolor translation to the screen of the kind of Broadway revues staged by impresarios such as George White and Florenz Ziegfeld in the 1920s and 1930s. In embracing the change from stage to cinema, however, *The King of Jazz* makes use of

2. Paul Whiteman and his orchestra in *The King of Jazz* (1930, Universal). Jerry Ohlinger's Movie Material Store, Inc.

all the possibilities of the newer medium, including double exposure, matting, and animation. Early in the film, for example, Whiteman arrives with a portable bandstand about the size of a doll house. He opens a small box and watches while tiny men use a ladder to climb out and assemble on the bandstand.

Perhaps the most memorable scene in *The King of Jazz* takes place immediately after the opening credits. Charles Irwin, the dapper announcer with a British accent, comes forth to tell us how Whiteman was crowned King of Jazz. The ensuing two-minute cartoon, created by Walter Lantz before Woody Woodpecker made him famous, has much of the pop surrealism that also flourished in the cartoons of Max and Dave Fleischer. The animated Whiteman first appears dancing with a musket in what the announcer has called "darkest Africa" even though the mise-en-scène has the colorful look of a comic book (Grant 1989). When he fires his gun at a lion pursuing him, the lion strips off his skin and allows the bullet to play on his ribs like mallets on a xylophone. When Whiteman fires a second round, the lion smiles broadly and the lead bounces along his teeth as if they were piano keys. After the lion has prepared to eat Whiteman by removing his teeth and stropping them on his elongated tongue, the bandleader soothes the savage beast by playing music on his violin. The lion falls to its knees and cries out, "Mammy!" A few caricatured African natives are briefly seen stepping to the music, but Whiteman mostly encounters animals in this cartoon Africa, including a rabbit, a monkey, an elephant, and a snake with a derby hat. Although the sequence begins by suggesting that Whiteman is in Africa to hunt for something, perhaps musical inspiration, the cartoon ultimately portrays Whiteman as bringing music to Africa.

The rest of *The King of Jazz* consists of musical numbers and short blackout sketches without a narrative thread to link them. An early number takes place in a stylized Louis XVI palace in which a white woman with blonde hair and white clothes sings of the joys of marriage. In dead seriousness, she watches as a procession of white women, also in elaborate white gowns and white feathered headdresses, descend a staircase. To extend the references to the court of Marie Antoinette, several children appear with ornate shepherd staffs. The orchestra plays a minuet by Mozart and "Long, Long Ago."

Later, in still another surfeit of whiteness, members of Whiteman's band coax a performance out of the white "prop man," whose name is Jeff White. They call him "Old Black Joe" in spite of his color and his name. As Henry Jenkins (1992b) has written, *The King of Jazz* draws heavily upon a "vaudeville aesthetic" that combines a variety of genres without any narrative thread (132–36). But the Jeff White episode also shows how vaudeville faithfully maintained the traditions of nineteenth-century minstrelsy. The non-narrative flow of musical numbers interrupted with comic sketches and short blackouts is firmly rooted in the minstrel tradition. So is a stage setting in which several musicians sit in a semicircle behind a single performer who delivers a "stump speech" full of images reaching back "to long-prohibited pleasure in nonlogical modes of thinking and speaking" (Lott 1993, 143). Very much the clever fool who was central to minstrelsy, the prop man in *The King of Jazz* narrates a stream-of-consciousness story that includes a boxing match between a tuna and a bass in a fish store. Like the endmen in the semicircle of minstrel performers, members of the band call out derisive remarks and produce vulgar sounds on their instruments.

In a sequence in still another theatrical style, Whiteman's vocal trio, The Rhythm Boys (Bing Crosby, Harry Barris, and Al Rinker), appear as black silhouettes against a bright background. They sing "Happy as a cow, chewing on a cud, when the darkies beat their feet on the Mississippi Mud" before the lights reveal their white faces. One member of the trio protests that the importance of this "super super special special production" demands a loftier song than the one they have been singing. They then perform a song about bluebirds and blackbirds. The exact message of the song is obscure—something about the need for cooperation to produce fair weather—but today, lines such as "The blackbirds said 'We're birds of a different feather,' so the bluebirds and the blackbirds got together" inevitably point to the missing black presence in a film with jazz in its title.

But black people are not completely absent from *The King of Jazz*. African American faces appear twice. About halfway through the film, in a song about lovers in a park, members of the band play their instruments, each dressed in a sailor suit and seated with an affectionate female companion. Whiteman, also in sailor drag, sits in front of the band with his back to the camera. When he turns to face the audience, he has a small, smiling black girl on his lap. He winks at her as she pinches his cheek. Later on, the second black character is indirectly introduced by Whiteman at the beginning of a major production number: "No record of American music would be complete without George Gershwin's *Rhapsody in Blue*, which was written for the Whiteman Orchestra and first played in Aeolian Hall in 1924. The most primitive and the most modern musical elements are combined in this rhapsody, for jazz was born in the

African jungle to the beating of the voodoo drum." After Whiteman has offered this introduction, the camera cuts to a coal-black, muscular body with a "voodoo" headdress dancing on a large drum with an animal hide stretched tightly over it. Reminiscent of the *faux* Africanist dancing of Josephine Baker, the black man's movements are accompanied solely by percussion and serve as the prologue to a spectacular, art-deco, all-white performance of Gershwin's well-known fusion of jazz and symphonic music. These two visions of African Americans in *The King of Jazz* show the degree to which blacks were contained in Hollywood even when they were physically present. The black female is sexualized at the same time she is comfortably infantilized; the black male is stigmatized as primitive and eroticized as all body. Any sexual threat of the black male body is defused by isolating the body on a huge drum, thus rendering it as impotent as a puppet.

But if blacks are present in these two short scenes, they are notably absent from the film's final number. "The Melting Pot of Music" is introduced by an announcer reading aloud the same words that are printed behind him: "America is a melting pot of music wherein the melodies of all nations are fused into one great new rhythm, JAZZ." As a huge, boiling cauldron takes center stage on a set that anticipates the stadium in Leni Riefenstahl's *Triumph of the Will*, large groups in the familiar garb of European nationalities sing and dance to their native music: "Italians" play accordions, "Scotsmen" bagpipes, "Russians" balalaikas; there is an Irish tenor, a Flamenco guitarist, and Frenchmen in Revolutionary garb. After the parade of Europeans, Whiteman stirs the cauldron while circles of colored light magically ascend from the steaming mix. Several images from the preceding processions are then superimposed over a vortex as the camera looks into the pot to see the different musical traditions melt together. At the grand finale, a group of female "Americans" emerge from the cauldron wearing Rough Rider outfits and performing a dance that is inflected with jazz age gestures and the clichés of an Indian war dance. Rows of men in derbies with saxophones sway behind them. Meanwhile, the Whiteman band plays a medley of songs previously featured in the film before breaking into "Stars and Stripes Forever." The "Melting Pot of Music" is especially remarkable in 1930, six years after the Aeolian Hall concert in which Whiteman had presented a similar "history of jazz" that also excluded African Americans. One of Whiteman's admirers wrote that the concert was an "Emancipation Proclamation, in which slavery to European formalism was signed away" (Goldberg 1931, 36). As Michael Rogin (1992b) has observed, Whiteman was also emancipating jazz from black Americans (1065). But if the sin of erasing black people from jazz was ever called to his attention after the 1924 performance, Whiteman clearly was under no pressure to atone for the omission when he made his film in 1930.[4] It should also be pointed out that Jews are not included in the Whiteman melting pot, at least not *as* Jews. In spite of the highly visible role in popular music assumed by performers such as Al Jolson and songwriters such as Irving Berlin, and in spite of the prominent place afforded George Gershwin in *The King of Jazz* itself, the film makes Jews as invisible as blacks.

This refusal to credit African Americans can and should be attributed to simple racism. However, we should accept that jazz held a different meaning for Whiteman's audience in the 1920s than it does for most consumers of the music today. A brief passage in Rogin's essay on *The Jazz Singer* shows the kind of confusion that results when definitions of jazz from different eras are invoked simultaneously. I would first insist that Rogin in "Blackface, White Noise: The Jewish Jazz Singer Finds His Voice" (1992a) Rogin undertakes psychoanalytic, structuralist, and sociocultural analyses that are a model of how a film ought to be read. In fact, when I first began a book on jazz and film some years ago, I had no intention of including a discussion of *The Jazz Singer.* I believed that the film had nothing to do with jazz in spite of its title. Many writers supported this conviction, including David Meeker, whose *Jazz on Film,* with its thorough listing of all films that feature some kind of jazz performance, has gone through two editions without devoting more than a few lines to *The Jazz Singer.* Most jazz writers, if they have treated the film at all, have done so only with contempt. But Rogin's essay convinced me that the film cannot be overlooked (see chapter 1 of this book).

I take issue only with a few brief sections toward the end of Rogin's essay. He writes, "The most obvious fact about *The Jazz Singer,* unmentioned in all the critical commentary, is that it contains no jazz" (Rogin 1992a, 447). Rogin first admits that "the 'jazz' of the jazz age, to be sure, was not the music of King Oliver, Louis Armstrong, Jelly Roll Morton, and Fletcher Henderson." He then criticizes the film for what he has just admitted was the received wisdom of its time: "Jazz may have been the jazz age's name for any up-tempo music, but that no more excuses *The Jazz Singer*'s missing sound than blackface compensates for its absence of blacks" (449). Without rejecting any substantial portion of Rogin's argument about the film, I would submit that he is reading a contemporary conception of jazz back into a text from the 1920s. I would also argue that he has posited a questionable model of a "pure" black jazz separate from what he considers racist imitations of the music by whites.

Rogin's insistence that *The Jazz Singer* ought to have embraced a jazz canon that was constructed more than thirty years later is especially surprising considering his accurate characterization of popular attitudes toward jazz at the time of *The Jazz Singer.* He correctly points out that most Americans in the 1920s associated jazz with Whiteman ("The King of Jazz"), Irving Berlin ("Mr. Jazz Himself"), and Sophie Tucker ("The Queen of Jazz"). Rogin also admits that, "almost without exception, popular culture writing in the 1920s treated Negro primitivism as the raw material out of which whites fashioned jazz. . . . Jazz was identified with freedom as emotional release rather than as technical prowess. Improvisational skill, instead of being recognized in African-American musicians, was overlooked as central to jazz, and attributed to such performers as Jolson instead" (448). The achievement of many African American artists has in fact been the ability to *improvise* new melodies on old ones, often creating solos of great beauty and complexity, even at breakneck speed. But, to return to the canon of black jazz artists that Rogin cites earlier in his article—Armstrong, Oliver, Henderson, and Morton—only Armstrong was known primarily as an improviser. The other three are now recognized for other achievements. Jelly Roll Morton has been called the "first great composer" in jazz (Schuller 1968, 134); Fletcher Henderson is considered "the pioneer of big band arranging" (McCarthy 1968, 128); and King Oliver is credited with perfecting a "musical whole greater than the sum talents of the individual members" (Williams 1983, 10). I take nothing away from these three artists by saying that their most celebrated achievements were other than and in addition to improvisation. I would add that white players such as Beiderbecke, Frankie Trumbauer, Joe Venuti, and Red Nichols were all accomplished improvisers playing a style of jazz in the 1920s that ought to be understood as something other than white theft of black capital. In chapter 2 I discuss Beiderbecke's importance as a jazz improviser who possibly developed his style without the direct influence of black musicians.

Rogin also supports his "no jazz in *The Jazz Singer*" claim by separating *urban* black music from other musical manifestations called jazz. He writes, "African-American jazz was the music of the urban, New Negro, from New Orleans to Chicago to Kansas City, Harlem, and San Francisco. Blackface minstrelsy in the jazz age, by contrast, ventriloquized blacks as rural nostalgia. Domesticating the primitive, in the renderings of Jolson and other songwriters and performers, the plantation supplied the lost-and-longed-for, innocent origins of jazz" (448). First, a long-standing tradition always existed of vocal black blues that was predominantly rural but without which the urban jazz of the New Negro would have been unthinkable: the first jazz instrumentalists were basically playing the blues on trumpets, clarinets, and trombones instead of singing it. These musicians definitely assimilated a great deal of other influences, but the blues, developed outside urban areas, was the single most important element separating early jazz from the white mainstream. More importantly, while Louis Armstrong is the only member of Rogin's pantheon of four who supports the portion of Rogin's jazz paradigm that privileges improvisation, Armstrong also stands as the most striking *refutation* of the portion that privileges the city. Although Armstrong grew up in New Orleans and spent his glory years in Chicago and New York, he also spent a large portion of his career perpetuating the same nostalgia for the mythological plantation that Rogin attributes to Jolson and *The Jazz Singer*. Rather than embracing an urban persona, Armstrong recorded "When It's Sleepy Time Down South" in 1930 and used it as his theme song right up until his death in 1971. He was even filmed singing the song in a 1943 "soundie" wearing the stereotypical garb of a slave. "When It's Sleepy Time Down South" is straight out of the minstrel tradition with "mammies falling on their knees and darkies crooning soft. . . . [I]n general [the song] celebrates the dear old Southland from which blacks were then fleeing by the tens of thousands into the ghettos of the cold cities of the North. . . . [Armstrong] went on singing about the joys of this mythical South for two generations, not even substituting another word for 'darkies' until he was pressed to do so by the civil rights movement years later" (Collier 1983, 245). Armstrong built much of his popularity on songs like "Sleepy Time Down South," "Shine," "Snowball," and "Shoe Shine Boy": he was content to please audiences even if he could be accused of embodying the black stereotypes that populated the minds of many of his white spectators. As I argue in chapter 6, however, Armstrong was a complex, even enigmatic man who was also capable of vehemently denouncing white racism.

If, as Rogin asserts, "*The Jazz Singer* emasculated revolutionary, black modern music," then so did numerous black artists who played the music, including those mentioned by Rogin. Not only Armstrong performed and recorded music associated with minstrelsy: in the 1920s, Fletcher Henderson recorded "Old Black Joe Blues," "Darktown Has a Gay White Way," and "Cotton Picker's Ball," and in 1927, the same year as *The Jazz*

Singer, King Oliver recorded a song called "Aunt Jemima." While this repertoire probably was forced on black entertainers by white impresarios, it is the only body of work through which we can come to know these black entertainers. There is no such thing as a pure, uncorrupted, uncommercialized black music that is somehow knowable without the apparatus of the culture industry. As any good deconstructionist can tell you, the "original" and the "copy" are not so easily distinguished.[5] Nor are the black urban original and the white nostalgic imitation so strictly delineated. What is more easily identified—and what Rogin justly emphasizes in his writings—is the gross power imbalance between black artists and the predominantly white industry that exploited them. An early history of jazz must include some black/white interactions if only because jazz could never have developed without a background of military marches, Tin Pan Alley songs, polite dance music, and other aspects of a predominantly white culture. Although *The Jazz Singer* ought not win praise for eliminating blacks from its presentation of "jazz," the film should not be held responsible for using the term in the same way that most whites would have understood it in the 1920s.

The history of jazz that Rogin implicitly accepts—and that was until the 1990s almost uniformly reified in the jazz histories—was developed primarily by critics such as Martin Williams, Marshall Stearns, and Barry Ulanov, all of whom learned formalist principles of literary criticism in university English departments. These critics applied their lessons to jazz, forging a romantic, Leavisite narrative built around a handful of genius composers and soloists who passed along a great tradition in isolation from cultural forces. In the terms of this idealized history, early jazz gives us Jelly Roll Morton, "the first great composer" and one of the music's "first theorists" (Williams 1983, 46), rather than the "sloppy" music of the legendary but unrecorded Buddy Bolden (Baraka 1963, 145). Or compare the canonizing language lavished on Morton with the account of jazz in turn-of-the-century New Orleans reported in the autobiography of the black bassist Pops Foster: "I only saw Buddy Bolden's band play once at Johnson's Park. That's where the rough people went. I knew all the guys in the band and later on played with them. Buddy played very good for the style of stuff he was doing. He played nothing but blues and all that stink music, and he played it very loud" (Foster 1971, 16).

The Jazz Singer's substitution of Jolson's plantation songs for more authentic jazz would seem to be consistent with the film's substitution of blackface for real African American performers. But what happens in a film when African Americans are in fact present along with whites in blackface? Is the result any less offensive than when blacks are entirely absent as in *The Jazz Singer*? Alongside *The King of Jazz*, I would offer a second test case, *Rhapsody in Blue*, Irving Rapper's 1945 biopic in which Robert Alda plays George Gershwin. An important scene in the film stages a re-creation of a composition that Gershwin wrote for *George White's Scandals* of 1922. Before the piece has been accepted for the show, White tells Gershwin that his blackface number will not be well received by audiences: "Harlem . . . dame shoots a guy . . . that's not for *The Scandals*." Gershwin, however, believes that the number must be a part of the show. Paul Whiteman, playing himself in the film, reluctantly expresses admiration for the number and agrees to conduct the pit orchestra. The film asks us to side with the daring Gershwin for having the courage to put a sequence on stage in which white actors in blackface perform his short operetta *Blue Monday*. The action takes place in a dicty Harlem nightclub populated by strutting, overdressed patrons. At the climax of the story a jealous woman stabs her man after he receives a letter she suspects is from another woman. The letter turns out to be from the man's sister, who has written to say that their mother is dying. As he

3. Whites perform in blackface in the *Blue Monday* sequence from *Rhapsody in Blue* (1945, Warner Bros.). Museum of Modern Art Film Stills Archive.

expires, the wounded man sings, "I'm going to see my mother, mother mine. God, how I miss my mother. . . ." The film first asks the audience to accept the stereotypical view that blacks are violent, uncontrollably passionate, and mother-fixated. But during the climax of the operetta, these images are validated by a reaction shot of two *real* African Americans. One appears to be an usher, the other a maid, both of them presumably at the back of the theater—the camera does not establish their precise whereabouts. What is clear is that the black man is spellbound and the woman is quietly shedding tears. Earlier the camera had cut to the well-dressed white audience responding uncomfortably to the display of passion in a Harlem nightclub. The shot of the black couple asserts that the operetta is an accurate representation of their lives, something that the affluent white patrons cannot understand. As Rogin has argued, *The Jazz Singer* capitalizes on "the surplus symbolic value of blacks" (417); this scene from *Rhapsody in Blue* doubly exploits African Americans, first as represented in blackface and then, allegedly, as the real thing.

The *Jazz Singer* is not unique in using the highly problematic term "jazz" to describe the songs of a white man in blackface at a time when, rightly or wrongly, most Americans understood jazz in this way. One does not have to look far, however, to find much more egregious exploitations of blacks in Hollywood's long history of making African Americans stand for, as Rogin puts it, "something other than themselves."

Policing Boundaries: The Forgotten Career of Kay Kyser

Popular understanding of jazz among whites began to allow for a greater black presence in the 1930s. Artie Shaw, John Hammond, and Benny Goodman deserve credit for their mixed bands of that decade. Their first steps in this direction, however, were tentative: Hammond saw to it that Billie Holiday did not appear in public with the white musicians with whom she recorded in the mid-thirties; when Goodman first brought Teddy Wilson and later Lionel Hampton on stage, he and Gene Krupa performed with them while his all-white orchestra was off stage; and a year passed after Goodman's first recordings with blacks before he would perform with them in public. Still, by the mid-thirties, few Americans enjoyed a popular music that was lily white. The popularity of Ellington, Lunceford, Calloway, and other black bands made whites even less likely to deny the centrality of black artists during a decade when the type of jazz known as swing was becoming the dominant popular music of the United States. Even if everyone was not aware that Benny Goodman's hugely popular band was playing the arrangements of Fletcher Henderson after 1935, they surely knew that many black bands played in styles similar to Goodman's. And many white Americans knew that the more exciting dance styles were derived from black vernacular dance, even if most whites also regarded the more extreme acrobatics of the jitterbugs as vulgar or silly. Goodman, Henderson, Ellington, Glenn Miller, Harry James and the rest were all considered to be jazz, then as now. But is "jazz" as a category today still capacious enough to include the various white bands that played "swing" in styles not so obviously derived from black arrangers and composers? Many Americans certainly thought so at the time, even if the official view today has shifted considerably. The question is especially crucial to a study of jazz and film. Although black jazz artists did find their way onto film throughout the 1930s and 1940s, Americans at the movies were much more likely to see white musicians holding the saxophones and drumsticks and snapping their fingers with hip insouciance. The career of Kay Kyser presents an opportunity for testing the limits of what belongs in a book on jazz and film. He also provides an ideal focus for an inquiry into how the large cinema audience actually experienced the music of the swing era.

Kyser, who had worked with a small jazz group as a student at the University of North Carolina, took a larger band on the road when he graduated in 1928. After struggling for several years, the band achieved its first success at the Blackhawk Restaurant in Chicago, where it had the good fortune to be hooked into a radio network. Seizing the opportunity, Kyser tried a number of gimmicks, including an attempt to appeal to the college crowd by reading football scores between musical numbers.[6] Success finally came with Kyser's idea of staging a quiz show about music, often with questions sent in by listeners whose names Kyser was careful to read on the air. Kyser struck it rich when his program was picked up in 1938 by the NBC radio network. His "Kollege of Musical Knowledge" became required listening in millions of American households, and he was soon the biggest box office draw in the country, receiving larger fees than any other band. By no means a musician himself, Kyser built his success upon clowning on stage and a savvy business sense off stage. Reading names of listeners on his radio program encouraged people to tune in hoping to hear their own on the air. A seemingly simple idea that vastly elevated the popularity of his band was the "singing song titles": as each number began, a vocalist would sing the title of the tune even if there was no other vocal work involved. Audiences loved it. Kyser also capitalized on his drawling accent and his country boy manner. His patter would always begin with a phrase such as "Evenin' folks. How y'all?" and he would often introduce a number with "So come on, chillun, le's dance!"

In the early 1940s, Kyser was one of the two or three most popular bandleaders in America in both record sales and popularity polls, often outdrawing Glenn Miller and Tommy Dorsey, not to mention the black bands. According to Grover Sales, in the late 1930s Kyser was outgrossing Ellington "better than six to one" (1984, 44). Merwyn Bogue, the dour, trumpet-playing comedian with bangs who as "Ish Kabibble" was a mainstay of Kyser's band for most of its life, attests to Kyser's popularity:

> From 1938 through 1941, *Billboard* magazine conducted annual polls among college students who selected their favorite bands and their band singers. In 1938 the first five bands chosen were those of Benny Goodman, Tommy Dorsey, Hal Kemp, Guy Lombardo, and Kay Kyser. In 1939 the first two were Artie Shaw's and Kay Kyser's. In 1940 the first two were Glenn Miller's and Kay Kyser's. In 1941 the first three bands were those of Glenn Miller, Tommy Dorsey, and Kay Kyser, and Ginny Simms of the Kay Kyser Band was voted top female vocalist. (Bogue 1991, 47)

Bogue's catalog ends in 1941, but Kyser's best years may have been yet to come. According to a chart in a September 1942 issue of *Down Beat*, three of Kyser's records ranked among the ten most often played in the country, holding first, second, and seventh places ("Your Automatic" 1942, 9). In 1943, at a dance at the civic auditorium in Oakland, California, Kyser drew the largest paid attendance ever by a band on a one-night stand; with a crowd of more than 20,000, he broke the previous record of 18,000, which also was set by his band ("Kyser Draws" 1943, 1). From 1939 through 1944, Kyser starred in seven feature films: *That's Right, You're Wrong* (1939), *You'll Find Out* (1940), *Playmates* (1941), *My Favorite Spy* (1942), *Swing Fever* (1943), *Around the World* (1943), and *Carolina Blues* (1944). He was also given prominent exposure in *Stage Door Canteen* (1943) and *Thousands Cheer* (1943). No other bandleader of the swing era could boast so substantial a filmography, at least in terms of the amount of time spent on screen. Although many of his most popular records were puerile novelty items such as "Three Little Fishies" ("And they thwam and thwam all over the dam"), his other hits included more durable songs such as "Slow Boat to China," "Indian Summer," and "Ole Buttermilk Sky."

And yet Kyser today is almost entirely forgotten and virtually unknown to anyone born after 1945. All that has kept his memory alive in recent years is the cable television service American Movie Classics which occasionally broadcasts his films.[7] There is no mention of Kyser, for example, in the standard reference work, *The New Grove Dictionary of Jazz* (Kernfeld 1988). In *Jazz in the Movies* (1981), David Meeker mentions only two of Kyser's films, in both cases because musicians such as Harry James and Marie Bryant make small appearances; no listing for Kyser appears in Meeker's index. Leonard Maltin, the best-known cataloguer of movies on television, who has even specialized in jazz on film (Maltin 1976, 382–86), does not list all of Kyser's films in his *Movie and Video Guide* (Maltin 1994). Jazz discographer Brian Rust cites only six records from 1929 in his listing for Kyser, explaining in a note, "Kay Kyser is best remembered today as an exuberant comedian parodying a schoolmaster or a college professor, but his first records are quite interesting as 'hot' dance items. His many subsequent Brunswicks and Columbias of the late 1930s are not of any interest as far as is known" (Rust 1978, 913). By the 1980s so little was known about Kyser that his short biography in *The New Grove Dictionary of American Music* (Sadie and Hitchcock 1986) and his brief obituary in the *New York Times* (July 24, 1985) both contained errors in dates and figures. In an otherwise scrupulously researched history of the swing era, David Stowe (1994) confuses Kyser with the obscure comedian Pinky Tomlin, incorrectly identifying Kyser as the star of the 1937 film *Swing It Professor* (134). Although all of Kyser's films can be considered musicals, there is no reference to any of them in the most important studies of the genre such as Altman (1989) and Feuer (1993). And in spite of Kyser's several million-selling records, as of this writing only two CDs of his music are in print. In Tower Records in New York City they are found not in the section on "Jazz" but in "Easy Listening."

But then, perhaps Kyser did not play jazz. Although he programmed a good many novelties and encouraged foolishness (such as the poetry of Ish Kabibble), Kyser's bands definitely played swing and hot dance music. When performing many of the charts of principal arranger George Duning, the Kyser band could swing just as hard as the orchestras of Glenn Miller and the Dorseys, who were just as likely, by the way, to program infantile vocal numbers. Of course, even the black bands were not above pleasing crowds with cute vocals—Ella Fitzgerald became a star singing "A-Tisket, A-Tasket" and "Coochi-Coochi-Coo" with Chick Webb, and Fletcher Henderson recorded with Baby Rose Marie. Purely in terms of the music it played, the Kyser orchestra has just as much right to be called a jazz band as do any of the bands of Glenn Miller, Artie Shaw, and the Dorseys, all of them categorized by discographers and record companies as jazz.[8]

The appearance of Kyser and several other popular orchestras in *Stage Door Canteen* (1943) provides revealing glimpses of the jazz bands of the period alongside what were called the "sweet" bands by their supporters and "Mickey Mouse" bands by their detractors. Embellishing a story about servicemen romancing hostesses in the famous New York club for men in uniform, *Stage Door Canteen* features a long list of popular entertainers including the bands of Count Basie, Xavier Cugat, Benny Goodman, Guy Lombardo, Freddie Martin, and Kyser. Basie and his orchestra are relatively restrained, primarily providing backup for a vocal by Ethel Waters. The Goodman band is presented to the best advantage as a young Peggy Lee sings "Why Don't You Do Right" before the band launches into Fletcher Henderson's arrangement of "Bugle Call Rag." Cugat, Lombardo, and Martin are in a different category altogether, playing with simple, almost mechanical rhythm and featuring lackluster vocalists. When Kyser performs, it is difficult to place him solidly in any of these camps. His rhythm section and soloists, especially tenor saxophonist Herbie Haymer, suggest that Kyser's band has more in common with Basie and Goodman than with Lombardo et al. But unlike Kyser, Goodman and Basie do not speak, dance, or make faces during their performances. Goodman is the model of the cool white hipster, nodding his head to the music and injecting carefully nuanced body language into his clarinet solos. Thanks at least in part to the sultriness of Peggy Lee, the scene with Goodman maintains a sexual tension completely lacking in Kyser's performance, even though Kyser does in fact interact with his female vocalists, lifting his trousers and dancing with mock suggestiveness. Totally without any quality we might call hip or cool, Kyser does not *act* like a jazz musician. Still, *Stage Door Canteen* brings some white jitterbugs onto the bandstand with Kyser, granting his performance a vision of "hot" that is not afforded the bands of Lombardo, Cugat, and Martin.

If there is today a consensus that Kay Kyser did not play jazz, then we have witnessed the triumph of an art discourse for the music. I will take up this issue in some detail in chapter 3, "Jazz Becomes Art." For now, I quote Gunther Schuller (1989), a prominent exponent of an aesthetic that places jazz in an elite sphere above the heads of what he calls "the great unwashed public" (199).

> Much of what was called jazz was, by some stricter definition of that term, merely "dance music" or "popular music". . . . But in looking back to the jazz of the thirties, especially in terms of critically assessing its *artistic* achievements, we must make just such distinctions. For when the "swing" styles reigned supreme, it was the swing music of Goodman, Miller, and Shaw, not Ellington and Lunceford, that became the popular music of the land. Perhaps even truer, it was the safer, more commercial dance bands— the Kay Kaysers [sic], Orrin Tuckers, Wayne Kings, and Sammy Kayes— that were the *real* beneficiaries of the swing craze. In a more critical time and with a more discerning audience, these countless mediocre dance bands would not have flourished, certainly not in such numbers. They plagiarized and trivialized the musical innovations and styles of the leading black musicians, reducing the content to a banal, lowest common-denominator of accessibility. (Schuller 1989, 199)

Although he seems uninterested in dissecting the "culture industry," Schuller has much in common with the theorists of the Frankfurt School of cultural critics who saw a large, benighted audience being denied the real thing by philistines. The audience swallows whole the "accessible" product and is impoverished by the lack of an art that is more challenging. But the tendency of Schuller and the Frankfurters to portray the mass audience as homogeneous should be considered alongside Raymond Williams's remark that there are no "masses," "only ways of seeing [other] people as masses" (1983, 300). Schuller does not consider the needs of audiences and how they actually consumed the music that was marketed to them: some learned the names of the soloists on each record; some built elaborate fantasy worlds around the lyrics; others just danced to it. The burgeoning new discipline of cultural studies has demonstrated that audiences are capable of resisting and even transforming what the culture industry offers them.[9]

Schuller implies that, in some utopian space, audiences will derive real benefits when they experience the music of Ellington and Lunceford. The fact that Ellington and Lunceford eagerly sought a mass audience or that their music is unimaginable outside the music industry does not prevent Schuller from ascribing to them a purity that seems to result as much from their "folk" origins as it does from their supposed existence outside the marketplace. Gary Tomlinson, in defending Miles Davis's electrified and popular post-1969 recordings against critics who claimed that he had ceased to play jazz, has called this position "elitism pure and simple" and "a snobbish distortion of history by jazz purists attempting to insulate their cherished classics from the messy marketplace" (Tomlinson 1991, 252). Those who embrace this view should instead "read recent nonhagiographical music histories that have Beethoven hawking the same opus to three different publishers, or Mozart conniving, with a sad lack of savvy, at one music-business killing or another. Music created with an eye to eternal genius and blind to the marketplace is a myth of European romanticism sustained by its chief offspring, modernism" (Tomlinson 1991, 253).

Schuller does not, however, maintain his contempt for Kyser throughout *The Swing Era*. After dismissing him in the earlier passage, he returns to the bandleader in a footnote much later in the book:

> Kyser, although he played no instrument, always maintained a fine orchestra, playing essentially in the late-thirties' Glenn Miller style, featuring good musicians and a stable of good pop and novelty singers, most of whom were superior technically to many of the more highly touted dance-band vocalists. The Kyser band had a remarkable blend and balance and could, when required, play with an infectious rhythmic swing, especially with the long-time Glenn Miller drummer, Maurice Purtill, driving it.[10] (Schuller 1989, 661)

Sometimes this clash between a crowd-pleasing novelty orchestra and a competent swing band was apparent in a single number. For example, in Kyser's 1945 recording of "Bell Bottom Trousers," a series of comic vocals, including a barbershop quartet and an imitation of the cartoon character Popeye, is punctuated by several tenor saxophone solos by Herbie Haymer that recall some of the better up-tempo playing of Lester Young and Bud Freeman.

Indeed, the World War II Kyser band bares little resemblance to Kyser's sweet bands of the late thirties and early forties. As was widely reported in 1942, the band lost its entire library of arrangements in a garage fire. George Duning quickly wrote an entire new book and essentially transformed the band's style. Many of the more maudlin items and "sweet" numbers that had been lost were never replaced. The post-1942 band traveled with as many as eight singers who performed their share of novelties, but it also specialized in up-tempo tunes with more solo space for improvisers such as Haymer, trumpeter Bobby Guy, and guitarist Buford Turner. The band that clowns its way through Kyser's early RKO films bears little resemblance to the tight ensembles on display in *Carolina Blues*, *Stage Door Canteen*, and *Thousands Cheer* just a few years later.

The development of Kyser's band through nine films and five years provides a vivid portrait of popular music during the final years of the swing era. If Schuller is correct that the dance music of this period was called jazz by most Americans, then Kyser's films extensively document the dominant view of jazz in the late thirties and early forties, just as *The Jazz Singer* represents what was widely considered jazz in the 1920s. As is always the case with Hollywood films, however, representations are highly selective, repressing and imperfectly reflecting much of what they represent. And as always, Hollywood functions as an "ideological state apparatus," presenting Americans with an image of how they imagine themselves in relation to their culture (Althusser 1977).[11] Most obviously, Kyser reflected the ideology of a music industry controlled almost exclusively by whites.

The narratives in Kay Kyser's films complement his music and the persona he projected in his radio broadcasts and personal appearances. If the jazz content of Kyser's recordings has been underestimated, a survey of his films offers ample material to explain his exile from jazz and film canons. In short, Kyser cleaned up swing music and made it acceptable to a large, Middle American, white audience. This process continued unabated in his films, some of which simply superimpose Kyser and his aggregation on the most familiar Hollywood plots. *You'll Find Out* (1940), for example, is a haunted house melodrama complete with secret passages, disembodied voices, and elaborately staged seances. The film even finds prominent roles for Boris Karloff, Bela Lugosi, and Peter Lorre. Kyser and the featured members of his band, such as Ish Kabibble, Sully Mason, Ginny Simms, and Harry Babbitt, take turns being puzzled and frightened by supposedly supernatural events before Kyser himself stumbles into the underground chamber where the villains have staged their ghost shows in an attempt to bilk a wealthy matron. In *My Favorite Spy* (1942), Kyser is called upon by government agents to infiltrate an espionage ring working in a nightclub. Although Kyser, as always playing himself, is at first a reluctant and incompetent spy, he singlehandedly captures every member of the Nazi spy ring at the end. Both films still find time for the band to play its benign music.

If, by the 1930s, swing and popularized jazz had acquired a "mulatto" quality in the minds of many whites (Roberts 1995), Kyser was reassuringly free of any trace of Otherness. He was not only a southerner; he was a blond, college-educated Anglo-American, exactly the right character to unmask the swarthy, thickly accented villains in *You'll Find Out* and *My Favorite Spy*. As a leader of a swing band, Kyser was not in any way ethnic or urban like Benny Goodman, Artie Shaw, or Gene Krupa, nor was he inscrutable and distant like Glenn Miller or Tommy Dorsey. Kyser was so removed from ethnic America that he passed through a large part of his youth bearing the nickname "Kike" before he was told what the word meant. As a bandleader and performer, he worked hard at playing the benevolent paterfamilias, establishing a reputation for fidelity to his musicians, many of whom stayed in his band much longer than was the custom for swing era musicians. He also put a wholesome face on the music, seeing to it that his musicians were "gentlemen." According to Merwyn Bogue, Kyser once said, "I'd rather hire a gentleman and make a musician out of him than hire a musician and try to make a gentleman out of him" (Bogue 1989, 35–36). If band members received any publicity, it was usually of the kind that Sully Mason acquired when he announced that he was marrying for the *twelfth* time—to the same woman. According to a story in *Down Beat,* Mason and his wife went through a marriage ceremony every year on their wedding anniversary "just for kicks" ("Sully Mason" 1942, 19).

There can be no doubt that many white Americans embraced swing because it contained elements associated with African American spontaneity, transgressiveness, and, most importantly, sexuality. These elements were clearly implied even when the music was played by an entirely white big band. A good example is the performance of the Goodman band in *Stage Door Canteen:* Peggy Lee appropriates vocal and performance styles from Billie Holiday; Benny Goodman plays the clarinet in a style associated with Jimmy Noone; and the band performs a hot arrangement by Fletcher Henderson. Together they bring a titillating quality to the music that helps explain why the band suddenly became so popular in 1935. Lewis A. Erenberg (1989) has written,

> When whites first encountered jazz in the 1920s, it had a dangerous as well as liberating aura, for the new music that first emerged in black urban areas in the early twentieth century had an enormous vitality and spontaneity. Segregated from white society, blacks had created their own expressiveness in the area that was less policed—their music and dance. Jazz bore the free, improvisatory energy of this one realm of freedom and expressed the body as a natural and divine feature of human existence. (223)

Although the white swing of the 1930s made black music seem less "dangerous," the African American underpinnings of swing may still have made a large portion of the white audience uncomfortable (Leonard 1962). It was for this group that Kyser probably had the greatest appeal. While Goodman, Dorsey, Krupa, and Shaw had all featured black soloists or arrangers by 1941, Kyser's band remained entirely white until it was disbanded in 1950. Blacks did, however, appear in Kyser's films, beginning with a feature for Lena Horne in *Swing Fever* (1943). In *Carolina*

Blues (1944), Kyser played catch-up with Glenn Miller, whose band had accompanied the extraordinary dancing of the Nicholas Brothers in both *Sun Valley Serenade* (1941) and *Orchestra Wives* (1942). By 1944, however, Fayard Nicholas had been drafted, so Kyser was only able to employ Harold Nicholas in a highly stereotypical Harlem number in *Carolina Blues*. But there were many ways in which Kyser kept the music white even when his band had mastered the jazz-inflected swing styles of the period. In the band's performance of "I Dug a Ditch" in *Thousands Cheer,* there are several short but pungent jazz solos by instrumentalists. When drummer Ormond Downes takes a Krupaesque drum solo, Kyser tries to stop him by tapping him on the shoulder. As jazz mythology demands, however, the White Negro drummer is too involved to notice. When he finally comes to his senses, Kyser stares at him reprovingly. The scene reveals a Kyser who could have it both ways: his band could swing, but certain implications of the sound were in conflict with his conservative nature. He visibly discourages those aspects of swing era performance that hinted at darkness.

To further defuse the mulatto connotations of swing, Kyser's persona carried little if any sexual menace. While Artie Shaw and Harry James were marrying movie stars, and Benny Goodman was seen escorting his female singers, Kyser only seemed interested in making funny faces at Ginny Simms, Julie Conway, and the rest. His male sexuality was further undermined by the medley of effeminate gestures in his stage routines and by the constant jokes about his first name: at the beginning of *My Favorite Spy,* for example, he is repeatedly confused with Kay Francis. Later in the film, after he marries a character played by Ellen Drew, his obligation to government counterespionage agents repeatedly prevents the consummation of their marriage.

There were rumors that Kyser was interested in marrying Ginny Simms, and he did in fact marry Georgia Carroll a few years after she had replaced Simms as the band's principal girl singer. In some cases, the films directly addressed Kyser's romantic relationships with his female vocalists, even though he was scarcely cast as the sexual aggressor. In *Playmates* (1941) he becomes jealous at the attention paid to Simms by John Barrymore (in his last film role, playing a broadly parodic version of himself). Kyser awkwardly expresses hurt when Simms herself tells him, "You're not the romantic type. Not everyone can have glamour." Later, at Barrymore's urging, Kyser is brazenly pursued by a sexual volcano played by Lupe Velez, a "beast of the Tropics" unleashed by the Good Neighbor Policy (López 1991, 412). At first terrified by Velez,

Kyser soon comes under her domination, in one scene following her tiny chihuahua on a leash. In *Carolina Blues,* after Georgia Carroll supposedly leaves the band to marry a lieutenant, she chides Kyser about being afraid of falling love with a singer played by Ann Miller, who is about to become the band's new vocalist. This last film in the Kyser canon ends with the hero and Miller kissing for the first time.

In his earlier films, however, Kyser was usually portrayed as the asexual head of a large family, his band. In his first film, *That's Right, You're Wrong,* the band is invited to Hollywood to make a movie. Playing the film's reluctant producer, Adolphe Menjou decides to sabotage the project by provoking Kyser to quit the picture. At first Menjou tells Kyser that he will replace Ginny Simms with a starlet played by Lucille Ball. He later announces that he will also replace Ish Kabibble, Harry Babbitt, and Sully Mason. Early in the film Kyser says that he is agreeing to make the trip to Hollywood only because the members of the band want to be in movies. Like all good fathers, he puts aside his own desires in the interest of the children. But as a wise patriarch, he sees trouble brewing when the band members begin to succumb to the more extreme aspects of the Hollywood life style. Once the film within the film begins to take shape as a solo vehicle for himself, Kyser seizes the opportunity to sabotage the project on his own. Anticipating generations of sitcom fathers to come, he pretends to "go Hollywood," affecting even more airs than anyone else in the band and demonstrating their folly to them for their own good. The picture never gets made, and in the final scenes, the band is back doing the radio program so beloved by Middle Americans.

During World War II, Kyser worked tirelessly at entertaining American troops. As early as *Playmates,* filmed a few months before the attack on Pearl Harbor, Kyser had already wrapped himself with the flag, staging a production number, "You Can Thank Your Lucky Stars and Stripes," that celebrated America amid militaristic trappings. At the climax of the number, members of the band march past the camera, each one shouting out some item of Americana worth celebrating: "Hot dogs / The county fair / Jeanie / With the light brown hair / The fox trot." Kyser sings, "And what's more, the grand old flag." The entire band joins in with "If you think it's worth your while to save it / wave it." Then at march tempo: "If you can sing / and believe in anything / you can thank your lucky stars and stripes."

By 1942, Kyser had canceled all his bookings and was performing exclusively at military bases, once visiting twenty-nine over a period of three weeks. On the one hand, his sincerity during this phase of his ca-

4. Is this the face of a movie star? Kay Kyser with Lupe Velez in *Playmates* (1941, RKO). Museum of Modern Art Film Stills Archive.

reer cannot be questioned if only because he accepted a huge drop in income and paid his band out of his own savings. On the other hand, he undoubtedly knew that this kind of exposure could help his record sales, which did in fact peak in 1942. Kyser was briefly embarrassed in 1943 when *Newsweek* reported that he had asked the Office of War Information to set aside his 1-A draft classification. The OWI ultimately exempted him from the draft, arguing that he was already doing more than enough for the war effort as a private citizen ("Kyser's Komplaint" 1943, 83). Nevertheless, Kyser's next two starring roles were his most explicitly patriotic. *Around the World* (1943) chronicles the band's travels as it entertains Allied troops in exotic locales. Although the tone is excessively facetious throughout most of the film, it becomes deadly serious at the end when Marcy, a lovable teenage girl traveling with the band, learns that her father has died in action. Recovering from her grief in the next

5. Is this a jazz orchestra? Kay Kyser and his band with Ish Kabbible in *Around the World* (1943, RKO). Museum of Modern Art Film Stills Archive.

and final scene, Marcy sings exhortations to victory with the band and two choirs of men in uniform. The plot of *Carolina Blues* (1944) involves Kyser's multiple attempts to deceive the members of his band into giving up their vacation time so that they can sell enough war bonds to build a battleship in Kyser's hometown of Rocky Mount, North Carolina.

His sincerity notwithstanding, there is no denying that the jingoism of Kyser's films has not aged well. Neither has his unironic homespun persona, the effete stage mannerisms, and the blandness of most of the music he played throughout his career. It is not surprising that, with the possible exception of American Movie Classics, none of the apparatuses of nostalgic fetishization, journalistic canonization, or academic categorization has been mobilized to revive his films. Kyser's popularity came too early to be part of baby boom culture, almost every aspect of which is now kept alive by some institution. Because of his blandness, whiteness, and asexuality, Kyser does not accommodate many of the principles of race-, sex-, and gender-based criticism developed since the 1970s for Hollywood in general and for the musical in particular. Nothing in his career is so transgressive as to recall the Three Stooges or Spike Jones, all of whom can be recuperated through the aesthetics of Bakhtin and/or Dr. Demento. And as a nonmusician who regularly deflected attention away from the music and onto spectacles of himself, Kyser destroyed any appeal his band might have held for jazz purists and canon-builders.

I have dwelled on Kay Kyser to demonstrate the powerful effect that a narrow definition of jazz has had on the writing of the music's earlier history. Similarly, the specific concerns of critics in the 1980s and 1990s—many of which I share—have determined what gets left out of cinema histories for the 1930s and 1940s. I would argue that Kyser belongs in both jazz and cinema histories, if only to illustrate the limiting effects of canonizing discourses. But rest assured, dear reader, musicians who have won places of honor in the canon are the subject of forthcoming chapters. In the second half of this book I devote a chapter each to the celebrated careers of Duke Ellington and Louis Armstrong.

As should be clear by now, race, gender, sexuality, and the discourses of art are central concerns of this study. Because Americans have always been fascinated with these issues in one form or another, filmmakers learned early on that jazz can be an ideal arena for exploring these obsessions. In the *Jazz Singer* films (chapter 1), these issues dominate an important tradition in the American cinema that can also be traced into the various jazz biopics (chapter 2), including those that are essentially remakes of *The Jazz Singer*. Accordingly, I devote large sections to the development of an art discourse for jazz (chapter 3) and to the articulation of male sexuality with that most phallic of instruments, the jazz trumpet (chapter 4). These early chapters cover some of the same territory, but each chapter adopts a different approach and moves successively closer to the present. In addition to writing the "other history" of jazz, I have also tried to construct at least the foundations for a psychoanalytic reading of the music. My methodology, however, has been eclectic, based where needed on a fluid model of psychoanalysis that can accommodate politics, ideology, and cultural history. This should be most apparent in chapter 4 when I look at the importance of masculine expression for jazz as well as for those who would represent the music.

Although the first half of the book is devoted to reading specific films within their historical and ideological moments, my goal in the sections on Ellington and Armstrong (chapters 5 and 6) has been to broaden an understanding of these two artists by chronicling their interactions with Hollywood. Both men were regularly marginalized by Hollywood, but in a few revealing moments they were able to "signify" on the movies or in some way to destabilize the carefully constructed products of the film industry. I have dealt with the shorter careers of Nat King Cole and Hoagy Carmichael (chapter 7) for different reasons. Rare among jazz musicians for actually pursuing a career in films, both managed to be known as something other than jazz artists. Although neither could overcome a certain stigmatization attributable to their careers in jazz, both had rare moments when they rose above their material in some of the same ways as Ellington and Armstrong. Still, the treatment they received at the hands of the film industry in the 1940s and 1950s reveals once again the crucial importance of race and gender expression in Hollywood, especially in the industry's depictions of musicians.

In the conclusion I am primarily concerned with the state of jazz after 1970, when the music no longer played an important role in American cinema. Martin Scorsese's *New York, New York* (1977) is an anomalous product of the American film industry—a large-budget musical that also tries to be an art film. Scorsese is sensitive to the paradoxes inherent in this project, and for this reason he may have chosen jazz as the central metaphor in a film that walks a fine line between art and commerce at a moment when American films were about to become much less challenging (*New York, New York* opened at roughly the same time as *Star Wars*). Robert Altman's *Short Cuts* (1993) may be just as ambitious as *New York, New York,* but it may also be more sophisticated in its handling of jazz. *Short Cuts* features the voice of jazz singer Annie Ross throughout the film, while Ross herself plays one of twenty-two major characters whose stories are obliquely related, if at all. The soundtrack music by Ross and her backup group, however, is a crucial element in the film's strategies for making the stories cohere. Although *New York, New York* is very much about jazz, it is also about why jazz lost its audience. *Short Cuts* is not explicitly about jazz, but it shows why jazz can still be highly evocative, perhaps because the music today has a small, devoted audience or perhaps even because it is in the process of building a new one. Together, these two films present an appropriate contrast for concluding this study.

ONE

The Ethnic Oedipus

The Jazz Singer *and Its Remakes*

Apart from its initial popularity, *The Jazz Singer* (1927) ought to have held little appeal for remakers: the novelty of introducing talking and singing to a mass audience must have worn off rather quickly; changing racial attitudes ought to have made a narrative involving blackface obsolete if not off limits; the title's reference to jazz should have discouraged studio bosses once jazz ceased to be a popular music in the 1950s; as J. Hoberman (1991a) has argued, the emergence of the state of Israel in 1948 drastically altered the issues of Jewish assimilation that are crucial to the film's plot; and the personality of Al Jolson weighs so heavily on the 1927 film that any re-creation would seem to be impossible without him. Finally, in the article that inspired this chapter, Michael Rogin (1992a) has shown that the original film dramatized several subjects that Hollywood abandoned after the 1920s, most notably the rags-to-riches ascent of American Jews who broke out of the ghetto, some of whom "invented Hollywood" (Gabler 1988).

Yet filmmakers repeatedly return to *The Jazz Singer.* Warner Bros. celebrated the twenty-fifth anniversary of the film's release with a 1953 remake directed by Michael Curtiz and starring Danny Thomas; playing a dramatic role for the first time in his career, Jerry Lewis appeared in a Ford *Startime* production directed by Ralph Nelson for NBC television in 1959; and Neil Diamond played the title role in a 1980 film directed by Richard Fleischer. Several other films also seem to have much in common with the first *The Jazz Singer,* even if they do not bear the same title. Films such as *The Jolson Story* (1946), *The Benny Goodman Story* (1955), *St. Louis Blues* (1958), and even *La Bamba* (1987) raise questions about biopics and remakes in general and about the pivotal role of *The Jazz Singer* in particular. Almost by accident, the 1927 *Jazz Singer* provided filmmakers with a uniquely American template for dealing with Oedipal, ethnic, and racial issues.

Cinderella, Semantics, and Syntax

In arguing that a number of films are unconscious or unacknowledged remakes of *The Jazz Singer,* I am cautioned by the exchange between Seymour Chatman and Barbara Herrnstein Smith (Mitchell 1981) that was first carried out in the pages of *Critical Inquiry.* Chatman posits a binary model of story and discourse, arguing that a "deep structure" or "basic story" can be transposed from one "discourse" to another, regardless of form, mode, or media. As an example of a basic story he cites *Cinderella,* which has existed "as verbal tale, as ballet, as opera, as film, as comic strip, as pantomime, and so on" (Chatman 1981, 18). Smith seizes on this example to charge Chatman with subscribing to a "versionless version" of *Cinderella* that resembles a Platonic ideal: "unembodied and unexpressed, unpictured, unwritten and untold, this altogether unsullied *Cinderella* appears to be a story that occupies a highly privileged ontological realm of pure Being within which it unfolds immutably and eternally. If this is what is meant by the basic story of *Cinderella,* it is clearly unknowable—and, indeed, literally unimaginable—by any mortal being" (B. H. Smith 1981, 212). After quoting several folklorists who have assembled international catalogs of *Cinderella* stories, Smith finds that no rules exist to distinguish versions with most elements of the "basic story" from versions with only a few. As folklorists pile up more and more *Cinderella* stories from around the globe, Smith begins to suspect that if one of the folklorists had continued long enough, "all stories would have turned out to be versions of *Cinderella,*" and that *Cinderella* would turn out to be basically all stories (216). Like Raymond Bellour (1979), I occasionally suspect that all films are versions of the Oedipus story, and after immersing myself in musical biopics, I sometimes believe that all Oedipus stories are versions of *The Jazz Singer.*

Smith is right that the term "basic story" is so highly contingent as to be of questionable value, especially if narratologists do not rigorously examine the "hierarchies of relevance and centrality" (217) that they construct to arrive at basic-ness. Smith ends her essay by asking for a more thorough theory of narration that is more attentive to the cultural contexts in which narratives take place: "individual narratives would be described not as sets of surface-discourse-signifiers that represent (actualize, manifest, map, or express) sets of underlying-story-signifieds but as the verbal acts of particular narrators performed in response to—and thus shaped and constrained by—sets of multiple interacting conditions" (222).

On the one hand, my attempt to establish common threads running through the first *The Jazz Singer* and its various remakes is not a search for basic-ness among texts composed centuries and continents apart. I will be looking rather at films produced in one country by a single industry over the relatively short span of fifty-three years. Furthermore, identifying the kernel of the 1927 film is somewhat different from positing a basic *Cinderella* since there is already a fully realized version of *The Jazz Singer* in contrast to some stripped-down, Platonic version of *Cinderella*. On the other hand, a psychoanalytic reading of the *Jazz Singer* texts suggests that elements of Oedipal tension and racial appropriation in the films constitute something like a consistent core. But these elements are inseparable from obsessions with popular music, ethnicity, assimilation, and reconciliation that have been prominent in the United States, especially in Hollywood. Furthermore, the Oedipal and racial dynamics of the films are deeply entwined not only with optimistic narratives of assimilation through music but with the specifics of each era in which filmmakers (and critics) operate. As Smith might argue, it is impossible to separate out a "deep structure" of Oedipal and racial themes from the "surface-discourse-signifiers" unique to each text. Smith might also argue that any paraphrase of *The Jazz Singer* says as much about the paraphraser as it does about the film. So, I lay a few cards on the table and declare my commitment to a flexible model of psychoanalysis that acknowledges the impact of cultural change on American obsessions as they are played out variously in popular narratives. I would also assert that the first *Jazz Singer* occupies a special role in American cinema, in effect establishing a set of conventions for narratives about race and Oedipal conflict in which the white hero transcends his ethnic background through success as a popular entertainer imitating African Americans. A large number of subsequent films have been based closely enough on these conventions to be called "remakes."

For my purposes, then, the defining plot elements of *The Jazz Singer* (1927) are (1) in early twentieth-century America, a boy from (2) a working-class (3) Jewish family with (4) strong feelings toward his mother wants to (5) sing popular songs or "jazz" much to the chagrin of (6) a father who is a cantor and who insists that his son follow in his footsteps. The father, who has disowned the boy, forgives him only (7) on his deathbed. Helping the son in his singing career is (8) a young and attractive Gentile woman who is more advanced in show business and who soon becomes the love interest for the son. At a crucial moment in the story the son (9) masquerades as an African American male just as he must simultaneously confront both his romantic ties to the Gentile woman and the Oedipal crises in his own family. As Rogin (1992a) has written, the blacking up of Jack Robin (Al Jolson) endows him with a more overt sexuality at the same time that it eases his path to assimilation by concealing his Jewishness. At the optimistic, multiculturalist conclusion, the son is able (10) to combine his commitment to "jazz" with his love for his family and their heritage by singing Kol Nidre with vaudeville body English. (Compare Jack's gesturing at the synagogue with the comportment of the eminent cantor Josef Rosenblatt who stands motionless when he sings in *The Jazz Singer*, unwilling to make any concessions to show business beyond appearing in the film.)[1]

Obviously, my scheme of ten elements can be expanded and numerous subcategories can be teased out of each element.[2] I have not, for example, mentioned any secondary characters, any details of the son's progress toward stardom, or any aspect of the film's racism and sexism. I have tried rather to identify the crucial constitutive elements of *The Jazz Singer* that are most likely to be restated in subsequent films and most relevant to my theses about the role of music and race in fables of Oedipus and assimilation. My scheme has the further practical advantage of lending itself to the following chart in which I have marked with an "x" each element that a "remake" shares with the original.

I have deliberately omitted from the chart the reference to the United States in the early twentieth century because all of the films occur at different times; like most remakes, the first three take place in the same present as when they were made, and the four biopics are anchored in the life history of a famous individual. There appear to be no films resembling *The Jazz Singer* that center on women, unless we include pictures such as *Coal Miner's Daughter* (1980) and *Sweet Dreams* (1985) in which a lower-class, rural milieu might supply the heroines' ethnicity. Given Hollywood's insistence on gender hierarchies, any female variant of *The*

Table 1 *The Jazz Singer and Its Remakes*

1. Movie	2. Class	3. Jews?	4. Does mother indulge son?	5. Does son sing jazz?	6. Does father oppose son at first?	7. Does father forgive son later?	8. Does son love a Gentile?	9. Does son wear black-face?
The Jazz Singer (1927)	lower x	yes x	yes x	yes x	yes x	yes x	yes x	yes x
The Jazz Singer (1953)	middle	yes x	yes x	no	yes x	yes x	lover may be Jewish	no
The Jazz Singer (1959)	lower x	yes x	yes x	no	yes x	no?	yes x	no, but clownface
The Jazz Singer (1980)	lower x	yes x	no mother	no	yes x	yes x	yes x	yes x
The Jolson Story (1946)	lower x	yes x	yes x	yes x	yes x	yes x	yes x	yes x
The Benny Goodman Story (1955)	lower x	yes x	yes, but opposes Gentile at first x	plays jazz x	yes, then dies early x	yes x	yes x	no, but plays with blacks
St. Louis Blues (1958)	lower x	no	close to Aunt Hagar	yes x	yes x	yes x	no, but Eartha Kitt appears	no, but sings with orchestra
La Bamba (1987)	lower x	no	yes x	no	competition with brother x	reconciled with brother x	yes x	no, but changes name

Jazz Singer would almost certainly have to focus on the moment in which the heroine upsets the gender apple cart by surpassing her male lover. The various versions of *A Star Is Born*, including the precursor *What Price Hollywood?* (1932), in which the success of a female star results in the suicide of her husband or mentor, is more typical of what happens when the gender roles of *The Jazz Singer* are reversed. If a single romantic male lead is omitted, however, a female version of the narrative may be possible. In a curious way the documentary of a tour by the pop singer Madonna, *Truth or Dare* (1991), vaguely recalls many of the conventions of the *Jazz Singer,* including a conflict with working-class ethnic parents, recuperation of the family's religious heritage into the star's performance, and the wary reconciliation with the father. The sexual capital of African Americans is also a crucial factor in this narrative—Madonna tours with a troupe of black male dancers and with two prominently featured female singer-dancers, one of whom is black. And like 90 percent of white pop singers today, Madonna relies heavily on vocal styles and body language steeped in African American traditions.

I have also omitted (10) the reconciliatory conclusion from the chart because I consider this to be the sine qua non for any remake of *The Jazz Singer;* virtually all of the films on the chart exhibit some version of it. If, to use Rick Altman's terminology, the chart summarizes the semantics of the film and its remakes, *The Jazz Singer's* conclusion is essential to the film's syntax (Altman 1986). To distinguish it from the "fairy tale musical" and the "folk musical," Altman describes the "show musical" as a narrative about a show business couple whose onstage romance and backstage love affair culminate in a final production number (Altman 1989). For Altman, the semantics of the show musical involve the production of a play, a revue, a film, or some kind of show, while the syntax involves the dovetailing of a love plot with the show's success. Representing the earliest stages of the show subgenre—Altman (1989) places the film first in his chronological listing of show musicals—*The Jazz Singer* splits the finale into two small production numbers instead of one large one. After Jack receives his father's blessing at the old cantor's deathbed, he observes the spirit of Yom Kippur and proceeds to the synagogue to sing his jazzy Kol Nidre; a title card then explains that "the season passes—and time heals—the show goes on" just before Jack is seen on the stage of the Winter Garden theater singing "Mammy" under cork while his mother and Mary Dale, his Gentile lover, look on adoringly. As David Desser (1991) has argued, "an overdetermined form of mother love represses the intermarriage component" (399), one of several elements in the conclusion that could easily disrupt the film's utopian view of assimilation. "Success in the American mainstream, a breakthrough into stardom, a breakout of the ghetto, 'naturally' brings with it the WASP woman. Intermarriage becomes secondary to assimilation" (Desser 1991, 399).

Significantly, Jack Robin's final return to the stage, along with the reaction shots of doting Jewish mother and Gentile lover, are not in Alfred A. Cohn's original shooting script for *The Jazz Singer.* Nor can these scenes be found in the principal sources for the film—Samson Raphaelson's 1922 short story, "Day of Atonement," and his play, *The Jazz Singer* (Carringer 1979). The shooting script ends with Jack in the synagogue where he may have ended his show business career by walking out on the opening night of a Broadway show. Although Raphaelson wrote "Day of Atonement" with Al Jolson's own story in mind (Carringer 1979, 11), the story ends with the hero actually choosing to remain a cantor. The triumphant but slightly incoherent "Mammy" finale was added to the film by Warners if only for the sake of a more upbeat ending. Like most show musicals, nearly all of *The Jazz Singer* remakes are more economical, placing the weight of the reconciliation primarily in a concluding stage act: the protagonist may in fact return to the synagogue or its equivalent, but the final stage performance is more clearly motivated, with the father usually surviving to enjoy the show along with the rest of his son's adoring fans. What the father eventually comes to understand is what the hero and most of the remakes have been saying all along, "that Jack's jazz singing is fundamentally an ancient religious impulse seeking expression in a modern, popular form" (Carringer 1979, 23). Or as the film itself states in its first title card, "perhaps this plaintive, wailing song of jazz is, after all, the misunderstood utterance of a prayer."

This kind of Oedipal reconciliation may be unique to American popular culture. In contrast to the reassuring ending of America's *The Jazz Singer,* Hoberman (1991a) has found a turn-of-the-century Yiddish tragedy from Poland that foreshadows the plot of the film, even though Raphaelson probably had no knowledge of it when he wrote "Day of Atonement." In *Der Vilner Balebesl,* later filmed in Yiddish as *Overture to Glory* (1940), a talented cantor's desire to see the world leads him to a successful career as an opera singer and eventually into the arms of a Polish countess. When he returns home to his village, however, he finds that his wife has gone mad and his child has died.[3] "In Europe, the fruits of assimilation were seen as madness, ruin, and death. In America, of course, it was a different story" (Hoberman 1991a, 64).

Robert B. Ray (1985) has placed Hollywood's paradigm of reconciliation alongside "American myths of inclusiveness," part of the fundamental belief that options are eternally available in the New World: "Often, the movies' reconciliatory pattern concentrated on a single character magically embodying diametrically opposite traits. A sensitive violinist was also a tough boxer (*Golden Boy*); a boxer was a gentle man who cared for pigeons (*On the Waterfront*). A gangster became a coward because he was brave (*Angels with Dirty Faces*); a soldier became brave because he was a coward (*Lives of a Bengal Lancer*)" (58). Similarly, a jazz singer who abandons his family for the stage can also lead the congregation in prayer on the most solemn of holy days, then return to the stage as a great success, and still have the love of his mother and a beautiful blonde. Although the myth implies that limitless possibilities are open to all Americans, the vast majority of American films suggests that Hollywood is willing to extend such wide-ranging freedom only to white males, even if they happen to be Jewish.

The Sexual Dynamics of Blackface Performance

Blacks in jazz were not only excluded from Hollywood's highly optimistic stories of assimilation; they were invariably confined to stories of alcoholism, drug abuse, and self-destructive behavior (see chapter 2). Although African American actors were simply not present in *The Jazz Singer* and other films about white jazz artists, the importance of blacks

6. In blackface, Jack Robin (Al Jolson) is masculinized so that he can become the lover of the hyperfeminine Mary Dale (May McAvoy) in *The Jazz Singer* (1927, Warner Bros.). Jerry Ohlinger's Movie Material Store, Inc.

to these films cannot be overstated. With direct links to nineteenth-century blackface minstrelsy, the 1927 *Jazz Singer* ought to be contextualized within the long history of whites impersonating blacks in mainstream American entertainment. In his brilliant study, *Love and Theft: Blackface Minstrelsy and the American Working Class* (1993), Eric Lott has explored the ambivalent view of blacks that white Americans held in the first half of the nineteenth century and in many ways continue to hold today. Although minstrelsy unquestionably allowed whites to indulge their contempt and even hatred for blacks, Lott argues that white people in the early nineteenth century, especially working-class males, regarded black men as sexual role models; the minstrel shows regularly played to white obsessions about the supposed hypersexuality, spontaneity, and phallic power of black men.

Although his major focus is not the present, Lott regularly shows continuity between minstrelsy and more contemporary practices. He points out, for example, that adolescent boys and boys of latency age today base a great deal of their behavior on their perceptions of African American males. Lott quotes writers such as Willie Morris and Leslie Fiedler who have emphasized the importance of African American styles of walking, talking, and dressing for white boys, and he observes that "this dynamic, persisting into adulthood, is so much a part of most American white men's equipment for living that they remain entirely unaware of their participation in it" (Lott 1993, 53). For the white minstrel man, "to put on the cultural forms of 'blackness' was to engage in a complex affair of manly mimicry. . . . To wear or even enjoy blackface was literally, for a time, to become black, to inherit the cool, virility, humility, abandon, or *gaité de coeur* that were the prime components of white ideologies of black manhood" (Lott 1993, 52). Of course, white fascination with black sexuality was not always so benign. Lott also writes, "Because of the power of the black penis in white American psychic life, the pleasure minstrelsy's largely white and male audiences derived from their investment in 'blackness' always carried a threat of castration—a threat obsessively reversed in white lynching rituals" (9). Lott's analysis is subtle enough to connect white fascination with black men to nineteenth-century ethnic and class anxiety. Significantly, many minstrel performers were Irish immigrants, perhaps the one ethnic group in the United States whose members could identify with the powerlessness and poverty of blacks during the first decades of the nineteenth century. Minstrel songs in the North, especially those that expressed a nostalgia for the plantation or "Old Folks at Home," were easily conflated with the Irishman's sentimental longing for his own homeland (Lott 1993, 191). In addition, "blackface acts had the effect of promoting socially insecure Irishmen (actors as well as audiences), an 'Americanizing' ritual by which they distanced themselves from the people they parodied" (96). During harsh economic times, white working-class males of all ethnicities found consoling pleasures in watching the counterfeit black men: the workingman, who frequently saw himself as a "wage slave," his masculinity in question, may have taken some comfort in the minstrel man's mimicking of the *real* slave who seems oblivious to hard times and indefatigable in his sexuality (104).

In "Just Asking," a brief essay from 1984, Martin Williams (1985, 93–95) raises questions about two popular musicians who have much in common in spite of the differences in their ages and audiences. Why, asks Williams, did both Benny Goodman and Mick Jagger choose careers built on imitations of black musicians? With no assurance that he would eventually achieve wealth and fame, Goodman chose to play the clarinet in the style of an obscure colored Creole from New Orleans named Jimmy Noone and to "form an orchestra that played like that of an American mulatto [sic] from Georgia named Fletcher Henderson" (93). Jagger, who might have continued his studies at the London School of Economics, decided to build a career singing in the style of a "relatively ignorant black man from Mississippi" (93). In each case, Williams then asks why the two white entertainers drew such large audiences. These are not rhetorical questions; Williams concludes his essay with assurances that he does not know the answers. "Why do we all, at whatever level, find such meaning in the musical culture of Afro-Americans? Why has their music so triumphed throughout the world? We invoke it to get through our adolescence and most of us then keep it, one way or another, central to our lives. As I say, I can't answer my question, but if I could, I think I'd know more about what we are and what we might become than any man alive" (Williams 1985, 95). Although he does not address Williams directly, Lott provides abundant material for answers to his questions. Like any number of "white Negroes" since the 1830s, Goodman and Jagger found something so deeply arresting in the manner of black musicians— including their expression of masculinity—that they built their young lives around pursuing it. The massive and largely unexpected rewards of this pursuit came later. It is not necessary to look for evidence that Goodman and Jagger expressed the universal fear of young men that they were not sufficiently manly. Lott is right to suggest that black male sexuality is so deeply imbedded in the white man's "equipment for living" that it remains invisible. The large audiences that applauded Goodman and Jagger were like the audiences for minstrelsy—male and female—who preferred to consume their fantasies of black male sexuality only when they were mediated through the bodies of white performers.

That Goodman and Jagger were more successful than innumerable other white imitators of black musicians testifies to their ability to perform in ways that accommodated more precisely the tastes of the American (and British) publics at their specific historical moments. But Goodman and Jagger were not exactly minstrel men. They lived in eras when the music of real African Americans was readily available, and they studied it. In doing so, these twentieth-century artists were even more invested in black males than were the minstrel men of the nineteenth century. As Amiri Baraka has argued in a somewhat different context, "the entrance of the white man into jazz at this level of sincerity and emotional legitimacy did at least bring him, by implication, much closer to the Negro" (Baraka 1963, 151). In his richly nuanced argument in *Blues People,* Baraka shows that the acceptance of jazz by whites marks a crucial moment when an aspect of black culture had become an essential part of American culture, that it was "available intellectually, that it could be learned" (155). Lott shows why it was so important for whites to undertake the intellectual labor of learning jazz.

Mick Jagger corresponds on some levels to what Lott has called "class mutineers." Raised in upwardly mobile Protestant families in the decades before the American Civil War, these men sought the freedom of expression, sexual or otherwise, in the world of minstrel entertainment (50). As John F. Szwed (1975) has observed, that Jagger performed without blackface "simply marks the detachment of culture from race and the almost full absorption of a black tradition into white culture" (7). Goodman came from an impoverished household of immigrant Jews. Because of his ethnicity, he had much in common with the unassimilated Irish immigrants in the minstrel troupes of the 1830s who felt most Americanized when they put burnt cork on their faces and acted out what they imagined to be the hypersexuality and transgressiveness of black males. As both Baraka and Szwed observe, however, by the time Goodman began learning the music in the 1920s, black music had become so much a part of American life that blackface and the antic foregrounding of the body were no longer necessary. The body *was* essential for both Al Jolson and Mick Jagger because one preceded and the other rejected the restrained, "artistic" performance practice that jazz was beginning to claim when Goodman came of age. It was Goodman, after all, who broke the color barrier by hiring Teddy Wilson, whose dignified, affectless persona anticipated the poker faces of jazz modernists in the next decade. Although his fans often moved their bodies with abandon at his dance dates, Goodman led one of the first bands of the swing era that large groups of people came simply to *watch* as they listened. Jazz took an important step toward art when fans stood in front of the bandstand and *observed* the Goodman orchestra, anticipating the large audience at the Carnegie Hall concert of 1938 that sat and listened while musicians played dance music. This was the jazz that Baraka says was "intellectually available" to whites. But for all its intellectual appeal, the music still carried with it the promise of black virility, poise, and abandon. In *The Jazz Singer,* Jack Robin (and Al Jolson) seek an even more mediated version of this fantasy, one that is still based on white imaginings about the lives of black people.

The Acknowledged Remakes

But black male sexuality was much less likely to be an issue as Hollywood remade *The Jazz Singer.* Career success and Oedipal reconciliation become more central as blackface and its ramifications subsided. Even after the upbeat ending was added to the 1927 *Jazz Singer,* the tragic possibility was still present that Jack Robin could lose the stage career he so desperately sought; when he arrives at the bedside of his dying father, both the producer of his show and Mary Dale come to caution him about walking out on opening night. The producer shakes his fist and warns him, "You'll queer yourself on Broadway—you'll never get another job." Mary Dale hangs on his neck and asks, "Were you lying when you said your career came before everything?" When Jack then chooses the synagogue over the theater, the evening's performance is canceled. In the remakes, however, the jazz singers face no such crises; rather, the heroes of the 1953 and 1980 versions arrive at their respective synagogues with little anxiety about career-ending absences on Broadway. In the 1953 version, when the summons to sing Kol Nidre comes on the same afternoon as the hero's important opening night, a quick call for the understudy is issued, and the heroine expresses only sympathy when the Danny Thomas character departs for home; no title card or expository dialogue is necessary to explain the jump from Danny singing in the synagogue to Danny singing in the theater. In the 1980 version, Jess Rabinovitch (Neil Diamond) has just ended a rehearsal by telling his musicians to take the day off for Yom Kippur when his father's friend arrives with the plea that

7. Danny Thomas, as the cantor's son who would break a family tradition, with Peggy Lee in *The Jazz Singer* (1953, Warner Bros.). Jerry Ohlinger's Movie Material Store, Inc.

Jess replace his ailing father back home; singing Kol Nidre has no effect whatsoever on the progress of the singer's career. Whereas the cantor in the 1927 film declares his love for his son but never articulates his acceptance of Jack's vocation as a singer, the father in almost all of the remakes comes to accept and actually appreciate his son's music.

As many critics pointed out, the path to reconciliation in the 1953 remake is so smooth that little tension remains to drive the narrative. Eduard Franz, who plays Danny Thomas's father in the 1953 version, is not a poor cantor in a Lower East Side ghetto, but the well-heeled leader of a congregation in an affluent section of Philadelphia. Not only is the cantor thoroughly assimilated into urban society; he also appears to be comfortable with popular culture, at one point singing every word of a rapid-fire soap commercial that his son recorded for radio. The father's demand that his son follow in a family tradition of several generations of cantors takes on the marks of a neurotic symptom, a familiar convention during Hollywood's romance with psychoanalysis in the 1950s (Gabbard and Gabbard 1987). Coming to his senses on his sickbed just before his son sings Kol Nidre, the cantor himself delivers the film's message that the popular entertainer can express a divine spirit. After giving his blessing to Jerry's show business career, the cantor adds, "Only I want you to remember that wherever you sing, always lift your head high and raise your voice to God, the way you did in the temple." Even the problem of intermarriage is solved by having Peggy Lee, Danny Thomas's love interest, drop a line about attending a seder to hint that she too may be Jewish.

Although Laurence Olivier's cantor in the 1980 *Jazz Singer* leads a less affluent congregation on Eldridge Street on the Lower East Side of Manhattan, and although he is never overheard equating popular music with religion, he is entirely won over when Jess shows the old man a photograph of his grandson, "Charlie Parker Rabinovitch." The reference to the canonical jazz saxophonist and composer seems motivated primarily by the anachronism of the film's title and by the vestiges of white appropriation of black culture that seem obligatory in a *Jazz Singer* remake. The largely perfunctory citation of Charlie Parker may also have stemmed from Diamond's desire to shore up his dubious claim to hipness. In the decidedly un-hip conclusion of the film, Olivier is caught up in the crowd's semi-Dionysian abandon while Diamond sings "Coming

8. Neil Diamond may not sing jazz, but he has a gentile girlfriend (Lucie Arnaz) in *The Jazz Singer* (1980, EMI). Jerry Ohlinger's Movie Material Store, Inc.

to America," a hymn to assimilationism so unproblematic that the Democratic party adopted the song for its national convention in 1988. Diamond's melting-pot American jingoism is expressed symbolically in the finale by his red, white, and blue outfit set off by a scarf worn like a prayer shawl.

In 1982 the SCTV troupe did a parody of the Diamond film on their NBC series in which the father—played by "Sid Dithers" (Eugene Levy) with dreadlocks—is a Jewish recording executive who wants his son to make hit records. The son, played by the African American vocalist Al Jarreau, wants to be a cantor. In still another *Jazz Singer* parody, Krusty the Klown told the story of his estrangement from his orthodox Jewish father on a 1992 episode of *The Simpsons;* as in so many of the remakes, the program culminates with the father accepting his son's profession and enjoying his performance, even to the point of heaving a pie into his son's face as the episode ends. For the sake of completeness, I should also mention a Warner Bros. cartoon from 1937, "I Love to Singa." A family of owls gives birth to several chicks, each of whom pleases the father by performing classical music as he emerges from his egg. To the father's horror, the final chick, named "Owl Jolson," breaks out of the egg singing

9. The assimilationist finale of *The Jazz Singer* (1980). Jerry Ohlinger's Movie Material Store, Inc.

the popular ditty, "I Love to Singa." Initially banished from the household, the industrious young owl wins over his father when he becomes a star on a radio talent show for singing animals.

Like these parodies, the 1953 and 1980 films tilt toward easy reconciliation. Jerry Lewis's 1959 television production, however, retains a sense of the tragic possibilities in the story of the ethnic Oedipus. Lewis plays a clown rather than a singer who is about to appear in his first national TV program when he is called back to the synagogue. With no time to wipe off his makeup, the son arrives at the last minute to sing Kol Nidre in *clownface* as his father expires and the film ends. Scott Bukatman (1991) has attributed the bizarre, nonresolution of the program's ending to Lewis's own "unresolved conflicts of identity" (192).[4] Whatever his reasons, Lewis remained true to the original spirit of Raphaelson's story and play, both of which emphasized the assimilating Jew's dilemmas rather than his successful negotiation of career and Oedipal conflicts. Like the authors of the 1953 remake, Lewis appeared to be uninterested in the original film's appropriation of black culture.

Even accounting for the inevitable changes that characterize the vast majority of remakes, the 1953 and 1980 *Jazz Singers* respond powerfully to agenda unknown to filmmakers in 1927. As Smith (1981) would argue, each new *Jazz Singer* was radically refashioned as its "narrators" formulated new stories to accommodate the profound changes in American culture. Danny Thomas appears in uniform at the opening of the 1953 remake, a G. I. faced with the problems of adjustment reminiscent of those in successful predecessor films like *The Pride of the Marines* (1945), *The Best Years of Our Lives* (1946), and *The Men* (1950). Although the film was also made in the shadow of several problem films that dealt with anti-Semitism, such as *Gentlemen's Agreement* (1947) and *Crossfire* (1947), hatred of the Jews is hardly an issue in Curtiz's film. In fact, the film is so careful to avoid Jewish stereotypes that the principals might as well be Episcopalians.

The 1953 film also omits any reference to African Americans, either real or mimicked through blackface. My research has turned up nothing to indicate that Warner Bros. made a conscious decision to eliminate blackface performance, and almost without exception the reviews of the film make no mention of the omission. By 1953, civil rights organizations may have been sufficiently successful with consciousness-raising to have made the practice forbidden, even in a film that must have quickly brought to mind Al Jolson, the best-known of all blackface performers, whose long and highly visible career had ended with his death just two years earlier.[5]

Richard Fleischer's 1980 version was motivated primarily by the personal fixations of Neil Diamond who insisted on script changes throughout production to bring the story more into line with his own life story (Wiseman 1987, 256). The most significant omission is the protagonist's mother, so essential to the Oedipal hysteria of the original and most of the remakes. Blackface, on the other hand, returns. Diamond and Fleischer may have intended a tongue-in-cheek homage to the 1927 film when they inserted an early scene in which Jess Rabinovitch reluctantly puts shoe polish on his face in order to replace the missing member of an African American singing group that is performing his songs in a black nightclub. At least initially, the scene is played for laughs as Jess tries to conceal his misgivings with the black makeup. At the dawn of the era of Reagan and Bush, however, the sequence is especially disturbing in its invocation of racial stereotypes that were soon to become more pervasive than they had been during previous decades. If in 1927 blackface authorized sexuality and emotional vulnerability, in the 1980 *Jazz Singer* blackface appears to authorize violence against obstreperous blacks and the fantasy of loyal retainers fighting alongside the white hero; after an angry black man in the audience notices that Jess has neglected to put color on his hands ("That ain't no brother; that's a white boy!"), he rushes the stage and sets himself up for a sucker punch from the hero. As members of the soul group come to his aid and the entire club breaks into pandemonium, the film activates clichés from bar fights in westerns as well as from myths about the natural inclination of black people to violence. The film also upholds Hollywood's old racial hierarchies by suggesting that a group of black singers is dependent on a white man for their music. Although there is no question that whites in general and Jews in particular have made substantial contributions to the evolution of jazz and black popular music, the film acknowledges the crucial role of African Americans in jazz history only in the name of Jess's son.

The Unacknowledged Remakes

If each of the three titled remakes departs substantially from the semantics and syntax of the original, the four biopics in the chart line up more consistently with the racial, ethnic, and gender obsessions of the 1927 film. On the one hand, this phenomenon may be related to the need for self-identified remakes to update their plots to separate themselves from the original. The frequently hagiographical biopics, on the other hand, tend to be more conservative and consequently fall back on well-established conventions. *The Jolson Story* (1946), for example, is part of a progression of *Jazz Singer* texts—story, play, screenplay, and final film—each of which moved closer to Jolson's own history. Almost all of the semantic elements of the 1927 film reappear in *The Jolson Story*, although the syntax begins to break down in the film's final third that chronicles the star's temporary retirement, his separation from his wife, and the beginnings of his comeback. The reconciliation with his father comes quickly and easily, even before the young Asa Yoelson changes his name to Al Jolson; after the child runs away from home, he is taken to a Catholic boys' home where his parents arrive to see him singing "Ave Maria." When the elder Yoelson complains, "singing without his cap on," an Irish priest strikes the principal ecumenical note of all *The Jazz Singer* films when he says, "It's not so much what's on the head as what's in the heart, is it, Cantor?" The father's smile indicates his agreement and concession to his son's wishes; with the film less than fifteen minutes old, the man becomes the ardent follower of his son's career, thus setting an example for the 1953 and 1980 titled remakes. On one of the boy's visits home, the father even tells his son that he need no longer wear a yarmulke.[6] The Oedipal aggressiveness of the first *Jazz Singer* surely became less appealing after so many Jewish fathers had died in the Holocaust, perhaps motivating the makers of almost all the post-1945 *Jazz Singer* films to allow the fathers to live on and achieve satisfying reconciliations with their sons.

In addition to anticipating the much greater attention to career progress that characterizes the remakes of *The Jazz Singer, The Jolson Story* goes farther than any of the films in exploring the significance of blackface and the "love and theft" relationship that whites have developed with blacks. The adult Jolson (Larry Parks) first blackens up while appearing in a variety show that features a blackface performer. When the white minstrel man is too drunk to perform one night, Jolson spontaneously replaces him, coincidentally while one member of the audience is Lew Dockstader, the leader of a well-established minstrel troupe at the end of the century. Jolson's desire to work in blackface appears to grow out of natural exuberance and his desire to succeed in show business. It may also be related to an interest in African American music, but the film offers no evidence that the young Jolson has previously heard blacks in performance, even though he begins improvising and syncopating his vocal solos early in his career. The film seems to regard minstrelsy as the unproblematic inclination of certain white performers, presumably those possessed with the joy of life and enough sensitivity to appreciate the musical accomplishments of blacks.

Only after he has joined Dockstader's minstrel show and become a featured performer does Jolson arrive in New Orleans and wander into a gathering of *real* black people where he hears a slick, anachronistic version of Dixieland jazz. Jolson has a revelation, that the staid repertoire of the minstrel troupe can be transformed by actually playing black music in blackface. He tells Dockstader that he wants to sing what he has just experienced: "I heard some music tonight, something they call jazz. Some fellows just make it up as they go along. They pick it up out of the air." After Dockstader refuses to accommodate Jolson's revolutionary concept, the narrative chronicles his climb to stardom as he allegedly injects jazz into his blackface performances. Like many of the biopics produced by Hollywood in the forties and fifties, Jolson's success is built on anticipating what Americans really want. Dockstader performs the inevitable function of the guardian of the status quo, whose hidebound

10. Al Jolson (Larry Parks) with Lew Dockstader (John Alexander) in *The Jolson Story* (1946, Columbia). Museum of Modern Art Film Stills Archive.

commitment to what is about to become obsolete reinforces the audience's sympathy with the forward-looking hero. The film reassures the majority culture that its comfortable notions of entertainment in 1946 are right and inevitable. George Custen (1992) sees this tradition as especially dear to the hearts of the men who made the movies. He describes the common scenario, in which the hero is vindicated for innovations that are initially greeted with resistance, as "extrapolations of the producer's own struggles to manifest and articulate greatness in his own histories. A Zanuck viewed the world in terms congruent with those that had brought him to power and nurtured him in his position of eminence; to question the basis of a biopic life would be to question the basis on which he had made his own life"(147). The struggle of the heroic protagonist who anticipates changes in cultural attitudes is central to other white jazz biopics such as *The Glenn Miller Story* (1954) and *The Benny Goodman Story* as well as to films as different as *Blossoms in the Dust* (1941) and *Sister Kenny* (1946) (Custen 1992, 147).

In *The Jolson Story* the audience is of course invited to appreciate Jolson's foresight in predicting the popularity of jazz, or at least its appropriation by whites. But the film also suggests that this ethereal music—picked out of the air by simple black folk—needs the genius of someone like Jolson to give it solidity and validity. After the brief scene in New Orleans, African Americans are never seen again, nor is there any other reference to jazz and Jolson's claims on black music. In subsequent scenes, however, the blacked-up Jolson is granted license to play the trickster, impishly but endearingly rewriting stage shows as they unfold in front of audiences. Blacking up allowed a certain freedom of sexual expression for Jolson in the first *Jazz Singer,* just as it did in *Swing Time* (1936) when Lucky (Fred Astaire) kisses Penny (Ginger Rogers) for the first time just as he is about to apply burnt cork for his performance of "Bojangles of Harlem." Perhaps because the Hays Office cast a much starker shadow over films in the 1940s, blackface in *The Jolson Story* becomes associated with harmless mischief. Unlike Jack Robin with Mary Dale, Jolson does not court the woman he eventually marries in blackface. He does, however, have a scene in which he hastens the conclusion of a show that has received bad reviews. He simply walks on stage under cork, summarizes the remaining moments of the plot, and brings together the reluctant leading man and leading lady for the final embrace.

Once we accept a semantic change from singing to playing the clarinet, *The Benny Goodman Story* becomes an almost transparent reworking of *The Jazz Singer.* The hero never puts on blackface, but he does have critical encounters with black musicians who seem to affect his sexuality and emotional expressivity. The mythological characteristics of African Americans that Jack Robin puts on along with burnt cork are acquired by Goodman when blacks are simply nearby. When the young Benny plays his first job with a white dance band on a riverboat in Chicago, he is introduced to a young woman who is about to become his first date. Their relationship ends almost immediately, however, when she ridicules him for wearing short pants. Still smarting from the insult, Benny wanders into a performance by the intermission band led by legendary New Orleans trombonist Kid Ory (played by Ory himself) and notices that the musicians have no music. Ory explains that he plays New Orleans style, just like Louis Armstrong, King Oliver, and Fletcher Henderson [sic]. "We just play what we feel," explains Ory. "Playing the way you feel," muses Goodman. "Say, could I sit in?" Immediately, the young clarinetist becomes an accomplished improviser, presumably finding in African American music the perfect means for overcoming his wounded feelings.

Donna Reed is later introduced into *The Benny Goodman Story* as Alice Hammond, the Gentile woman from New York society whom the mature Goodman (Steve Allen) eventually marries. Their romance is off to a slow start until Benny has returned to Chicago at the pinnacle of his first great success. Standing next to Fletcher Henderson (Sammy Davis, Sr.), the black bandleader whose arrangements contributed mightily to Goodman's success, Goodman is reintroduced to Kid Ory, who offers the praise, "You have the best band I ever heard anyplace." At this moment, Alice walks in, and Benny is about to approach her in earnest. Reversing the situation of his first sexual humiliation, Benny quickly thanks Ory for his compliment and then hands his clarinet to Henderson, adding, "Fletch, could you hold this, please?" Now a more fully sexualized individual, Goodman no longer needs black musicians to tutor him about feelings, although the film does seem to relate their proximity (and easy dismissal) to his romantic energies.

That Benny should hand his long black instrument to an African American musician just before a romantic encounter shows the limiting effect of the Hays Office on a film's ability to forge a connection between black music and sex. The scene is also an example of how subjects "return from the repressed" regardless of whether or not the filmmakers consciously intended to present the clarinet as a symbol for Goodman's sexuality. The instrument is first charged with phallic qualities when Goodman learns to play jazz from black artists. Even though the mature Goodman never abandons the clarinet in his public life, he eventually becomes sufficiently confident as a sexual being to put the object aside. Handing the phallic instrument to Fletcher Henderson while Kid Ory is present completes a process that began when Ory taught Goodman the full potential of the clarinet while twice mentioning Fletcher Henderson's name in conversation. Hollywood's racial codes may have demanded that a woman like Donna Reed/Alice Hammond should require a suitor more sophisticated than one tutored by blacks, who simply "play what they feel." According to this logic, Goodman can successfully approach Alice only after he has put his large black prosthesis aside. He no longer needs it because he has renounced black male sexuality and embraced the white male fantasy that white women can only be won by sublimating sexual urges associated with black men.

For all the patronizing and marginalizing of black jazz artists in *The Benny Goodman Story,* the film does in fact acknowledge the contribution of Henderson as well as Teddy Wilson and Lionel Hampton (both played on screen by themselves) to Goodman's career. The appearance of Wilson, Hampton, and Buck Clayton with Goodman at the re-creation of the triumphant 1938 Carnegie Hall concert that ends the film is a dramatic

11. Relying on his clarinet, Benny Goodman (Steve Allen) romances Alice Hammond (Donna Reed) in *The Benny Goodman Story* (1955, Universal/International). Jerry Ohlinger's Movie Material Store, Inc.

change from the mimicking of black performers that concludes the 1927 *Jazz Singer.* The end of *The Benny Goodman Story* with its several black performers is one of the most inclusive of the many reconciliatory finales in the cycle of show musicals. As in *The Jazz Singer,* this unorthodox performance by a jazz musician is presented as a gamble that might endanger his career. Appropriately, the romance plot culminates at this concert when we are told that Goodman is asking Alice to marry him by means of a clarinet solo, a proposal she accepts by nodding her head. This wedding proposal doubles the marriage of jazz and classical music symbolized by a Carnegie Hall concert attended entirely by socially prominent New Yorkers, who depart from their usual behavior at concerts by tapping their feet in rhythm. Goodman's adoring mother is seated next to the clarinetist's fiancée at the concert, recalling the reaction shots of Jack Robin's mother and lover at the end of *The Jazz Singer.*

As another film about successful assimilation by a Jewish musician, *The Benny Goodman Story* owes a perhaps unconscious debt to *The Jazz Singer* and suggests that the 1927 film had definitively established the rules by which such a story should be told, even one alleged to be true. Although there is no Kol Nidre at the conclusion of the film, *The Benny Goodman Story* also follows *The Jazz Singer* in forging a rapprochement between Jewish culture and the mainstreams of American popular culture. The word "Jew" is never uttered in the film, though the accents of Benny's parents provide one of several obvious references to the family's Jewishness. At another point, Mrs. Goodman has a brief moment of hesitancy about Benny's courtship of the upper-class, Gentile Alice in which she tells her, "You don't mix caviar and bagels." Generally, the film displaces anxieties about social class and ethnicity into a conflict over musical tastes—a conflict much more easily resolved both here and in the *Jazz Singer* narratives in which music is the preferred path to assimilation. Since Alice prefers classical music to jazz, her admiration for Benny grows substantially when she discovers that he is capable of what the film identifies as an expert reading of Mozart's clarinet concerto.[7]

A number of other subtle signs indicate that Benny has retained his Jewish heritage in his "hot music." At several transitional moments in *The Benny Goodman Story,* he plays a melancholy tune alone at night on the rooftop of his building. Anyone with a passing knowledge of Goodman's music would be able to recognize the song as "Goodbye," a tune written by Gordon Jenkins that became the Goodman band's closing theme. When played solo by Goodman (who dubbed in all clarinet solos for Steve Allen), the minor melody of the song also bears the signifiers of

Jewish folk music. Even more strikingly, the final Carnegie Hall concert features a performance of "And the Angels Sing" with the famous trumpet solo by Ziggy Elman that quotes from the Jewish klezmer tune, "Der Shtiler Bulgar," part of an earlier version of the song entitled "Frahlich in Swing" (Sapoznik 1987). With the *echt* WASP Martha Tilton taking the vocal chorus on "And the Angels Sing," Jewish is married to American, even if klezmer does not precisely accomplish the mixture of the sacred and the profane that ends *The Jazz Singer.*

A case can be made that remakes of *The Jazz Singer* can involve non-Jewish groups so long as they are sufficiently marginal. With slight semantic changes, *St. Louis Blues* (1958) and *La Bamba* (1987) address many of the same questions as the original 1927 film. In *St. Louis Blues,* Nat King Cole plays W. C. Handy, the African American who was the first great popularizer of the blues. Handy's father is a minister who strongly disapproves of secular music and insists that his son pursue a respectable career as a schoolteacher. Although the hero's mother is dead, he is frequently indulged by his Aunt Hagar (Pearl Bailey). Like all the mothers

12. A typically multicultural moment in a remake of *The Jazz Singer*: with Buck Clayton to his left, Ziggy Elman plays a klezmer trumpet solo at the finale of *The Benny Goodman Story.* Jerry Ohlinger's Movie Material Store, Inc.

in the *Jazz Singer* texts, surrogate mother Aunt Hagar inevitably sides with the boy in his Oedipal struggles with his father.

In *St. Louis Blues,* the young Handy is fascinated by the work songs he hears from black laborers, and he begins writing tunes that show the influence of these sources. Even when the protagonist is black, American cinema is able to find an otherness in black music. Handy is soon playing and singing his songs in a cabaret whose featured performer, Gogo Germaine, is played by the sensually purring Eartha Kitt. Her otherness from Handy's strict Christian background puts her in much the same relationship to the hero as Mary Dale bears to Jack Robin. It is also suggested that whatever sexual attraction Handy feels for Gogo is facilitated by his exposure to secular black music. At any rate, Kitt is certainly more outside the protagonist's tribe than was Peggy Lee in the 1953 *Jazz Singer.* In the final moments of *St. Louis Blues,* Handy appears in a tuxedo—in some sense, a cultural disguise—and sings the title tune before a symphony orchestra while his father stands backstage, accepting at last his son's vocation. The film's religious crisis is displaced into issues of social class and the sacralization of the concert hall; when the father arrives in

13. Nat King Cole, Eartha Kitt, and Cab Calloway (foreground) in *St. Louis Blues* (1958, Paramount). Museum of Modern Art Film Stills Archive.

New York from Memphis to discover that the symphony is playing "St. Louis Blues" and not his son's hymns, he denounces the music as "cheap dance hall." Gogo Germaine, however, is there to instruct him otherwise. "This is Aeolian Hall, Reverend, no dancing, no drinking. People pay three dollars and thirty cents a seat to sit and listen to great music." He is eventually won over, at least in part by the majesty of the symphony hall and the spectacle of white men in tuxedos playing violins. The ending resembles that of other *Jazz Singer* remakes in its suggestion that the son can be true to his artistic convictions *and* to his father's demands. *St. Louis Blues* also has much in common with biopics about white jazz musicians (see chapter 2), and Nat King Cole was one of the few black performers who could effectively function as "white" in a narrative about black music.

In *La Bamba,* Ricardo Valenzuela (Lou Diamond Phillips) grows up playing rock and roll in southern California in the 1950s with a highly supportive mother who takes an active role in his career. Although the boy's father is dead, the protagonist must deal with an older brother, an ex-convict given to violent outbursts, in ways that adumbrate the conflict between father and son in earlier *Jazz Singer* films. The film creates additional Oedipal tension by indicating that Ricardo feels affection and later sympathy for the woman who is married to his brother. Before he crosses over to success under the name Ritchie Valens, the Mexican-American hero has already established a relationship with Donna, a blonde girl whose father strongly disapproves of the young man's ethnic and lower-class origins. Significantly, Ritchie has grown up in America listening to rock—specifically, to black artists such as Little Richard—and never learned to speak Spanish. When his older brother takes him on a trip to Tijuana he hears a *norteño* band playing the old folk tune "La Bamba." The trip was arranged by the brother to take Ritchie to a brothel for his first sexual experience, part of the brother's attempts to acquaint Ritchie with the cultural heritage that Ritchie regards ambivalently. (The jazz singer's bar mitzvah?) In the film's multicultural solution, Valens sings the Spanish words to "La Bamba" while transforming the song with a rock beat and stage mannerisms borrowed from black rhythm-and-blues performers. As an assimilated Hispanic American, Valens draws his sexual power from blacks and his ethnic legitimacy from the Mexican band that he first heard in a bordello. The film ends when Ritchie dies in a plane crash at the height of his popularity, still adored by his mother and his blonde girlfriend and recently reconciled with his brother. Like the

14. Ritchie Valens (Lou Diamond Phillips) with Donna (Danielle von Zerneck) in *La Bamba* (1987, Columbia). Jerry Ohlinger's Movie Material Store, Inc.

various jazz singers before him, Ritchie has successfully negotiated his ethnic and Oedipal crises before the end of his short life.

Expiating the Oedipal Crime

By adding the "Mammy" finale to the originally scripted ending for *The Jazz Singer*, Warner Bros. helped cement a tradition that we now call the Classical Hollywood Cinema. Hoberman (1991a) quotes one reviewer who attributed the revised ending to the persona of Jolson: "No audience would really expect to see Al Jolson give up show business—even in a film" (65). A more general explanation of the change has been offered by Carringer (1979): "The story is transformed from a fable of adjustment (how the new generation finds its place in a cultural tradition) to a more characteristically American fable of success—open revolt against tradition, westward movement, the expenditure of energy, triumph, and the replacement of the values of the old by the values of the new" (27). I would qualify this characterization by adding that the resolution of Oedipal tension must accompany the revolt against tradition if the fable is to be sufficiently appealing. Furthermore, the hero's appropriation of black American music may also be an essential part of the original *Jazz Singer's* lasting influence; like Louis Armstrong, Jack Robin sings of a nostalgic return to the mythological plantation with its infantilized black slaves. He puts on a mournful demeanor with the burnt cork that is highly inconsistent with the cheerful opportunist we first meet at Coffee Dan's, where Jack practically dances as he eats his breakfast. Along with everything else it offers, blackface gives Jack a dimension of solemnity and filial piety that are otherwise absent in his single-minded pursuit of assimilation. The hero's return to the stage at the end is substantially less abrupt because of Jack's impersonation of a mournful and loyal mama's boy. The crime of Oedipus becomes less abhorrent. And by simultaneously hiding his Jewishness and putting on the satyr's mask, Jack can move closer to his Gentile love object. If the upbeat finale of *The Jazz Singer* is crucial to the film's syntax, so is the borrowing of emotional and sexual capital from African Americans. This exchange of sexuality is especially significant in a culture that stereotypes blacks as hypersexual at the same time that it characterizes Jewish men as undersexed.

In this sense, the 1953 and 1980 remakes are not as close to the original as are *The Benny Goodman Story* and, to a large extent, *St. Louis Blues.* In the W. C. Handy film, the hero's final success resolves the Oedipal crisis with his father; although Benny Goodman's father is absent at the end, the culture of the father is never abandoned as the son moves into Gentile society. The regular proximity of Goodman to black musicians like Wilson and Hampton allows him to make this move without losing his soul, just as in *St. Louis Blues* the devotion of W. C. Handy to the folk art of "simple" African American workingmen preserves his authenticity even as he stands in his tuxedo before a symphony orchestra. And as in *The Jazz Singer,* an idea of an assimilable black vernacular music provides both protagonists with an acceptable context for their sexualization. By contrast, Danny Thomas and Neil Diamond have only the most tenuous

connection to black culture both inside and outside their respective narratives. (Steve Allen had substantial ties to jazz artists, and Nat Cole has
always been considered a first-rate jazz pianist.) It has not been my intention to valorize films that exploit the "surplus symbolic value of blacks"
(Rogin 1992a, 417) or for that matter the surplus symbolic value of Gentile women. I am interested rather in how a seemingly unique film like
the 1927 *Jazz Singer* can become a paradigm for American success stories, regardless of what they are called.

Black and Tan Fantasies

The Jazz Biopic

A "black and tan" was a speakeasy of the 1920s, particularly one in which whites and African Americans mingled in ways that were effectively forbidden under more conventional circumstances. In April 1927, Duke Ellington recorded the first of his several versions of "Black and Tan Fantasy." When asked about the title, Ellington expanded upon the definition by explaining that a black and tan was a place "where people of all races and colors mixed together for the purpose of fulfilling their social aspirations" (Dance 1963). Ellington was ironically acknowledging the miscegenetic interactions among black and white audiences, but he might just as well have been describing the relations between black and white musicians of the 1920s. Indeed, from the first moments that the first notes of "jazz" were played in or around New Orleans in the early twentieth century, black and white musicians have listened to each other and borrowed ideas. Just as Paul Whiteman had been inspired early on by the black and Creole artists of New Orleans and later by musicians including Ellington himself, black artists such as Ellington, Fletcher Henderson, and Don Redman, all of whom wrote for the first African American big bands, surely learned a great deal about "symphonic jazz" from Whiteman's orchestra. The arrangements that Ferde Grofé wrote for Whiteman in the 1920s may have been especially important for the first black jazz orchestras (Collier 1988).

Ellington himself always spoke highly of Whiteman, in spite of the contempt in which "The King of Jazz" has been held by many jazz enthusiasts, both black and white. Ellington's regard for Whiteman goes back to his days at the Kentucky Club in the mid-twenties: "Whiteman came often as a genuine enthusiast, listened respectfully, said his words of encouragement, very discreetly slipped the piano player a fifty-dollar bill, and very loudly proclaimed our musical merit" (Ellington 1973, 103). Of course, Ellington's knowledge of "symphonic jazz" was not only the result of his exposure to Whiteman. As Mark Tucker has written, Ellington was already well acquainted with an African American symphonic tradition during his youth in Washington, D.C., where he could have heard Will Marion Cook, James Reese Europe, and Ford Dabney (Tucker 1993b, 119). All of these African American composers led large groups of musicians at one time or another, although their music probably would be considered "pre-jazz" in our contemporary, narrow sense of the music's evolution. Nevertheless, Ellington surely absorbed crucial lessons from these artists that he would combine with what he later picked up in Harlem from more overtly jazz-inflected composer/arrangers. In particular, Ellington listened to the work of Noble Sissle and Eubie Blake, who wrote the successful Broadway show *Shuffle Along,* and Will Vodery, who did arrangements for the Ziegfeld Follies and who orchestrated George Gershwin's *Blue Monday* for *George White's Scandals* in 1922.[1] Fletcher Henderson, who arrived in New York in 1920 to study on the cusp of Harlem at Columbia University, was exposed to many of the same black influences as Ellington. He would also have known African American symphonic groups such as the New Amsterdam Orchestra, which gave concerts in 1921 with fifty-two Negro musicians, including William Grant Still, Ralph Escudero, and Russell Smith (Allen 1973, 1). Henderson too, however, even before he left Georgia for New York, enjoyed listening to the music of Paul Whiteman (Allen 1973, 4), and much of the symphonic music he heard that was played by blacks in the 1920s was closely modeled on European musics. Don Redman, who arrived in New York in 1923 at roughly the same time as Ellington, was the son of a music teacher. A child prodigy who played multiple wind instruments including oboe before he was twelve, Redman later received an extensive education in European classical music at the Chicago and Boston conservatories. His arrangements for Fletcher Henderson's band preceded those of Henderson himself and show the utility of "white" musical training for a jazz arranger. Although it is indisputably true that much of the white swing music of the 1930s and 1940s was derived from black idioms, it is also true that these same black idioms emerged from the interaction of blacks with European music and white American performers.

Needless to say, these interactions were not always as benign as Ellington deftly implies in his characterization of the black and tans. In the early decades of the century, for example, blacks in New Orleans were not allowed to join the American Federation of Musicians; when the light-skinned trombonist Dave Perkins married his black childhood sweetheart and stopped passing for white, the local union official saw to it that he lost his union card (C. E. Smith 1939, 45). Later, white bandleaders and impresarios either ignored black artists entirely, underpaid them, or swindled them out of large portions of their legitimate earnings. In the minds of many jazz enthusiasts, whites have played a primarily parasitic role in the history of jazz, becoming rich with their imitations of black innovators. As Lester Young is rumored to have said, "Stan gets the money." Although the image of white parasites is much too simple, without question white musicians have reaped greater rewards from the long history of interracial musical borrowings. The early histories of jazz even denied the extent to which whites borrowed from blacks. For example, Henry Osgood's *So This Is Jazz* (1926), the first published book to use the word "jazz" in its title, is devoted almost entirely to praising Whiteman and George Gershwin for improving the "quaint" folk music of blacks. One year later, with the appearance of *The Jazz Singer,* Hollywood made the first of many talking films that repress the role of black musicians in the development of jazz. In this chapter I am concerned with films that narrate the life histories of jazz artists. I pay special attention to the elaborate maintenance of white hegemony through several decades of filmmaking, especially when jazz is involved. In making my case, I will necessarily return to several films discussed in chapter 1.

"The Story"

The Jazz Singer provides the basic narrative for the lives of jazz and popular musicians in the movies. If this argument means that sometime after 1959 the narrative must belong to pop rockers, it only proves the power of the original 1927 film to determine how Hollywood tells the stories of popular musicians. It is no secret that this basic narrative is marked "Whites Only," allowing only exceptional performers like Nat King Cole to cross the line. For black artists, crossover success has never seemed as inevitable as it did for Jolson and his successors, and American mythology has never been so deeply invested in stories about blacks achieving the American dream. Although Jewish men in the movies regularly achieve that part of the dream that includes marriage to a Gentile woman, Hollywood has never celebrated interracial marriage as the sign of a black artist's success. (Compare, for example, *Bird* to *The Benny Goodman Story*.) For African American musicians, the basic narrative has been very different. Vance Bourjaily has called it "The Story."

> The Story goes like this: a musician of genius, frustrated by the discrepancy between what he can achieve and the crummy life musicians lead (because of racial discrimination, or the demand that the music be made commercial, or because he has a potential he can't reach), goes mad, or destroys himself with alcohol and drugs. The Story might be a romance, but it is a valid one. (Bourjaily 1987, 44)

In the oral traditions of American jazz, "The Story" probably begins with Buddy Bolden, the legendary, unrecorded trumpeter whose name appears in the recollections of many New Orleans jazz pioneers. In 1907, at age twenty-nine, Bolden was institutionalized for insanity at the East Louisiana State Hospital, where he remained until his death in 1931. According to legend, he never played again after his institutionalization. But no one built a novel or a film around the story of Bolden's life until much later. Both Bourjaily and Michael Jarrett (1996) consider Michael Ondaatje's fanciful treatment of the Bolden legend, *Coming through Slaughter* (1976), to be one of the finest of all jazz novels. For Bourjaily, "The Story" first appears in print as *Young Man with a Horn*, Dorothy Baker's 1938 novel about a white jazz musician. The 1950 film adaptation of the novel, also called *Young Man with a Horn*, was directed by Michael Curtiz for Warner Bros. in 1950. The substantial changes "The Story" underwent as it made the transition from novel to film provide the beginnings for a larger discussion of jazz biopics, especially those that, like *Young Man with a Horn*, must protect white subjectivity from the overwhelming black presence in the history of jazz.

Wrong Man with a Horn

In a note at the opening of her novel, Dorothy Baker says that she was inspired by the *music* of cornet player Leon "Bix" Beiderbecke but not by his life. Beiderbecke, who was twenty-eight years old in 1931 when he died of pneumonia and the effects of his habitual drinking, shares Buddy

Bolden's initials as well as his death date (Garber 1995, 79). Today, Beiderbecke is almost universally regarded as the first important white jazz musician. Baker probably insisted that she was not writing a life of Beiderbecke because little had been written about him during the decade in which he died. Bourjaily has said that the best thing about the novel is its title (1987, 44). In fact, Baker took her title, along with much of the Beiderbecke myth, from a 1936 *New Republic* piece by Otis Ferguson.[2] In this essay, "Young Man with a Horn," Ferguson became one of the first critics to write about Beiderbecke. Ferguson did not exploit the Keatsian potential in the musician's life, but as Baker discovered, his story is easy to romanticize. As the mythologized progenitor of several generations of young whites aspiring to play jazz, Beiderbecke occupies a unique place in the history of the music. The phrase "Bix lives!" preceded the appearance of the graffito "Bird lives," a reference to another self-destructive jazz genius, now also part of Hollywood myth.[3]

Because the film of *Young Man with a Horn* subjects the life and music of Beiderbecke to even more blatant transformations, my facetious working title for this chapter was "Bix dies." To my surprise, I subsequently discovered that those are almost the exact words that open Hoagy Carmichael's book *The Stardust Road* (1946). This first of Carmichael's two autobiographies begins and ends with the death of Beiderbecke, whom Carmichael knew and recorded with frequently (Beiderbecke's last recordings were made at a Carmichael session). My research took me to Hoagy Carmichael because he plays a role in the film of *Young Man with a Horn* that is curiously both diegetic and extradiegetic.[4] As the piano-playing character Willie Willoughby (the name has the same rhythm as "Hoagy Carmichael"), he invites the audience to perceive him both as the well-known musician-songwriter and as a character in the film. Carmichael opens and closes the film as the narrator, but he also appears as a friend of the hero within the diegesis. Although Carmichael was an accomplished player, his piano solos were dubbed in for the film by pianist Buddy Cole, who was called in early to prerecord the film's musical selections. Just as Carmichael is both inside and outside the story, both an actor and not an actor, he is both a musician and not a musician in the film. Since he steps out of the real world of Bix Beiderbecke, Carmichael's presence creates tensions in a film that is even less about Beiderbecke than was Dorothy Baker's novel. As always, classical cinema is capable of effacing such tensions, and in fact Carmichael's appearance provides a bit of what Roland Barthes (1972, 50) calls "inoculation," ultimately furthering the anti-jazz project of the film by acknowledging flaws in its mythology. Specifically, Carmichael refers to jazz as "mumbo jumbo" in his opening narration, but his unproblematic devotion to the music grants it a legitimacy that is otherwise repressed. At the same time, Carmichael helps solve the film's major problem of a white protagonist who is effectively the child of a black father.

Many white musicians embraced the delicate lyricism of Beiderbecke's playing as an alternative to the dramatic, often brash sounds of the early black trumpet masters such as King Oliver, Bubber Miley, Freddie Keppard, and, most importantly, Louis Armstrong. Born in Davenport, Iowa, in 1903, Beiderbecke could play the piano by ear at age five. In 1917, like many other young people in the United States, he acquired the recordings of the Original Dixieland Jazz Band. Although the musicians in the ODJB were white, they undoubtedly were influenced by the black and Creole musicians of New Orleans. Beiderbecke repeatedly listened to these records, memorizing the parts and playing them first on the piano and eventually on a cornet. It is possible that he also was directly exposed to African American trumpeters, perhaps even Louis Armstrong, as early as 1919 when the Fate Marable band was touring the Mississippi on a riverboat and disembarking at towns like Davenport to play concerts.[5] But Beiderbecke's style was probably fully formed by the time he began listening to Armstrong, which may not have happened until 1922 or 1923 when both men were in Chicago.[6] This is not to suggest that Beiderbecke did not learn anything from Armstrong; for example, Sudhalter, Evans, and Myatt (1974) discuss Armstrong's practice of building "correlated choruses" that made a significant impression on Beiderbecke (100). Even cursory listening to the recordings of the two musicians, however, reveals that they played in completely different styles. Collier's metaphor for comparing Beiderbecke to Armstrong is "sonnets instead of epics" (1978, 172).

Even black artists fell under Beiderbecke's spell—the Fletcher Henderson band recorded a version of "Singin' the Blues" based on a transcription of a performance of the tune by Beiderbecke and Frankie Trumbauer (Allen 1973, 255). But for white jazz musicians and followers of their music, Beiderbecke's records have been uniquely fetishized. I know of no other jazz artist, for example, whose admirers can purchase records with the title "Sounds Like Bix," collections of recorded scraps that compilers believe *might* bear some trace of Beiderbecke's cornet. Since Bix Beiderbecke has become the great white jazz father, pre–1950s American racial ideology had to erase the possibility that this key figure had a mixed musical parentage. One strategy for denying any black influence on Beiderbecke has been to suggest that he transcended mere jazz and was more closely related to European forebears. In his 1946 autobiography, Carmichael acknowledges the influence on Beiderbecke of "the black men who plied the river," but he subsequently emphasizes Beiderbecke's interest in the music of Debussy and Ravel (29, 48). Dorothy Baker began her novel with a prologue in which Rick Martin, the Beiderbecke character, is compared to Bach and to Thomas Mann's Tonio Kröger (Baker 1938, 4–5). And in a foreword to a reprint of Baker's novel, Clifton Fadiman likens Rick Martin to Christopher Marlowe and then praises Baker for "knowing quite well that Kreisler is a greater genius than Louis Armstrong" (Fadiman 1943, viii).

In Baker's novel, Rick Martin socializes frequently with black jazz musicians, who give him the first taste of the gin that is implicated in his destruction. After a prologue, the novel's first sentence reads, "In the first place maybe he shouldn't have got himself mixed up with negroes." Equally important to his downfall, however, is Amy North, the socialite who takes a perverse interest in Martin and eventually marries him. Here the novel partakes of the "primitivist" myth of jazz according to which childlike, uncomplicated people—usually but not necessarily black—create a music that flows naturally from the soul, unobstructed by intellection (Gioia 1988, 19–49). Martin is initially portrayed as a naïf who wishes to express himself only through his music. Amy North, significantly, is studying psychoanalysis, a complicating discourse that she marshals in her attack upon Martin's innocence. Since the novel is not totally devoted to promoting the Beiderbecke cult, Rick Martin is portrayed as an anomalous figure with no heirs waiting in the wings. He is a doomed poet, easily brought down by those two major sources of otherness, women and blacks, and to a lesser degree by the philistinism of American culture.

The film of *Young Man with a Horn* was released in 1950, by which time a Bixian cult was more fully developed than when Baker's novel appeared twelve years earlier. The ideological project of devaluing the black figures in Beiderbecke's musical parentage complements the film's efforts to transform Rick Martin (played by Kirk Douglas) into a more conventional hero for classical cinema. Two of the principal black characters from the novel turn up as whites in the film: Smoke Jordan, a black drummer, becomes Willie Willoughby, nicknamed "Smoke" (Carmichael); Jo Jordan, a black jazz singer and Smoke's sister in the book, becomes the big band vocalist played in the film by Doris Day. Rather than mixing regularly with blacks, the Rick Martin of the film has a long apprenticeship with a single African American character, the trumpeter Art Hazard (Juano Hernandez).[7]

In chapter 4 I discuss how the trumpet functions to establish the virility of those who play it. I argue that the instrument is not just a phallic symbol, but that it effectively functions as the phallus (as opposed to the penis), the grand signifier of power and masculinity that all men seek but can never really possess (Silverman 1988). The phallic discourse of *Young Man with a Horn* extends not just to the vaguely Oedipal relationship between Rick Martin and the older black trumpeter. When Art Hazard buys the young Martin his first trumpet, the boy presents the black man with a cigar. When the adult Rick Martin decides to leave his mentor and begin a career on his own, he once again makes a gift of a cigar. Although both men play the phallic instrument, the student must acknowledge his own multifaceted lack by repeatedly giving up the dark-colored cigar, an overdetermined symbol that also evokes racial and homoerotic associations. At least here, a cigar is more than just a cigar. Later in the film, Martin achieves his first real success just after he reencounters and in a sense vanquishes Art Hazard in a New York nightclub. After handing a third and final cigar to Hazard, Rick plays a number with the band, inspiring the teacher to announce to the audience that Rick has surpassed him as a player: "I taught him how to hold that trumpet he just played for you, but I didn't teach him how to play it—not the way he does." Within a few moments Rick is hired by a character modeled after Paul Whiteman, who employed Beiderbecke from 1927 until 1929.

After Rick becomes successful and appears to be on the verge of *possessing* the brass phallus, the aged Hazard becomes his plain-speaking companion, gently chiding him about his increasingly self-destructive behavior but receiving no cigar for his efforts. Art Hazard and Rick Martin establish a relationship very much like the one between Sam (Dooley Wilson) and the hero of *Casablanca,* another Rick in another Curtiz film. Far from being a black master to Rick Martin's white apprentice, Art Hazard and his proximity to the hero now validate Rick's independence from the false values of his culture. At the same time, Hazard takes on a feminized, mother-hen function that black companions have fulfilled for white heroes in American popular entertainments at least since Huck Finn and Nigger Jim. We know that Rick Martin has mastered an African American Other after Hazard is run down by a car, and in a funeral scene that recalls nothing so much as *Green Pastures,* Rick plays "Swing Low, Sweet Chariot" with virtually no jazz inflections.

By this time, however, Rick has become entangled with a new threat to his authority: the upper-class, dilettantish femme fatale Amy North (Lauren Bacall), who attempts to dominate the trumpeter by destroying the purity of his relationship with his instrument. Her overdetermined malevolence imbricates class prejudice, suggestions of lesbianism, and the more skeptical currents in Hollywood's long fascination with psychoanalysis.[8] It is Amy who teaches Rick how to drink hard liquor (previously his drink had been milk) and to notice, finally, the complexities of life that his single-minded obsession with the trumpet had spared him. When their doomed relationship reaches its nadir, she even smashes his beloved collection of Art Hazard records. After he collapses in the street from alcoholic despair over the death of Hazard and the cruelties of his wife, Rick's castration becomes most explicit when the wheels of a passing car flatten the battered trumpet he has been carrying. Earlier in his decline, at a recording session with Jo Jordan, he had repeatedly failed to hit a high note, a privileged signifier in the film's phallic discourse of the trumpet. The real Bix Beiderbecke, by the way, was almost perversely uninterested in high notes, playing consistently in the middle registers of the cornet. I should also point out that Art Hazard is denied access to the high notes throughout the film.

In many ways, *Young Man with a Horn* is the story of Harry James rather than Bix Beiderbecke. James, who is prominently listed as "musical adviser" in the opening credits, achieved most of his success in the thirties and forties, first as a featured soloist with the Benny Goodman orchestra and later as the leader of his own swing band. James possessed great technical facility and played in a bravura style heavily influenced by Louis Armstrong. It was nevertheless James who dubbed in the glitzy, anti-Beiderbeckian trumpet solos for Kirk Douglas in the film. (Jimmy Zito, an interesting trumpeter who made his mark with Les Brown's band in the late 1940s, dubbed in the trumpet solos for Art Hazard but is uncredited in the film [Meeker 1981, #3705].) Just as Harry James married the blonde actress-singer Betty Grable, Rick Martin at the end of the film seems to be married to the blonde actress-singer Doris Day. Like James, the Rick Martin of the film survives the jazz life by being more than a jazz musician and, of course, less than a jazz musician.

The year 1950 was an exceptionally appropriate release date for *Young Man with a Horn*. Almost all of the important big bands from the late forties were in serious trouble by that time. Duke Ellington's orchestra was the only major big band that continued touring through 1949 and into 1950—even Count Basie and Woody Herman were reduced to leading small groups. Kay Kyser, unerringly savvy throughout his career, retired from the music business in 1950. Many reasons have been offered to explain the sudden end of the big band era—the postwar suburban migration away from the inner-city dance halls, mothers and fathers staying home with their baby boom children, the rise of television. At least partially responsible for killing the big bands—and for bringing about the popular decline of the kind of jazz that Harry James had been playing—was the rise of the vocalists whose names began to appear above those of the bandleaders, a process that is explicitly represented in Martin Scorsese's *New York, New York* (1977). Unlike Scorsese's film, however, *Young Man with a Horn* ends with a jazz instrumentalist accepting the role of accompanist to a singer heroine. At the end of the film, Kirk Douglas is centered in a shot while Doris Day sings "With a Song in My Heart" in the background. There is no doubt, however, that this is a singer's recording session. Still, the film does not suggest that Rick has failed to achieve phallic authority at the end. *Young Man with a Horn* is careful to imply that Rick's heterosexual liaison with Doris Day has allowed him once again to master those high notes that Amy North had taken away from him and that Art Hazard could not teach him.

The presence of Hoagy Carmichael in *Young Man with a Horn* both disrupts and promotes the film's projects. In the first place, Carmichael occupies that space in classical cinema for nonactors whose wooden line readings and lack of polish undermine the *illusionistic* realism of a film at the same time that their real-life links to some relevant, profilmic expertise strengthen the film's claim to *documentary* realism. We might cite Babe Ruth's appearance in *The Pride of the Yankees* (1942) as an extreme example of this dual process. But if we consider, say, Oscar Levant in *Rhapsody in Blue* (1945), we see a nonactor moving into the realm of conventional Hollywood performance practice and losing some of his exteriority. Carmichael is closer to Levant than to Babe Ruth in this respect, but his historical relationship to Beiderbecke represents a much more profound contribution to the film's documentary basis.

Born in Indiana rather than Iowa, Carmichael had a great deal in common with Beiderbecke, even before the two men met and began their decade-long musical association in 1922. Both musicians learned jazz directly or indirectly from New Orleans players but reworked the music to accommodate white, Middle American sensibilities. Carmichael's understated, detached performance as an actor gives a much better sense of

Beiderbecke's music than do Harry James's histrionic trumpet dubbings. As he implies in his 1965 autobiography, Carmichael did some writing for *Young Man with a Horn*, allowing aspects of his public persona to color his screen character of Willie "Smoke" Willoughby. For example, when Rick Martin and Smoke drive between gigs, they are shot in an open car very much like the "open job" that Carmichael bought as a young man and that is prominently mentioned and pictured in both of his autobiographies. Smoke even invites Rick to visit his relatives in Indiana, an association that was well known to Carmichael's radio audience. Rick says, with a mock Indiana accent, "And meet Aunt Maaary?" At the end of the film, Smoke explains to the audience how Rick Martin managed to survive the hard times that are so vividly portrayed at the end of the film:

> You see, Rick was a pretty hard guy to understand, and for a long time he didn't understand himself. But the desire to live is a great teacher, and I think it taught Rick a lot of things. He learned that you can't say everything through the end of a trumpet, and a man doesn't destroy himself just because he can't hit some high note that he dreamed up. Maybe that's why Rick went on to be a success as a human being first—and an artist second. And what an artist.

Near the end of his 1946 autobiography, Carmichael makes similar statements about Beiderbecke: "Bix, the incomparable genius, but a human being with it all, subject to the ills of the flesh, the tortures of the spirit. And no way to say it except with the horn and the horn wouldn't say it all" (23).

In his direct address to the audience at the beginning of *Young Man with a Horn*, Carmichael implies that Rick Martin is dead as he speaks, suggesting that an earlier draft of the film's script ended with the hero's death. In his second autobiography Carmichael's recollections suggest precisely that: "Dorothy Baker's story was fine except for one thing—no ending. The story conferences became so intense that they even called me in to see if I could think up an ending. Mike Curtiz's idea of just letting Kirk die of alcoholism finally won out" (Carmichael 1965, 273). Carmichael has forgotten that the novel, not the film, ends with the death of the hero.[9] By keeping Martin alive at the end, the film is simply being true to classical Hollywood, but to a large extent the film's *actual* ending appears to be Carmichael's own solution to Beiderbecke's problems, as if Carmichael were erasing Beiderbecke's death along with Rick Martin's. The love of a good woman that Jo Jordan/Doris Day offers Rick is Hollywood's alternative to what Beiderbecke apparently experienced at the hands of a female companion at the end of his life. Carmichael speculates that the woman did not even know who Beiderbecke was. On the one occasion that he met her, Carmichael made her promise to keep in touch: "if Bix ever gets sick, if anything happens, *let me know*" (Carmichael 1946, 136, emphasis in text). When Carmichael recalls the day when he learned that Beiderbecke has died of pneumonia, he injects great pathos into the question, *"Little girl, why didn't you call me? Maybe a hospital, oxygen tent, little girl . . . "* (1946, 143, emphasis in text). This pain at the death of Beiderbecke that resonates strongly through both autobiographies may have led to the cinematic resurrection of the trumpeter.

In keeping with "The Story," jazz musicians with artistic aspirations often end up with some kind of chemical dependency, a topic best-suited to the social problem film, not to mention film noir, out of which the character of Amy North certainly emerges. Carmichael, who functions as an important element in the therapeutic dialectic of that social problem film *The Best Years of Our Lives* (1946), brings some of this quality into *Young Man with a Horn*. This process of generic exchange also helps disentangle Rick Martin from his black parent figure by pointing him in the same direction as the character in *The Best Years of Our Lives* played by Dana Andrews. As Michael Wood has noted, Andrews only has to pull himself together at the end of *Best Years* in order to find a job, even though the film clearly states that jobs for veterans like Andrews simply do not exist (Wood 1975, 38).

In his own unassuming way, Hoagy Carmichael transforms *Young Man with a Horn* into something entirely different than it would have been without him. Because he is more outside the film than within it, he can safely and positively signify "jazz" in a film that has no real use for the music. On a variety of levels he is instrumental in moving the white protagonist out of the castrating orbit of blacks and film noir women and into a more secure position, one occupied both by himself and by Harry James. The public probably perceived these two figures as jazz musicians, but also as much more. Their association with *Young Man with a Horn* in essence validates their ability to *transcend* the degraded world of jazz and to move into the unproblematic domain of post-big band show business in 1950. The judgments about jazz that are implied in the film's final scene are, in a sense, self-fulfilling prophecies. An even more appropriate ending for *Young Man with a Horn* would have shown Rick Martin ten years later, dubbing in the trumpet solos for a movie about a dead jazz musician.

Questions of Influence in the White Jazz Biopic

The cycle of films about actual jazz musicians probably begins with Al Jolson playing a character very much like himself in *The Jazz Singer* (1927). We might also include the cartoon that narrates how Paul Whiteman was "crowned" at the beginning of *The King of Jazz* in 1930. At the beginning of the 1940s, Bing Crosby starred in *Birth of the Blues* (1941), based loosely on the rise of the Original Dixieland Jazz Band, the group that recorded the first widely known jazz records in 1917 and changed the life of the teenage Bix Beiderbecke. Another film that ought to be mentioned in the early history of the genre is the Ted Lewis biopic, *Is Everybody Happy?* (1943). Lewis led an extremely popular dance band from the 1920s through the 1940s. He did in fact record with a handful of canonical jazzmen such as Benny Goodman, Fats Waller, and Muggsy Spanier, but his success was primarily based on his image as "The High-Hat Tragedian of Song" (Simon 1981, 497). On many levels, especially the Oedipal tension between father and son, the film is still another remake of the 1927 *Jazz Singer*. Although *Rhapsody in Blue* (1945) strives to carve George Gershwin's career to fit the European paradigm of the classical composer, even manufacturing for him a Viennese piano teacher who believes that Gershwin can become another Schubert, the film devotes a few scenes to his appropriations of blues and jazz. I will return to *Birth of the Blues* and *Rhapsody in Blue* later in this chapter.

The white jazz biopic did not become well established until Columbia Pictures scored a sizable hit with *The Jolson Story* (1946), directed by Alfred E. Green (Custen 1992, 84). The film inspired a sequel, *Jolson Sings Again* (1949), and may also have been responsible for the decision to film the lives of Tommy and Jimmy Dorsey in *The Fabulous Dorseys* (1947), also directed by Green. After the abrupt demise of many big bands and the rise of the pop vocalists at the end of the 1940s, the cycle of white jazz biopics took an elegiac turn with most of the subsequent films building their appeal primarily on nostalgia. *The Glenn Miller Story* (1954) ends naturally with the trombonist's death in 1944, but the diegesis of *The Benny Goodman Story* (1955) concludes with Goodman's 1938 performance at Carnegie Hall, even though Goodman was still an active performer. The success of *The Glenn Miller Story* led to the Goodman biopic as well as to films such as *St. Louis Blues* (1958), *The Gene Krupa Story* (1959), and *The Five Pennies* (1959), the story of the premodern jazz cornetist Red Nichols.

For most audiences in the 1950s, what I am calling "the white jazz biopic" was probably indistinguishable from films about entertainers with only marginal jazz associations, such as *The Eddy Duchin Story* (1956), *The Helen Morgan Story* (1957), and *I'll See You in My Dreams* (1951), in which Danny Thomas played songwriter Gus Kahn. As George Custen (1992) points out, most of these films rely on the same conventions that dominated the white jazz biopics. Much the same can be said of a number of fictional films about jazz musicians, including *Pete Kelly's Blues* (1955), *All the Fine Young Cannibals* (1960), and Michael Curtiz's 1953 remake of *The Jazz Singer*. After 1960, the cycle of white jazz biopics definitively came to an end. Black artists have dominated jazz biopics in more recent years, including Billie Holiday (*Lady Sings the Blues* [1972]) and Charlie Parker (*Bird* [1988]). In France, Bertrand Tavernier contributed to the cycle with *Round Midnight* (1986), in which a figure based on Bud Powell and Lester Young is assisted by a French admirer. The stories of white jazz artists are occasionally told today in documentary films such as *Let's Get Lost* (1988) and *Talmadge Farlow* (1981), although here, too, the vast majority of jazz documentaries have dealt with black artists.[10] After 1960, when jazz had ceased to be a popular music and the nostalgia for swing had played itself out, Hollywood had no real use for white jazz biopics, especially as jazz became reconfigured as an art music practiced most expertly by African Americans.

Before the preeminence of African Americans in jazz became received wisdom, the white jazz biopic presented Hollywood with a dilemma concerning the place of blacks in the lives of the white subjects. Because blacks could not entirely be denied their role in the genesis of jazz and swing, filmmakers had to acknowledge their importance without departing from the entrenched practice of denying black subjectivity. *Pete Kelly's Blues* dispensed with the problem early by showing an all-black funeral behind the opening credits. While a choir sings, the cornet of a recently deceased jazz musician is placed on the coffin on its way to the cemetery. When the instrument falls off the wagon, a small child picks it up. Cut to close-ups of hands exchanging the horn, first in a pawn shop and then in a poker game. The camera then draws back to reveal that the last hands to hold the cornet belong to Pete Kelly (Jack Webb), who goes on to be one of the few unambiguously macho males to play jazz trumpet in the history of the American cinema.[11] Although black instrumentalists are absent from the film after the prologue, the film has effectively solved the problem of acknowledging black influence without actually incorporating it into the plot.

Before *Pete Kelly's Blues*, Hollywood developed less adroit methods for dealing with the problem, most commonly the stigmatization of black jazz as a primitive, undeveloped form perfected by whites. This strategy was already operative in 1941 in *Birth of the Blues,* in which the white child who grows up to become Bing Crosby can already improvise on his clarinet more expertly than the folk artists who provide music for cakewalking blacks on the levee at the end of Basin Street. Surreptitiously accompanying the band from behind a wall of cotton bales, the white boy plays elaborate contrapuntal lines while a black cornetist, trombonist, and clarinetist simply play the melody to "Georgia Camp Meeting." The black clarinet player cannot understand how "his own hot licks" can be emerging from his horn even after he has stopped playing. But as soon becomes apparent, the child is not simply copying the black musician's licks. When he is discovered behind the bales, he is asked where he learned to play. "Oh, I just picked it up hanging around Basin Street." The black clarinetist then tells him, "White boy, come set beside me. There's a few things I want to pick up." Just by listening, the white child has acquired enough musical knowledge to surpass his mentors.

The idea that whites are more accomplished than blacks in the performance of jazz becomes explicit in *The Jolson Story* when the hero decides to inject black music into blackface performance practice. By contrast, the film has shown Dockstader's performers singing in an unsyncopated style more reminiscent of Stephen Foster than King Oliver. Jolson is portrayed as a visionary who understood the appeal that "jazz" could hold for a large white audience. He has also *improved* on a music that was naïvely made up "out of the air" by unsophisticated blacks. An even more elaborate version of this same narrative appears in *The Benny Goodman Story* (1955) when young Benny hears Kid Ory. Ory, playing himself and speaking words he probably would never have spoken on his own, tells the young hero that the band simply plays "New Orleans style." "It's nothing special. All the guys down in New Orleans play this way. . . . Most of these guys can't read music. They just swing on out and play the way they feel." As in *Birth of the Blues,* a young white clarinetist can hold his own with mature blacks. In *The Benny Goodman Story,* however, the young white musician actually plays with as much expertise as a professional jazz musician.

The Benny Goodman Story does go out of its way to acknowledge the role of black artists in Goodman's career.[12] Still, young Benny's easily acquired jazz competence in the scene with Kid Ory is only one of several racist fabrications in this early portion of the film. Most of the musicians in Ory's band did in fact read music, and viewers with some musical so-

15. Benny Goodman (Steve Allen) meets Fletcher Henderson (Sammy Davis, Sr.) in *The Benny Goodman Story* (1955, Universal/International). Jerry Ohlinger's Movie Material Store, Inc.

phistication can tell from the scene that Ory and his band are playing music that has been carefully worked out ahead of time—it's not just "swinging on out." And even if members of the band are in fact improvising some of what they are playing, a child does not learn the art of improvisation simply by being told to "play what you feel." More importantly, the film shows how the child grows up to be much more than a mere improviser. Like Jolson, he is a visionary who understands what Americans need to hear, and he is sufficiently dedicated to keep a band together until the public catches up with his vision. Again, Hollywood suggests that it takes a white person to bring substance to something that anyone—black or white—can do simply by instinct.

Often films in the white jazz biopic genre wait until the end to elevate white music over black music. *The Fabulous Dorseys* (1947) makes no reference to African Americans until the film is approximately half over and one of the battling brothers says that he is off to a nightclub to hear some "real jazz." This real jazz turns out to be a performance by Art Tatum, the revered black pianist. The one scene with an African American artist takes place in a dark, basement-like club, where Tatum is eventually surrounded by white players who have clustered around his piano with their horns. Tatum's dark, claustrophobic domain is in stark contrast to the film's finale in which both Dorseys play on a mammoth stage behind a string orchestra. The marks of Eurocentric high art are recruited to lift white jazz out of its degraded roots. That same year, in *New Orleans* (1947), several scenes with black artists take place in a backroom while the finale, in which a white opera singer performs a song that she learned from her black maid (played by Billie Holiday), is set in a concert hall with a symphony orchestra. *The Benny Goodman Story* also ends with the clarinetist playing in Carnegie Hall before a sold-out audience of well-dressed white concertgoers. Even the black jazz biopic *St. Louis Blues* ends in a concert hall with W. C. Handy (Nat King Cole) singing with a symphony orchestra.

The most memorable moments toward the end of *The Glenn Miller Story* (1954) also function to elevate the bandleader's music, this time by associating it with America's military might and the all-important morale of her fighting men. In one scene the men in Miller's band, looking sharp in their crisp uniforms, continue playing fearlessly while the English audience ducks at the sound of a rocket falling from the sky. The men in Miller's band are clearly soldiers and not mere jazz musicians. Later, Miller is equally fearless in instructing his band to play "St. Louis Blues" at march tempo while a general is reviewing the troops. As his commanding officer upbraids Miller for violating the military's rules of decorum, the visiting general arrives to congratulate the bandleader for doing so much to elevate morale.

Like Goodman and the Dorseys, the Miller of *The Glenn Miller Story* plays with black musicians in an early and crucial scene: the open spaces of the parade ground, like the dignified stage of the concert hall, contrast with the cramped jazz clubs to which black artists are invariably relegated. When the trombonist sits in with Louis Armstrong and an all-star group, Gene Krupa is also present, playing himself. The archetypal white Negro, Krupa was the subject of a biopic a few years later in which he would be portrayed by Sal Mineo, thus adding a homoerotic subtext to the many subtexts already associated with his character. The luridly colorful lights that wash over Krupa in the nightclub sequence in *The Glenn Miller Story* suggest these subtexts, especially his reputation as a user of marijuana, presented in *The Gene Krupa Story* in a manner reminiscent of *Reefer Madness* (1936). A more revealing example of how black and white jazz musicians must exist in different spaces takes place in a studio where Glenn Miller and the band record "Tuxedo Junction" while a pair of black dancers are marginalized as black-and-white images projected onto a screen.

Young Man with a Horn is especially interesting in terms of how it handles the question of a black man's impact on the playing of a white artist. Nick LaRocca, the trumpeter with the all-white ODJB and the first jazz trumpet player that Bix Beiderbecke would have heard, undoubtedly developed a portion of his style from listening to black musicians in New Orleans. LaRocca's own playing does not sound much like the canonical black New Orleans trumpeters such as Armstrong, Freddie Keppard, and King Oliver. Beiderbecke was also influenced to some degree by Paul Mares, the cornetist with the New Orleans Rhythm Kings, another white group that toured and recorded extensively. NORK's first records date to 1922, but Beiderbecke heard the group live the previous year in Chicago when he was playing hooky from the Lake Forest Academy (Sudhalter 1974, 67). Basing his early style on white trumpeters like LaRocca and Mares, Beiderbecke sounds even less like a black jazz artist from New Orleans. If Hollywood was interested in erasing blacks from the history of jazz, the industry could have found no better subject than Bix Beiderbecke. A film about Beiderbecke could have moved seamlessly from Bix listening to records of white musicians to his encounter with the New Orleans Rhythm Kings in Chicago and then to his recording sessions with Hoagy Carmichael, Paul Whiteman, and other white groups. Such a film would have overlooked Beiderbecke's high regard for black performers such as Armstrong, with whom he probably played in Chicago clubs in 1923, but it would not have been a complete misrepresentation of his stylistic development. In 1950, with Hoagy Carmichael available as a highly knowledgeable resource on Beiderbecke, *Young Man with a Horn* could have been tilted in this direction.

A film made in 1990 did in fact tell Beiderbecke's story without bringing a black musician before the camera. *Bix: An Interpretation of a Legend* was shot on many of the original locations in Iowa, Illinois, and Wisconsin by an Italian unit. Written by Antonio Avati and Lino Patruno and directed by Pupi Avati, the film starred Bryant Weeks as Beiderbecke.[13] Although the film took a few small liberties with Beiderbecke's life, the music, supervised by Bob Wilber, was extraordinarily accurate in recreating the music of Beiderbecke and several of the ensembles with which he recorded. Told in a series of flashbacks, the diegesis never ventures back before 1921, so no mention is made of the ODJB or of Beiderbecke's early encounters with their records. *Bix: An Interpretation of a Legend* does depict the cornetist's exposure to Paul Mares in Chicago, his meeting with Carmichael, an early performance of the Wolverines at a dance at Indiana University, and numerous sessions with Paul Whiteman, Jean Goldkette, and other all-white groups. In a scene at the Cinderella Ballroom in the New York of 1924 a house musician brags that the Cinderella is always packed, even though "Henderson's orchestra" has been filling Roseland every night since the addition of "that kid who was with Oliver's band." A voice off screen gives the name: "Armstrong." The house musician continues, "Everybody's going nuts over him. He's pretty tough to beat." End of conversation. Although numerous black servants and laborers appear throughout the film, there are no black musicians, and this one bit of dialogue is the only time that even the name of an African American artist is introduced.

Young Man with a Horn could have, with some justification, adopted this same approach to excising the black musical presence from Beiderbecke's life. And yet the film takes the black Art Hazard out of Dorothy Baker's novel and makes him into Rick Martin's father, mother, teacher, and musical inspiration. As with Kid Ory in *The Benny Goodman Story,* the black mentor eventually delivers the obligatory speech in which the white student is congratulated for outclassing the mentor. *Young Man with a Horn* demonstrates that Hollywood had a genuine need to bring forth black characters so that white musician/heroes could surpass them. This was the case even when, as in the case of Beiderbecke's life, it was not actually necessary.

Black Music and the Sexual Maturation of the White Jazz Hero

The Jazz Singer is not just about Oedipal reconciliation and successful assimilation into the great American mainstream. The film is also about Jack Robin's sexual coming of age; he wins the love of Mary Dale, although (and perhaps because) he is still singing passionately to his mother as the film ends. The liaison between Mary and Jack is visibly facilitated by his borrowing of sexuality from African Americans. As Michael Rogin (1992a) points out, at a crucial moment in their relationship Jack puts on burnt cork while Mary is effectively also in disguise.

> Neither Jack nor Mary appear in the everyday clothes that signify sexual difference. Jack wears black skin as his costume; in tightfitting pants and shirt, he is blacking his face and putting on a black wool wig. Mary, undressed in scanty dance costume, is all white. Her visible limbs convey a phallic power that, her availability for the male gaze notwithstanding,

accentuates the blackface performer's passivity. To complete the disorienta-
tion, Mary wears a giant tiara on her head. Standing as Jack sits in the
scene's opening, Mary towers above him. (Rogin 1992a, 442)

Her exaggerated femininity complements his grinning black satyr's face.
As a blackface minstrel, Jack covers over the Jewishness that might block
his sexual assimilation. And as Rogin suggests, Jack's blackface passivity
adds pathos more than menace to his sexuality.

Many of the white jazz biopics are somewhat more explicit about the
impact of black sexuality on the white hero. Rather than allusions
through blackface, many of the films bring on real black musicians to
transfer sexual power to the protagonist. Sometimes this sexual subtext
is linked to the moment when the white hero wins the admiration of the
black artists he has surpassed. Benny Goodman's reunion with Kid Ory,
who was present at young Benny's first sexual humiliation, takes place
just as Benny is about to begin seriously romancing Alice. Similarly, in
Young Man with a Horn, Art Hazard's declaration of Rick Martin's superiority as a trumpeter comes just before the hero begins his liaison with
Lauren Bacall. There are similar scenes in *The Glenn Miller Story* and *The
Five Pennies.* In fact, the young white protagonists in both films come of
age in remarkably similar encounters with Louis Armstrong.

In *The Glenn Miller Story,* the eponymous hero (James Stewart) and
his wife are on their wedding night when they arrive at Connie's Inn, the
legendary jazz spot in the Harlem of the 1920s. They imbibe bootleg
liquor in teacups as they listen to Armstrong and his band work their way
through "Basin Street Blues." Miller's cloyingly wholesome wife (June
Allyson) appears uncomfortable in this foreign locale with its lurid lighting, racially mixed patronage, and illegal spirits, not to mention Gene
Krupa. Eventually, Armstrong invites Miller and several other white musicians to join him on the bandstand and then cheers them on as they
solo. Miller has only this one interaction with a black artist, as if Armstrong were preparing him for the sexual initiation of his wedding night.
Miller's acquisition of sexual maturity is associated with his acceptance
by Armstrong at a Harlem nightclub.

Armstrong plays a slightly larger role in *The Five Pennies.* Like Beiderbecke, Red Nichols developed his style from listening to recordings of
white groups as he grew up in Utah. Nichols played briefly with Beiderbecke at the end of the Iowan's life, and together the trumpeters mark
the beginning of a jazz tradition in which the instrument is played with
less of the intensity associated with black trumpeters. In *The Five Pennies,*

16. As in most jazz biopics, romance is in the foreground with music in the background. James Stewart with June Allyson in *The Glenn Miller story* (1954, Universal/International). Jerry Ohlinger's Movie Material Store, Inc.

as in *The Glenn Miller Story*, a young, soon-to-be-famous white musician once again journeys up to Harlem to hear Armstrong, and once again the hero consummates a romantic relationship with a woman immediately after he performs with the black trumpeter and drinks liquor from a teacup. Specifically, Danny Kaye as Red Nichols receives a lover's kiss from Barbara Bel Geddes on their way out of the Harlem club, even though she is portrayed as a nice girl from Brooklyn on her first date with Nichols.

What is new in *The Five Pennies* is the latitude given Armstrong as he amuses himself at the expense of a white person. Nichols has just arrived from Utah with the conviction that he can outplay any trumpeter in New York. (Although Armstrong himself arrived in New York to play with Fletcher Henderson at roughly the same time that Nichols came to the city, the film shows Armstrong leading his own band and singing "Bill Bailey.") Drunk on bathtub gin, Nichols insists on joining in with Armstrong and his band.

Nichols: I'd like to show you how to really play this thing.

Armstrong: You look a little shaky there, son. You better sit this one out. We'll get to the volunteers later.

Nichols: . . . I happen to be the second greatest cornet-player in Ogden, Utah.

Armstrong: North Ogden or South Ogden? . . . If you ain't Gabriel, you in trouble. Play!

Nichols: Where's the arrangement?

Armstrong: Arrangement? Man, nobody writes down Dixieland. You just let it happen.

Nichols: Suppose it happens great one time and you'd like it to happen exactly the same way. What do you do then?

Armstrong: Just like tappin' a nightingale on the shoulder, sayin' "How's that again, dickie bird?"

Although *The Five Pennies* once again presents the motif of the intuitively improvising black artist versus the carefully trained white musician, the film grants Armstrong a position of at least temporary superiority, even allowing him to deliver the line about the "dickie bird" with its sexual mockery directly into the white man's face. Finally granting him permission to play, Armstrong warns Nichols, "Don't look back or you'll be trampled to death." Too intoxicated to perform adequately, Nichols is further humiliated when Armstrong tells the audience, "Excuse it, folks. Somebody must have put alcohol in our liquor." Needless to say, Armstrong does not remain critical of Nichols in the first scene at the Harlem club. After dashing to the men's room and presumably vomiting out his liquor, Nichols returns to join Armstrong in a convincing chorus of "Battle Hymn of the Republic." Suitably impressed, Armstrong calls after the departing cornetist, "Yeah! Get that boy's license number. He caught the nightingale." The moment is sexualized by the lover's kiss Nichols then receives from the woman he has just met as well as in the continuation of the bird imagery with its long history of phallic connotations.[14]

Armstrong is even present at the finale when Red Nichols is reconciled with his daughter, whose attack of polio Nichols had blamed on his own negligence and excessive devotion to his career. The original *Jazz Singer* had separated out family reconciliation from the hero's blackface adventures in crossover sexuality. In most of the jazz biopics, black sexuality is important only at the hero's sexual awakening; in Hollywood myth, white family harmony is not an issue that involves black males (unless the black man is retarded, as in *The Hand That Rocks the Cradle* [1992]). But the climax of *The Five Pennies*, given even more importance than the trumpeter/hero's return to playing after a long absence, shows Nichols's daughter suddenly recovering from polio and taking a few tentative dance steps with her father. Armstrong is not necessarily crucial to this process, but his presence tells us a great deal about the ambiguous nature of his role in American culture, especially as he grew older. At least in *The Five Pennies*, Armstrong takes on the qualities of the asexual loyal retainer that are still essential to Hollywood's conventions for depicting African Americans. (I will have more to say about Armstrong in chapter 6.)

The moment in which black people validate the white artist's achievement and/or his coming of age is repeated in numerous films besides the white jazz biopics. In *Carnegie Hall* (1947), the son (William Prince) of the female protagonist (Marsha Hunt) has left home to become a jazz pianist, much to the chagrin of the mother who wants him to play only classical music. A black actor appears in the film only when the heroine's maid plays and dances to the son's records on the phonograph. Significantly, the maid is an attractive young female. When discovered by the mother, the maid praises the son's music, adding that she and her friends in Harlem have even formed a fan club for the white pianist. This trope is still present in *Adventures in Babysitting* (1987), when a white teenager from the suburbs with no experience as a singer performs the "Babysitting Blues" with bluesman Albert King and wins the adulation of an initially wary audience of black blues fans. In *Back to the Future* (1985), a black rhythm and blues guitarist in 1955 named Marvin Berry is so impressed with the performance of Marty (Michael J. Fox), the boy from 1985, that he calls his cousin Chuck on the telephone, thus allowing the film to suggest that a white teenager is in some way responsible for the guitar style of Chuck Berry.[15]

An even more startling attempt to recruit real blacks as apologists for white imitations of their music is the *Blue Monday* scene in *Rhapsody in Blue*, which justifies a blackface operetta about a jealous black murderess and her mother-fixated lover by showing a pair of real African Americans becoming seriously involved in the action. Paul Whiteman, who has conducted the music from the pit, subsequently declares that he has decided to schedule a concert in Aeolian Hall in which he will "make a lady out of jazz." He invites Gershwin to write "a serious concert piece based on the blues." In a moment that is inevitable in most artist biopics, Gershwin has an epiphany in close-up. He will write a "Rhapsody in Blue." Although several scenes in the film show Gershwin learning the European masters from a teacher with a goatee and a *Mitteleuropa* accent, he is not shown actually listening to a black artist until late in the film when he sees Hazel Scott performing in Paris. Nor does the film suggest that Gershwin must listen more acutely to African American musical forms if he is to accomplish his project of marrying jazz and classical music.[16]

The white jazz biopic performed a great deal of cultural labor for white Americans in the 1940s and 1950s. Most of these films were typical of what Jane Feuer has identified as the need of the Hollywood musical to justify its own existence and by extension the popular entertainment industry of which it is a part. Just as popular music and jazz must win out over classical music in Judy Garland films such as *Babes in Arms* (1939) and *Presenting Lily Mars* (1943) (Feuer 1993, 58), so must the popular white musicians surpass their black influences. The African American Other has always been a source of fascination for white audiences, and the culture of blacks has been the subject of cinematic voyeurism at least since Edwin S. Porter's *Uncle Tom's Cabin* in 1903. Well before the birth of cinema, blackface minstrelsy was the most popular form of American entertainment and allowed whites an opportunity to both envy and despise their constructions of African American spontaneity and sexuality. Likewise, the white jazz biopic allowed a highly mediated view of the black Other at the same time that it reassured white audiences that their own cultural rituals could survive the comparison.

White Subjectivity and the Black Jazz Biopic

Except for the made-for-television movie, *Louis Armstrong—Chicago Style* (1975), the life of Armstrong has never been dramatized on film. Nor are there full-scale American films in which actors interpret the lives of Duke Ellington, Jelly Roll Morton, Miles Davis, or Thelonious Monk. There is, however, Clint Eastwood's biopic of Charlie Parker, *Bird* (1988). Clocking in at 160 minutes, *Bird* puts many demands on the viewer, including leaps back and forth in time that have much more in common with what David Bordwell (1985) has called "art cinema narration" than with the perfectly clear narrative progression of most Hollywood product. Eastwood and his cinematographer Jack N. Green also agreed upon an exceptionally dark mise-en-scène for the film so that details in apartments and nightclubs are often lost. If Parker emerges from the film as a somewhat inscrutable figure, it is at least in part because he is so often in the dark—or at least backlighted, much in the way that the body of director Eastwood has been presented in many of the films in which he acted. But if the lighting techniques developed for Eastwood idealized his body, the effect for Forest Whitaker was entirely different. For Paul Smith (1993), the ways in which the body of Parker/Whitaker signifies "decadence and dissolution" bear a significant relationship to "the ways in which Eastwood's own body both represents and signifies whiteness" (241).

One of the more controversial aspects of *Bird* was the aural presentation of Charlie Parker's improvisations, mimed on screen by Whitaker. Working with musical director Lennie Niehaus, Eastwood chose a computer process that effectively lifted the sound of Parker's alto saxophone out of its original recorded context. Working jazz musicians were then brought in to play along with the isolated alto solos. Although Parker's sound was enhanced by the computer, it still bears some of the thinness and fuzziness of the old Parker records, home recordings, and airchecks. In some cases the fidelity is so low that it jars with the crisp sound of the trumpeters, pianists, bassists, and drummers playing in the present. At other moments, Parker's saxophone has been mixed in at such low volume that he could be playing in a different room. On the most basic level, as Stanley Crouch (1989) has observed, Parker always made an effort to play *with* the other musicians (27), and much is lost by destroying the group rapport that once existed. And the living musicians with whom Parker is made to perform play in a much smoother, neobop style than many of the musicians with whom he actually recorded. Thus is Parker's difficult music tamed and made more accessible.

Indeed, the extreme fetishization of Parker's sound—digitally reengineered to eliminate much of the ambience and surface noise of the original recordings—does have its appeal. As Corbett (1994) has argued, recordings of music hold an almost erotic appeal, allowing the music to supply an imaginary wholeness in spite of the obvious lack of a performing body. The music in *Bird* is of course clearly attached to images that would reintegrate sound with sight—although Forest Whitaker does not comport himself very much like Parker did in performance, he does manage at moments to *look* a great deal like Parker in his later years. But the authentic sound of Parker, the grain of his alto's voice intact and completely unlike any other sound in the film, takes on a life of its own. The soundtrack album for the film sold well and gave many people their first and only taste of Parker's music. When the laser disc of the film was released, home viewers could use their remotes to skip directly to specific musical selections. In the end, the "aura" of Parker sticks to his sound even to the point of blotting out the images it was supposed to serve.[17]

Bird was also widely criticized for basing the story of Charlie Parker almost exclusively on the accounts of two white witnesses: the trumpeter Red Rodney, who toured and recorded briefly with Parker, and Chan Richardson, who was Parker's common-law wife in the years just before his death. While Parker himself remains a cipher, the motivations of Rodney and Chan are always clear. In an early scene when Parker is institutionalized after a suicide attempt, he confronts a white inmate playing chess. When the two come to blows, there is no obvious reason why Parker has deliberately picked a fight with an apparently random victim. Chan, however, explains to a hospital psychiatrist that because Parker has given up drugs and alcohol he needs to feel *something,* even if it is the pain that comes with a fight. Only in the explanation of a white character does Parker's behavior become coherent in spite of the fact that the audience never sees this particular character trait again. Similarly, Red Rodney has a special relationship with Parker, who is more concerned about the white trumpeter's narcotics abuse than about the drug habits of any of his black acquaintances.[18]

Black jazz biopics like *Bird* inevitably belong to traditions outside the mainstreams of Hollywood. Eastwood knew this when he filmed a life of Charlie Parker, regarding it as a labor of love rather than as a business venture (Giddins 1992). Historically, comparable films have usually been independent productions, or in the case of *Round Midnight* (1986), European ones. Nevertheless, even these films seem devoted to establishing the centrality and sameness of white observers alongside the marginality and otherness of the black jazz artist. This is the case in two films from 1966, *Sweet Love Bitter* and *A Man Called Adam,* as well as in the French film, *Round Midnight.* In all three, as well as in *Bird,* the life of a black jazz artist is framed within the gaze of white subjects, much in the same way that all views of Gandhi originate with white narrators in Richard Attenborough's 1982 biopic (Sharma 1996).[19]

A Man Called Adam concerns a trumpeter-singer loosely based on Miles Davis. The presence of Cicely Tyson, who appears on the cover of the trumpeter's 1967 LP *Sorcerer* and who would eventually marry Miles Davis in 1981, gives an uncanny air to the film, especially since the film foreshadows Tyson's troubled relationship with Davis in its depiction of the love affair between Claudia (Tyson) and Adam (Sammy Davis, Jr.). The hard-drinking protagonist abuses Claudia and virtually every other character. Not until the film is almost over does the narrative reveal that Adam still feels pain because he was the driver in the automobile accident that killed his wife and child and blinded the man who played piano in his group. But Adam's anger is not simply the result of this misfortune. The civil rights movement is very much a factor in *A Man Called Adam*. We are told, on the one hand, that Claudia had spent the night in a Southern jail as a freedom rider. Adam, on the other hand, has no use for the movement or for any organized activity outside jazz, and even then he regularly disrupts the harmony of his group. Nevertheless, he speaks the language of black liberation, and the film takes the 1960s liberal stance of justifying his irascibility as a legitimate reaction to the racism and philistinism of American culture. Surprisingly, Adam has taken on a white student, Vincent (Frank Sinatra, Jr.), who tours with Adam's group as second trumpet. Except for Claudia, Vincent has a stronger rapport with Adam than any other character in the film. In one of his many outbursts Adam speaks harshly to his white idolator, but Vincent is shown to be sympathetic—he understands that the attack is not personal.

A Man Called Adam also departs from Hollywood practice by showing that racism is not simply the result of a few bigots in the South but that it is a systemic part of American culture. The personification of institutionalized racism is Manny (Peter Lawford), the booking agent who has ultimate control over Adam's career. Adam asserts that Manny abuses

17. Sammy Davis, Jr., Frank Sinatra, Jr., and Hank Jones in *A Man Called Adam* (1966, Embassy). Jerry Ohlinger's Movie Material Store, Inc.

musicians because he was not able to succeed as one himself. Because Adam has recently walked out on a tour of clubs, Manny is reluctant to set him up with the kind of all-star bookings that Adam feels he deserves. To teach Adam "discipline," Manny has decided to send him on a six-week tour of one-nighters in the South. In a rage, Adam threatens Manny with a broken bottle and insists that the white man crawl on his hands and knees. Adam subsequently pays for his outburst, losing all opportunities for regular work. In desperation, Adam eventually tracks down Manny and, crawling on his hands and knees, attempts to shine his shoes as a gesture of contrition. On the tour of the South that Manny still insists he must take, Adam, along with Vincent and the rest of his group, appears in a montage of one-nighters playing to consistently appreciative audiences. At the end of the sequence, however, Vincent is attacked backstage in an alley and brutally beaten by white thugs. Adam stands helpless and watches while Claudia urges him to do something. The beating of Vincent begins Adam's final decline.[20] A few scenes later he collapses during a club date and dies. As Adam is carried off to the ambulance, Vincent surreptitiously takes the mouthpiece out of his horn and puts it in his pocket, a slightly displaced but striking example of the trope of the white jazz musician appropriating black sexuality. In spite of the less than heroic fate of its protagonist, black artists did participate in the making of the film: *A Man Called Adam* was made by Sammy Davis, Jr.'s production company, and Ike Jones, one of the film's two producers, is an African American. Mark Reid (1988) considers the film to be a forerunner of the black exploitation films of the 1970s.

Sweet Love Bitter has more in common with *A Man Called Adam* than a 1966 release date. Just as Vincent relays the gaze of the audience to the self-destructive trumpeter-protagonist, in *Sweet Love Bitter* the story of the self-destructive saxophonist-protagonist takes place almost entirely under the eyes of an obsessed college professor played by Don Murray. Richie "Eagle" Stokes (Dick Gregory), based loosely on Charlie Parker, is looked after by the Murray character much as Vincent attempts to keep Adam from destroying himself. In both films a black jazzman fights with racist cops, overindulges in drugs and alcohol, refuses to accept the rules by which normal working people function, and exhibits wildly irrational behavior that is implicitly justified by his sufferings at the hands of American racism.

A white hero, however, is even more dominant in *Sweet Love Bitter* than in *A Man Called Adam*. In fact, it is the white college professor, Dave (Don Murray), who was driving when *his* wife was killed in an automo-

18. Dick Gregory as Richie "Eagle" Stokes in *Sweet Love Bitter* (1966, Film Three). Jerry Ohlinger's Movie Material Store, Inc.

bile accident! The film opens with Dave hocking his wedding ring in a Lower East Side pawnshop to finance a night of heavy drinking. There he meets Eagle who strikes up a conversation in spite of the fact that Dave studiously avoids him. Moments later the two meet in a bar, and again Eagle, who later shows little regard for any other white person, initiates conversation. Presumably because Eagle recognizes a fellow sufferer, the two become close friends, and Eagle sees to it that Dave has a place to sleep when their drinking session ends on a city street. Later, as Dave begins to pull himself together, he returns to the upstate New York college where he once taught. The president of the college, who understands that Dave's breakdown was a legitimate reaction to personal tragedy, offers him his old job back. Eagle has tagged along on Dave's journey upstate, and as the professor consults with the college president, Eagle is assaulted by a white policeman. Fearing for his newfound job security, Dave stands by and watches the beating. Dave later feels that he has doubly betrayed Eagle by not intervening and by moving to a place where he will no longer be able to take care of Eagle. The jazz saxophonist appears even more devastated by these betrayals at the hands of his white friend—another similarity with *A Man Called Adam,* although the races in the two parallel scenes are reversed. Still another similarity involves the black musician's final decline shortly after a crisis with the central white figure.

The third major character in *Sweet Love Bitter* is Keel (Robert Hooks), the black owner of a jazz club where Eagle occasionally performs. After Eagle insists that Dave join him when Keel comes to take the drunken saxophonist home with him, Keel gives Dave a job waiting tables and cleaning up in his club. The two become co-caretakers for Eagle, at one point struggling together to undress him and then drag him into a bathtub full of ice in hopes of saving him from an overdose of heroin. In a significant subplot, Keel has a white girlfriend, Della (Diane Varsi), with whom he has become impotent. He even has a dream in which he finds himself in a movie theater watching her face enlarged to enormous proportions on the screen. A tiny figure emerges from the margin of the screen playing a saxophone; the figure turns out to be Keel, whose saxophone solo breaks off when he can no longer make the notes flow.[21] Dave and Della have a conversation in which she details the rough treatment she receives from strangers as part of an interracial couple. Keel and Della are still together at the end of the film, but there is no indication that Keel has recovered from his impotence or that he and Della have decided what to do about it. At the end of the film, after Eagle has died of an overdose, the two are simply there to bid farewell to Dave as he returns to college teaching.

If *A Man Called Adam* and *Sweet Love Bitter* have not aged well, there is still much to recommend in these two independently produced jazz films.[22] Both take the music seriously, even seeing to it that jazz is heard exclusively on the extradiegetic score. Benny Carter was hired to write the music for *A Man Called Adam,* and Mal Waldron wrote the score for *Sweet Love Bitter.* In both cases, the use of jazz to fulfill the emotive functions of the background score gives an authenticity to these two films that more mainstream jazz films have lacked. The sound of Adam's trumpet in *A Man Called Adam* was dubbed by Nat Adderley, a talented but self-effacing musician whose sound does not have the earthiness and bite that one might have expected from the Adam character. *Sweet Love Bitter,* however, makes excellent use of the alto saxophone of Charles McPherson, who dubs in the sound of Richie's horn. McPherson also worked with Lennie Niehaus on *Bird,* playing the various Parker solos that were not lifted off the records. McPherson's imitations of Parker are extremely convincing, and his fleet, lyrical dubbings for Dick Gregory in *Sweet Love Bitter* offer good reasons why the other two principal characters should be so devoted to keeping the saxophonist alive.

The dreary but well-intentioned *Round Midnight* operates on the myth that European connoisseurs understand jazz better than do the actual practitioners, and, once again, the fortunes of a self-destructive black artist become episodes in the life of a sensitive white admirer. Francis (François Cluzet) is the commercial artist who takes Dale Turner into his apartment because Turner's black girlfriend-manager Buttercup does not treat him with enough sympathy. While Dale Turner is based on both Lester Young and Bud Powell, Francis is based on Francis Paudras, who looked after Bud Powell during his last years. The black-white homoerotic subtext that is also present in *Sweet Love Bitter* and *A Man Called Adam* is most explicit in *Round Midnight*. At one point, Francis tells his estranged wife that he must devote his time to Dale Turner because he "inspires" him. The wife asks the legitimate question, "Did I ever inspire you?" Black women do not fare well in the black jazz biopics either. As Stanley Crouch has observed, Charlie Parker had positive working relationships with Mary Lou Williams, Sarah Vaughan, and Ella Fitzgerald, but the only black female performer in *Bird* is a fictitious blues singer who disparages Parker's early attempts at developing his style with the words, "Nigger, don't be playing that shit behind me while I'm trying to *sang*" (Crouch 1989, 26). Nor does the film acknowledge that two of

19. Forest Whitaker as Charlie Parker in *Bird* (1988, Warner Bros.). Jerry Ohlinger's Movie Material Store, Inc.

Parker's wives prior to Chan were black. Although Cicely Tyson is given some sympathetic moments in *A Man Called Adam,* the trumpeter's other black girlfriends are savaged. Much the same can be said of the black bimbos in *Sweet Love Bitter* and the castrating Buttercup in *Round Midnight.* The real love affairs in these films are between white men and black men.[23]

A significant exception to the misogyny of the black jazz biopic is *Lady Sings the Blues* (1972), if only because it takes as its subject the life of Billie Holiday (Diana Ross). For obvious reasons, few critics and film historians have embraced *Lady Sings the Blues.* Based on William Dufty's ghosted autobiography (1956) that Holiday herself probably never read, the film repeatedly throws historical accuracy to the winds. Nevertheless, Robert O'Meally (1991) is probably correct when he says that Holiday would have liked the movie (197). As O'Meally argues throughout his book, *Lady Day: The Many Faces of Billie Holiday,* the singer encouraged myths about her life, especially when they brought her fame and badly needed cash. Many of the distortions in the film can be traced back to Holiday herself. For example, the scene in which the teenaged Billie fails in her attempt to find work as a dancer at a Harlem club but unexpectedly succeeds when the piano player encourages her to sing, is straight out of a paid interview that she gave to Frank Harriott of the left-wing tabloid *PM* in 1945 (O'Meally 1991, 64). But O'Meally has turned up evidence that Holiday had been singing along with records in a Baltimore brothel and performing at amateur shows and after-hours clubs at least since the age of eleven.

Holiday also liked to cast herself as a victim in the self-fabricated versions of her life story, another reason why the film might have appealed to her. Throughout the film Billie is primarily reactive, coping with burdens placed on her by others. Her heroin addiction is blamed on enticements from the pianist in the white big band with which she travels. (Holiday did in fact travel with Artie Shaw in 1938, but Shaw refused to lend his name to the movie [Clarke 1994, 450].) After steadfastly refusing, she one day succumbs in hopes of overcoming the exhaustion of travel and the pain she endures from racism, brought home by the sight of a lynching victim and a Klan rally she encounters in her travels.

Louis McKay, Holiday's last husband and the inheritor of a small fortune in royalties when her death brought renewed interest in her recordings (Chilton 1975, 197), was an adviser to the producers of *Lady Sings the Blues* (Clarke 1994, 450). For O'Meally, McKay was one of sev-

20. Diana Ross as Billie Holiday in *Lady Sings the Blues* (1972, Paramount). Museum of Modern Art Film Stills Archive.

eral "rogues" that Holiday took as lovers, "neurotically choosing men who would reenact the desertion of her father" (18). In the film, however, he is a paragon played by the "Black Clark Gable," Billy Dee Williams. In *Lady Sings the Blues*, McKay functions for Holiday in some of the same ways that whites function for black jazz artists in *Bird*, *Sweet Love Bitter*, and *Round Midnight:* McKay is the reliable center to which the jazz musician can return whenever life's impossibilities bring about a self-destructive episode. Like Chan in *Bird*, McKay even interprets Billie's behavior for the audience. It is not entirely clear, for example, that Billie is newly under the influence of heroin when McKay arrives after she has been away on tour; it is, however, clear to McKay. Ultimately he functions as the audience's surrogate as he looks at and after the heroine. It is McKay who relays a voyeuristic gaze at the appalling but mesmerizing sight of Billie taking down the top of her dress as she prepares to inject herself with the drug. The entire scene is played out in terms of McKay's reaction. At the climax, when he sees her glassy-eyed and nodding from the effects of heroin, Michel Legrand's overripe love theme swells on the soundtrack, further enhancing the eroticism of the spectacle.[24]

Portraying Billie Holiday as a helpless waif substantially enhanced her erotic appeal, but it did little to clarify her real gifts as a singer, including her ability to create what Michael Jarrett (1994) has called the "authenticity effect." Holiday was undoubtedly a shrewd artist, always aware of the emotional shadings she gave her performances. In studio patter that has been released on a number of discs, Holiday can even be heard having fun with material that she would later perform with real conviction. On a rehearsal tape made at bassist Artie Shapiro's house the day before a Verve studio session, Holiday can be heard working out a version of Matt Dennis's "Everything Happens to Me."[25] The first lines of the song are written as "I make a date for golf, and you can bet your life it rains." On the rehearsal tape, however, Holiday sings "you can bet your ass it rains" and then breaks out laughing.

Nevertheless, *Lady Sings the Blues* suggests that her songs were straightforward expressions of her emotional states. Here, too, she is portrayed as entirely reactive. Stumbling upon the lynching victim, she is heard extradiegetically singing "Strange Fruit" as if the song were the instantaneous result of the experience. Although Billie Holiday wrote the music for the song, the lyrics ("Southern trees bare a strange fruit / Blood on the leaves and blood at the root") were written by poet Lewis Allan. In 1939, Allan brought the poem to Barney Josephson, the owner of Café Society, a unique club of the time that catered to a biracial audience. Josephson recommended that Allan show the lyric to Holiday, who was then a regular attraction at Café Society. "At first, Lady was slow to understand the song's imagery, but her bewilderment decreased as Allan patiently emphasized the cadences, and their significance" (Chilton 1975, 68–69). Soon she was convinced of the song's importance and decided that she must record it. Her moving performance of "Strange Fruit" endowed her career with a powerful anti-racist element and transformed her in the minds of many listeners. Although "Fine and Mellow," the song on the flip side of "Strange Fruit," was a bigger hit on jukeboxes (Feather 1979), a great deal of Holiday's cachet then and now rests upon this song of social protest. In 1939 the lyrics were so daring that Columbia, Holiday's record company at the time, refused to release the recording (Chilton 1975, 70). In the film, however, the song seems to grow organically out of her shock at seeing a lynching victim. Similarly, when Louis McKay throws her out of his apartment because of her drug use, the next scene shows her singing "'Tain't Nobody's Business If I Do" and then "Lover Man (Oh, Where Can You Be?)" as her divided reaction to the breakup.

Holiday's image as a naïve transmitter of lived experience was already established at the outset of her career. In 1935 she appeared with Duke Ellington and his orchestra in *Symphony in Black* as a rejected woman who sings a blues after her lover has shoved her to the ground and walked off with another woman. Unlike Ellington, who is pictured composing his music throughout the short film, Holiday appears to be producing music "naturally" without a text or a thought. Holiday was of course complicit in the myth that her songs transparently reflected what was inside her. She herself would make statements such as "Anything I do sing, it's a part of my life" (quoted in O'Meally 1991, 11). Coming at the end of the brief era of "blaxploitation" films in the late 1960s and early 1970s, *Lady Sings the Blues* might have given Billie Holiday some of the same resourcefulness and wit that Pam Grier and Tamara Dobson displayed in *Coffy* and *Cleopatra Jones,* both of which were released one year after *Lady Sings the Blues* in 1973.[26] O'Meally's book goes a long way toward restoring some of Holiday's subjectivity. A revealing companion piece to *Lady Sings the Blues* is Stuart Goldman's 1992 documentary *My Castle's Rockin',* which tells the story of blues singer Alberta Hunter as the refutation of the myth of the fragile and doomed black female singer. Even now, however, it is difficult to imagine any other Billie Holiday than the one that she herself created and that has been deeply inscribed in jazz myth.

The W. C. Handy biopic, *St. Louis Blues* (1958), represents a striking exception to the conventions of films about black jazz artists. Released at the high water mark of the white jazz biopic, the film stands on the other side of a cultural gulf from *A Man Called Adam, Lady Sings the Blues,* and *Bird.* From the outset, the film makes a point of showing Handy's fascination with the work songs of black laborers. As the observer of black vernacular music, the celluloid Handy has more in common with Stephen Foster, who probably spent time listening to the songs of black boatmen and wharf workers as a youth in Pittsburgh (Foster 1932, 83), than with someone like Sidney Bechet, who described the music as part of his blood and the air he breathed rather than something he had to learn (Bechet 1978). After apparently absorbing the laborers' songs through listening, the Handy of *St. Louis Blues* plays along with them on a cornet. Handy's father, a respected minister, discourages his son from listening to the secular music of poor folk, preferring that the boy play the piano in church.[27] He even "castrates" the boy by throwing his horn under the wheels of a passing wagon. The film is unremarkable in suggesting that Handy is better off following his own instincts and that he transforms simple folk music into something much more sophisticated. As the privileged spectator and auditor of black music, Handy/Cole was granted the kind of subjectivity usually extended only to whites, at least in part because he functioned as white within the discourses of the genre. This would not have been possible if the syntax of the white jazz biopic had not been so well established by this time— almost all of the films in the cycle were made before *St. Louis Blues* appeared in 1958.

The fact that the black W. C. Handy's story is *not* seen through the eyes of, say, his best friend the white drummer has much to do with the persona of Nat King Cole, whose career is treated in much greater detail in chapter 7. In spite of his modest talents as an actor, Cole may have been one of the few blacks in Hollywood who could meet at least some of the generic requirements of the white jazz biopic. In particular, Cole functioned as a healthy alternative to the unsavory image of the drug-crazed, psyched-up black jazz artist that had been thoroughly inscribed on the American mind by the late 1950s. It is also likely that the culture industry presented him as a wholesome alternative to the white (and black) rockers who were then scandalizing the more squeamish guardians of American morals.

Still, *St. Louis Blues* puts Cole in a marginal position. W. C. Handy was born in 1873, and although he lived until 1958, he had written most of the songs for which he would be remembered before the end of the 1920s. Significantly, Handy was a composer, not an improviser. He fits more easily into the biopic's Eurocentric aesthetic that valorizes composed "art" above the ephemeral solos of jazz musicians. For the same reasons, the Glenn Miller, the Benny Goodman, and even the Al Jolson of the biopics are more like composers than soloists as they seek to conceptualize the right *sound* to which audiences will eventually respond. And because Handy represents the ancient history of jazz and swing, he can safely be canonized without in any way undermining the importance of the popular white musicians of the late 1950s. As always in the 1940s and 1950s, black musicians were welcome in the jazz biopic, but only so long as dominant racial hierarchies were strictly observed. More specifically, early jazz musicians (blacks) were subordinated to the popular swing musicians (whites) as, for example, in *New Orleans* and *A Song Is Born* (1948), both of which are discussed in chapter 3.

Like *The Jazz Singer*, *St. Louis Blues* ends with a scene of reconciliation between the son and his more conservative father. As has been the case with white jazz biopics since the original *Jazz Singer* of 1927, the hero finds that popular music provides a means for great success at the same time that it allows the hero to preserve important ties with his wife, parents, and children. This strongly contrasts with the high prices that black musicians like Billie Holiday in *Lady Sings the Blues*, Charlie Parker in *Bird*, and Dale Turner in *Round Midnight* must pay for their art. For African American jazz musicians the only success is the kind that leads to self-annihilation. For white artists the conditions for success are much less dire.[28]

THREE

Jazz Becomes Art

oday, many jazz enthusiasts believe that their music is art. They support this conviction with a history of the music built around a pantheon of composers and instrumentalists within a great, evolving tradition. They even break careers of some canonical jazz musicians into early, middle, and late phases on the model of Beethoven and other European masters.[1] Wynton Marsalis, who today practically embodies the idea that jazz is art, has brought jazz into the realm of American high culture through his stewardship of the jazz division at New York's Lincoln Center.

Few general listeners, however, are likely to connect jazz with high art. A quick glance at the artists who dominate *Billboard's* lists of best-selling jazz records, or who appear on the cover of *Jazziz,* might suggest a broader notion of a music that overlaps with rock and roll, New Age, and the nostalgia industry. Although listeners undoubtedly consume music in their own highly personal ways, few have endowed Kenny G, Tony Bennett, or George Winston with the same seriousness that followers of classical music have brought to Mozart, Beethoven, and Bartók. Even the most canonical albums from jazz history have often been contextualized as something distinct from art. In Hollywood films, for example, classic jazz has been cast as the music of sexual chemistry. In *Zebrahead* (1993), a white teenage boy completes his seduction of a young black woman by playing the John Coltrane quartet's recording of "Say It Over and Over Again" from the 1962 *Ballads* album. In *Rising Sun* (1993), Duke Ellington's 1959 recording of "A Single Petal of a Rose" plays extradiegetically as Wesley Snipes and Tia Carrere show the first signs of mutual attraction. As early as Joseph Mankiewicz's *No Way Out* (1950), in which Sidney Poitier plays a young doctor accused of murdering a white patient, compositions by Ellington waft from a radio in two separate scenes as Linda Darnell must decide whether or not to overcome her suspicion of Negroes and help out the Poitier character. During these two moments in the film, Darnell smokes, paces, and listens to "In a Sentimental Mood" or "Sophisticated Lady." Although she is probably contemplating the dangers of supporting a Negro in an explosive situation, she may also be moved by the allure of an attractive, dynamic black man, an implication reinforced by two of the most sensual compositions by another attractive, dynamic black man.

More recently, jazz has been configured not so much as art but as the signifier of elegance and affluence, an association the music seldom if ever carried before the early 1980s. In *Indecent Proposal* (1993), for example, the multimillionaire played by Robert Redford brings a tuxedoed Herbie Hancock aboard his yacht to provide the appropriate background of tasteful jazz piano for his well-heeled guests. In television commercials of the early 1990s, Benny Goodman's 1952 recording of "How Am I to Know" accompanied ads for the Chase Manhattan Bank; Ellington and Strayhorn's "Chelsea Bridge" played behind an American Express commercial; and Louis Armstrong's recording of "A Kiss to Build a Dream On" was recruited to sell Diet Coke. In all of these advertisements the accent was on comfortable prosperity. In Woody Allen's *September* (1987), musical taste is the basis for a Chekhovian differentiation between troubled but sensitive intellectuals (Sam Waterston and Mia Farrow) who admire the classic Art Tatum/Ben Webster album of 1955 and the boorish survivor (Elaine Stritch) who prefers Glenn Miller.

Although a small group of supporters may think of jazz as something akin to high art, others have held the music in contempt *because* of lofty claims made for the music. Many jazz fans can recall being accused of snobbism when they expressed a preference for Sarah Vaughan over Linda Ronstadt, Charles Mingus over Bob Wills, or Lambert, Hendricks and Ross over Crosby, Stills and Nash. Elvis Presley's encounter with snobbish jazz lovers at a faculty party in *Jailhouse Rock* (1957) may be the most arresting example of how jazz and its adherents can be portrayed as pretentious and elitist.[2]

The Battle Between the Ancients and the Moderns

The view of jazz as art probably began with disputes in the jazz press of the 1940s. As Bernard Gendron (1993) has convincingly argued, a schism developed among jazz aficionados during the height of the swing era when a number of record collectors and serious students of the music began publishing magazines such as *The Record Changer* and *H.R.S. Rag*. These journals extolled the "hot" music of New Orleans in the 1920s as the authentic jazz and condemned swing as "counterfeit" and "commercially degraded." The defenders of swing, writing primarily in *Metronome* and *Down Beat*, fought back, claiming that Dixieland, as the older music was usually called, was technically backward and "corny." The more pugnacious opponents of Dixieland, most notably Leonard Feather, referred to writers of the revivalist, pro-Dixieland journals as hysterical cultists and musical ignoramuses. Feather coined the term "moldy fig" to describe the revivalists and took his attacks to such levels that fistfights and even lawsuits took place between the two camps.

No sooner had this dispute begun to cool down than a new war flared up between traditionalists and modernists, this time around a set of young, African American musicians known as beboppers—Charlie Parker, Dizzy Gillespie, Thelonious Monk, Bud Powell, Howard McGhee, Kenny Clarke, etc. Retrospectively, we now see bebop's emergence in the mid- to late 1940s as a revolution that permanently transformed jazz into an art music. At the time, however, an important aspect of bop's emergence was the ability of the music's defenders to adapt quickly to the discursive strategies previously devised in the disputes over Dixieland and swing. All the arguments that were once made for swing—it is complex, it is progressive, it requires great talent—could just as easily be applied to bop.

Counterarguments were advanced for Dixieland—it is authentic, it is emotionally powerful, it is the music of the folk. As Gendron argues, then, the notion that jazz is art did not so much originate with bop as it did with the earlier battle between Dixieland and swing. Whether it was Dixieland versus swing or boppers versus moldy figs, both sides engaged in the creation of an art discourse, something that was never needed when jazz simply meant dance music and fast living. In Gendron's words, "both contests were fought on much the same discursive terrain—the same field of concepts, issues, aesthetic standards, and opposing theories." He appropriates Foucault and discourse theory to show how the debates in the jazz press established the premises within which an aesthetics of jazz could coalesce. Specifically, the discourse was developed around binary oppositions such as art versus commerce, nature versus culture, technique versus affect, European versus native, authenticity versus artificiality, and, of course, black versus white.

The oppositions, however, were often slippery. That between art and commerce, for example, could be used by either side; Dixieland was never as popular as swing and was thus easily separated from commerce, but the champions of swing could point to the relative lack of success for bands that reputedly played *real* swing compared to the hugely popular "sweet" bands like Kay Kyser and Guy Lombardo. Revivalists could use the fashionably leftist concept of *folk music* to distinguish Dixieland from its unauthentic, bourgeois counterparts, while modernists could insist that their music had more in common with the great art of Europe than with the simpler forms of America, and so on.

Both groups—almost without exception made up of white writers—insisted in an often patronizing way that jazz possessed the greatest authenticity when it was played by blacks, but even this apparent area of agreement led to further debates about authenticity. The fact that most young African Americans in the late 1940s played in a modern rather than an older style led one revivalist to complain, "How tragically the Negro trades his own music for only another sort of slavery" (Blesh 1958, 262). Many white writers dispensed with their posture of racial tolerance, however, with the 1943 appearance of *The Music Dial,* a short-lived black jazz journal. The editors of *Metronome* denounced *The Music Dial* for bad spelling and shoddy production values but reserved most of their scorn for the tendency of black jazz writers to introduce political matters such as an article about rape charges made against a black G.I. in France "that have no business in a music magazine" (Gendron 1993, 42). The myth of jazz's autonomy was already being enforced even as an art discourse was still emerging. Jazz history was becoming, in the words of Scott DeVeaux (1991), "a means of framing and justifying aesthetic judgments" (542). Questions of race and politics had no place in an enterprise that was about separating the genuine from the ersatz and the geniuses from the also-rans.

The binary oppositions identified by Gendron were densely intertwined, and different groups often laid claim to the same half of a pair. Obviously this unified discourse of jazz aesthetics owes much to the various European avant-gardes and modernisms. The "modernist" practices of Picasso, Bartók, Milhaud, and the surrealists publicized and valued their debt to the folkloric and the primitive; when revivalists claimed that their music was an *authentic* folk music, they were participating in a modernist discourse even though their debates with the boppers demanded that they repress the term "modernism." And of course the claim that art is separate and should be *kept* separate from politics is a basic tenet of high modernism in all of its forms.

From today's perspective, neither camp vanquished the other. Dixieland never really went away—it is still being played by men in straw hats and arm garters in virtually every major city throughout the world. Record companies such as Stomp Off and Arbors regularly add new discs to their large catalogs of traditional and New Orleans–style jazz, much of it played with great finesse and authority. The bebop of the postwar era, which held immense appeal for jazz critics but practically none for audiences,[3] has recently become the conventionalized, canonical style of a group of earnest young musicians following the lead of Wynton Marsalis, and Charlie Parker has been sanctified in Clint Eastwood's *Bird* (1988). The agonistic environment in which the two musics functioned dissipated long ago when both the revivalists and the modernists consented to an accommodation in their mutual interest. The idea that jazz was undergoing an *organic* growth process helped to reconcile the two forms. "In the long run, it proved as much in the interests of the modernists to have their music legitimated as the latest phase of a (now) long and distinguished tradition, as it was in the interests of the proponents of earlier jazz styles (whether New Orleans jazz or swing) not to be swept aside as merely antiquarian" (DeVeaux 1991, 539). Along with the binary discourses identified by Gendron, this notion of an organic, evolutionary history of the music has become an essential article of faith in the claim that jazz is art.

But if there is a sine qua non for an art discourse for jazz, it is the claim of autonomy. With few exceptions, the mainstreams of jazz criticism today are still devoted to an internalist aesthetics that closes out sociocultural analysis, as when the editors of *Metronome* denounced the political reporting in *The Music Dial*. There were and are, however, significant exceptions, such as John Hammond, Leonard Feather, and Nat Hentoff, all of whom wrote journalism that went beyond the formalism of a writer such as Martin Williams. Black writers such as Ralph Ellison (1964), Amiri Baraka (1963, 1967), and Albert Murray (1976) continued *The Music Dial*'s practice of writing socially conscious jazz criticism. Today, scholars and critics such as Henry Louis Gates, Jr. (1988), Houston A. Baker, Jr. (1984), Cornel West (1990), Stanley Crouch (1990), and Gerald Early (1989) regularly incorporate jazz criticism into larger arguments about the oral, literary, political, and cultural traditions of Africans and African Americans.[4]

I need not belabor the fact that the concept of "art" is a construction, perpetuated and mystified by those who have an investment in placing certain activities within a separate sphere. The awe-inspiring "aura" that many perceive around a work of art represents the anachronistic persistence of a tradition in which art was created for and consumed within a religious context (Benjamin 1969). A text, a painting, a musical composition, or any other artifact possesses nothing within itself that necessarily distinguishes it as a work of art. Creative people may understand the qualities a culture considers "artistic" and then strive to incorporate them into their work, but the work must then appear in a museum, a concert hall, a university syllabus, an anthology, or some other appropriate place before its status as art is validated. Even then, those who bestow the imprimatur of art are constantly dismissing works that once were sanctioned, and finding new value in works that were previously ignored.

If there ever was a stable canon of art works that was universally accepted, it is certainly not the case today. Members of ethnic, economic, and sexual minorities have described the processes by which works are denied the status of real art because they are considered sacrilegious, primitive, pornographic, trivial, propagandistic, dated, regional, sentimental, or in some other way unlike what the dominant culture calls art. The art of the dominant culture, meanwhile, is asserted to be universal and timeless, possessing eternal and essential artistic merit, regardless of whether or not anyone outside of an elite finds it to be of interest.[5]

Although jazz is fast becoming an acceptable fixture in various pantheons of art, it was often denied the status of art because it did not meet standards of decorum developed for classical music. This has less to do with eternal verities of music than with issues of race, class, and established traditions of music aesthetics, traditions that were themselves still in the process of formation only two centuries ago. And of course, many of jazz's practitioners were not white. Although blackness was essential to the art discourse of the jazz press, it has always been an obstacle to the acceptance of jazz by white, majority culture. This does not prove the reverse, however. Jazz is not unequivocally art just as nothing can unequivocally be characterized as art. I am profoundly suspicious of *any* claims for or against a work being "art" and have no desire to debate the artistic merits of the music. I am more interested in how Hollywood confronted this problem when it began to adopt at least portions of the art discourse for jazz.

The Movies Look at Art

As DeVeaux (1991) has observed, the major task for jazz critics who insist that music is art is the separation of the real thing from the degraded imitation. They must evaluate all working musicians, whether established or not, in terms of their contributions to the art form. The critics are the connoisseurs who can tell good from bad and who can communicate their discriminations to a larger group of fans. The musicians most deserving of condemnation are the ones who "sell out" or play music that is "commercial." American movies, and the ideology of entertainment that drives them, have little use for the connoisseur's judgments, however. If a handful of American films in the 1940s began to assert that jazz was art, this new view had to conform to Hollywood's sense of what a mass audience would and would not accept. A significant component of such mass acceptance involved the industry's categories of race, gender, sexuality, and the artist's life. These categories, however, were never entirely stable—they were the subject of constant negotiations and renegotiations between filmmakers and their audiences. More often than not, Hollywood could only configure jazz as an art form if the music or the musicians were portrayed negatively. When exceptions were made, they tell us a great deal about the ways in which the racial and gender hierarchies of the film industry were negotiated to accommodate shifts in the perception of jazz.

There were attempts, both inside and outside Hollywood, to cast jazz as an art with a history before the jazz wars of the 1940s that Gendron has so thoroughly described. When Paul Whiteman performed in Aeolian Hall in 1924, he made a travesty of the history of jazz (see my discussion of *The King of Jazz* in the Introduction), but the mere suggestion that jazz even *had* a history was a significant step toward the claim of art. By the early 1930s a handful of classical music critics were asserting that certain works of African Americans in New York were highly artistic, even more so than the works of Gershwin.[6] R. D. Darrell and Constant Lambert compared Duke Ellington in unpatronizing terms with contemporary European composers such as Stravinsky and Delius (Tucker 1993a, 57–65, 110–11).

In 1938 Benny Goodman made an attempt to sum up the history of the music when he brought his band and a number of black musicians into Carnegie Hall. A section of the concert, "Twenty Years of Jazz," worked in a vaguely chronological manner through the famous recordings of the Original Dixieland Jazz Band, Bix Beiderbecke, Ted Lewis, Louis Armstrong, and Duke Ellington before culminating with the Goodman band's rendition of "Life Goes to a Party." John Hammond's series of "Spirituals to Swing" concerts in 1938 and 1939 also mark an attempt to dignify the music through claims of a great tradition.

Although Goodman and the "Spirituals to Swing" concerts featured black artists, they were mounted by white impresarios and represented a view of jazz history rooted in the writings of white critics and promoters. How else do we explain the presence of Ted Lewis in Goodman's survey?[7] Two films from the black film industry of the era, *Broken Strings* (1940) and *Paradise in Harlem* (1939), offer fascinating examples of how jazz and art could be mixed outside the confines of Hollywood and the white jazz establishment. *Broken Strings,* starring Clarence Muse as a concert violinist who opposes the desire of his son to play "swing," can be considered still another remake of *The Jazz Singer.* As in so many of the "race films" of the 1930s and 1940s, *Broken Strings* creates a world where white people are, for all intents and purposes, nonexistent: bankers, factory owners, judges, classical musicians, and all who pass before the camera are black. Like many of the films made for black audiences during this era, *Broken Strings* creates a permissible space for the acceptance of jazz at the same time that it works hard to enforce "bourgeois ambition" in hopes of bringing dignity to the race (Cripps 1977, 339). Earlier, in a film such as Oscar Micheaux's *Veiled Aristocrats* (1932), the aspirations of the black bourgeoisie listening to "art songs" suffer by comparison with the lively, down-to-earth parties of their servants, who sing and dance to jazz. *Broken Strings,* however, upholds the decorum of the black bourgeoisie. When the patriarch, Arthur Williams (Clarence Muse), loses the movement in his hands and can no longer play the violin, he insists that his young son carry on in his place by practicing the classics for long hours. But because the father needs funds for an operation, the son secretly earns money playing jazz on his violin in a nightclub. Shortly after he learns that his son has been supporting him with swing, Arthur attends a talent contest in which the son stops in the middle of a classical piece and spontaneously leads the stage orchestra in a jam session. As in most of the *Jazz Singer* remakes, the father finds himself clapping loudly at his son's performance. In *Broken Strings,* he also regains the use of his hands at this moment. At the conclusion, he declares, "My heart still belongs to the masters, but look what swing has done for me." No grandiose claims are made for jazz, but the music is recognized as valid even by its natural antagonists.

Paradise in Harlem (1939) charts the career of Shakespearean actor Lem Anderson, whose goal is to play Othello. Frank Wilson, who plays Anderson, also wrote the original story for the film. The choice of *Othello* seems an odd one since, once again, no white people are in the film, and all the actors in the production of Shakespeare's play, including Desdemona, are African American. When the *Othello* drama is finally staged, hecklers disrupt the performance by shouting out wisecracks. In an extraordinary finale the entire audience joins in as Othello is about to throttle his black Desdemona. To compete with the hecklers, Lem begins overstating, even chanting his lines. In response, the heroine sings and chants as well. When she croons, "Ay, but not yet to die," a female voice from the audience responds in the same key, "Yes, yes, tell him, Desdemona." When Othello chants, "Thou art to die," the same female spectator sings, "No, no, she shan't die." Soon the entire audience is singing "No, no, she shan't die," complete with harmony and soft wailing. Desdemona and Othello sing their lines as a jazz counterpoint above the refrain, while the black Emilia calls out in gospel tones, "My lord, my lord." A pit orchestra led by Lucky Millinder joins in, and soon the entire audience is clapping and dancing in the aisles. At the conclusion of the film, the Shakespearean hero receives an offer to appear on Broadway with *Othello*, a jazz band, and a choir. While both *Broken Strings* and *Paradise in Harlem* acknowledge a separation between jazz and European high art, they also delight in mixing the two: playing jazz on a violin or singing Shakespeare with a jazz band provide satisfying denouements. And unlike many Hollywood films of the 1940s, they do not attempt to justify the mixture by arguing that the classics can be "improved" by injecting them with jazz.

The remarkable *Jammin' the Blues*, a ten-minute film from 1944, contains a highly self-conscious attempt to connect jazz with art just as the wars in the jazz press were getting under way and young musicians in Harlem jam sessions were giving birth to bebop. In the opening voice-over of the film, an announcer says, "This is a jam session. Quite often these great artists gather and play, ad lib, hot music. It could be called a midnight symphony." "Symphonic jazz" had been a cliché since Whiteman introduced it in the early 1920s. Two years before *Jammin' the Blues*, the concept was mocked in *Syncopation* (1942). But in its specific connections between art and the symphony, *Jammin' the Blues* looks back to *Symphony in Black* (1935) with Duke Ellington, perhaps its only cinematic predecessor in evoking Eurocentric art forms to dignify music played by African Americans.

Jammin' the Blues begins with a view of Lester Young with the porkpie hat that was soon to become a major jazz icon. Francis Davis (1992b) exaggerates only slightly when he writes that Young was "the first black musician to be publicly recognized not as a happy-go-lucky entertainer . . . but as an artist of the *demi-monde* whose discontents magnified those felt in general by his race" (16). Although the portrait of Young eventually gives way to more conventional representations of jazz, specifically the smiling visage of Jo Jones that ends the film, the dour tenorist indelibly marks the film with the image of an avant-garde, hipster artist. Shot by Gjon Mili, who had already endowed jazz with a unique aura through his photographs in *Life* magazine, *Jammin' the Blues* adopted many of the expressionistic camera techniques that Americans knew best from foreign films, especially those from Weimar Germany that were among the first to be considered "art films." Some of these same techniques were regularly featured in the work of Hollywood craftsmen such as Fritz Lang, Billy Wilder, and Jacques Tourneur, who learned their trade in Europe before emigrating to the United States. In austerely presenting the musicians in front of a white cyclorama without set decorations of any kind, the film provided an early visual analog to the evolving idea that jazz was an autonomous art.[8]

But there was no history in *Jammin' the Blues*. In mainstream Hollywood films, something like a history of jazz was presented amid the startling naïveté and unrepressed racism of *Birth of the Blues* (1941). In the final moments of the film, after Bing Crosby tells Mary Martin, "I'm crazy about you, honey," she inquires, "As much as you are about your blue music?" Crosby responds, "That ain't mine. That's gonna be everybody's blue music." The film then concludes with a montage of faces associated with jazz while Crosby sings the title song. The successive images of Ted Lewis (born 1892), Duke Ellington (b. 1899), Louis Armstrong (b. 1901), the Dorseys (b. 1904 and 1905), Benny Goodman (b. 1909), George Gershwin (b. 1898), and finally Paul Whiteman (b. 1890) vaguely imply a historical development. As in Benny Goodman's Carnegie Hall history of three years earlier, Ted Lewis continues to play an important role, but his precise place in the music's chronology seems to shift. The finale of *Birth of the Blues* was probably designed to suggest that jazz was developed by both white and black artists but that the music did not come of age until the maturation of composers such as Gershwin and impresarios such as Paul Whiteman.[9] Osgood made this argument in *So This Is Jazz* (1926). At least in *Birth of the Blues* the notion still had force fifteen years later. The presence of dancing couples behind the final reverse zoom of Whiteman, however, tends to undermine any attempt to redefine jazz as an art form.[10]

As for the actual representation of jazz musicians as artists, filmmakers used conventions already in place in artist biopics. The most obvious paradigm is of course racial. In films such as *The Jolson Story* and *The Benny Goodman Story* the opposition "nature vs. culture" was inscribed over the opposition "black vs. white." This process appeared at least as early as Anatole Litvak's *Blues in the Night* (1941). The hero, significantly named Jigger (Richard Whorf), first appears at the piano in a noisy bar where a drunk demands that he play "I'm Forever Blowing Bubbles." Rather than consent to the request and place commerce before art, Jigger punches first the patron and then the owner of the bar. Carted off to jail with his sidemen, Jigger declares his intention to play *real* music, "the way it comes out of people." He then hears the African American prisoners in the next cell singing "My Momma Done Tole Me," as if it were an authentic black folk song and not in fact "Blues in the Night," written specifically for the film by Johnny Mercer and Harold Arlen. Declaring that this music is the "real, low-down, New Orleans blues," Jigger and his men—all of them white—are inspired to take to the road and perform the music for audiences. The possibility that the black jailhouse singers might be able to join them or otherwise make a living playing real music for real people is never raised.

Blues in the Night is also interesting in terms of how it establishes gender roles. Jigger is obviously no wimp as indicated by his quick willingness to put up his fists. Although Jigger's pugnacity suggests the art versus commerce dichotomy, it is just as much about masculinity at risk. The insistence on the hero's phallic maleness must be seen as an attempt to ward off the obvious suspicion that artists in general and musicians in particular are feminized. As McClary (1991) has pointed out, "the whole enterprise of musical activity is always already fraught with gender-related anxieties" (17). As I argue in chapter 4, adding the burden of "art" to the already perilous position of musician requires even more textual work if the hero's masculinity is to be preserved. At least some of the contempt that is heaped upon Paul Whiteman is related to his desire "to make a lady out of jazz": for some, this must have meant emasculating a virile music historically associated with black male sexuality.

Using *Blues in the Night* again as a tutor text, I would point to the only character in the film who uses the word "artist," the talented but shiftless trumpeter, Leo (Jack Carson), whose self-aggrandizing and ironic use of the term is related to his strutting but dubious masculinity. He first appears playing an impressively high and fast solo just before his trumpet is wrested away from him by a bartender to whom Leo has apparently traded the horn for money. As he picks up a pool cue and begins a game of billiards, Leo complains that he, "an artist," must submit to the financial demands of the philistine publican. Later, Leo accompanies members of Jigger's band to a New Orleans restaurant where the Jimmie Lunceford band is performing. Declaring that the musicians are "not so hot," and that he could "blow them all right out of the joint," Leo picks up his trumpet and plays another impressive solo while the band continues to play along obligingly.

The sound of Carson's trumpet in *Blues in the Night* is dubbed in by the black trumpeter Snooky Young, a regular member of the Lunceford band. Like Al Jolson and a century of minstrel men before him, Carson draws on the sexuality as well as the music of black men. Seldom, however, is the appropriation as direct as when Snooky Young supplies phallic trumpet solos for the white actor. In many ways Young "dubs" in sexuality along with the sound of his trumpet; Leo (Carson) seems much more "manly" playing his trumpet than he does merely boasting about his prowess. This practice of allowing the sound of black musicians but not their images was a common practice in Hollywood. Even Duke Ellington suffered the indignity of playing off camera and unbilled behind harmonica player Larry Adler in *Many Happy Returns* (1934) while the Guy Lombardo orchestra received the credit (Stratemann 1992, 85).[11] Later, MGM would prevent the young Charles Mingus from appearing on camera with the white members of Red Norvo's group in *Texas Carnival* (1951) (Priestley 1982, 44). But Snooky Young is not entirely invisible in *Blues in the Night*. He can be seen sitting in the trumpet section of the Jimmie Lunceford band, depicted here as extremely receptive to musical interjections from the audience. In a typically conflicted view of African Americans, the film first presents black prisoners who speak about "the miseries" and whose musical abilities appear to emanate from their primitive souls. This stereotype is scarcely compatible with the sharp, technically accomplished members of Lunceford's band. The orchestra would have even *looked* sharp if the film had not put casual costumes on the Lunceford musicians, ordinarily known as the best-dressed of all the black bands of the 1930s and early 1940s. *Blues in the Night*,

however, makes no attempt to account for these contradictory representations.[12]

Appearing just one year after *Blues in the Night* and *Birth of the Blues,*
Syncopation (1942) offers a fascinating counterexample to the earlier
films' attempts to elevate the achievements of white musicians over those
of blacks. Based on an original story by Valentine Davies (who would
later direct *The Benny Goodman Story*), *Syncopation* makes a sincere effort
to narrativize jazz history. It even begins with a montage that opens on a
map of Africa, followed by a dissolve to natives dancing while a white
trader presents an African chief with various gifts. As the music takes on
ominous tones, the chest of gifts is closed, and a second chest is opened
to reveal chains and leg irons. After a shot of Africans filling the hold of
a slave ship, the scene changes to a cotton field with slaves singing a
work song, and then to the title, "New Orleans 1906," superimposed on
a final montage of black Americans attaining stature as educators and
businessmen. One of the black educators is trying to teach Rex, a young
cornetist, how to read music. The boy insists, however, that he is better
off playing by ear. Rex begins his career as a jazz musician when he meets
"King Jeffers," played by the eminent jazz trumpeter and author Rex
Stewart. Impressed by the boy's trumpet technique, King Jeffers hires him
to play in his band, no doubt a reference to King Oliver's hiring of Louis
Armstrong. Ella, the mother of Rex (also called Reggie), tries to prevent
him from joining Jeffers. "I want him to study music like the white folks
do," she tells him. King Jeffers's reply shows that the filmmakers have
already internalized some concept of jazz as an art form with a history.

> Listen, Ella. Reggie's got somethin' that no teacher can give no one no how.
> Every once in a great while the Lord takes a tiny little spark and drops it
> inside of someone. That spark can be snuffed out—one, two, three. But if
> you leave it alone, it can grow into a great big ball of fire, just a-burnin' so
> bright, just a-givin' off so much heat that after the man die, folks can still
> set around that fire and keep warm. Let Reggie be with me, and I'll watch
> over the spark of his.

Rex grows up to be a "hot" jazz player and an inspiration for other trumpeters, but he is hardly the main character in the film.

The main plot of *Syncopation* revolves around Kit (Bonita Granville)
and Johnny (Jackie Cooper). As a child in New Orleans, Kit had known
Rex because Ella was her father's maid. Kit herself had picked up some
New Orleans licks along with her classical training at the piano. As a
young woman in Chicago in 1916, Kit wanders into a Chicago bar and

plays her boogie-woogie piano solo with such fervor that she causes a small riot and is arrested. At her trial, Ella testifies in her defense, suggesting that Kit had learned jazz from "around the river front." The prosecutor then cries out that jazz is "the music of the low places, iniquitous place." Hearing these code words for racism, Ella tearfully insists that jazz is "trouble music, that's all it is, trouble music. When folks has got trouble they get it off their minds by singing." Although Ella's outburst does not do much to save Kit, the jury finds her innocent after she plays a piano that has been brought to the court. During her performance, all the spectators including the judge tap their feet.

Rex soon moves to Chicago after New Orleans' Storyville is closed. When a band of newly arrived black jazz musicians passes by Kit's house in a parade for liberty bonds, a woman asks, "What kind of music is that?" When a man turns to her and says, "jazz," she promptly slaps his face. Soon, Johnny has found Rex, and, in a scene that would not have been possible a few years earlier, he sits in with Rex's group while insisting that he is not in the same league as the black musicians. Later, when Johnny tells Kit that he will never be able to play as well as Rex, she reassures him: "You've got a style of your own. Rex is New Orleans, Basin Street, and you're Chicago. You pick up where Basin Street leaves off."

The rest of the film develops the notion that a white jazz, soon to be called swing, is fundamentally different from the "hot" music of New Orleans. *Syncopation* even denigrates the overblown orchestra of Paul Whiteman by creating a bandleader with a small Whitemanesque moustache called Ted Browning, who presents a "Symphony of Jazz" with a string section and an elaborate stage setting. When Kit and Johnny stumble on the theater where Browning is performing, they meet Rex on his way out. The black cornetist has quit the band because he cannot stand to play set routines instead of "what he feels." Johnny joins the large aggregation hoping to change the sound by adding his own jazz licks. In a montage that vividly dramatizes the art versus commerce dichotomy, Johnny becomes increasingly frustrated by playing the same arrangements and fruitlessly begging Browning to allow him to insert some jazz into the performances. At one point, Johnny hallucinates that the written music he plays night after night becomes huge and three-dimensional and starts to strangle him.

When Johnny is finally fired by Browning, he begins leading a small band that Kit characterizes as "more than jazz." Always the apologist for white music, Kit says that the band "swings." Anticipating films such as

The Glenn Miller Story and *The Benny Goodman Story* in the next decade, Johnny's band in *Syncopation* struggles to find its audience. When the creative impulses and dedication of the musicians are finally rewarded with large audiences of dancers, Kit again delivers the justification for the allegedly white music of the swing era. Looking out over the crowd of appreciative dancers, Johnny says, "Rex must have had nights like this in New Orleans." Kit tells him that he is not just experiencing a single night's success; his music is here to stay. Gesturing at the dancers, she says, "They're not dancing just to forget their troubles. They're getting something they can carry away. They're dancing to music that comes from the heart—music that's American born. And you'll go on, Johnny, just as great names in music will always go on." Kit's speech completes Ella's testimony in the courtroom scene—if jazz serves black people by taking their mind off their troubles, then it has a higher function for white people. It enriches their lives and creates a canon of great musicians, in part because it is truly American. The appeal to American chauvinism was of course typical of films made during World War II, just as the invocation of the "folk" was a trope in the art discourse for early jazz. Kit also speaks of popular music as an American institution worth fighting for, even if it includes a Negro element (Cripps 1993, 35–63).

As soon as Kit has explained how swing has transcended jazz, however, there is a lap dissolve to a jam session with an all-white group of musicians identified in the credits as winners of a *Saturday Evening Post* poll: Jack Jenny, Joe Venuti, Harry James, Alvino Rey, Charlie Barnet, Benny Goodman, and Gene Krupa. Swing has totally transcended jazz. Rex and the black musicians had disappeared a good half-hour before the end of the film. Nevertheless, *Syncopation* shows filmmakers catching up with the popular music industry where black and white musicians had been performing together for two decades. It is also significant that the film shows a white jazz musician expressing envy of a black artist even at the moment of his greatest success, in stark contrast to the tendency in many subsequent films to have a black musician pronounce the superiority of the white musician.

An Art Without Autonomy

The first hints that an art discourse for jazz had arrived in Hollywood began to appear in 1947, although these hints incorporated few of the discursive practices from the jazz press. In *Carnegie Hall* (1947), for example, the argument persists that classical music can be improved by the addition of "jazz" (Feuer 1993, 58). In many ways still another remake of *The Jazz Singer*, *Carnegie Hall* involves a young pianist who plays somewhat in the style of Art Tatum and who leaves home to pursue a passion for swing. At the finale, however, he brings great joy to his mother by merging jazz with the classical music to which she had hoped he would devote his life. At a triumphant concert in Carnegie Hall, an orchestra plays his vaguely Gershwinesque "Rhapsody for Trumpet and Orchestra" with Harry James as featured soloist.

Similarly, in John Cromwell's *Night Song* (1947), the blind pianist Dan Evans (Dana Andrews) goes from playing Dixieland in a nightclub to writing a piano concerto that is performed at the end by Artur Rubinstein, Eugene Ormandy, and a symphony orchestra. Dan initially plays in a band led by Chick Morgan (Hoagy Carmichael) who specializes in New Orleans jazz, typical of Hollywood's tendency to side with the moldy figs during the jazz wars. In 1947, as big band swing was becoming less associated with "jazz," filmmakers had to choose between Dixieland and be-bop, and the familiar music of New Orleans, not to mention the predominance of white musicians among the revivalists, made Dixieland a much more likely choice. In *Night Song*, as in *The Best Years of Our Lives* from the previous year (1946), a character played by Hoagy Carmichael becomes the caretaker for a character played by Andrews. In a scene near the beginning, Dana Andrews/Dan Evans sits at the piano between sets and plays a piano solo that sounds much more like Ravel than Fats Waller. Evans's pianistic impressionism plus the presence of Carmichael points in the direction of Bix Beiderbecke. In 1927, Beiderbecke recorded a piano solo, "In a Mist," that many critics compared to the work of Ravel and Debussy. Beiderbecke's single piano recording provides a crucial link between jazz and classical music in the plot of *Night Song*.

Later, when the heroine Catherine (Merle Oberon) begins romancing the reluctant hero, she tells him that she likes jazz, specifically "Gershwin, Duke, and Bix." Dan perks up when he hears the last name. "Beiderbecke. You know his stuff?" Catherine then says exactly what Dan wants to hear, "People think he was just a man with a horn, but he played a good piano. He died too soon." (This was three years before the release of *Young Man with a Horn*.) Now that she has his interest, Catherine begins quizzing the blind pianist about the classical music that she had heard him play in the nightclub and that inspired her to pursue him. Dan tells her that he has given up on classical music, largely because the blinding he experienced in the war has left him without hope. "I don't play anymore. I just trade boogie woogie for beer and a hamburger." Thanks to the efforts of Catherine, however, Dan gets back his eyesight and the courage to write his concerto. Although he leaves jazz behind, Carmichael is with him all the way. Anticipating a slew of films that associate jazz with castration (see chapter 4), *Night Song* charts the progress of a musician who goes from blindness, despair, and jazz to sightedness, success, and the classics. The final prize for the remasculinized hero is Merle Oberon. As is often the case in Hollywood films, jazz is not autonomous but entirely the result of a character's pathology. Nevertheless, the film connects the jazz of the tragic white genius Beiderbecke with the classical music of the damaged hero.

Two other films from this period show an even greater awareness of the newly refined claim that jazz is art, *New Orleans* (1947) and *A Song Is Born* (1948). Both made the significant decision to include Louis Armstrong in their casts, even though the trumpeter found no favor among the beboppers *or* the revivalists during the 1940s. Because he began recording with a mediocre swing band in the 1930s, Armstrong was considered a traitor by the revivalists. His mugging and servile stage manner alienated the young boppers, who developed their impassive stage mannerisms at least in part as a reaction to Armstrong. Nevertheless, by the time Hollywood appropriated the idea that jazz was an art form, Armstrong was available, an experienced performer who by the late 1940s had appeared in twelve American feature films as well as in numerous shorts and foreign films. Hollywood had the perfect commodity in Armstrong, a certified giant from jazz history who was also capable of charming audiences with skills that had little to do with the unrepresentable aspects of jazz. Compared to Armstrong, even the most popular jazz and swing musicians, including Benny Goodman, Harry James, and Gene Krupa, were almost devoid of stage presence. And, of course, Armstrong always appeared to be so obsequious that his artistry—or for that matter his masculinity—could scarcely be conceived as threatening.

Scenes in both *New Orleans* and *A Song Is Born* attempt to recount the history of jazz. Although neither of these accounts has much in common with today's canonizing histories of jazz, they are more thoughtful than the odd montage of faces that ended *Birth of the Blues* in 1941. The plot of *New Orleans* revolves around the mythological end of the Golden Age of jazz, the closing of Storyville in 1917. The film also charts the acceptance of black music among a conspicuously educated group of whites. When the white protagonist is asked to explain where jazz originated, he replies, "Well, it comes from work songs, the gold coast of West Africa, little Christian churches, river boats. . . . They made up the music as they

21. Arturo De Cordova explains jazz to Dorothy Patrick while Red Callender, Zutty Singleton, Charlie Beal, Kid Ory, Louis Armstrong, Billie Holiday, Bud Scott, and Barney Bigard dwell in the background. *New Orleans* (1947, United Artists). Museum of Modern Art Film Stills Archive.

went along." In *A Song Is Born*, directed by Howard Hawks as a remake of his *Ball of Fire* (1941), the professor of folk music played by Danny Kaye assembles Armstrong and a group of swing musicians for the purpose of recording a history of jazz to accompany a multivolume musical encyclopedia on which Kaye and his colleagues have been working for nine years. The film itself seeks to bring legitimacy to jazz while the diegesis recounts a parallel process in which the music becomes a suitable academic subject for the professorate.

The cockeyed history of jazz that Danny Kaye narrates in *A Song Is Born* begins in Africa with a drum, "the first musical instrument." The camera cuts to white drummer Louis Bellson playing a simple tom-tom rhythm. As Kaye continues, different musicians join in to give the effect of the evolving music. Very little corresponds to current jazz history, not to mention published histories that predate the film. Here is the ungrammatical narration that Kaye is supposedly reading into a massive reference work on music:

22. Literature elevating jazz to the status of art: Dorothy Patrick holds Louis Armstrong's first autobiography in *New Orleans*. Museum of Modern Art Film Stills Archive.

To the basic rhythm was added the human voice. Next, the first wind instrument, the shepherd's flute. The basic beat of the tom-tom and the same thematic strain of the chant that was carried across oceans and contained in early Spanish music after the invention of the guitar [*sic*]. It spread to countries that shared the Spanish language—Cuba, West Indies, and South America, where the rhythm or beat assumed a new form of expression. The ever-widening cycle finally reached the shores of southern United States where the beat was momentarily lost, but the melody was woven into pure Negro spiritual.

A black vocal group, the Golden Gate Quartet, then sings a chorus of the film's title tune in gospel style. "A Song Is Born," written specifically for the film by Don Raye and Gene de Paul, invokes the mockingbird as still another forerunner of jazz. The tune's melody is very close to "Going Home" and the theme from Dvořák's *New World Symphony*. The "art" of jazz is retrospectively validated by referencing the American folk song that supposedly inspired the European master.

When Kaye announces, "Then the beat returned," the gospel quartet sings another verse, this time in dance tempo with guitar accompaniment. The film's account of jazz's development suddenly arrives at the present when the swing musicians (Tommy Dorsey, Charlie Barnet, Louis Armstrong, Lionel Hampton, and Mel Powell) play a familiar introductory vamp. The vamp has only lasted four bars before it makes way for a vocal performance by Virginia Mayo, who sings more of "A Song Is Born." All suggestions of racism, not to mention the slave trade, are scrupulously avoided in this history; jazz seems to have been transported to American shores by Spanish explorers via Cuba and the West Indies. In addition to citing the mockingbird and the "tinkling rain" as inspirations for early jazz musicians, Virginia Mayo sings that "the blues must have come from a sigh." Eventually, Mayo yields the floor to Louis Armstrong, who sings another verse of the tune. Armstrong, the canonical master from jazz history, fits right in with a "revisionist" history that also includes Tommy Dorsey and the white nightclub vocal style of Virginia Mayo.

The progress of *New Orleans* from concept to final film is a revealing and dispiriting example of how African Americans fared in the studio system of the 1940s. Initially the film was to star Armstrong and Billie Holiday as jazz artists who leave New Orleans and take their music on the road.[13] As Thomas Cripps (1993) has shown, Armstrong and Holiday became progressively less important in each new rewrite of the script (208). Ultimately they became secondary characters in a story about a white cabaret owner and his romance with a white opera singer. Nick Duquesnes (Arturo De Cordova) is the "King of Basin Street," owner of the town's most elegant casino as well as a connoisseur of jazz. The film begins with what any jazz initiate would find to be a startling anachronism: as the title "1917" is superimposed over a New Orleans street scene, we hear the unmistakable sounds of the trumpet cadenza that began Armstrong's 1928 recording of "West End Blues." The camera pans across the room to land on Nick listening to Armstrong and his band, who appear to play in the cellar of the casino entirely for their own amusement and only coincidentally for Nick. Eventually, Nick falls in love with Miralee Smith (Dorothy Patrick), the daughter of a New Orleans dowager who frequents Nick's casino. Mrs. Smith does everything she can to prevent the love affair, hypocritically denying to her daughter the very pleasures she herself enjoys. The mother especially disapproves of jazz and has planned a career for her daughter as an opera singer. Miralee, however, is taken with the sound of New Orleans jazz and asks her maid, Endie (Billie Holiday), to take her to the cellar where Armstrong performs for Nick. (Although Holiday is given a character's name, Armstrong is called "Satchmo" and "Louis Armstrong.") They are joined by the conductor of the local symphony orchestra, who also has a taste for jazz, even accompanying Armstrong on piano at one point. Miralee possesses all of the tolerance that her mother lacks, observing that classical music is similar to jazz—it was once new and it too "sprang up in a variety of places." In one of the more romantic conceits of the film, the closing down of Storyville results entirely from the clout of Mrs. Smith, who uses her political connections to distance her daughter from the cabaret owner.

On the same night that Nick leaves New Orleans to become a music promoter in Chicago, Miralee chooses to perform her rendition of "Do You Know What It Means to Miss New Orleans?" before an audience of classical music enthusiasts, most of whom make booing noises and walk out. The lovers are then separated for several years, although the exact amount of intervening time cannot be determined because of several additional anachronisms. We see both Armstrong and Miralee performing in Paris, the former clad in a tuxedo and winning approving nods from royalty in the audience. Armstrong's first European tour took place in 1932, but the film suggests that the simultaneous overseas tours of Miralee and the trumpeter take place only shortly after the closing of Storyville in 1917. But when Miralee greets Louis at one of his concerts, she congratulates him for his success and holds up a copy of *Swing That Music*, Armstrong's first autobiography, published in 1936.

The lovers are united at the finale, a concert back in the States that culminates with another of Miralee's out-of-tune renditions of "Do You Know What It Means," bolstered by Woody Herman's band and a symphony orchestra. In its attempt to engulf jazz with the high art trappings of the concert hall, *New Orleans* anticipates the white jazz biopics *The Fabulous Dorseys* (1947) and *The Benny Goodman Story* (1955), both of which conclude with the heroes performing on the stages of concert halls, as if white jazz artists had brought dignity to a primitive music. And as with *Syncopation,* the black artists around whom the film was originally built have been off screen for some time by the final credits.

Both *A Song Is Born* and *New Orleans* use a variety of tropes to associate jazz with art. Never before in an American film had Armstrong appeared in a tuxedo or on what was supposed to be a European stage. The shot of Armstrong's book in *New Orleans* functions as literary evidence of jazz's seriousness in much the same way that Winthrop Sargeant's *Jazz, Hot and Hybrid* (1938, 2nd ed. 1946) is produced in *A Song Is Born* to enable the professors first to understand and then actually to play the music.[14] What is most important is the specific purpose that an art dis-

23. A professor (Danny Kaye) holds forth on the history of jazz while the Golden Gate Quartet looks on in the background. *A Song Is Born* (1948, Samuel Goldwyn). Museum of Modern Art Film Stills Archive.

course serves in these two films: Hollywood has opportunistically appropriated the new idea that jazz is serious art in order to promote the white swing bands with which the movie industry had established a symbiotic relationship (Feuer 1993, 54). Most of the white bandleaders regularly appeared in films during the 1940s, and it was no coincidence that bandleaders such as Harry James and Artie Shaw were married to movie stars, in Shaw's case more than once. If an older, black musician like Armstrong was an artist, that became one more reason to celebrate the white swing bands as a later—perhaps even more advanced—stage of the music. Off screen, Armstrong himself had been complicit in the perpetuation of this myth, insisting that jazz and swing were really one and the same (Armstrong 1936). When jazz and swing ceased to be popular in the 1950s, Hollywood no longer had any need to make the claim that Armstrong or any other jazz musician was creating "art."

For many jazz lovers, however, *New Orleans* and *A Song is Born* are striking examples of how jazz artists could transcend even the most banal material. The forgettable vocals of Dorothy Patrick, presented as the climax of *New Orleans,* provide little competition for the extraordinary performance of "The Blues Are Brewing" by Armstrong and Holiday. The charm and grace that Holiday lacked in her dialogue scenes as Endie she more than regains in her vocal duet with the trumpeter. Similarly, Armstrong's effortless crooning of "A Song is Born" in Hawks's film provides a striking contrast to the minor singing talent displayed moments earlier by Virginia Mayo in what was intended to be a culminating moment in the professors' recorded history of jazz. Rather than being recognized as autonomous art, jazz serves the conventional Hollywood project of giving audiences a reason to like the music they already like.

A Popular Art Loses Its Audience

After a brief moment in the movies as an art form, however compromised this distinction may have been, jazz had no place to go but down. The music quickly became a much more free-floating signifier as its popular audience drifted away. By 1950 the pursuit of art by a jazz musician was explicitly condemned by Hoagy Carmichael himself at the conclusion of *Young Man with a Horn;* the hero survives his bout with alcohol and hard times by "becoming a human being first and an artist second." But most films in the final days of jazz's popularity did not bother with such polemics. In *On the Town* (1949), black jazz musicians and dancers are interchangeable with commodified Brazilian and Chinese exotics as the sailors and their dates experience three almost identical scenes from New York nightlife. In *The 5,000 Fingers of Dr. T.* (1953), with a story by Dr. Seuss and set designs inspired by drawings in his books, jazz is explicitly associated with much of what society has tried to cast out. This child's fantasy of a possessed piano teacher's stylized domain confines all non-piano-playing musicians to what a Dantesque inscription calls "dungeon for scratchy violins, screechy piccolos, nauseating trumpets, etc., etc." This mock-Freudian underground of repressed behavior seems a combination marijuana den and gay bar. March music dominates the score as various groups of flutists, trombonists, and percussionists perform their dances, but jazz harmonies begin to dominate when five dancers emerge connected to a fantastic instrument that is part hookah and part saxophone.

More conventional notions of criminal behavior are tied in with jazz in *The Big Combo* (1955) when a hoodlum refers to a drum break as "real crazy" before he blasts it through a hearing aid into the ear of a policeman he is torturing. And in the "Girl Hunt Ballet" scene in *The Band Wagon* (1953), jazz is an essential part of a satirized noir underworld inhabited by the hard-boiled detective "Rod Riley" (Fred Astaire); all of the dancer-gangsters are dressed in black as they contort their bodies to the music in a jazz club called "Dem Bones Cafe."

All of these films had fun with jazz at the same time that it was developing an elite group of enthusiasts who associated the music with the other avant-garde movements of the twentieth century. But the identification of jazz as a modernist art form seldom appeared in the movies during the 1940s and 1950s unless it was presented as a joke as in the introduction of Jervis Pendleton III (Fred Astaire) in *Daddy Long Legs* (1955). The film begins with a tour of a museum, built presumably with the Pendleton fortune and containing portraits of three generations of Pendleton heirs, all looking like Fred Astaire. We are told that the portrait of Jervis Pendleton I was painted by James Abbott McNeill Whistler and that John Singer Sargent painted Pendleton II. Although the name Picasso is never uttered, Astaire's fractured features in the portrait of Jervis Pendleton III bear an unmistakable resemblance to the painter's work. The film then cuts to a shot of Astaire improvising jauntily on a drum kit while the recording of a large jazz band blares out of a phonograph. The film associates the same irreverent but trivial impulses to both Picasso and the jazz musician.

An even more striking association of jazz with modern art creates a memorable moment in the 1957 film *Jailhouse Rock*. Here the opposition "nature vs. culture" has been resurrected to favor the authenticity of Elvis Presley over the effete pretensions of jazz lovers. Shortly after his release from prison, Vince Everett (Presley) is discovered by Peggy (Judy Tyler), a young record producer, who quickly takes him to his first recording session. When she subsequently brings him to a party at the house of her college professor father, the conversation turns to a record by "Stubby Ritemeyer," a fictional musician probably based on the West Coast trumpeter-composer Shorty Rogers. "I think Stubby's gone overboard with those altered chords," says one of the pompous guests. "I agree," says another, "I think Brubeck and Desmond have gone just as far with dissonance as I care to go." "Oh, nonsense," says a man, "have you heard Lennie Tristano's latest recording? He reached outer space." A young woman adds, "Some day they'll make the cycle and go back to pure old Dixieland." A well-dressed, older woman says, "I say atonality is just a passing phase in jazz music." Turning to Presley, she asks, "What do you think, Mr. Everett?" He answers, "Lady, I don't know what the hell you're talking about," and storms out of the house. Followed and scolded by Peggy, Everett protests that he was being forced into a corner by a stupid question from "some old broad." After Peggy tries to assure him that the woman was only trying to bring him into the conversation, Everett says he wasn't sure "that she was even talkin' English." He then kisses her forcefully. She protests, "How dare you think such cheap tactics would work with me?" Everett kisses her again and adds, "I ain't tactics, honey. That's just the beast in me." As the young antihero walks off into the night, the camera dwells on Tyler's face while a bluesy trumpet plays over a background of strings on the soundtrack. It is a strange moment indeed when extradiegetic music inflected with jazz follows the hero's stinging *rejection* of jazz. Or to conceptualize the scene in another way, a popularized white appropriation of black music (Presley) is privileged over an elite white appropriation of black music (West Coast jazz) to the unobtrusive accompaniment of a middle-brow appropriation of black music (the background score).

Jailhouse Rock's dizzy mix of black and white music and their imitations is not at all untypical of American culture. Andrew Ross (1989) gives numerous examples of the practice including:

> Howlin' Wolf—an "authentic" bluesman (most revered by sixties R & B purists in the suburbs of London), whose name is taken from his failure to emulate the yodeling of Jimmie Rodgers, the white hillbilly musician of the thirties whose own vaudeville-inspired yodeling was spliced with a variety of powerful blues influences; and Elvis's rockabilly hair, greased up with Royal Crown Pomade to emulate the black "process" of straightening and curling, itself a black attempt to look "white" (68)

As Ross points out, black musicians have never been as financially successful as whites. As a result, it is easy to understand why white imitators are often called thieves. Still, Ross is correct in throwing a monkey wrench into the project of sorting out the genuine article from the imitation in the long history of black-white musical interactions.

The extradiegetic jazz on the soundtrack of *Jailhouse Rock* also marks a moment in film history when rock and youth culture were beginning to find a place in Hollywood films. In fact, jazz and rock were often conflated as emblems of rebellion. In *The Wild One* (1954), released just three years before *Jailhouse Rock,* Marlon Brando and the members of his troupe of outlaw motorcyclists listen to big band jazz and talk about bebop as an expression of their youthful rebellion. In *The Girl Can't Help It* (1956), both Abbey Lincoln and Ray Anthony have their featured moments in a sequence of popular music acts that also includes Little Richard, Gene Vincent, and Eddie Cochran. In *Jamboree* (1957), Count Basie is just one more act among a collection of rock and rollers, and Lionel

Hampton, serving as "musical director," sings the extradiegetic prologue for *Mr. Rock and Roll* (1957), a vehicle for Alan Freed and the rock acts he presented on his radio program.[15] All of the films make no real distinction between the youthcult music of the mid-fifties and mainstream jazz. Although "bebop" would become part of the slang of fifties rock and roll, no room was found for Parker, Gillespie, et al. in these films. Perhaps this is why in *Jailhouse Rock* bop-inflected cool jazz has become emblematic of bourgeois superficiality. Once again, jazz is linked metonymically to sexuality, although this time the spurning of jazz is marked as sexual. Here the primitive can be valorized when the primitive is white rather than black.

A more subtle stigmatization of jazz takes place in *Kings Go Forth* (1958), in which Tony Curtis plays Britt, a sergeant with the American forces in the south of France during the last days of World War II. Much to the chagrin of Sam (Frank Sinatra), Britt wins the attentions of Monique (Natalie Wood) when he plays a hot trumpet solo in a jazz club called "Le Chat Noir." Sam has been pursuing Monique even after she has told him that her late father was black and her mother was white. (The couple had emigrated to France from the United States to seek greater tolerance. Because Monique was raised abroad, Natalie Wood speaks with a painful attempt at a French accent.) Britt is portrayed as a spoiled rich kid who has never experienced self-doubt. He says that he learned how to play the trumpet by hanging out on 52nd Street when he should have been attending classes at Cornell, one of the four colleges from which he was expelled before the war. When Sam tells Britt about Monique's mixed parentage, he seems slightly intrigued. "What do you know," he says. Britt soon begins a serious romance with Monique, even saying he will marry her. He later reneges on the promise, explaining to Sam that being with Monique was "like a new kick for me." Appalled at Britt's treatment of her daughter, the mother calls him "scum." Britt replies, "That's a funny term coming from someone like you."

Britt is unmasked as a thrill-seeker with a touch of Negrophilia who is attracted to jazz and mixed-race women but without any real feelings for either. In depicting Britt as a skillful jazz musician, the film joins many others in casting improvisation as an easily acquired skill, the kind of thing that some people—usually but not necessarily black—achieve effortlessly, perhaps even by nature. But in *Kings Go Forth*, Pete Candoli dubs in an extremely convincing bop solo for Britt that does not sound like the work of someone who merely dabbles in jazz. The film, written by Merle Miller, suggests that Britt's talent as a jazz artist must be under-

24. Tony Curtis plays bop on the trumpt with Frank Sinatra and Natalie Wood (left) in the audience. *Kings Go Forth* (1958, United Artists). Jerry Ohlinger's Movie Material Store, Inc.

stood in terms of his racist fascination with black culture. One thinks of the love/hate relationship for blacks that minstrelsy encouraged in its white spectators.[16]

Tony Curtis also appears as an aspiring jazz saxophonist in *The Rat Race* (1960). Hoping to find work with "Frankie Jay and His Red Peppers," supposedly a well-known combo, the Curtis character arrives at the audition carrying four saxophones, three flutes, and a clarinet. The three other musicians sound accomplished, and they give some slight encouragement to the Curtis character. After some elaborate jive talk in which they refer to one another as "daddy," the other musicians send him out for beer. When he returns, they have disappeared with his instruments. They have even stolen his sports jacket.

In *Some Like It Hot* (1959) Curtis was again cast as a saxophone player, this time one who verbally imitates Cary Grant in order to win the affections of Marilyn Monroe. Curtis succeeds even though Monroe says that she always falls for sexually appealing saxophonists who later break her heart. In the context of so many Tony Curtis films from the fifties in which jazz is associated with sociopaths, thieves, and satyrs, *Sweet Smell of Success* (1957) is an anomaly. Directed by the Scottish-born Alexander Mackendrick, written by Ernest Lehman and Clifford Odets, photographed by James Wong Howe, and with a jazz-inflected score by Elmer Bernstein, the film is one of the American cinema's most unrelentingly negative portraits of U.S. culture at the same time that it is one of the most flattering portraits ever of a jazz musician. The entire film is set in motion by the desire of J.J. Hunsecker, an egomaniacal gossip columnist played by Burt Lancaster, to keep his sister away from Steve (Martin Milner), a jazz guitarist.

Steve is shown performing with his group at several moments in the film. Jim Hall dubbed in the guitar solos for Martin Milner in the group that Chico Hamilton was leading at the time. Along with Hall and Hamilton, the band included Fred Katz, Paul Horn, and Carson Smith. Since the film idealizes the Milner character, the choice of Hamilton's group was an especially intelligent one. On the one hand, the band plays in an intellectual style, featuring the slightly outré compositions of Katz, one of a handful of musicians who played jazz on the cello. On the other hand, the presence of the African American Hamilton, as well his aggressive drumming, keep the band from sounding "too white." Operating at the nexus of thoughtful music and borrowed black manliness, the fair-haired Steve is perfectly constituted to be the film's one exemplary character.

J.J. knows that Steve, unlike virtually everyone else in the film, cannot be bought or corrupted. He also knows that the guitarist is one of the few people who can separate him from his sister Suzie, for whom J.J. has an almost incestuous passion. When J.J. enlists Sidney Falco (Tony Curtis) to turn Suzie against Steve, Sidney first plants a story in the column of another gossipmonger to label Steve as not only the leader of a "highbrow jazz quintet" but also as a marijuana smoker and a communist. Suspecting that J.J. is behind the story, Steve confronts him in the presence of Suzie. Steve's denunciations indicate his understanding of the moral corruption of J.J. and his milieu, including the gossip columnist's hypocritical claim that he speaks for the American people. Eventually, J.J. has corrupt police detectives sent out to beat Steve, who is hurt badly enough to require hospitalization. In spite of all of J.J. and Sidney's efforts, however, Suzie finally stands up to her brother, and the film ends as she goes off to the hospital to be with her jazz guitarist. Although *Sweet Smell of Success* never makes any explicit claims for jazz as art, it associates the music with idealism and a refusal to compromise with the mediocrities represented by Sidney, J.J., and most of the film's other char-

25. The only character in the film with integrity, a jazz guitarist (Martin Milner), confronts the sociopathic gossip columnist (Burt Lancaster) in *Sweet Smell of Success* (1957, United Artists). Museum of Modern Art Film Stills Archive.

acters. It places Steve very much on the right side of the art versus commerce binarism.

The Cult of the White Jazz Artist

The character of Steve in *Sweet Smell of Success* acknowledges a tendency in American culture of the 1950s to idealize white jazz musicians. Dave Brubeck, Stan Kenton, Gerry Mulligan, Shorty Rogers, and Terry Gibbs were all photogenic men with followings among jazz enthusiasts. Although these artists were in no way effeminate, they provided alternative models of masculinity based more in creativity and feeling than in the conventional codes of phallic dominance that characterized mainstream male heroes of the era. These musicians also provided an entry into jazz for Americans who may have felt threatened in some way by black male artists and for whom the white swing musicians of the 1930s and 1940s seemed out of date. Needless to say, the standard jazz histories have not been kind to these musicians of the fifties, casting them in the shadow of players with more distinctive and/or "original" voices. Furthermore, in spite of their popularity, limited though it was, in the 1950s, only a relatively small number of white male players had substantial careers in the movies, usually as studio musicians. For a variety of reasons, many white jazz musicians did not seek work in Hollywood. Chet Baker, whose early similarities to James Dean later made him an ideal subject for Bruce Weber's fetishizing documentary *Let's Get Lost* (1988), landed a few roles, including speaking parts in *Hell's Horizon* (1955) and *Urlatori alla Sbarra* (Italy, 1959). Baker can also be seen playing his trumpet, wearing dark glasses, and looking mysterious during a party scene in *Stolen Hours* (1963). As Weber's documentary suggests, Baker might have had a more important career in films if he had not run into legal problems because of his drug use.

Gerry Mulligan was one of the few white jazz artists with a significant following to achieve some visibility in Hollywood films. He provides a good example of the cult of the white jazz artist, which must be kept in mind as we look at the careers of Ellington, Armstrong, and Nat King Cole in the chapters that follow. As a tall, red-haired, handsome young musician in the late 1940s and early 1950s, Mulligan already had a certain cachet, at least as a photographic subject for the cover of *Metronome*. But Mulligan deserves real credit for pioneering the pianoless quartet and for reaching out to record with older black musicians such as Ben Webster, Johnny Hodges, and Thelonious Monk. He also formed an integrated big band called the Concert Jazz Band which if nothing else carried a highly significant title for the discourse of jazz as art. For the jazz initiate, Mulligan reached an apex of sorts when he played a solo on "Fine and Mellow" in the classic television program *The Sound of Jazz* (1957) alongside canonical black figures, including Billie Holiday, Lester Young, Coleman Hawkins, Ben Webster, and Roy Eldridge. Mulligan subsequently worked regularly in Hollywood, his saxophone heard on the soundtrack of at least a half-dozen films. Perhaps because of a relationship with actress Judy Holliday, he even landed a few speaking parts, including a short, undistinguished moment with her in *Bells Are Ringing* (1960) and a somewhat more professional scene in *The Rat Race,* during which he exchanges a few lines with Tony Curtis. (Mulligan also dubbed in Curtis's baritone saxophone solos in *The Rat Race.*) In addition, Mulligan can be seen intensely blowing his baritone in the opening scene of *I Want to Live* (1958) while expressionistic camera angles—tilting as much as 45 degrees at one point—set the tone for the out-of-control life of Barbara Graham (Susan Hayward). As Barbara becomes more sympathetic throughout the film, she has a scene in her death row cell listening to jazz on the radio. She identifies one of Mulligan's solos and adds that she has collected all of his records. In spite of her reputation as a prostitute and possible murderer, Barbara has cultivated an aesthetic sophistication in her private moments. As the film has already taken pains to demonstrate, she can't be all bad.

By far the most idealized image of Mulligan appears in *The Subterraneans* (1960). In this attempt to bring a Jack Kerouac novel to the screen, jazz as modernist art is associated with the San Francisco bohemian scene and its struggling novelists, improvising poets, bearded bongo players, interpretive dancers in leotards, and overdressed fops, all of them white.[17] Mulligan, who appears in several club sequences playing his horn with both black and white sidemen, is not, however, lumped with the other weirdos. In fact, Mulligan has a speaking part off the bandstand in which he functions as a hip cleric without denomination, protecting fellow Beats from the police when their emotional lives become too tumultuous. In one scene he gives shelter to Leslie Caron who, in the midst of a nervous breakdown, has run into the street naked. When the police follow her to Mulligan's door, one officer addresses him as

26. Gerry Mulligan performs with Buddy Clark, Art Farmer, and Dave Bailey in *The Subterraneans* (1960, MGM). Museum of Modern Art Film Stills Archive.

"Mac, I mean Reverend." Sincerely but firmly, Mulligan informs the police that the girl was in need of help, as well as in need of clothes, and that his mission is simply to help her. In spite of or perhaps because of the limitations of *The Subterraneans*—and they are many—the film accepts the status of Mulligan as a serious musician and connects a clerical calling with his devotion to art. Significantly, Mulligan also stands outside the sexual politics of the plot; compared to the other characters in *The Subterraneans,* he seems to have transcended the need for lovers and sexual dalliances. But his association with the hyperphallic baritone saxophone, with the black artists of *The Sound of Jazz,* and with the white leading lady Judy Holliday gave him as much subjectivity as Hollywood allowed jazz musicians in 1960. *The Subterraneans* may not exactly position the white Mulligan as an artist, but it endows him with an aura never available to black artists such as Louis Armstrong and, as I hope to demonstrate in chapter 7, even Nat King Cole. The old binary oppositions were still in effect at the end of the 1950s, but the most important binarism was still black versus white.

The Jazz Soundtrack

Other discursive practices contributed to the progress of jazz toward art status after the 1940s. Another book could be written about the jazz fiction of James Baldwin, Jack Kerouac, Eudora Welty, and John Clellon Holmes, to name just a few.[18] In particular, Holmes perfected a discourse in which jazz retained its rough edges at the same time that it was indisputably conceptualized as art. In *The Horn,* published in 1958, Holmes is explicit about the music's stature:

> For Billie James Henry was one of those solemn, pretentious younger jazz-men who were everywhere now, who had all been to Juilliard for composition, talked intelligently to Milhaud, and used the Schillinger method in their labored, atonal scores that carefully never swung *too* much; who all felt that jazz could *be* an art (forgetting that it was), and frowned on those who liked a hard beat, and worked the clubs reluctantly; who wrote arrangements with names like "The Thinking Reed," and really felt more comfortable in Europe. (Holmes 1988, 118–19) [emphasis in original]

In a much more subtle fashion, the presence of jazz in film scores of the 1950s indicates that jazz had become established as an art music, even in Hollywood. Claudia Gorbman (1987) has spoken of the "epic feeling" that late Romantic music is said to inspire (81). Perhaps the single most significant legacy of European art music from the late nineteenth century has been its impact on film scores, and by extension, on how Americans have come to perceive the emotional codes of music. Film music by Erich Wolfgang Korngold, Max Steiner, Alfred Newman, and within the last two decades, John Williams, draws heavily on the lush, overheated traditions of Wagner, Mahler, and Rachmaninoff. The Romantic repertoire became entrenched during the early years of cinema, at least in part because most of it was not copyrighted and therefore cost nothing when played as an accompaniment to silent films (Kalinak 1992, 61). Because of the reverential mood that such music can induce, and because the high art associations it has acquired have only reinforced its power, late Romantic music can, as Gorbman suggests, transform "The Particular into The Universal, The Prosaic into The Poetic, The Present into Mythic Time, and The Literal into The Symbolic" (Gorbman 1987, 82). And because it is ordinarily not associated with a literary text or a visual image, music more than any other art seems to transcend the everyday and speak a "universal language" of emotions, specifically those emotions that are *outside* the audience's quotidian activities. But since music for the classical Hollywood cinema must be "inaudible,"[19] because it is meant to be felt rather than listened to, movie scores do not lose their aloofness from specific plots and images. The music may seem to remain in the domain of "art," even when it swells up at the climax of a film that has been about secret agents, baseball players, or reformed hoodlums.

There are numerous examples of jazz being used extradiegetically in Hollywood films from the beginning of sound cinema, not to mention the many cartoons that have made prominent use of jazz. Scholars of film music have argued that musical strains derived from jazz are an important part of the scores for *The Plainsman* (1937), *Laura* (1944), and *Force of Evil* (1948) (Kalinak 1992, 185). The actual institutionalization of jazz on the soundtrack happens around the midcentury mark with films such as *Pinky* (1949), *Panic in the Streets* (1950), *The Strip* (1951), and *A Streetcar Named Desire* (1951). In some cases, jazz enters the film score through a kind of narrative justification—both *Panic in the Streets* and *Streetcar Named Desire* take place in New Orleans where jazz is in a sense inevitable (Kalinak 1992, 103). At the beginning of *Pinky,* the eponymous heroine walks among the run-down shacks of the black community in a small southern town while an extradiegetic soprano saxophone plays the blues. At least at first, composer Alfred Newman must have considered this the appropriate sound for the milieu. But jazz disappears from the soundtrack as Pinky both accepts her place in this community and overcomes its associations with poverty and idleness. By the conclusion of *Pinky,* jazz, blues, and saxophones have been replaced with the more familiar strains of Hollywood Romanticism. Although Newman can hardly be called a daring advocate of jazz, using the music here in a culturally patronizing way, his willingness to write at least a few passages in an American idiom indicates his relative independence from the elitist traditions of nineteenth-century European Romanticism in which virtually all of the other major film composers of classical Hollywood were schooled.[20]

Although jazz had lost its mass popularity by 1950, those who would cast jazz as an art music had scored another victory as the music made its way into the background score. Jazz had always carried with it a strong Romantic element. Louis Armstrong, who had obviously listened to a few arias from European opera (Berrett 1992), may have been the first jazz soloist to bring an "epic feeling" into his performances. He infused his solos with drama and structured them around emotional climaxes, even in recordings as unlikely as "Struttin' with Some Barbecue" (1927). The "symphonic jazz" of the early 1920s was also highly inflected with Romantic influences and influenced much of the big band jazz that followed. The rise of jazz on the film soundtrack represents the growing acceptance of jazz as an art music that can signify emotions as successfully as late-nineteenth-century European music. Jazz was useful when plots in the 1950s took on "social problems" such as drug abuse, alcoholism, and juvenile delinquency. When Otto Preminger's *The Man with the Golden Arm* opened in 1955, many, including the Hays Office, were shocked by the protagonist's addiction to heroin, but few were distressed by composer Elmer Bernstein's decision to base the film's music on jazz elements. Jazz was becoming the preferred and even appropriate music to express contemporary urban disaffection and turbulence.

A more complex argument can be made for extradiegetic jazz as an art music. The most common critique of film music among cinema scholars is that the extradiegetic score in the classical cinema functions "ideologically" to soothe the viewer into an uncritical acceptance of the film's values, even when the viewer ought to know better (Kalinak 1992, 36). Once the music of late Romanticism became entrenched as the zero-degree vehicle of emotional realism, it became the ideal means for sugarcoating whatever pill filmmakers wanted their audiences to swallow. Hanns Eisler and Theodor Adorno's *Composing for Films* (1947) charges Hollywood films with denying the contradictions in their narratives as well as in the heterogeneity of their technological basis. It indicts music in particular for contributing to the film's illusion of reality and concealing its own remoteness from other components.

Eisler, who had composed music for the plays of Bertolt Brecht before writing music for films, subscribed at least initially to the hope of enlightening audiences to the actual economic and political conditions under which they live. He wanted a film music practice that would expose the contradictions of the film, and by extension, the contradictions of life in a capitalist state (Gorbman 1987, 106). But because Eisler wrote with Adorno, who was deeply pessimistic about the possibility of art having a real effect on people's lives, *Composing for Films* does not spell out an alternative practice for filmmaking; rather it limits itself to describing the actual nature of Hollywood film music.

Still, Eisler/Adorno as well as subsequent theorists such as Gorbman (1987), Kalinak (1992), and Flinn (1992) are helpful in conceptualizing the jazz soundtrack. In this context, a jazz soundtrack can succeed by calling attention to itself and *disrupting* the illusion that the action in a film is natural and unproblematic. Jazz should be the ideal tonic for rousing audiences out of their imaginary relationship to the film and their unreasoning acceptance of its values. Of course, the jazz connoisseur will easily pick out the signature sounds of soloists and the names of familiar songs when jazz plays in the background. The jazz buff inevitably watches these films in a state of heightened awareness, hearing the music as something with a history and an ontology outside the film. But even the noninitiate might have a more complex reaction to films such as *Sweet Love Bitter* (1966) or *She's Gotta Have It* (1986), where the music of Charles McPherson and Mal Waldron or Bill Lee and Kenny Barron is difficult to ignore since it is not always carefully cued to the action. The improvising jazz artist, who answers to a private sense of which sounds are right for which moment, is almost by definition incompatible with standard film music practice. Jazz soundtracks at times seem to spin along on their own, seemingly oblivious to the action. While it is of course debatable whether or not the audience experiences some sort of Brechtian distanciation from the action in such circumstances, the jazz film score at least offers the viewer an opportunity to experience the film more critically as a modernist, even fragmented, work of art.

John Cassavetes's *Shadows* (1960) takes jazz extremely seriously in the lives of the characters, in the extradiegetic score, and even in the director's approach to filmmaking. At least two of the film's principal characters are jazz musicians, and the film boasts a limited but complex score by Charles Mingus and saxophone improvisations by Shafi Hadi.[21] What

is most interesting about *Shadows*, however, is its valorized use of improvisation to create dialogue. At the very end of the film, a title card announces, "The film you have just seen was an improvisation."[22] Jazz had
now become a model for an avant-garde filmmaking, and Cassavetes and
a number of other innovators would continue to develop this model as a
countertradition in the American cinema.

It is no coincidence that the Actors studio and the improvisational
practice of Method acting flourished in the 1950s at the same time that
jazz was being embraced as another form of modernist art. There is also
a definite relationship between psychoanalysis and modernist intuitive
practices such as jazz and the Method. At least in theory, both practices
drew heavily on theories of the unconscious in which truth was to be
found through free association and the uncovering of buried emotions.
Jazz and its mystique of improvisation were related to and perhaps an
influence on the technique of many actors in the 1950s who brought an
ad-lib aesthetic to both theater and film.[23] A jazz aesthetic had grown
beyond music and taken on a life of its own.

The importance of jazz for the Hollywood film score declined after the
1950s. By turning over the soundtrack of *The Graduate* (1967) to Simon
and Garfunkel, Mike Nichols set the stage for several decades of films
that featured a nonstop succession of recordings by pop artists. In the
1990s, however, the jazz score may be on the rise again. The popularity
of Wynton Marsalis and the cultural ascendance of jazz in the 1980s and
1990s has had its impact even in Hollywood. Several films from 1994
used jazz in ways interchangeable with those of the well-established Romanticism of the Hollywood film score. In *Quiz Show*, when Herb Stempl
jauntily arrives home in Queens after another winning performance on a
television quiz program, Mark Isham's score features a walking bass and a
muted trumpet. In *Mrs. Parker and the Vicious Circle*, a growling, plunger-
muted trumpet and a Venuti-esque violin evoke the urbanity of the Al-
gonquin Round Table. And most remarkably, in *Vanya on 42nd Street*, the
high art of Anton Chekhov and the faded glory of New York's old New
Amsterdam Theater, once the home of the Ziegfeld Follies, are accompanied by the jazz of Joshua Redman's quartet. Redman was a logical choice
for this project. His father, Dewey Redman, is a member of the jazz aris-
tocracy with a substantial following among connoisseurs. Joshua Redman is a Renaissance man who graduated summa cum laude from Harvard University and was accepted by the Yale Law School but who
ultimately deferred his admission to become a professional jazz musician
(Cole 1993, 17). Louis Malle, the Frenchman who directed André Grego-

ry's workshop production of David Mamet's adaptation of *Uncle Vanya*, undoubtedly shares the tendency of many Europeans to regard jazz as a legitimate art form. A director of American as well as European films, including *L'Ascenseur pour l'échafaud* (*Elevator to the Gallows,* 1957) with an improvised score by Miles Davis, Malle is likely to understand the artificiality of conventional distinctions between high and low art. In *Vanya on 42nd Street,* Malle demonstrates that a young black artist playing neobop is entirely compatible with an informal but highly faithful performance of a modernist classic.

FOUR

Signifyin(g) the Phallus

Representations of the Jazz Trumpet

> Virgil Thomson had compared the performances of famed jazz
> trumpeter, Louis Armstrong, to those of the great *castrati* of the
> eighteenth century.
> —Theodor Adorno, "Perennial Fashion—Jazz" (1981)

Adorno's appropriation of Virgil Thomson's comment on Armstrong is typical of Adorno's notorious and possibly uninformed attacks on jazz.[1] Although he argues both in "Perennial Fashion—Jazz" and in his earlier essay "On Jazz" (1989–90) that the music brings about the castration of the *listener,* Adorno supports this thesis by suggesting that one of the music's most prominent *producers* was in some way emasculated. Earlier in "Perennial Fashion—Jazz," Adorno had associated the jazz performer with "the eccentric clown" and "the early film comics" (Adorno 1981, 129). If Adorno had Armstrong in mind in these remarks, he was probably aware that, like many African American performers, the trumpeter was frequently asked to play the epicene clown when he appeared in American movies. But Adorno ignores the patterns of racism in the culture industry that demanded the demasculinization of black jazz performers. Other than castration, he admits no alternative—positive or negative—to an undefined masculinity just as he makes no attempt to distinguish the diverse forms of masculine expression among different races and social classes. Adorno also appears unaware of the many ways in which a performer like Armstrong found his way around Hollywood's constraints. How Armstrong accomplished this feat is an important topic in chapter 6. For now, suffice it to say that Armstrong was a master of "signifying," an African American term for the art of talking about, criticizing, ridiculing and/or putting one over on the audience. Henry Louis Gates, Jr. (1988), has made this practice—which he writes as "Signifyin(g)" in order to distinguish it from the Standard English sense of the word—a central concept in his work on African American literature.[2]

Although many Americans now recall Armstrong as a smiling clown, he regularly used his trumpet to express phallic masculinity along with a great deal of the sexual innuendo that was already an essential element of jazz performance. When Hollywood's racial codes allowed, Armstrong was even given license to represent his sexuality in more conventional ways as, for example, when he performed erotically charged duets with Dorothy Dandridge in *Pillow to Post* (1945) and with Billie Holiday in *New Orleans* (1947). Adorno's association of Armstrong with castration has not been defended, even by Adorno's most tenacious advocates. While Miriam Hansen (1981–82) has brilliantly constructed a positive aesthetics of cinema out of Adorno's largely negative writings on film, no one is likely to tease a corresponding jazz aesthetic out of essays such as "Perennial Fashion—Jazz."[3]

Louis Armstrong was only the first of many African American jazz artists to attract international attention by establishing phallic authority with that most piercing of instruments, the trumpet. Dizzy Gillespie, a celebrated musical descendant of Armstrong who frequently spoke of the "virility" of black jazz, may have been signifying on the phallic nature of his instrument when he bent the bell upward as if to simulate an erection. In the forty years since Gillespie bent his bell, however, a new generation of trumpet players has emerged who, while not abandoning the libidinal recesses of jazz, have moved away from the more explicitly virile possibilities of the instrument. Although these younger musicians have in no way embraced castration, they seem much less interested in phallic display. Their stylistic orientations might be called "post-phallic."[4]

As writer and director of *Mo' Better Blues* (1990), Spike Lee has confronted this tradition if only because he hired Terence Blanchard to dub in the trumpet solos for his protagonist, Bleek Gilliam (Denzel Washington). The choice is significant because Blanchard plays in a style with distinct post-phallic qualities. But as has long been the case, the codes of sexual signification developed through the history of jazz have been profoundly repressed within the traditions of classical cinema. *Mo' Better Blues,* Spike Lee's most personal film before *Crooklyn* (1994), falls back on a well-established pattern in Hollywood films that calls into question the masculinity of jazz trumpet players, white and black. Adorno's thesis that jazz leads to some type of symbolic castration is validated by *Mo'*

Better Blues as well as by several American films that preceded it, including *Young Man with a Horn* (1950), *The Five Pennies* (1959), and even *New York, New York* (1977). Probably without intending to do so, Lee has brought Terence Blanchard's sound into his film, even though Blanchard's post-phallic trumpet undermines the film's reaffirmation of the traditional sexual roles that Hollywood has promoted throughout the century.

A term such as post-phallic may be even more problematic than words such as phallic, masculine, and castration, especially now that increasingly large numbers of critics have addressed the inevitable slippage of such terms. Among the many useful articles addressing "male trouble" in the journal *Camera Obscura*, I find Thomas DiPiero's "The Patriarch Is Not (Just) a Man" (1991) to be especially helpful in formulating a discourse of the phallus among jazz artists. DiPiero argues that possessing a phallus (in the sense of social and cultural empowerment) and being male are not necessarily the same thing: phallic entitlement is just as dependent upon "one's racial and class identity, along with one's sexual orientation, national identity, and a host of other qualities" (103).[5] For DiPiero, masculinity is by no means monolithic and ought to be understood "as an unstable nexus of social and political phenomena, rather than as a mystified, consistent source of power and control" (118). Given the long history of violence and disempowerment endured by African Americans, there is no question that black masculinity constitutes an even more unstable nexus. With its complex history of signifying and encoding, jazz offers abundant examples of how black artists have refused to abide by prescribed and proscribed notions of phallic masculinity. A striking but not exceptional example is Cecil Taylor, a gay jazz pianist who has for several decades played an unrelentingly aggressive, experimental music.

As Eric Lott (1993) has demonstrated, white America's view of black masculinity has always been riddled with contradictions. As was often the case with Louis Armstrong, the black male was a figure of hypermasculinity at the same time that he was considered pathetically unmanly (Fredrickson 1971). This must have been especially true for Armstrong in the 1920s and 1930s when the jazz trumpet was most flamboyantly representative of sexuality among African American musicians. As with many aspects of black culture, jazz provided its practitioners with wide latitude for expressing masculinity while avoiding the less mediated assertions of phallic power that were regularly punished by white culture. If it is true that no one ever possesses the phallus of the father—the first phallus that anyone desires—then all us of us, male and female alike, are castrated.[6] The trumpet can then be conceptualized as a compensatory, even hysterical, mechanism to ward off castration. By extension, as Di-Piero has argued (118), *any* display of masculinity is essentially hysterical. The inescapably hysterical underpinnings of the jazz trumpet must be acknowledged even for a figure such as Armstrong, who deftly negotiated racial and sexual taboos by carefully coding his phallic display. One of my purposes here is to distinguish the joyous and subversive if compensatory phallicism of musicians such as Armstrong from the castration (as in loss of subjecthood) that Adorno broadly attributes to jazz but *not* to what he calls autonomous art.

On the most obvious level, the phallicism of the jazz trumpet resides in pitch, speed, and emotional intensity, all of which Armstrong greatly expanded in the 1920s.[7] The many artists who followed Armstrong have found numerous ways of dealing with these dimensions of the trumpet. By contrast, we may not choose to characterize the Eurocentric virtuoso who can play high and fast as necessarily phallic: what a symphony player might call bad technique—an extremely wide vibrato or a "smeared" note, for example—can become a forceful, even virtuosic device of a jazz trumpeter. Stage deportment and the musician's clothing can also become part of a phallic style. Consider the pelvic thrusts that Dizzy Gillespie performed in front of his bands in the 1940s and 1950s.[8] Consider also the "Prince of Darkness" mode in which Miles Davis clothed himself during his final two decades. Steven Cohan (1993) has argued that all such displays constitute a kind of performative masculinity, in spite of the fact that our culture has traditionally designated women, not men, as the object of the gaze. In this sense, the actor, the dancer, or the jazz artist who claims for himself the quality of "to-be-looked-at-ness" runs the risk of feminization. But as Cohan convincingly demonstrates in his analysis of Fred Astaire, under certain circumstances masculinity itself can be based in spectacle (48). Similarly, a great deal of what I have called the phallic trumpet style depends on how the trumpeter displays himself.

If African American artists have understood how to manipulate musical codes of masculine sexuality,[9] they have also been aware on some level of the artificiality of phallic display. Although most jazzmen would probably not agree with DiPiero's (1991) thesis that masculinity "can only ever be hysterical" (118), they have been capable of signifying on received notions of the masculine. One of the most common ways in which trumpeters have played on the phallic nature of their instrument is by adopting the role of self-effacing *eiron* where the strutting *alazon* is expected. Gillespie, for example, would fend off other trumpet players—especially young, ambitious ones—by underplaying; when preceded in a sequence of solos by a flashy young trumpeter, Gillespie would "cut" his opponent with short, piquant, often humorous phrases. Cat Anderson, who for many years played extraordinarily high notes in trumpet solos with the Duke Ellington orchestra (Ellington would tell audiences that Anderson's final stratospheric note was "a high C above Hyannis Port"), is signifying on his own reputation as well as on his audience's expectations in a 1976 recording with a band led by Bill Berry. Anderson is about to solo on "Boy Meets Horn," a tune that Ellington and Rex Stewart wrote in the late 1930s to feature Stewart's playful, half-valve cornet style. Berry announces that Cat Anderson will perform "Boy Meets Horn" and then adds, "although in this case it's more like Superman." In his solo, however, Anderson stays almost exclusively within the middle register, frequently offering a precise imitation of Stewart's original reading of the tune.

A useful contrast to the signifying black artist is the white jazz trumpeter Maynard Ferguson, who simply plays as high as possible in order to establish his power unself-consciously and without irony. This is not to say that whites or women cannot signify or play a role in the history of the jazz trumpet. On the one hand, many have internalized and transformed styles originally associated with African American males. The black female trumpeter Valaida Snow, who flourished in the 1930s and 1940s, recorded in a distinctly Armstrongian style as did the white Harry James, who grew up playing in traveling circus bands directed by his father. In the 1920s, white trumpeters like Bix Beiderbecke and Red Nichols, whose middle-class, midwestern backgrounds provided few of the conditions that prompted black artists to develop phallic styles, created distinct paradigms of their own.

Today a number of talented female trumpeters are regularly disrupting any attempt to mark the instrument as exclusively male. I would specifically cite the case of Rebecca Coupe Franks, a white woman who is fully in control of the phallic elements of the tradition at the same time that she is capable of substantial lyricism. Although not at all unserious, Franks appears to enjoy herself as she addresses the history of the jazz trumpet, often quoting from canonical recordings and clearly signifying on her predecessors as well as on her audience's gender expectations.

Still, the dominant figures in the history of the jazz trumpet have been African Americans, especially those who used the trumpet to express masculinity at historical moments when other, comparable expressions were dangerous, to say the least. What separates a "trumpet jock" like Maynard Ferguson from a figure such as Louis Armstrong is Armstrong's ability to do more than simply overwhelm the competition with pitch, volume, and speed. Like many African American entertainers of his generation, Armstrong made signifying a regular feature of his performance persona, engaging in a great deal of ribaldry and self-deprecation. Part of Armstrong's success was surely related to his ability to play the sexual *and* the asexual jester in different registers and at different moments in a performance. Although Armstrong did not give the impression that he was a sexual threat to all the women in his audience, he often kept a teasing edge on his ribaldry. Along with the poetry and pathos, there was a libidinal energy in Armstrong's solos that could create a kind of foreplay leading up to climaxes. Accordingly, members of his band are said to have referred to their accompanying figures on Armstrong's 1931 recording of "Star Dust" as "the fucking rhythm" (Radano 1992).

Most of the important trumpeters who came of age in the 1930s and 1940s—Roy Eldridge, Buck Clayton, Frankie Newton, Hot Lips Page, Charlie Shavers, Dizzy Gillespie—were the aesthetic progeny of Armstrong, all of them adopting styles with phallic elements. In fact, almost all of Armstrong's disciples relished the opportunity to establish their authority, regularly taking on challengers in "cutting contests."[10] In the years after World War II, when jazz was about to establish itself permanently as an art music, Fats Navarro, Clifford Brown, and Miles Davis were all poised at one time or another to become the most prominent inheritor of the Armstrong-Gillespie legacy. Navarro died a drug addict in 1950 at the age of twenty-six, and in 1956 Clifford Brown was killed on the Pennsylvania Turnpike at age twenty-five. The field was effectively left open for Miles Davis, already well-established since the mid–1940s and undoubtedly the most influential trumpeter since Armstrong. As the son of a dentist in East St. Louis, Illinois, Davis may also have been the first important black trumpeter from a comfortable, middle-class background. Many phallic elements persisted in Davis's playing, including spikes into the upper register, fast runs throughout the range of the instrument, and an often exaggerated feel for climaxes. He was also conspicuous in refusing to develop an ingratiating performance persona, often turning his back on audiences, ignoring their applause, and leaving the stage when other musicians were soloing. Always attentive to sartorial elegance, Davis adopted a highly ornate style of dress at roughly the same time in the late 1960s that he began using electrified instruments in his band and embraced forms of music closer to the popular mainstream.[11] Although one of the platitudes of jazz history posits a decline in Miles Davis's playing after the late 1960s, many qualities that surrounded his playing enhanced the phallicism of his image. The heavily amplified volume of his final bands is only the most obvious example of this change.

In spite of Davis's desire to create an almost exaggerated masculine identity, as early as the 1940s he was using his trumpet to reveal emotional depth and introspection, even vulnerability. When Davis made a "mistake"—when his tone faltered or he seemed to miss a note—the cause was soulfulness and sensitivity rather than some shortcoming of technical prowess.[12] (Davis's ability to aestheticize the "clam," or missed note, should be considered alongside the Hollywood trope discussed below in which failure to hit the right note symbolizes a trumpet player's sexual impotence.) Without attempting to explain the complex development of Miles Davis's style over some forty-five years,[13] I would point out that what came to be known as the "cool" aspect of his playing has influenced a great many players in a great many ways. Since the 1950s many of the most critically acclaimed black trumpeters have been ironists (Clark Terry, Don Cherry, Lester Bowie, Olu Dara) and introverts (Art Farmer, Clarence Shaw, Booker Little, Ted Curson) rather than dominators and extroverts.[14] Art Farmer may be the best example of an artist working in a post-phallic style derived from emotional codes developed by Davis. While Davis was a man of slight stature who nevertheless posed provocatively in boxing gear for a notorious album cover,[15] Art Farmer is tall and large-boned. His lyricism, soft tone, hesitant delivery, and lack of stage mannerisms all represent a retreat from phallic bravado.[16] Farmer's style might be called post-phallic rather than nonphallic because, on the one hand, it in no way suggests that Farmer has accepted castration, lost his subjecthood, or refused the sexuality of the idiom; on the other hand, there is no obvious hysterical edge to Farmer's self-presentation that spills over into showy displays of technique or extra-musical affectation.

In the last few years a post-phallic style has become the norm among a group of young musicians who have taken the fantastically successful Wynton Marsalis as their model.[17] Marsalis, Wallace Roney, Marlon Jordan, and Terence Blanchard all play in a frequently understated manner that conventionalizes—a more severe critic might say commodifies— Miles Davis's modal improvisations from the mid-1960s. Like many jazz musicians of recent decades, the younger musicians have transformed the withdrawn but elegant performance image of Davis's middle period into an affectless stage presence and a highly conservative dress code. Without renouncing the romance and sexuality that have always been fundamental to jazz, and without completely abandoning speed and high pitch, these trumpeters have substituted finesse and control for theatrics and ostentation.

The emergence of a post-Davis, post-phallic style in the 1980s is surely overdetermined. Recalling DiPiero's statement that maleness is manifested differently within different races and social classes (and at different historical moments), we might associate the rise of the post-phallic trumpet style with a group of African Americans who are more affluent, better educated, and/or more class-conscious and who thus feel less impelled to demonstrate their masculinity with the provocative gestures of ostensibly working-class musics such as rap and hip-hop. By avoiding the flamboyant displays of more popular and more visible forms, jazz artists have maintained the obligatory "otherness" of their music. At the same time, a large population of fans has nourished the music of Wynton Marsalis, Marcus Roberts, and their peers; it is an upscale music that bears marks of both the contemporary and the classical but favors smooth elegance over the rough-edged forms of more experimental and/or progressive jazz.[18] Revealingly, in the early 1990s the New Old Jazz began to grace television advertisements as a signifier of affluence and sophistication. For example, a Marsalis clone can be heard playing trumpet on the soundtrack of a commercial for the Infiniti, a luxury car. We might also consider the possibility that musicians like Marsalis and Blanchard are signifying on old and/or lower-class notions of masculinity by retreating from phallic posturing.

At any rate, Marsalis is disproportionately more popular than someone like Jon Faddis, an exceptionally phallic trumpeter who *might* have been a better choice to dub in Bleek Gilliam's solos in *Mo' Better Blues*. In stature and carriage Faddis even resembles Denzel Washington, in stark contrast to the diminutive Blanchard. A protégé of Dizzy Gillespie, Faddis regularly appeared on the same stages with his master and evoked gestures of approval from Gillespie whenever the younger man negotiated particularly impressive improvisations.[19] Blanchard, on the other hand, could trace his parentage almost entirely to Miles Davis. Unlike Gillespie, Davis was a highly problematic father figure, who regarded with suspicion a generation of young players who took up a style that he had abandoned twenty-five years earlier.[20]

If Harold Bloom's (1973) theories of the dynamics of influence among post-Enlightenment poets are applicable to jazz history, both Faddis and

Blanchard might be considered weak poets, anxious about their influences. Playing with confidence and expansiveness as he rifles through the legacy of the strong poet Gillespie, Faddis's style might be understood in terms of Bloom's trope *apophrades:* the work of the precursor is completely absorbed by the ephebe, who identifies with the strong poet to the point of replacing him or re-creating him as if he never existed. By contrast, Blanchard's work suggests the ratio of *askesis* as he turns inward with a pared-down, resigned version of Davis's more sweeping vision. Blanchard sometimes appears unusually self-effacing in his recordings and appearances, especially in the years before Spike Lee began shooting *Mo' Better Blues.* In fact, according to Lee's companion volume for the film, Blanchard was not performing in public during the filming because he was in the process of developing a more effective embouchure (Lee 1990, 158). But Blanchard must not be written off because he has not reached Faddis's level of technical flash. In addition to complementing and perhaps enhancing our understanding of signifying in jazz, Bloom's work offers the advantage of placing the two trumpeters within a system that is free of value judgments. In terms of how masculine codes are articulated in music, however, Blanchard may in fact be more interesting for pursuing the complicated legacy of Miles Davis. On *Black Pearls* (1988), the last recording he made before changing his embouchure, Blanchard provides one of the most convincing demonstrations of how the trumpet can be made to speak a compelling, romantic language devoid of phallic bravado.

Spike Lee probably did not come up with the original idea to hire Terence Blanchard as the trumpet voice of Bleek Gilliam in *Mo' Better Blues.* Blanchard more likely was recommended to Lee by saxophonist Branford Marsalis (Wynton's brother), who acted in Lee's 1988 film *School Daze,* contributed much of the music for *Mo' Better Blues,* and recorded the saxophone solos that are dubbed in for Shadow Henderson (Wesley Snipes). On one hand, Blanchard's restrained playing is appropriate to the obsessive artistic personality that Lee gave to Bleek Gilliam. On the other, Blanchard's decidedly post-phallic style is not what we might expect from a character who declares, "It's a dick thing," when asked to justify his need for two regular sex partners. Bleek Gilliam is presented first as a musician too obsessed with his art to develop real feelings for either of his two women; at the end of the film, after he gives up the jazz life, he is "saved" by one and becomes a bourgeois patriarch. While it can be argued that the first role leads to nagging, castrating behavior by both women and that the second involves the emasculating act of begging for salvation from one woman, little in Bleek's character is consistent with the self-consciousness and sexual complexity of Blanchard's playing.

In his interviews and in the companion volume to *Mo' Better Blues*, Spike Lee (1990) has singled out *Round Midnight* (1986) and *Bird* (1988) as films that do not accurately portray the lives of jazz artists (39–40). But these are not the only films about jazz musicians, including jazz trumpet players as in *Mo' Better Blues*. In fact, the phallic symbolism of the jazz trumpet has not been lost on Hollywood filmmakers. For example, when Robert Wagner in *All the Fine Young Cannibals* (1960) reencounters his lover after a long absence, he thrusts the bell of his trumpet into the air and executes a long glissando into a high note. Although Goldie Hawn refuses Kurt Russell's advances for five months in *Swing Shift* (1984), she takes him home to her bed the first night she hears him play the trumpet. Christine Lahti, *Swing Shift's* other heroine, also succumbs to Russell's allure after her first experience of his music. In *I Dood It* (1943), an early film directed by Vincente Minnelli, Lena Horne appears in a production number that invokes the biblical story of Jericho. When a black jazz trumpeter joins Horne on stage in the Jericho segment, the (hymen) walls come tumbling down after the musician reaches his highest note. The trumpeter then collapses as well, his body drained of tumescence after the musical climax.

In other films, however, the trumpet's obvious phallicism is connected with impotence or vulnerability to castration in much the same way as in *Mo' Better Blues*. A more general comparison here would cite a long history of narratives in which excessive masculinity is constantly undermined by performance anxiety as well as by the fear that sex with a woman will limit a man's strength in a variety of "manly" pursuits such as sporting events. In *Raging Bull* (1980), for example, Martin Scorsese (for whom Spike Lee has expressed admiration) drew attention to Jake LaMotta's conviction that sexual intercourse would hinder his success as a boxer. When this trope is translated into the plots of jazz films, the trumpet brings substantial fragility to an otherwise highly masculine male. In *Birth of the Blues* (1941), for example, when Bing Crosby comes to blows with Brian Donlevy, Crosby is urged not to hit cornetist Donlevy in the lip. More revealingly, a common scene occurs in which the trumpet player's inability to hit the right notes is a metaphor for his sexual or masculine inadequacy. Examples of this situation can be seen in at least two films that preceded *Mo' Better Blues: Young Man with a Horn* (1950) and *The Five Pennies* (1959).

As some reviewers of *Mo' Better Blues* observed, Rick Martin (Kirk Douglas), the eponymous hero of *Young Man with a Horn*, bears a certain resemblance to Bleek Gilliam in that both trumpeters are obsessive artists torn between two women. In part because he has married the emasculating Amy North (Lauren Bacall) instead of the nurturing Jo Jordan (Doris Day), *Young Man with a Horn*'s Rick cannot command the upper register at a recording session with singer Jordan. Later, after he has collapsed and Jo has nursed him back to health, Rick once again ascends to the higher registers of his instrument at the same time that we are told he has renounced the desire to be "an artist." Rick regains the phallus through normative monogamous sexuality rather than through art, not at all unlike Bleek Gilliam in Spike Lee's film.

In *The Five Pennies*, Red Nichols dubbed in the trumpet solos for Danny Kaye in Nichols's own film biography. In the middle of the film, after the protagonist blames himself and the excesses of his career for his daughter's crippling attack of polio, he destroys his horn and takes a job as a common laborer. Years later, Nichols is provoked into playing when several teenagers, who have come to celebrate his daughter's birthday, express ignorance of his earlier achievements. One young man says, "My father told me all about you. . . . He said you were smart to get out of the

27. Dizzy Gillespie with his trademark trumpet. Jerry Ohlinger's Movie Material Store, Inc.

business before the parade passed you by." Outraged at this slight and intent on proving that he is still musically potent, Nichols is conveniently handed a cornet by his wife, who sees an opportunity to bring him back to the music after many years. Although he plays a highly embellished version of "Indiana" for a few bars, Nichols stops in frustration when he fluffs a high note. All of his daughter's friends then leave the house in embarrassment, one of them explaining, "I have homework to do." Nichols's eventual comeback performance is marked not by renewed success as a musician but by the realization that the love of his family is what really matters. At the climactic moment in the final scene, Nichols

28. Ish Kabibble (Merwyn Bogue) with his nonphallic trumpet. Photo courtesy of Janet Bogue Arnot.

is invited to dance by his daughter who has suddenly regained the near complete use of her legs. Again, love and family sustain the musician where jazz cannot.

I should also point out that Jackie Gleason's Ralph Cramden, one of the most castrated males in the history of television, continually fails to hit the high notes on his old trumpet in an episode of the *Honeymooners*. Similarly, in the 1960s and 1970s comedian Jackie Vernon presented himself as a resigned loser, often bringing a battered cornet into his stand-up routine. Appropriately, Vernon's range was limited to the lower registers. There is, finally, the character of Ish Kabibble (Merwyn Bogue), a tall, solemn comedian with a bowl haircut who was regularly featured with Kay Kyser's band in the 1930s and 1940s. Kabibble has posed holding a damaged horn with the bell bent upward (Bogue 1989), slightly reminiscent of the trademark trumpet of Dizzy Gillespie. Here, however, the resemblance ends; rather than phallic power, the broken horn of Ish Kabibble jokingly symbolizes his lack of conventional manliness. I would argue that the hypermasculine image of premodern black trumpeters is a structuring absence in the personae of all three white comedians.

Spike Lee resurrects the trope of the impotent trumpeter at the climax of *Mo' Better Blues* when Bleek Gilliam walks into the Dizzy Club where his old group is performing, now led by his musical and sexual rival Shadow Henderson. Bleek has just undergone a long recovery from a severe injury to his lip, and as is often the case in a narrative when the hero has been out of circulation for a while, important issues are about to be resolved. Earlier scenes in *Mo' Better Blues* suggested that these issues would involve the debate between Bleek and Shadow over what kind of music the band ought to be playing. In an initial scene, Bleek had accused Shadow of "ego-grandstanding" during a solo, as if the saxophonist were compromising his art to please the unsophisticated listeners in the house. Later, at a party, Shadow had called Bleek "a grandiose motherfucker" for playing his own personal brand of jazz and then complaining because audiences ignored the music. None of these issues, however, are directly addressed at the film's conclusion.

When Bleek walks into Dizzy's, the group is playing behind a vocal by Clarke Bentancourt (Cynda Williams), formerly one of Bleek's two lovers, now a bedmate of Shadow. Bleek had earlier declared Clarke to be unprepared to sing jazz, and in fact her singing recalls Joni Mitchell rather than canonical female jazz vocalists such as Billie Holiday, Sarah Vaughan, Betty Carter, or Abbey Lincoln, who appears in *Mo' Better Blues* in the nonsinging role of Bleek's mother. The audience in the club, however, appears to be enjoying her singing while Lee's camera glamorizes her with star close-ups. When Bleek joins his old group on the bandstand, the film might have shown the two horn players squaring off in a cutting contest, or Bleek might have rallied his old sidemen to play a more complex or more soulful form of jazz after the bland performance by Clarke. When he takes his solo chorus, however, Bleek finds himself unable to maintain command over his trumpet and suffers the same humiliation as the protagonists in *Young Man with a Horn* and *The Five Pennies*. In all three films (as well as in *I Dood It*), the analogies with sexual performance are reinforced by placing the narratives' key women in close proximity to the infirm trumpeters.

In disgrace, Bleek walks out of the club and hands his trumpet to Giant, his incompetent manager played by Spike Lee. In a striking scene that exhibits what Michael Wood has called the "perfectly overblown" qualities of classical Hollywood, Giant walks after Bleek in a heavy rainstorm. As the camera rises to shoot down from a great height and as the diegetic music from the club becomes empathically extradiegetic, the Chaplinesque Giant holds up the trumpet and shouts, "I won't sell it, Bleek, I won't sell it." Bleek then appears at the apartment of his other girlfriend, Indigo (Joie Lee). After he asks her to save his life, a montage shows them married and raising a son while the John Coltrane quartet's recording of the "Acknowledgement" section of *A Love Supreme* plays on the soundtrack.

The presence of Coltrane's music is one of the film's several problematic appropriations of jazz. Recorded in 1964 to celebrate his discovery of God, saxophonist Coltrane presented *A Love Supreme* as a single suite, a unique addition to his discography at that moment. Lee says that his film was originally titled *A Love Supreme* but that Coltrane's widow refused him permission unless he excised absolutely all foul language from the film, a compromise Lee was unwilling to make (Holley 1990, 54). Coltrane purists might object that the film relegates the saxophonist's expression of his religious conversion to the background of a largely secular account of marriage and family and that Coltrane's music accompanies the hero's renunciation of jazz, even though it is in the language of this tradition that Coltrane chose to communicate his most profound convictions. And as Kalamu ya Salaam (1990) has written, at the time that Coltrane recorded *A Love Supreme* he was successfully raising a family with a "Black woman who was both wife and musician" (13).

A certain incoherence also is evident in the film's suggestion that Shadow has succeeded as a musician (and as the lover of Clarke) by embracing a compromised form of jazz scorned by Bleek. In fact, however, the Marsalis/Blanchard style of jazz trumpet has proven to be highly successful with real-life audiences, and the film shows Bleek to be a crowd-pleasing entertainer with a substantial following.

According to the published script for *Mo' Better Blues,* Bleek becomes a music teacher sometime after the incident at the Dizzy Club (Lee 1990, 283), but we are not told what kinds of music or what approaches he teaches, and the film itself provides no information at all about Bleek's

29. Joie Lee, Denzel Washington, and Cynda Williams in a publicity photo for *Mo' Better Blues* (1990, Universal). Jerry Ohlinger's Movie Material Store, Inc.

new career in its last scenes. What we do know is that Bleek, like the
hero of *Young Man with a Horn,* has chosen the less sexual of his two
women, given up his obsessive artistic aspirations, and become a better
person. Bleek Gilliam is still another of Hollywood's jazz artists who runs
the risk of castration—on several levels—so long as he remains devoted
to his music. Early on, he makes a great fuss when Clarke bites his lip
in their love play and actually draws blood. This hint of castration is a
foreshadowing of the climactic scene in which Bleek's mouth *and* trumpet are brutally maimed when he tries to save his manager from two
toughs hired to punish Giant for falling behind in his gambling debts. In
spite of his public statements that *Mo' Better Blues* would correct the
myth of the doomed jazz artist presented in *Bird* and *Round Midnight,*
Spike Lee has made another film about a self-destructive jazz musician.
The hero is not a drug addict or an alcoholic, but he can only be saved
by abandoning jazz. Once he renounces the music, the film suggests, his
masculinity is restored as he ascends to the role of strong father.

The final scene of *Mo' Better Blues,* designed to parallel closely the
opening moments of the film, reveals much about Lee's attitudes toward
jazz and masculinity. Both scenes are shot in the same Brooklyn brown-
stone, and the same actor plays both the young Bleek and Miles, the son
of Bleek and Indigo. When young Bleek is urged by his peers to join them
in a game of baseball in the opening scene, the boy's mother forbids it,
insisting that he stay in and practice the trumpet. Bleek's father is unable
to prevent the mother from denying the boy his time with his friends.
The film then cuts from a shot of young Bleek practicing to the mature
Bleek performing in a club. From the outset, *Mo' Better Blues* has linked
the life of the jazz artist to matriarchy and the denial of normally sanctioned masculine behavior. The final scene precisely duplicates dialogue
and camera setups of the opening scene, but it ultimately shows the
young trumpeter being allowed to put down his horn and play with his
friends. Unlike his father, Bleek successfully intervenes when the mother
insists that the boy continue his practice session. Although the son is
named Miles, and although Bleek is seen teaching him to play the trumpet, the ending suggests that the boy will not be forced into the jazz life
with its attendant hazards.

The idealization of baseball in *Mo' Better Blues* has been noted by Viveca Gretton (1990), who has published a perceptive article on the renaissance of baseball films in the 1980s. As in *The Natural* (1984), *The
Slugger's Wife* (1985), *Long Gone* (1987), *Bull Durham* (1988), *Eight Men
Out* (1988), *Stealing Home* (1988), *Major League* (1989), and especially

Field of Dreams (1989), *Mo' Better Blues* uses baseball as a vehicle for the reestablishment of patriarchy.[21] Hollywood has found in baseball—especially the baseball of a premodern era—a domain in which an old-fashioned paradigm of phallic masculinity can be presented as natural and uncomplicated. *Field of Dreams* in particular identifies this beleaguered form of masculinity as not merely benign but actually as the key to reforging ties with the problematic fathers whose values were rejected in the 1960s. As Gretton points out, however, the guilty nostalgia of the new baseball films represses a number of ugly subtexts. For our purposes, the most glaring is the racism of premodern baseball that excluded African Americans from the major leagues until 1947.

In *Mo' Better Blues,* Lee largely ignores the racist aspects of baseball history that correspond closely to the exploitation of black jazz artists portrayed in the film. Houston A. Baker, Jr. (1991), has applied a Fanonian reading to Spike Lee's *Do the Right Thing* (1989) in which Sal, the owner of the pizzeria, can be understood as a typical white colonizer: "These are my people. They grew up on my pizza. I love these people, especially the attractive young females." Similarly, in *Mo' Better Blues,* the Flatbush brothers have colonized black jazzmen while presenting themselves as honest businessmen doing their job. In a gesture of friendship, they offer their cousin to Bleek as a new manager at the same time that they refuse to give him a larger portion of the receipts from his performances. The jazzman is condemned to the degraded life of an alienated laborer, his subjecthood at risk. But the film forgets the exploitation of black athletes that has long been central to the institution of baseball. Significantly, the protagonists in Lee's films wear jerseys associated with Jackie Robinson and Willie Mays. As in *Field of Dreams,* early baseball suggests a maleness that is unapologetic and unambiguous rather than contested; it is to a ball game, not to music, that Bleek sends his own son at the end of the film, just as Bleek had earlier bonded with his own father as they played pitch and catch.

A number of reasons are possible why Spike Lee would make a film that portrays sports and patriarchal family life as healthy alternatives to jazz. On one level, *Mo' Better Blues* marks the inevitable movement of an independent filmmaker toward familiar models of sexuality and cultural behavior as his budgets and audiences expand; the concluding montage, with its earnest portraits of masculinity and femininity based in child-rearing marriage, would have been unthinkable in Lee's earlier films. With *Mo' Better Blues,* Lee also may have been extending the role of spokesperson bestowed upon him by the media after his extremely effective commercials for Jesse Jackson's presidential campaign appeared on television in 1988 and even more so after *Do the Right Thing* became linked to contemporary events in New York City during the summer of 1989. Lee has accepted this advocate's role by appearing frequently on news and talk shows and consenting to regular interviews. He may still be the only black filmmaker to make this transition: it is difficult to imagine Mario van Peebles, Charles Burnett, or the artist formerly known as Prince (the auteur of two films in his own right) discussing race relations with Ted Koppel on ABC Television's *Nightline*. Certainly because of this public image, Lee was widely criticized for making films that were not sufficiently "realistic" by people with widely different takes on reality. This kind of criticism may have impelled Lee to end *Mo' Better Blues* with the portrait of a black family led by a strong father.[22] In *Do the Right Thing*, by contrast, Lee himself had played a father who neglected his son and the boy's mother. A similar trajectory toward "positive images" characterizes the progress of Lee's character Mars Blackmon, the streetwise trickster figure who first appeared in Lee's *She's Gotta Have It* (1986). After playing Mars in his witty television commercials for Nike shoes with basketball star Michael Jordan, Lee eventually made a public service message in which Mars and Jordan urge young people to stay in school.

In addition, Lee appears to harbor an ambivalence toward jazz that may be related to feelings about his father's career as a jazz artist. In the companion volume to *Mo' Better Blues* the filmmaker has said that his father, Bill Lee, an established jazz bassist, refused to play the electric bass during the 1960s and was thus unable to find regular employment (Lee 1990, 163). Consequently, Spike Lee's mother went to work as a schoolteacher, the same profession practiced by Indigo, the character played by Spike's sister (Joie Lee) who "saves" Bleek Gilliam. Spike Lee has also written that his mother was "the heavy" in the house while his father was a passive figure (43), the same constellation we see in young Bleek Gilliam's family. As Sharon Willis (1991) has written, "Giant happens to have Spike's face, but the film seems to want to say that the real 'Spike Lee' figure is Bleek" (250). Although the son hired his father to provide jazz scores for all of his films before *Jungle Fever* (1991), the younger Lee apparently remains conflicted about the music and about his father's unwillingness to compromise by playing something other than jazz.[23] Accordingly, one can choose to portray Bill Lee as a principled artist refusing to sell out or as a stubborn man clinging to an anachronism in spite of his family's needs. Spike Lee's account of his family must be regarded as one more text to be interpreted rather than as the real-life situation that explains the film. In this context, *Mo' Better Blues* can be understood as Spike Lee's attempt to rewrite his own story: jazz may have a place in this revised version but not if it interferes with family harmony. Significantly, Bleek Gilliam's sympathetic if passive father is a former professional baseball player rather than a jazz artist. Furthermore, no real jazz community exists in *Mo' Better Blues* outside Bleek and his sidemen, and Bleek never interacts with a "strong poet" and/or trumpet mentor. Thus, Bleek can give up jazz without disturbing some larger tradition that is inseparable from his performance career.

If Spike Lee is more comfortable with codes of masculinity connected with baseball than with jazz, he has also gravitated toward the highly representable codes of masculinity established for rap music. The most memorable performance scene in *Mo' Better Blues* takes place when Bleek turns around his baseball cap and sings "Pop Top 40 R 'n' B Urban Contemporary Easy Listening Funk Love" while adopting the body language of a rapper rather than a jazz artist, a strong contrast to the post-phallic stance he adopts while playing the trumpet elsewhere in the film. It is extremely difficult to imagine Wynton Marsalis or Terence Blanchard crossing class boundaries to abandon their affectless stage poses for more than a moment. The film ends, revealingly, with the rap group Gangstarr singing "Jazz Thing" while the credits roll. Lee's own view of jazz is probably summarized in Gangstarr's lyrics that position jazz as the revered but obsolete forerunner of more contemporary—and more provocative—forms of African American expression. Baseball is supremely representable; its codes have been thoroughly conventionalized in several decades of films and in the heroic close-ups we know so well from watching the game on television. Similarly, rap has quickly developed a highly conventionalized mode of performed masculinity that has become a regular feature of music videos, some of which have been directed by Lee himself.

Lee's affinity for rap and sports must be understood in the context of the choices he faces as a filmmaker. Unlike baseball and rap, jazz operates with a set of codes that are extremely difficult to represent, especially those forms that work against familiar models of masculinity. (The Hollywood convention that "missed" notes can only symbolize a trumpeter's impotence provides a strong case in point.) David James (1990) has identified the qualities that prevent the representation of a cultural development when it cannot be commodified in several intertextual, complementary depictions. James cites Madonna, Ronald Reagan, and the Olympics as easily represented phenomena that can be recognized in television, magazines, posters, and any number of other media and discourses. By contrast, "any social program that is not reducible to the priorities of this totalized machine is effectively unrepresentable" (79). James lists "the British miners' strike, AIDS, systemic judicial racism in the United States," and the U.S. defeat in Vietnam as phenomena that cannot be assimilated within the mythologies of contemporary culture industries (79). Certainly, all avant-garde forms of art belong in this list, with the post-phallic codes of jazz a legitimate if less conspicuous example.

Spike Lee was acting within prescribed cultural/cinematic practice when he equated the jazz life with self-destructiveness (the attack on Bleek's mouth is the most gripping moment in the film) and then indicated his hero's redeemed masculinity through the perennially effective spectacles of a wedding and the birth of a child. Speculating about the life that Bleek accepts after his embouchure has been damaged by the two toughs, Lee has written, "Out of the devastation that comes from not being able to play professionally, Bleek finds himself. And he finds that he can love and be loved. I really don't think Bleek could have been a happily married family man if it weren't for the accident" (Lee 1990, 68). An alternative ending to Mo' Better Blues in which Bleek can love and be loved *and* play jazz would have required a radical if not impossible revision of mainstream American cinema.

Several films provide relevant comparisons to this theme that the jazz life is incompatible with sustained romantic love. *Young Man with a Horn,* in which the protagonist becomes "a human being first and an artist second," is the clearest example. *Paris Blues* (1961) ends with its protagonist—an American jazz artist (Paul Newman) living in Paris—confirming his commitment to jazz by sending his lover (Joanne Woodward) back home to the States. In *Swing Shift,* Kurt Russell leaves behind both of his lovers to go on the road with a group of black jazz musicians. Martin Scorsese, who may be Spike Lee's strong poet, contributed to this tradition in *New York, New York* (1977) by attributing the central couple's breakup at least in part to the uncompromising desire of Robert De Niro to play modern jazz rather than the more commercial forms that emerged after the big band era.

As I suggested earlier, the post-phallic trumpet of Terence Blanchard is and is not a logical choice for the sounds that appear to emanate from the horn of Bleek Gilliam in *Mo' Better Blues.* On the one hand, the confidence and swagger of a Jon Faddis would have been inconsistent with the protagonist's decision to give up his craft after one humiliation. (In fact, as John Gennari [1991] has observed, no experienced jazz artist would have ventured into a club in the first place if he had any doubt about the condition of his embouchure [517]). On the other hand, the complex rethinkings of phallic masculinity implicit in Blanchard's music are inconsistent with the conclusion of the film; its idealization of sports and normative gender roles represses the vulnerability, sensuality, and introspection of Blanchard's trumpet solos. Lee celebrates the same modes of masculinity on which Blanchard may in fact be signifying.

Adorno's thesis that the audience for jazz is told, "give up your masculinity, let yourself be castrated," is especially relevant to the issues raised by the history of the jazz trumpet in general and by *Mo' Better Blues* in particular. In "Perennial Fashion—Jazz," Adorno creates a scenario that recalls the opening and closing scenes of Lee's film: "A child who prefers to listen to serious music or practice the piano rather than watch a baseball game or television will have to suffer as a 'sissy' in his class or in the other groups to which he belongs and which embody far more authority than parents or teacher. The expressive impulse is exposed to the same threat of castration that is symbolized and mechanically and ritually subdued in jazz" (Adorno 1981, 131). Like Adorno's theorized child, the young Bleek is condemned by his peers for accepting a practice session with his trumpet rather than a game of baseball. But Lee and Adorno submit their similar scenarios to sharply different interpretations. For Lee, the child can resist castration by moving toward baseball; for Adorno, sports and jazz are virtually identical in their regressive character.[24] The two interpretations intersect only in the association of castration with the child's move toward jazz.

Although he was critical of Freud's bourgeois privileging of normative genital sexuality (Huyssen 1986, 27), Adorno reveals a familiar bias, associating good, autonomous art with manliness and consumer art with femininity.[25] Most importantly, Adorno has confused jazz with the truly industrialized music of popular culture.[26] Even when he was writing his essays on the music, there were a great many jazz artists whose work could pass muster according to his definition of autonomous art. In the late 1950s and 1960s, musicians such as Cecil Taylor, Ornette Coleman, John Coltrane, and Charles Mingus were producing musics that fit many of the categories of "protest," "inaudibility," and "nonsubsumability" that Adorno created to license the music of Arnold Schoenberg in his *Philosophy of Modern Music* (1973). Even earlier, jazz musicians had developed expressive modes that strongly undermined Adorno's dichotomy of masculine autonomous art and castrated jazz. Ironically, Hollywood—which

Adorno held in contempt—has been as reluctant as Adorno to look past the uncritical association of jazz with castration.

Discography

Berry, Bill. "Boy Meets Horn." Rec. July 1976. *Hello Rev.* Concord.
Davis, Miles. "My Funny Valentine." Rec. February 12, 1964. *My Funny Valentine and Four More.* Columbia.
————. *Tune Up.* Prestige.
Faddis, Jon. *Legacy.* Rec. August 1985. Concord.
Franks, Rebecca Coupe. *Suit of Armor.* Rec. February 2, 1991. Justice Records.
Harrison, Donald, and Terence Blanchard. *Black Pearl.* Rec. 1988. CBS.
Snow, Valaida. *Hot Snow.* Foremothers, Vol. 2. Rosetta Records.

Videography

Charles Mingus's Epitaph. Rec. 1989 at New York's Lincoln Center by British Television Channel 4 and broadcast on Bravo.
David Murray Quartet Live at the Village Vanguard (1986). Directed by Bruce Buschel. Video Artists International 60094.
Art Farmer: Jazz at the Smithsonian (1982). Kultur 1272.
Dizzy Gillespie's 70th Birthday, Live at Wolf Trap. Rec. June 6, 1987. Directed by Phillip Byrd and broadcast on PBS in 1988.
Jivin' in Be-Bop (1947). Directed by Leonard Anderson. Jazz Classics JVCV-115.
Saxophone Colossus (1986). Directed by Robert Mugge.
Trumpet Kings. Video Arts International 69036.

Duke's Place

Visualizing a Jazz Composer

uke Ellington once used the phrase "Beyond Category" to describe Ella Fitzgerald, a singer who is probably much easier to categorize than Ellington. Appropriately, the phrase is evoked today to describe Ellington himself as in John Hasse's biography, *Beyond Category: The Life and Genius of Duke Ellington* (1993). Ellington was a bandleader, a pianist, a composer, an arranger, and much else. He was also, on a few occasions, an actor. But early in his career Ellington had already begun to find his place as a jazz composer, specifically a composer of music related to the experience of the Negro in America. That Ellington could derive real stature from this designation was apparent when he appeared in his first film, *Black and Tan* (1929). For many Americans, however, a Negro composer was an oxymoron. Ellington's career in films richly demonstrates how much an African American genius can achieve even when a racist culture tries to belittle his accomplishments. In fact, he may have designed some of his more remarkable musical effects to critique the work of white filmmakers.

The Composer on Film

In his autobiography, *Music Is My Mistress* (1973), Ellington wrote that he turned down a fellowship to study art at the Pratt Institute in Brook-

160

lyn because he was making too much money as a piano player in his hometown of Washington, D.C. (32). The decision to work as a professional musician may have been only the first of several crucial choices that Ellington made during his extraordinary career. Some twelve years after he gave up art for music, Ellington may also have considered a career in films. In 1929 his manager Irving Mills landed him a speaking part in the eighteen-minute film, *Black and Tan,* shot at the RKO studio in Astoria, New York, probably in August (Stratemann 1992, 14).

Ellington's debut appearance in films was directed by Dudley Murphy, who was, in the words of Thomas Cripps (1977), "the most unlikely *and* the most successful" of the white Negrophiles who worked in early cinema (204). Although Murphy directed Gloria Swanson in *The Love of Sunya* (1927) and signed a number of light comedies, most of his work as a writer and director in mainstream films was unremarkable until his films with black artists. Outside the industry he gained a degree of renown for making the avant-garde short *Ballet Mécanique* with painter Fernand Léger. But Murphy may have most impressed the executives at RKO by bragging of his connections with eminent blacks and of his sexual conquests of African American women (Cripps 1977, 205). Whatever his qualifications, a few months before Murphy made *Black and Tan* he was given the green light at RKO to direct Bessie Smith in *St. Louis Blues.* The strikingly different meanings of African American musicians in these two black-cast films was an early indication of Ellington's uniqueness. *St. Louis Blues* is about a victimized woman (Bessie Smith) whose dapper lover romances her only long enough to extract money from her garter. The film ends with Smith leaning against the bar, holding a stein of beer, and mournfully singing the title song; earlier, after failing to prevent her lover from leaving by clinging to his leg, she sings the blues while drinking gin on the floor of her apartment. The blues singer does not "play" a blues singer. Rather, she is entirely contained within a narrative of unrequited love and its spontaneous, unmediated expression in song. But in *Black and Tan,* Ellington plays a man very much like himself (he is called "Duke" in the film) who is in complete control of the music he produces. The contrast between two films made in the same year by the same writer-director surely reflects the rigidly defined roles then available to black men as opposed to black women. (It also shows how filmmakers treated women of different *shades* of color: the dark Bessie Smith plays a more "primitive" character than the much lighter Fredi Washington in *Black and Tan.*) But Ellington's role as a talented composer with dignity and principles also reveals how much Ellington was able to rise above the conventional depictions of African Americans. In the first decades of the century, such transcendence was virtually unprecedented for a black actor; Ellington was neither a Tom, a Coon, or a Buck, to use the categories established by Donald Bogle (1992).[1]

From the first moments of *Black and Tan,* Ellington is presented as a composer in the process of creation. No suggestion is made that he, like the Bessie Smith of *St. Louis Blues,* is simply expressing his emotions "naturally" through music. Ellington sits at the piano giving instructions to Arthur Whetsol, the trumpeter who was in fact a boyhood friend of Ellington and subsequently a member of his orchestra. The men's clothing already says a great deal about the film's intentions. As a man with a professional calling, Duke wears a tie, a vest, and a white shirt, but perhaps because he has immersed himself in the work of composing, he has taken off his coat and loosened his tie. The Whetsol character, who seems to have just arrived at Duke's apartment, wears a suit, a tie with a stick pin, and a well-blocked hat.

Although the tune the men are rehearsing is presented as a new composition, the song would have been familiar to anyone who had been listening to the Ellington band for the past two years. "Black and Tan Fantasy" had been in the orchestra's book since early in 1927, and before the end of that year the band recorded it for three different record labels. Many Americans also had heard the piece on the regular radio broadcasts from the Cotton Club in Harlem, where the band was in residence after December 1927. The opening section of "Black and Tan Fantasy" that Duke appears to be teaching Whetsol has been attributed to James "Bubber" Miley, the bluesy, growling trumpeter whom Ellington himself credited with much of the hot, "jungle" sound that drew so much attention to the band in the 1920s.[2] More than anyone except for Ellington himself, Miley defined the sound of the early Ellington bands. Miley, however, was a heavy drinker and highly unreliable. Ellington, in effect, fired him a few months before the filming of *Black and Tan* (Hasse 1993, 116).

If Miley had remained in the orchestra just a little longer, he might have played the trumpet solo in *Black and Tan* that he first recorded in 1927. His replacement by Arthur Whetsol, however, makes a substantial difference in the racial politics of the film. Resembling the sophisticated New Negro of the Harlem Renaissance, Whetsol had a lighter complexion than Miley as well as Freddie Jenkins and Cootie Williams, the band's other trumpeters. In *Music Is My Mistress,* Ellington (1973) praised Whetsol for his "clean appearance and reliability" and reported that Whetsol corrected a member of the orchestra who made a mistake in grammar (54). When Whetsol left the band for several years during the 1920s, the trumpeter let it be known that he was going to Howard University to study medicine. A search of the records at Howard turned up no evidence that he did so (Tucker 1991, 293 n.14), but Whetsol's desire to associate himself with the medical profession reveals a great deal about the image he projected in *Black and Tan* as well as the image that Ellington himself presented in his first film appearance.

Ellington and Whetsol are definitively separated from familiar racist stereotypes of African Americans when *Black and Tan* introduces two black comedians, one large and one small, who have come to repossess the piano. Edgar Connor and Alec Lovejoy play illiterate, shiftless piano-movers. In a quotation from King Vidor's *Hallelujah!* (1929) that is probably not ironic, they reveal their inability to tell time when one answers the question "What time is it?" by looking at his watch and saying, "There it is," after which the other laughs and says, "Sho is." At first they cannot find the right apartment because they are unable to read the numbers on the repossession papers and the doors of the apartments. They find the room only because they hear the sounds of the piano played by the character Duke. Lovejoy, considerably larger than Connor, picks up the piano stool and a feather duster, stating that he has two pieces and that his partner must now carry out the one remaining piece, the piano. Throughout their scene, the black comedians speak in Joel Chandler Harris dialect, as when Lovejoy tells Duke that he is behind in his payments: "Why, you ain't paid nothin' on it since last Octuary." Lovejoy refers to Connor as "Action," "EcZEEma," and "Sasparilla."

As Ellington watches the men helplessly, Fredi Washington makes her dynamic entrance. Already an accomplished performer at twenty-six, Washington later played opposite Paul Robeson in *The Emperor Jones*, also directed by Dudley Murphy. In 1934 she created the definitive film version of the "tragic mulatto" when she played Louise Beavers's daughter in John Stahl's *Imitation of Life*. Her first appearance in *Black and Tan* again emphasizes the difference between the light-complected, poised musicians and the darker proletarians played by Lovejoy and Connor. When Fredi, also called by her own name in the film, bribes the movers with a bottle of gin, they happily leave the apartment, accepting her instructions to tell their boss that no one was home.

Having saved the piano, Fredi tells Duke that she has found jobs for herself as a dancer and for him as her accompanist. Duke, who appears to be living in the apartment with Fredi, says that she ought not to dance because of her weak heart. She refuses to acknowledge her condition,

30. The romance of jazz composition: Arthur Whetsol, Fredi Washington, and Duke Ellington in *Black and Tan* (1929, RKO). Institute for Jazz Studies, Rutgers University at Newark.

however. Whetsol returns to play along as Duke performs his new composition, and Fredi listens appreciatively. The scene changes to a nightclub where the twelve-piece Ellington band is playing on a small bandstand in front of a dance floor that includes a large, mirrored section. A group of five male dancers in tuxedos (the Five Hot Shots) perform their close-order dance while the band plays two compositions by Ellington and his sidemen, "The Duke Steps Out" and "Black Beauty." Fredi watches from the wings in her scanty costume, already showing the effects of her weakened condition. Adopting Fredi's point of view, the camera shows multiple, overlapping images of the band and the dancers, an effect that adds an expressionistic, arty quality to the film. When Fredi has her turn on stage, she dances frenetically to the band's "Cotton Club Stomp" before collapsing on the mirrored floor. The club's manager quickly emerges and orders stage hands to carry her away: "Hey, boy. Get her out of here, quick." He then says to Duke, who has risen from the piano to watch Fredi being carried into the wings, "Sit down, Duke, and play something. Play the girls' number. Get this show on. Keep the show on." After a contingent of six female dancers from the Cotton Club have gyrated to a few bars of Ellington's "Flaming Youth," the manager prevents one of the stagehands from approaching the bandstand to speak to Duke. In a two-shot, the manager instructs the stagehand, "Don't tell him now—wait till after the show." At this point Duke storms off the stage shouting, "Come on, fellas, let's go. Pack up. Close that curtain!" Ellington has been cast as a bandleader who will not work for a heartless manager. Few other black performers have ever played characters with such scruples and assertiveness.

In the final sequence the Hall Johnson Choir sings while Ellington and several of his musicians perform at Fredi's deathbed. Again, a self-conscious artiness is created as tall, high-contrast shadows of the musicians appear on the rear wall. When Fredi requests that Duke and his musicians play "Black and Tan Fantasy," the choir sings along, the only time in Ellington's many recorded performances of the piece that singing was included. Once again, the camera shifts to Fredi's point of view as she watches Duke at the piano. His image fades into a blur as she expires. As the film ends, the band plays the few bars of Chopin's "Marche Funèbre" that end all recorded versions of "Black and Tan Fantasy."

Ellington does not make an auspicious debut in his first appearance as a screen actor. It is not surprising that he seldom again acted in films. The only other full-length fiction film in which he had a speaking role was *Anatomy of a Murder* (1959), where he is on camera for less than a minute and speaks a total of fifteen words. Nevertheless, in *Black and Tan*, Ellington makes the dignified impression that he and at least a few others hoped he would make. Irving Mills, who receives prominent billing in the opening credits, was happy to give exposure to the musician whose composing skills and "sophisticated image" he had regularly proclaimed ever since he first heard the band at the Kentucky Club in 1926 (Tucker 1991, 201). And Ellington, who had been carefully cultivating his persona long before he arrived in New York, was surely eager to record that image on film. The image of the elegant but thoughtful artist persisted throughout his career and beyond. Ten years after Ellington's death, Francis Ford Coppola included several brief scenes depicting Ellington in *The Cotton Club* (1984); when the audience first sees Coppola's Ellington, he is immaculately dressed and dispensing musical instructions to his sidemen. This scene in *The Cotton Club* is set close to the same year that the historical Ellington was filming *Black and Tan*. Coppola might have seen *Black and Tan* as part of his research, but it was hardly necessary. The image he reproduces had already been constructed both outside and inside the film industry.

Dudley Murphy was also pleased to show Ellington in the best light, no doubt because of his genuine admiration for the man and his music. His simultaneous willingness to bring the minstrel figures Lovejoy and Connor into his film was consistent with the fragmented view of blacks that many whites held in the 1920s. Like Carl Van Vechten, who may have contributed to the scripts for both St. Louis Blues and Black and Tan,[3] Dudley Murphy was fascinated by the combinations of sophistication, savagery, and buffoonery that Harlem nightspots such as the Cotton Club served up to white audiences in the 1920s. In this sense, Murphy resembled many Negrophiles of that decade who did not distinguish between what we now consider to be positive and negative images.[4] Murphy packed a wide range of myths about black Americans into the eighteen minutes of Black and Tan. The juxtaposing of sophisticated artists of the Harlem Renaissance with minstrel stereotypes at the opening of the film is comparable to the moment in the middle section when Cotton Club dancers clad primarily in animal feathers shimmy while black men in tuxedos gracefully perform on shiny brass instruments. In the deathbed scene, the "folkloric" view of African Americans as simple, rural, hymn-singing Christians is layered over the urban, profane sounds of the Ellington band.[5] Murphy may not have intended to exploit all of these discourses, but he probably did not see any contradiction in placing the idealized image of Ellington amid so many conflicting representations. There is, after all, a certain racist logic in Murphy's willingness to elevate Ellington only within a milieu that is repeatedly characterized as "primitive."

Nevertheless, Black and Tan marked a crucial moment in Ellington's career. At the time of his first film appearance he was on the verge of realizing a variety of possibilities that the film itself directly or indirectly suggests. The role that he most fully realized and that constituted his most lasting contribution was of course that of composer-arranger and orchestra leader. But Ellington also may have considered mixing other ventures with music in 1929. By 1929, Ellington had blossomed into a mature jazz composer, but at the Cotton Club the emphasis was more on spectacle and crowd-pleasing, both of which Ellington was learning to master. Just before the filming of Black and Tan, the band appeared on stage in the Gershwin musical Show Girl, produced by Florence Ziegfeld. While continuing to play nightly at the Cotton Club, the band was earning an additional $1,500 a week on Broadway (Hasse 1993, 122). The stock market crash later in the year quickly put an end to this kind of largesse, but to the Ellington who acted and performed in Black and Tan, the promise of wealth and celebrity may have seemed almost limitless. Ellington surely had no intention of leaving music in 1929, but he also must have been interested in exploring new regions such as the movies, just as he had recently achieved success on the Broadway stage.

In spite of his legendary personal charm and magnetism in one-on-one situations, however, Ellington had always been nervous about speaking in public (Collier 1987, 98). Tom Harris (1994) quotes Ellington as admitting to "stage fright" before important performances. Although he eventually became accustomed to acting as his own announcer and master of ceremonies, Ellington's fundamental unease can be detected throughout his career in the slight awkwardness and patterns of repetition ("And now . . . ") that always characterized his public appearances. Although he was capable of great charm and spontaneous wit, he was slightly intimidated by larger audiences. In 1929 his nervousness was more than evident in *Black and Tan.* Although he plays the piano with his usual panache, he tends to be stiff in his acting scenes, especially in comparison to the lively Fredi Washington and the seasoned vaudevillians Lovejoy and Connor. When Fredi announces that she has found them jobs in a club—surely important news for a musician who cannot even keep up payments on his piano—the character Duke barely registers recognition let alone pleasure. When he is on camera with Connor and Lovejoy and then with Washington, he stands uncomfortably smoking a cigarette, regularly allowing others to stand between him and the camera. His charisma returns when he leads the orchestra from the piano in the nightclub sequence, but it must have become clear to Ellington— as well as to Irving Mills—that a significant career as a speaking actor in movies was not a strong possibility. Still, *Black and Tan* prophetically introduced several themes that would persist throughout Ellington's career and that are almost always central concerns in his films, specifically the clash of discourses about African Americans and the ambiguous status of jazz as both art and popular entertainment.

In Hollywood

One year after *Black and Tan,* the Ellington band performed on screen in the Amos and Andy vehicle *Check and Double Check,* shot in Hollywood in 1930. This appearance was another landmark moment for Ellington. Never before had a black band been granted a credited performance in an otherwise all-white film (Stratemann 1992, 35). (Under cork, Amos and Andy were played by the same white actors who did their voices on the popular radio program.) Ellington, however, does not speak during his time on camera, although this was surely not a decision left up to him. At the time it was sufficiently daring to put black artists on the same screen with whites. The Hollywood filmmakers were somewhat less daring in their decision to put blackface makeup on Barney Bigard, the Creole clarinetist from New Orleans, and Juan Tizol, the Puerto Rican trombonist, both of whom were deemed too light-skinned to maintain the film's racial balance.

In *Bundle of Blues,* a nine-minute film from 1933, Ellington speaks only one line, a typically awkward announcement that the band is about to play "that haunting melody, 'Stormy Weather.'" Ellington is a much more confident performer than he was in *Black and Tan,* gesturing at the piano with real flamboyance. But after the band plays its first number, "Rockin' in Rhythm," the same disparity of racial discourses occurs that was present in *Black and Tan.* When the elegant Ivie Anderson stands by a window and sings "Stormy Weather," the camera cuts to a number of rustic scenes, including a ramshackle cabin into which a chicken enters by the front door. The urban sophistication of the tuxedoed Ellington orchestra and its vocalist somehow seem to demand a reminder of rural poverty. Similarly, in the next number, Florence Hill and Bessie Dudley dance to "Bugle Call Rag" in the energetic, seemingly spontaneous "jungle" style of the Cotton Club, clashing with the image of Ellington as the leader of a disciplined group of musicians. As in the scene with the Cotton Club dancers in *Black and Tan,* however, the uninhibited performances of Hill and Dudley provide a small but revealing glance at how audiences actually experienced the Ellington band in a live performance.

Shortly after Ellington filmed *Bundle of Blues* back in New York, the orchestra made its first trip to Europe. Ellington found that Europeans regarded him as a composer rather than as a bandleader or piano player; audiences came to hear the musicians as a concert orchestra, not as a dance band. *And* Ellington drew crowds, even breaking the box-office record at the London Palladium. At the Palladium, audiences could read about the band in a 24-page program that referred to Ellington's compositions as valid works of art. He was even introduced to the Prince of Wales. The critic Richard O. Boyer, who later wrote a three-part article on Ellington for the *New Yorker,* saw the band at the Palladium and declared that their show had "truly Shakespearean universality" (Hasse 1993, 170–72). These declarations on the artistic nature of Ellington's work must be understood in light of the regular presence in his nightly shows of Bessie Dudley's shake dancing and the tap dancing of Bill Bailey and Derby Wilson. Even working within a vaudeville context, Ellington managed to win over a number of critics. Boyer's designation of the Ellington revue's "Shakespearean universality" surely reflects the critic's ability to see beyond the Eurocentric aesthetic to which Ellington never measured up according to his harsher critics. After all, even Shakespeare had his clowns.

If, as Collier has written, Ellington returned from Europe in 1933 with "a sense of his importance as an artist" (1987, 160), the groundwork for this conviction was already in place before he left. In 1931 he had taken the audacious step of recording "Creole Rhapsody," a single composition that was highly unusual among jazz records for taking up both sides of a 78-rpm record. But this risk was not so great for so well-established a bandleader. In the same year Herbert Hoover invited him to the White House along with a group of black dignitaries, and in 1932 he was invited to lecture at New York University by Percy Grainger (Collier 1987, 101). Also in 1932 critic R. D. Darrell wrote a long appreciation of Ellington in *disques,* a magazine aimed at consumers of classical recordings; names such as Delius, Sibelius, and Elgar were regularly mentioned alongside Ellington's, and Darrell found much in Ellington's work that he preferred to compositions by Gershwin and Copland (Tucker 1993a, 57–65). The canonization of Ellington as a composer was under way even before he left for Europe.

But canonization becomes problematic when the artist is American and not European, and especially when he is African American. Very few Americans, and for that matter very few Europeans, could regard any black performer as an artist. Surely Ellington, as well as anyone else, knew what he was up against. He was always reluctant to speak of himself in the terms that his learned admirers had chosen. In the many revealing articles that Mark Tucker collected in his *Duke Ellington Reader* (1993a), Ellington consistently appears unmoved by comparisons between himself and European composers. In England in 1933 he told a Scottish interviewer that he played "folk music" (80), and he later made statements such as "a black man feels [a] black man's music most, and that's what I want to write" (113). When a reporter came backstage in 1935 and read some of the accolades that Constant Lambert had lavished upon Ellington in his book, *Music Ho!* (1934), Ellington remained skeptical and ironic. Told that Lambert put him in the same league as Ravel and Stravinsky, Ellington responded, "Is that so? Say, that fellow Lambert is quite a writer, isn't he?" When he was praised for the "texture" of his records, Ellington told of transposing a piece to a different key so that it would sound better when recorded by "a goofy mike" with a "loose plunger." After the interviewer read a phrase that compared Ellington's music to "the opalescent subtleties of Debussy," he responded, "Opalescent subtleties. Don't those London fellows push a mean pen?" (113). Ellington was always adept at handling the press, but his reluctance to accept such Eurocentric praise was surely related to his genuine desire to represent the experience of African Americans in his music, even though he allegedly went out and spent $100 on Delius's records when critics first started making the comparison. According to Derek Jewell (1977), Ellington had never even heard of Delius (48). Ellington had grown up with black music, and it had provided him with a living for almost twenty years up to that point. As Billy Strayhorn said later, Ellington's instrument was his orchestra; none of the European composers to whom he was being compared ever had the luxury of regularly hearing their new music played just hours after they had written it. Ellington definitely thought of himself as an artist, but not the kind of artist who goes looking for symphony orchestras to play his compositions. Rather, he saw himself as an artist working regularly with a band (and dancers, comedians, and the rest) and within a Negro idiom, not unlike his childhood idols Henry Lee Grant, Will Marion Cook, and James Reese Europe (Tucker 1993b, 111–27).

Ellington pursued his mission as a black artist seriously, even zealously. In an unguarded moment in 1935, he attacked Gershwin's *Porgy and Bess* for its failure to capture the real spirit of the Charleston Negroes it portrayed. Responding to questions from Edward Morrow, a reporter for *New Theatre*, Ellington insisted that Gershwin's music did not "use the Negro musical idiom." As a more accurate alternative, Ellington mentioned a scene from *Symphony in Black*, a short film that he had recently made but that had not yet been released (Tucker 1993a, 114–17). Significantly, Ellington made no mention of his appearances in two films from the previous year, *Murder at the Vanities* and *Belle of the Nineties*.

Although Ellington and his musicians continued to make the kind of dramatic progress in mainstream films that they had earlier achieved in *Check and Double Check*, they nevertheless provided brief moments of exoticism in otherwise conventional films. Back in Hollywood, the Ellington band's one scene in *Murder at the Vanities* (1934) succinctly offered the other side of the argument that Ellington was the equal of Sibelius and Delius. In "The Rape of a Rhapsody," a production number within this backstage musical, a symphony orchestra is playing the "Second Hungarian Rhapsody" by Liszt. Ellington and his men pop up from behind the symphony players to interject stereotypically jazzy phrases. As the black musicians become more intrusive, the white symphony players leave the stage in disgust. The Ellington band is left on stage to perform its elaborate arrangement of Johnston and Coslow's reworking of the Liszt tune, entitled "Ebony Rhapsody."[6] They are joined by a chorus line of black female dancers and by singer-dancer Gertrude Michael who sings lyrics such as

> It's got those licks, it's got those tricks
> That Mister Liszt would never recognize.
> It's got that beat, that tropic heat
> You shake until you make that ol' thermometer rise!

The scene concludes with the symphony conductor returning to the stage to strafe the entire assemblage with a machine gun. In one sense, the joke is on the intolerant and fanatical symphony conductor. As Jane Feuer (1993) has shown, Hollywood regularly assured audiences that classical music could be "improved" with injections of "jazz," the popular music of the day (54–65). In *Thousands Cheer* (1943), for example, audiences could enjoy the spectacle of Judy Garland teaching José Iturbi how to swing. And yet the jazz that was preferable to classical music in films of the 1930s and 1940s seldom featured black artists. One wonders if the same comic violence would have been necessary if the band had been led by someone like the popular and respectable white bandleader Hal Kemp.

The appearance of the Ellington ensemble with Mae West in *Belle of the Nineties* (1934) reflected West's desire to sing with a group that could put more punch into her vocal performances. To her credit, she saw to it that the band playing on the soundtrack was the same one appearing with her on camera. The band performs most memorably when West sings "My Old Flame" in a saloon while Ellington and a handful of his sidemen lounge around the piano. Stratemann has pointed out that Ellington's musicians contribute to the ambience of the scene "to an extent not experienced by any other black band of the time" (96). Later, when West sings "Memphis Blues" on stage, the camera cuts repeatedly to the orchestra pit to show the Ellington men; in another unprecedented editing decision, the camera dwells much longer on the black artists than was customary in white Hollywood. In the most striking of these scenes, Sonny Greer pitches a drumstick at Ellington who catches it and then returns it to Greer with a jaunty, behind-the-back toss. As always, the band's attire is extremely formal and elaborate. A touch of dignity is also evident in their relaxed demeanor during the "My Old Flame" scene. But as in *Murder at the Vanities,* none of the black musicians speak in *Belle of the Nineties,* and they are entirely marginal to the plot.

A Rhapsody of Negro Life

Although Ellington again has no lines in the nine-minute *Symphony in Black,* the film is a much more evocative portrayal of the world-class composer who had returned from Europe two years earlier. Subtitled "A Rhapsody of Negro Life," *Symphony in Black* was shot in late 1934 and early 1935 at Paramount's Eastern Service Studios in Astoria by the same crew that had shot *Bundle of Blues* (Stratemann 1992, 119 and 122). After the credits, an anonymous hand places a letter into a mail slot just beneath raised letters that read, "Duke Ellington Studio." The letter is from "The National Concert Bureau," and it reads: "Just a reminder that the world premiere of your new symphony of Negro Moods takes place two weeks from today. I trust that work on the manuscript is nearing completion so that you may soon start rehearsals." For the first time in Ellington's career in movies, there is a clear connection with "art" both in the word "symphony" and in the phrase "world premiere" as well as in the association with some fictional agency, perhaps governmental, that would administer and schedule orchestral concerts. In the next shot, the camera looks over Ellington's shoulder at a collection of score paper on which he is writing with a pencil. Ellington is then shown in profile from head to toe as he sits writing music and playing the piano. Dressed with casual elegance, his cigarette burning in an ashtray nearby, Ellington is at home composing the commissioned symphony. Although we do not actually see Ellington's own handwriting, the camera suggests that Ellington has written in florid script

Symphony in Black
Part One
The Laborers

The camera cuts back to Ellington as he begins to play more rhythmically and with greater flamboyance. Without a break in the music, there is a lap dissolve to Ellington at a grand piano in a black tuxedo, his tails draped over the back of the piano stool. Behind him is his orchestra, playing the piece we had just seen him composing. As in *Black and Tan,* Ellington is depicted from the outset as a working composer, but in *Symphony in Black* he gets a much bigger buildup—the film viewer first sees

his name, then the back of his head, his profile in casual dress, and finally
his formally draped body in front of a large orchestra. Ellington is further
dignified and even mythified by the decision not to have him speak on
camera. In fact, no spoken dialogue of any kind occurs in this film, distinguishing it as more artistic than standard fare.

As the camera draws back from Ellington and his orchestra, initiates
can see that the band has been expanded from its usual fourteen pieces
to twenty-four, including tympani and vibraphone in addition to the typically elaborate drum kit of Sonny Greer. The camera's reverse zoom continues, revealing the backs of men and women in an auditorium, all of
them in formal attire and all of them white. Another lap dissolve shows
a group of black men ("The Laborers") shoveling coal and hauling heavy
sacks up a flight of stairs. Throughout the film, shots of Ellington at
home composing are intercut with scenes of the full band in performance
and with a series of dramatizations based on the music. The central section of the film is introduced by another glance at the sheet music with
the following titles:

> A Triangle
> Dance
> Jealousy
> Blues

In "Dance," Bessie Dudley (who also appeared in *Bundle of Blues*) and
"Snake Hips" Tucker, both dressed in fancy street clothes, cavort in a
living room while a young, portly Billie Holiday looks up at their window
from the alley below. The music is "Ducky Wucky," a piece that Ellington
wrote with Barney Bigard in 1932. In the section titled "Jealousy," Holiday approaches Tucker as he leaves the apartment with Dudley. After
Tucker pushes her away and ultimately onto the pavement, Holiday sings
the section called "Blues." This was Holiday's first film appearance, and
only her fourth recording session. Lying on the concrete, she sings a version of Ellington's "Saddest Tale."

Part three of Ellington's "symphony" is called "A Hymn of Sorrow." In
a return to the folkloric myth of simple, African American piety, the film
shows a white-haired minister with a large, flowing beard leading a congregation in prayer. There are several close-ups of black hands and faces,
and at least one face shedding tears. As the camera dollies back through
the pews, the minister leads the worshippers in raising their hands upward as one. Like the theme for "The Laborers" segment, "Hymn of Sor-

row" was written specifically for *Symphony in Black*. This is the section of the film that Ellington had referred to in his interview with the reporter for *New Theatre* who coaxed out his reactions to *Porgy and Bess*.

> In one of my forthcoming movie "shorts" I have an episode which concerns the death of a baby. That is the high spot and should have come last, but that would not have been "commercial," as the managers say. However, I put into the dirge all the misery, sorrow and undertones of the conditions that went with the baby's death. It was true to and of the life of the people it depicted. The same thing cannot be said for *Porgy and Bess* (Tucker 1993, 116–17).[7]

Ellington's uncharacteristically frank statements hint at what he may have intended to show in *Symphony in Black*. In the studio's dramatized inserts for "Hymn of Sorrow," a small, open casket can be detected in front of the pulpit, but it is not at all obvious that a small corpse could be inside of it. Without understanding that the scene involves the death of a child, viewers might wonder what the congregation is mourning; the black actors seem to be simply engaged in a set of stylized movements. It is significant that Ellington wrote new music especially for this sequence; of the six pieces played by the band in *Symphony in Black*, only three were new, and "Hymn of Sorrow" may be the most moving. Most likely, Ellington had hoped for an opportunity to provide a humanizing view of black Americans, whose sufferings were seldom treated with any seriousness in American popular entertainment. The studio executives who edited the "Hymn of Sorrow" segment no doubt assumed that audiences were more comfortable watching the pain of the jilted lover played by Billie Holiday (or by Bessie Smith in *St. Louis Blues*) than they were watching black parents grieve over the loss of a child.

In the final section of *Symphony in Black*, "Harlem Rhythm," the images become more expressionistic as multiple scenes from uptown nightlife are superimposed over one another. "Snake Hips" Tucker reappears in a performer's costume and does his unique set of lower-body movements while the band plays Ellington's "Merry-Go-Round." Four chorus girls undulate in silhouette above couples with glasses and bottles at the bottom of the screen. The words "Harlem Hot Spot" flash diagonally in one corner of the frame. Eventually the camera splits the image of Tucker so that he seems to be dancing with a mirror image of himself. The film ends as "Merry-Go-Round" reaches its conclusion and the camera focuses once again on the pianist's hands.

Symphony in Black was not treated sympathetically by Barry Ulanov in his 1946 biography of Ellington:

> Right out of Oscar Hammerstein's lyric for *Ol' Man River,* big, black colored men sweated and strained, loading heavy bales into storehouses on river wharves; they stoked blast furnaces. And then for surefire audience appeal, there was a brief little story, the eternal triangle, the theme of jealousy underlined heavily and the figurative blues accompanied by blues figurations. (Ulanov 1975, 161)

What Ulanov does not mention is the portrait of Ellington the artist that these images may trivialize but not erase. It should also be pointed out that the film is organized entirely around music by Ellington. At some point, as the article in *New Theatre* makes clear, he even had some say in what scenes ought to accompany his music. While "Black and Tan Fantasy" may have been chosen as the central melody for *Black and Tan* because of its mournful quality (not to mention the quotation from Chopin's funeral march that perfectly accommodated death and the end of the film), everything in *Symphony in Black* hangs on music that Ellington himself chose for the film.

Of course, outside the cinema Ellington had not been commissioned to write a "symphony of Negro moods" or for that matter any other kind of symphony before 1935. He had, however, been contemplating such a work at least since 1930 (Tucker 1993c). Unlike the scene in *Murder at the Vanities* that makes a joke out of the artistic aspirations of jazz, *Symphony in Black* inflates Ellington's status as a composer. But eight years later, Ellington would write something very much like a "symphony of Negro moods," the 44-minute suite *Black, Brown, and Beige: A Tone Parallel to the History of the Negro in America* that premiered in Carnegie Hall on January 23, 1943. The structure of *Black, Brown, and Beige (BBB)* strongly recalls that of *Symphony in Black;* both begin with a work song and include "dances," a religious section, and a blues sung by a woman.[8] The theme for "Work Song," the opening movement of *Black, Brown, and Beige,* has many melodic and structural similarities to "The Laborers." When *Symphony in Black* and *BBB* are combined with *New World a-Coming* (1943), *Harlem* (1951), *My People* (1963), and even the sacred concerts (not to mention countless shorter and less ambitious compositions), we can see continuity in Ellington's project of making "serious" music out of African American vernacular traditions. In spite of his legitimate objections to the rearranging of music and images in *Symphony in Black,* Ellington succeeded in combining "high art" with "low art," effectively undermining the hierarchies that separated the two. In his own tactful and often ironic manner, Ellington continued to work at upsetting these kinds of dichotomies throughout his career, and as we shall see, he often did this most effectively in his work in films.

In 1937 the Ellington band performed memorably in the Republic feature *Hit Parade*. Also in 1937 Ellington made a brief appearance on film in "Paramount Pictorial, No. 889," a magazine-like newsreel that was shown in theaters along with feature films. In one of the pictorial's three segments, Ellington and his band are shown making a record of "Oh Babe! Maybe Someday" for the soon-to-be-defunct Variety label. An off-screen voice narrates what is effectively a detailed documentary of how a record is made, from the recording session to the pressing of discs available to the public. Once again, the focus is on Ellington the composer-conductor, who gives instructions to his band at the beginning of the segment. Unlike every other bandleader of the time, Ellington was regularly shown in the act of creating—he was not simply a performer in front of an orchestra. This image was even acknowledged in a newsreel devoted primarily to technological fetishism.

By 1938, Ellington was competing with numerous other "swing" bands, both black and white, for a young audience for whom he may have been too familiar as well as too challenging. Although he had always encountered resistance to his music, Ellington was suffering from a broader range of criticisms in the late 1930s. Black commentators were increasingly uncomfortable with the style of his manager Irving Mills, who had grown wealthy from Ellington by treating him more as an employee than as an employer. Adam Clayton Powell, Jr., for example, charged that Ellington was "just a musical sharecropper" (Hasse 1993, 219). At least in part because of financial disagreements, Ellington left Mills in 1939 and signed with the William Morris Agency. Morris and company respected Ellington's artistic aspirations, but they did not immediately land Ellington the more prestigious engagements that he coveted. His friend Edmund Anderson (1993) has spoken of the uncharacteristic anger that Ellington expressed during Benny Goodman's 1938 landmark concert at Carnegie Hall. It should have been Ellington's concert. To his credit, Ellington allowed three of his musicians to perform on stage with Goodman.

Cabin in the Sky

In spite of the warnings of war, Ellington in 1939 took his orchestra back to Europe, where once again he played mostly concerts and where his stature as a composer was more widely recognized. No doubt this experience gave him new inspiration, for he returned to the United States and quickly began what many critics consider to be his years of greatest achievement. By the end of the year, Billy Strayhorn, Ben Webster, and Jimmy Blanton were all members of the Ellington organization.

There is precious little Ellington on film from this important period. The most important items are the Ellington "soundies," the result of a brief craze for jukeboxes that ran moving images of the musicians along with their music. From December 1941 into February 1942 the Ellington orchestra recorded music for five soundies in four of which members of the band appeared on camera.[9] By far the most remarkable is the one made first, most commonly known as "Hot Chocolate." The camera cuts between the band's performance of "Cottontail," with a solo by the debonair Ben Webster, and Whitey's Lindy Hoppers accomplishing their gravity-defying dance steps.[10] Two of the soundies, "Bli-Blip" and "I Got It Bad and That Ain't Good," give a frustratingly brief glimpse of the musical revue *Jump for Joy*, the rest of which now exists only as a few minutes of home movie footage (Stratemann 1992, 171). In 1941, however, the show had the potential of becoming a watershed in the representation of blacks on the American stage. *Jump for Joy* opened in Los Angeles as a series of sketches written primarily by Paul Francis Webster and Sid Kuller, but with contributions by a handful of others, of whom the most eminent was Langston Hughes. Ellington conducted his orchestra in the pit and contributed eleven songs. The subject of the skits was primarily the situation of blacks in the United States, and the tone was consistently witty and urbane without being abrasive. At least that was the intention. One of the numbers that made a wry attempt at discarding the old minstrel stereotypes was called "Uncle Tom's Cabin Is a Drive-In Now." According to Ellington, the original script showed Uncle Tom about to expire with "a Hollywood producer on one side of the bed and a Broadway producer on the other side, and both were trying to keep him alive by injecting adrenalin into his arms!" (Ellington 1973, 175). In another sketch, a black African king and queen, dressed in elegant Western clothes and dining in a tastefully furnished apartment, receive a telephone call warning them that another expedition was on its way from the United States to find the origins of jazz. "Oh, damn," says the queen.

"Yes, my dear," the king says, "we shall have to get out our leopard skins again" (Ulanov 1946, 242).

The show closed after only three months and never arrived on Broadway as many of the participants had hoped. A number of reasons have been offered for *Jump for Joy*'s untimely demise. Ellington himself wrote that the draft whisked away too many of the "young show-stoppers" to World War II (1973, 176). Barry Ulanov, who gives a thorough overview of the show in his biography of Ellington, insists that *Jump for Joy*'s ironic approach to black stereotypes was simply too subtle for large audiences (Ulanov 1946, 239–46). Other biographers have mentioned the constant rewriting that went on after virtually every performance, which created unevenness in the show as well as dissatisfaction among its backers (Collier 1987, 211; Hasse 1993, 248). Stratemann (1992) has documented the severe competition confronting the show from productions at the Biltmore Theatre, just six blocks away; the road show company of the phenomenally successful *Hellzapoppin* was in residence for two and a half weeks, and Ethel Waters drew large audiences in a revival of *Mamba's Daughters* (170). Ironically, another Biltmore attraction was the original Broadway cast of *Cabin in the Sky*. Although this show was precisely the kind of entertainment that *Jump for Joy* was designed to criticize, in 1942 *Cabin in the Sky* was made into a major motion picture with a prominent feature for the Ellington band.

Cabin in the Sky came at a peculiar moment in American film history. As part of the war effort, Hollywood was trying to pay more attention to African Americans, largely because they were difficult to ignore when so many were fighting and dying in World War II. The Roosevelt administration itself explicitly encouraged Hollywood to produce films with black casts. At the same time, however, Hollywood was still uncomfortable with the idea of blacks in dominant roles. Partially in response to pressure from Walter White, the articulate spokesman for the NAACP, MGM decided in 1942 to put together an all-black film, the first to be made in Hollywood since *Green Pastures* of 1936 (Cripps 1993, 80–82). *Cabin in the Sky* was chosen as the script because it had achieved some success on the Broadway stage in 1940 as well as in the road show incarnation that contributed to the demise of *Jump for Joy* in Los Angeles. The film starred Lena Horne, Ethel Waters, Eddie "Rochester" Anderson, and many well-known black performers in smaller roles, including Louis Armstrong, Butterfly McQueen, Rex Ingram, and the dance and song team of Buck and Bubbles.

As many feared, however, *Cabin in the Sky* did little to dispel the plantation stereotypes of black people that were a regular feature of Hollywood product. Words that commonly appeared in reviews in the black press were "insulting" and "patronizing" (Cripps 1993, 83). The film, however, did receive a few positive reviews from the white press, and it even made a modest profit, especially among black audiences in the South and at army camps where Lena Horne was extremely popular (Bogle 1992, 132).[11] As Adam Knee (1995) has suggested, *Cabin in the Sky* is in some ways an African American remake of *The Wizard of Oz* (1939). It even uses footage of a hurricane that was left over from *The Wizard's* twister scene (Naremore 1992, 106). Like the 1939 film, *Cabin in the Sky* consists of a brief framing story surrounding a long dream sequence in the mind of the main character. "Little Joe," played by Eddie Anderson, is near death from a gunshot wound he has suffered while gambling at Jim Henry's Paradise Café. He dreams that the representatives of God and the Devil are fighting for possession of his soul. The supernatural characters agree that if Joe does not stray from the righteous path for six months, the prayers of his wife Petunia (Ethel Waters) will be answered,

31. Duke Ellington and Sonny Greer (drums) in foreground. In back, left to right, Ray Nance, Rex Stewart, Joe Nanton, Harry Carney, and Johnny Hodges, the core of the band that performs in *Cabin in the Sky* (1943, MGM). Jerry Ohlinger's Movie Material Store, Inc.

and Joe will accompany her to heaven. The agents of the Devil fight for Joe's soul by arranging for him to win the Irish sweepstakes and by sending the temptress Georgia Brown (Lena Horne) to help him spend his fortune. Although Joe does not immediately succumb to Georgia Brown's allure, Petunia is convinced otherwise. After Petunia reluctantly throws Little Joe out of the house, we see him dressed uncomfortably as a millionaire escorting Georgia to Jim Henry's, the same nightclub where he had only recently escaped death. This is also Ellington's moment; the band is identified on the marquee as "Duke Ellington and His Famous Orchestra."

Ellington had just added a fourth trumpeter to a band that plays a

32. Lena Horne and Eddie "Rochester" Anderson in *Cabin in the Sky*. Jerry Ohlinger's Movie Material Store, Inc.

new, richly orchestrated version of Mercer Ellington's composition, "Things Ain't What They Used to Be." The second number is a brand-new composition, significantly titled "Goin' Up." The sequence features a large group of dancers in zoot suits and stylish dresses, many of them veterans of the stage presentation of *Jump for Joy*. Until this point the film has portrayed African Americans primarily in terms of "folkloricism," that is, as simple, plantation-style darkies who vacillate between singing hymns and shooting craps. At its most basic, the film opposes the values of simplicity, religion, and the country to those of big city sophistication and decadence. As in *Green Pastures*, God himself demands that black people sing in church rather than dance in nightclubs. In *Cabin in the Sky* this dichotomy is played out in clearly racist terms. The agents of the Lord are dressed in white, while those of the devil are clothed in black; the Lord's men even tell Joe that his affection for Georgia Brown is a "black mark" on his record (Knee 1995, 198). But other discourses of negritude are also operating in the film. In the first place, as Naremore points out, the film was based on a "mostly liberal, 1930s-style folkloricism" (1992, 102)—the songs of Leadbelly and the dances of Katherine Dunham rather than the Walt Disney studio's notorious *Song of the South* (1946). But director Vincente Minnelli was even more committed to the discourse of "a chic, upscale 'Africanism,' redolent of café society, Broadway theater and the European avant-garde" (107). Hence, the presence of Ellington.

On some levels the clash among these discourses makes the film incoherent, what Naremore has referred to as the film's "ideological schizophrenia." Long before Ellington actually appears on screen, the film has betrayed its basic folkloric dichotomy by disclosing a much greater fascination with urban decadence than with simple piety. Inside their modest cabin, Petunia sings "Taking a Chance on Love," using the metaphors of the gambling den to describe her God-fearing marriage with Joe. In addition, the camerawork is much more elaborate in the early scene at Jim Henry's Paradise than it is for the humble buildings such as the village church. When Petunia first hears the cries of Little Joe after he is shot at Jim Henry's, she is centered by a stable camera in front of the church. A long tracking shot traces out a street and then seamlessly becomes a high-flying crane shot when the camera arrives at Jim Henry's. The camerawork alone makes the nightclub more intriguing than the church.

Before *Cabin in the Sky*, Vincente Minnelli had not directed an entire film on his own. He had, however, achieved some success directing Broadway revues featuring black entertainers such as Josephine Baker.

Minnelli also had directed Louis Armstrong and Martha Raye in the "Public Melody Number One" sequence in the 1937 film *Artists & Models,* and he had created settings for Ellington's band at Radio City Music Hall (Naremore 1993, 60). Minnelli would eventually go on to make some of MGM's most memorable musicals, including *Meet Me in St. Louis* (1944), *The Pirate* (1948), *An American in Paris* (1951), *The Band Wagon* (1953), *Brigadoon* (1954), *Gigi* (1958), and *Bells Are Ringing* (1960). Undoubtedly Minnelli was not at ease with *Cabin in the Sky's* folkloric approach to blacks. The choice of Duke Ellington for the scene at Jim Henry's was much more typical of Minnelli's own Africanism. This is not to say that Minnelli's uptown Negrophilia was any less racist than Hollywood's more conventional folkloricism. Minnelli, however, did not subscribe to the idea that blacks must struggle to separate the sacred from the profane. As for Ellington, just a few months after he filmed *Cabin in the Sky* he achieved a much grander synthesis of the supposedly incompatible dichotomies that inform the film when he premiered *Black, Brown, and Beige* at Carnegie Hall.

The folkloric approach was one of many strategies used by Hollywood to contain African Americans. The film industry would give work to black actors, but it would confine them to stereotypes. There was even grumbling at MGM simply because Minnelli wanted to cast the beautiful, sexually appealing, black nightclub performer Lena Horne in a major role. (Katherine Dunham had played the part in the stage version, but her role was much smaller.) Of course, the film's dichotomies *must* break down in a film that is very much a part of the entertainment industry and the cosmopolitan values that the film *seems* to condemn. Hollywood could not afford to insist too strongly that people devote their leisure time to church and other simple pleasures because, if that message becomes too convincing, the entertainment industry might then cease to exist—or at least lose some money. In *Cabin in the Sky,* as in numerous films before and after, Hollywood tried to strike a balance between the explicitly stated message of the film—do not drink and gamble in nightclubs—and the less obvious but in some ways more powerful message—going to nightclubs is great fun.

Until the Ellington orchestra appears, the film almost succeeds in concealing this contradiction. But from the moment the band plays its first notes, folklore is forgotten. Although Ellington performs at Jim Henry's Paradise—the site most closely associated with the corruption that Little Joe must overcome if he is to get to heaven—the music is consistent with what Richard Dyer (1981) has called the "utopianism" of the Hollywood musical. At Jim Henry's the musicians and the dancers have the kind of grace and energy that all of us would have in the best of all possible worlds. Their spontaneity and enthusiasm as well as the group spirit of their choreographed dancing undermine the film's explicit message that Jim Henry's is a despised alternative to simple Christian piety and that it must be destroyed by the end of the film.

Cabin in the Sky's audience first sees Ellington after the band has finished "Things Ain't What They Used To Be." The camera had lingered exclusively on the dancers throughout the number. When the song ends, the dancers applaud and rush toward the bandstand. The camera follows them right up to Ellington, who smiles back at a young couple leaning over the edge of his piano. After he finishes the piano introduction to "Goin' Up," the camera pans left to show the entire band, and the crowd once again breaks into dance. All movement quickly stops, however, when Lawrence Brown takes a preacherly trombone solo. As with Arthur Whetsol in *Black and Tan,* the choice of a specific musician creates an effect that would have been less powerful with some other band member. Born in Kansas, Brown was the son of a minister and acquired his first musical training in church. His earliest musical desires were directed toward the cello, and he told Stanley Dance (1970) that he took up the trombone because he believed it to be the cello of the brass family (118). Brown worked hard at producing a smooth, majestic sound on the trombone in imitation of the string instrument. Even when he became a full-time jazz musician, he never smoked, drank, or took drugs. Rex Stewart (1991) has said that Brown "resembled the Baptist minister who has wandered into the wrong place seeking converts" (153). Had he never become a professional musician, Brown, like Whetsol, said that he might have practiced medicine (Dance 1970, 117–21).

All of these elements in Brown's character and appearance are relevant when he takes his solo on "Goin' Up." After jiving to the song's early, up-tempo sections, the congregation of dancers stands in rapt attention from the moment that the trombonist plays his first, clearly enunciated notes. Brown soon involves the crowd in a call-and-response pattern. After each phrase of his sermon, the crowd shouts back. This performance of "Goin' Up" is remarkable for the concise way in which it undermines the folkloristic dichotomies of urban/rural, decadence/piety, and saloon/church. More intriguingly, Ellington's choice of a song title also seems designed to frustrate the distinction. When the song with Brown's solo was first recorded, it was identified as "Ellington Composition." As an MGM Recording Program dated September 28, 1942, makes clear, Ellington wrote the song specifically for *Cabin in the Sky* without at first giving it a title (Stratemann 1992, 205). Ellington may have chosen to call the song "Goin' Up" because of a line that Little Joe utters early in the film when he is trying to convince the agents of the Lord that he belongs in heaven. He says that he can operate the elevator in heaven, and then he adds as an important qualification, "goin' up." In the stage version of *Cabin in the Sky*, Little Joe worked as an elevator operator; in the film, however, he works in a cotton mill. The line is a little out of place, an example of the screenwriters' imperfect adaptation.

Nevertheless, Ellington could easily have heard Joe's line and decided to use it to name his new composition. If he had wanted to work within the folkloric plan of the film, which must necessarily associate his band with the work of the Devil, he would have called his tune "Goin' Down." Of course, I am speculating about intentions that Ellington would have been uncomfortable discussing in public. Recall the attempts by Ellington and his manager to retract most of what he had said about *Porgy and Bess* in 1935. But a strong possibility exists that Ellington may have sought to gently sabotage the film industry's racial stereotyping. This is exactly what he had tried to accomplish in the 1941 production of *Jump for Joy* and what he would achieve just a few months later in *Black, Brown, and Beige*. He may have regarded *Cabin in the Sky* as a step backward in racial progress after *Jump for Joy*. In fact, the title song for *Jump for Joy*, which the band recorded for RCA Victor, contains the line, "*Green Pastures is just a Technicolor movie*." Actually, *Green Pastures* is *not* a Technicolor movie. It was filmed and exhibited in black and white. When they wrote the lyrics to "Jump for Joy," Webster and Kuller probably combined their recollections of *Green Pastures* with scenes from *Gone with the Wind* (1939), which *was* in Technicolor and which went to some lengths to reinscribe plantation stereotypes. Regardless, the song tells us to reject the images of Negroes in *Gone with the Wind*, *Green Pastures*, and perhaps even *Cabin in the Sky*. Ellington may have decided to put the preacherly trombone solo into his composition and then call it "Goin' Up" in full knowledge that it confounded the folkloricism of the film. In any case, he was continuing the practice of combining different "Negro moods" in a musical program, something that has long been typical of African American music. As in the suites, *Symphony in Black* and *Black, Brown, and Beige*, religious themes are juxtaposed with the music of nightlife. In the performance of "Goin' Up," the two are combined in the same piece.[12]

The Composer for Film

Ellington made several film appearances in the 1940s and 1950s. The band was filmed on a train (not a subway car) in a carefully staged performance of "Take the 'A' Train" in *Reveille with Beverly* (1943): Betty Roché did her famous hip vocal ("Hurry hurry hurry—take the 'A' Train"); Ben Webster took a gruff solo on tenor; and Ray Nance strutted through one of his crowd-pleasing dances. The band also appeared in a handful of short subjects and newsreels during the period. Perhaps the most memorable example of Ellington's post-*Cabin* film work in the 1940s was his appearance in the George Pal "Puppetoon" *Date with Duke,* a seven-minute short bearing the subtitle "Presenting Duke Ellington Playing his *Perfume Suite*" (1947). Although Ellington awkwardly utters a few scripted lines from his seat at the piano, most of the film is devoted to the antics of a set of anthropomorphic perfume bottles that dance to "The Perfume Suite," an appealingly fanciful work by Ellington and Strayhorn that premiered at Carnegie Hall in December 1944. After his "comeback" at the Newport Jazz Festival of 1956, Ellington also began appearing regularly on television programs. Audiences saw a relaxed, personable, and affluent Ellington exchanging unscripted patter with Edward R. Murrow on *Person to Person* in a broadcast of March 15, 1957.

In 1959, Ellington achieved another historic breakthrough—he was commissioned to write a film score for Otto Preminger's *Anatomy of a Murder,* a major Hollywood film based on a best-selling novel and starring James Stewart. Ellington had not written music specifically for a film since *Symphony in Black* (1935). Each of Ellington's biographers devotes about a sentence to the film of *Anatomy of a Murder,* usually ignoring everything except the Grammy Award–winning music. In his autobiography, Ellington had more to say about the film, but he seemed to recall most fondly the meals that Billy Strayhorn prepared in the Hollywood penthouse where Preminger installed the two while they worked on the music (Ellington 1973, 193–94).[13] The culinary praise for Strayhorn is part of a short section in *Music Is My Mistress* where Ellington discusses all of his Hollywood films: he alludes in a single parenthesis to *Check and Double Check, Murder at the Vanities, Belle of the Nineties, Cabin in the Sky,* and *Reveille with Beverly;* he then devotes about a paragraph each to the four Hollywood films for which he wrote complete scores, *Anatomy of a Murder, Paris Blues* (1961), *Assault on a Queen* (1966), and *A Change of Mind* (1969). At one point, Ellington ruefully recounts the fate of his music for *Assault on a Queen,* in particular a flamboyant piece for the climactic moment when the thieves open the door to the safe on the H.M.S. *Queen Elizabeth.* The music was never used, and as of this writing it has never turned up on a recording (nor has much of the music for *A Change of Mind).* In this brief filmographical section of his memoirs, Ellington gives an accurate and telling description of how music functions in Hollywood films and how he tried to comply with the industry's rules: "But maybe we overdid it. The music, of course, is supposed to be an accompaniment, and must not overshadow the picture" (194).

A great deal of well-researched and theoretically sophisticated criticism on music for movies began to appear in the late 1980s. Claudia Gorbman (1987), one of the most important of these critics, has identified the principles of "classical Hollywood practice" for extradiegetic music:

> *Invisibility:* the technical apparatus of extradiegetic music must not be visible.
> *"Inaudibility":* Music is not meant to be heard consciously. As such it should subordinate itself to dialogue, to visuals—i.e., to the primary vehicles of the narrative.
> *Signifier of Emotion:* Soundtrack music may set specific moods and emphasize particular emotions suggested in the narrative (cf. #IV), but first and foremost, it is a signifier of emotion itself.
> *Narrative Cueing:*
>   *—referential/narrative:* music gives referential and narrative cues, e.g., indicating point of view, supplying formal demarcations, and establishing setting and characters.
>   *—connotative:* music "interprets" and "illustrates" narrative events.
> *Continuity:* music provides formal and rhythmic continuity—between shots, in transitions between scenes, by filling "gaps."
> *Unity:* via repetition and variation of musical material and instrumentation, music aids in the construction of formal and narrative unity.
> A given film score may violate any of the principles above, providing the violation is at the service of the other principles. (Gorbman 1987, 73)

Gorbman has also coined a memorable phrase to describe how music seeks to deny the technological basis for its presence: "Sound is just there, oozing from the images we see" (75).

As Ellington implied in his brief analysis, music in dominant cinema essentially restates what is already spelled out in some other register of the film. Gorbman (32) calls this the "ancrage" effect of the film score, adapting a term that Roland Barthes employs to describe the process by which captions in magazines *anchor* the troubling polysemy of photographs to specific meanings (Barthes 1977, 39). Max Steiner, for example, anchors the concluding scene of *Casablanca* with a few bars of "La Marseillaise." After Rick shoots the Nazi Major Strasser, the anthem accompanies Renault's observation that Rick is after all a patriot and that he should repair to the Free French garrison at Brazzaville. The strains of "La Marseillaise" assure us that the adventurous and rebellious impulses of Rick (and of Renault) are now exclusively at the service of France.

Kathryn Kalinak (1992) argues that film music does more than simply underscore what is already on the screen. She uses the creation of suspense as an example: "Thus when *tremolo* strings are heard, the music is not *reinforcing* the suspense of the scene; it is a part of the process that creates it. Indeed, one might argue that without the music, the suspense might not be as compelling or in certain cases perhaps even exist! (Would the ocean seem menacing without the shark theme in *Jaws*?)" (31). Kalinak's project is to reclaim film music from a limbo created by two thousand years of prejudices against music itself. She cites a tradition that began with the ancient Greeks and persisted as an accepted part of scientific discourse on sound until the nineteenth century. For Empedocles, Democritus, Anaxagoras, and Heraclitus, as well as for Plato and Aristotle, what is *seen* is solid and rational, while what is *heard* tends to be emotional and irrational.

This preference for the eye against the ear is still with us, especially in the popular sense that music is somehow feminine. Or as Susan McClary (1991) has written,

> The charge that musicians or devotees of music are "effeminate" goes back as far as recorded documentation about music, and music's association with the body and with subjectivity has led to its being relegated in many historical periods to what was understood as a "feminine" realm. Male musicians have retaliated in a number of ways: by defining music as the most ideal (that is, the least physical) of the arts; by insisting emphatically on its "rational" dimension; by laying claim to such presumably masculine virtues as objectivity, universality, and transcendence; by prohibiting actual female participation altogether. (17)

Film music has suffered doubly, on the one hand for its subsidiary nature, on the other for its supposed femininity. Many jazz scholars may have passed over Ellington's film music for related reasons. It is easier to insist upon the universal, transcendental splendors of his music than to deal with the idea that Ellington wrote something marginal or "feminized." There is also little pleasure for the initiate in hearing Ellington's music pushed far into the background behind plots that seem to become more dated each time the films are viewed. For the Ellington devotee the music is already *anchored* in a series of associations that are not so easily banished to the margins. For those of us who listened repeatedly to the soundtrack LP for *Anatomy of a Murder,* the music conjures up images of Ellington and specific sidemen such as Johnny Hodges, Paul Gonsalves, and Ray Nance. How demeaning that the film anchors the "Flirtibird" theme primarily with Laura Manion (Lee Remick), the kittenish wife of the defendant in a murder trial. Although I would argue that Remick gave a fine performance in *Anatomy* and numerous films thereafter, Johnny Hodges's typically lush solo for "Flirtibird" is reduced to what sometimes

33. Lee Remick and Duke Ellington in a publicity still from *Anatomy of a Murder* (1959, Columbia). Jerry Ohlinger's Movie Material Store, Inc.

may seem the inevitable function of the jazz saxophone in Hollywood—
the signification of "sleaze" (Berg 1978, 12). This is hardly the context
in which to present "a vernacular American symphony," the phrase that
Tom Piazza (1988) has used to describe the music for *Anatomy* (39).

In this sense, the score for *Anatomy of a Murder* qua movie music falls
short of success. To use Gorbman's terms, the music does provide a degree of unity and emotional expression, but it seldom does much for
continuity and narrative cueing. This is not to say that film music is good
or bad depending on how well it meets a series of criteria based on past
practice. (I will argue below that Ellington and Strayhorn achieved much
in *Paris Blues* by *violating* the principles of Hollywood music at the film's

34. Always the composer, Duke Ellington poses with Billie Holiday. Jerry Ohlinger's Movie Material Store, Inc.

climax.) But with *Anatomy of a Murder* the music sounds randomly tacked on, as for example when Paul Biegler (James Stewart) is in Quill's bar trying to convince the dead man's daughter to help with his client's defense. Johnny Hodges's lovely solo on "Haupe" is barely audible, while the chords laid down by the band are virtually imperceptible. At the end of the scene, Ellington can be heard vamping on the piano as if he had run out of ideas. This is of course the fault of music editor Richard Carruth. Otto Preminger, who chose a celebrity to compose music for his film and then displayed him on camera, also must share some of the blame for the music's shortcomings. It is also difficult to evaluate the music for *Anatomy* when so little of it was actually used. Ordinarily a composer is handed an edited print of a film and contracted to write music for specific scenes. Ellington and Strayhorn, by contrast, wrote a good deal of music without knowing exactly how it would turn up in the film. According to Walter van de Leur (1994), who has exhaustively catalogued the three large boxes of music for the film now in the Duke Ellington and Ruth Ellington Collections at the Smithsonian Institution, only shards of the music were used. It is difficult to imagine where much of the music could have fit into *Anatomy's* mostly music-less design. During the film's long courtroom scenes, for example, no music is played whatsoever.

Indeed, the choice of Ellington to compose for *Anatomy of a Murder* was probably not purely musical. Preminger often combined moral courage and pure showmanship. He made a name for himself by releasing *The Moon Is Blue* (1953) with its scandalous use of the word "virgin" and thus without the film industry's seal of approval. He also listed Dalton Trumbo in the credits of *Exodus* (1960) to help break down the practice of blacklisting alleged leftist radicals. The director surely saw an opportunity to gain publicity for the film by bringing in an honored bandleader who had recently enjoyed a comeback, complete with a cover story in *Time*. Preminger also may have hoped to attract attention by hiring a black artist who had never before composed a major film score. In addition, Preminger was perhaps hoping for the kind of coup he had achieved a few years earlier by using Elmer Bernstein's jazz-inflected score for *The Man with the Golden Arm* (1955), the story of a heroin addict that was also released without the blessing of the Motion Picture Producers and Distributors of America. In his autobiography, Preminger (1977) even admits to exploiting Ellington as an unestablished talent in the film industry; the director knew that the most sought-after composers would not have traveled to the Upper Peninsula of Michigan and willingly involved themselves in the film's early stages (156).

At first hearing, Ellington's music does not seem at all compatible with the appearance of James Stewart at the beginning of the film. Ray Nance's plunger-muted trumpet solo accompanies footage of Stewart driving home from a fishing trip wearing a rumpled hat and a self-satisfied look on his face; Paul Gonsalves takes a dark, heavy-breathing solo as Stewart saunters into his banal, rural home; then Ellington does a modernist take on barrelhouse piano as Stewart runs tap water on his fish and prepares to wrap them in newspaper. The music simply fades away as Stewart picks up the telephone to get the plot under way. To further inject jazz into this unlikely domain, the script establishes that Paul Biegler (Stewart), the former district attorney for the Upper Peninsula of Michigan, relaxes by playing jazz piano in a style that is an exact replica of Ellington's.

Biegler is also said to have a large collection of jazz records. Early in the film, when he returns to find Laura Manion waiting for him in his office at home, Biegler's secretary (Eve Arden) says that Laura "has been through all your albums, from Dixieland to Brubeck." The Paul Biegler of Robert Traver's 1958 novel, on which the film is otherwise closely based, does not play the piano. Neither is any suggestion made that he has a taste for jazz. At one moment in the novel, when he feels the need to unwind at the end of a difficult day, Biegler puts on a record of a piece by Debussy (Traver 1958, 110). Laura Manion's musical tastes are never mentioned in the novel.

Ellington's music begins to make sense only when the character of Paul Biegler has been thoroughly established. It soon becomes clear that he is entirely capable of cynically manipulating judge and jury for the sake of his client in spite of abundant evidence that the defendant may not be telling the truth. As Dennis Bingham (1994) has persuasively argued, *Anatomy of a Murder* makes startling use of the populist codes that Stewart displayed to great effect in films such as Frank Capra's *Mr. Smith Goes to Washington* (1939) and *It's a Wonderful Life* (1946). For Bingham, Preminger's film marks "the breakdown of the Stewart persona's sincerity and idealism" (91). At a crucial turn in the courtroom drama, Biegler/Stewart plays the "humble country lawyer" in the same style that he once employed in Capra's films—"I beg the court, I *beg* the court"—but he later acknowledges that it was all an act to introduce evidence that would cloud the real issues in the case. In this sense, as Bingham points out,

Biegler is a "wily trickster" (93), whose passion for jazz may be entirely consistent with a level of sophistication well beyond the typical denizen of the Upper Peninsula of Michigan. The music of Ellington and Strayhorn also underlines and in some ways romanticizes the outsider nature of Biegler and his best friend Parnell (Arthur O'Connell), an unemployed, alcoholic attorney. There is an oddball bond between the two, both of them confirmed bachelors. Audiences generally knew that the offscreen Stewart was a "wholesome" family man with a long-lasting marriage. But what Bingham calls the "bisexual" quality of Stewart's character was further enhanced by the omission of a romance between Biegler and Mary Pilant—played in the film by Kathryn Grant—that is promised at the end of the novel. Bingham is right that, in spite of his roles in films such as *Harvey* (1950) as well as *Anatomy of a Murder*, the American film industry succeeded in keeping the bisexuality of the Stewart persona out of the public's consciousness. Nevertheless, the industry always allowed for a complexity in his articulation of masculinity that was seldom available to other stars. Perhaps unwittingly, Preminger invited Ellington and Strayhorn to write music that was a curious complement to Stewart's unique image.

Anatomy of a Murder has other felicities. Toward the end of the film, Biegler noodles at the piano while he and the Irish-American Parnell wait for the jury to bring in its verdict. Parnell complains, "Do you have to play that stuff? Can't you play 'Danny Boy'?" Ellington then dubs in a few priceless bars of a boogie-woogie "Danny Boy" before he is interrupted by the message that a verdict is imminent. And Ellington himself has his few seconds on screen as "Pie Eye," the leader of a small group called The P.I. Five (Ray Nance, Jimmy Hamilton, Jimmy Woode, and Jimmy Johnson).

Shortly after *Anatomy* was released, Ellington admitted that he was less than satisfied with his work as a composer for films. He is quoted in an article in the *American Weekly Entertainment Guide:* "Music in pictures should say something without being obviously music, you know, and this was all new to me. I'll try another one and then I'll show them" (Stratemann 1992, 407). This is exactly what Ellington accomplished with *Paris Blues,* his next Hollywood project. Ellington did in fact "show them."

Paris Blues

Largely because *Paris Blues* is about jazz musicians, it was a much more appropriate project than *Anatomy of a Murder.* Ellington and Strayhorn

succeeded to a remarkable degree in bringing unity to the story and enhancing the emotional expression of the characters. Using what they
learned with *Anatomy,* they showed complete mastery of the conventions
of scoring for classical Hollywood. With the subsequent *Assault on a
Queen* and *A Change of Mind,* the music was more extensively edited and
recorded by many non-Ellingtonian musicians. Only Ellington and not
his band were contracted for *Assault,* and although Ellington revived several of his classic compositions for *A Change of Mind,* the film features
only fragments of extradiegetic music.[14] But for *Paris Blues,* producer
Sam Shaw granted a great deal of control to Ellington and Strayhorn.
What one hears on the screen is almost exactly what the two intended.

As with *Anatomy,* Ellington took an extended vacation from touring
with his orchestra to work on the film. After recording about six titles in
Hollywood, Ellington flew to Paris, the first time that he had sufficiently
overcome his legendary fear of flying to make the Atlantic crossing by
air. In Paris he recorded most of what is heard when Paul Newman's band
performs on screen. Paul Gonsalves dubbed in Sidney Poitier's tenor saxophone solos, and several other Ellingtonians supplied the sounds of the
rhythm section.

And as with *Anatomy,* Billy Strayhorn played an extremely important
role in composing the music for *Paris Blues.* At least at first, *Paris Blues*
seemed like an ideal project for Strayhorn. As his biographer David
Hajdu (1996) has observed, Strayhorn was a major figure among the expatriate American jazz musicians in Paris. He regularly traveled to Paris
where he spent a good deal of time with pianist Aaron Bridgers, Strayhorn's lover in the 1940s when the two men shared an apartment in New
York. Like Strayhorn, originally from North Carolina, Bridgers settled in
Paris in 1948 and still lives there as of this writing. In the 1950s he was
the house pianist at the Mars Club, a small Paris cabaret that on any
given night was approximately "60/40 straight/gay" (Hajdu 1996).
Bridgers actually appears in *Paris Blues* as the pianist in Ram Bowen's
band (although Ellington and Strayhorn are the only pianists heard on
the soundtrack). The presence of Bridgers as well as the gay couples who
appear in the opening scene of *Paris Blues* suggest that the club in the
film may have been at least in part inspired by the Mars Club.

Other aspects of *Paris Blues* initially must have made it especially appealing to Strayhorn. The attempt to place jazz within an art discourse
was probably as important to him as it was to Ellington. Strayhorn
worked closely with classical musicians in Paris, and one of the few LPs
that he released under his own name (*The Peaceful Side,* May 1961) was

recorded in Paris with a string quartet. His solo compositions were always much closer to the classical mainstream than were Ellington's. Strayhorn's "Suite for the Duo," recorded by the Mitchell-Ruff Duo in 1969 (Mainstream) is a good example of his ability to fuse jazz with more European forms. Some of the early work on the music for *Paris Blues* was directed by Strayhorn, who arrived in Paris a month before Ellington. A close inspection of the scores for *Paris Blues,* most of them in the Smithsonian, reveals a large portion in Strayhorn's hand.

Most of what Ellington and Strayhorn wrote and recorded during the *early* stages of their work on the film was for the actors who play musicians on camera. Paul Newman and Sidney Poitier convincingly mime the playing of a trombone and tenor saxophone because they could practice with recordings supplied to them before rehearsals began in Paris. Most of this music was probably recorded in Hollywood during the summer of 1960. One year later, when all filming had been completed and Ellington had resumed touring with his band, he took his augmented orchestra into the Reeves Sound Studios in New York and recorded about thirty minutes of extradiegetic music for the film. By this time Ellington and Strayhorn, like the great majority of film composers, had received a copy of the edited film along with a transcript of the dialogue. As I will argue shortly, the composers took this opportunity to register, albeit with great subtlety, their ambivalent feelings about certain aspects of the film.

Paris Blues is based on Harold Flender's novel of the same title, published in 1957. The novel's main character is an African American tenor saxophonist named Eddie Jones who plays regularly in a Paris nightclub. Entertaining no desire to be anything other than a working musician, he plays mostly Dixieland and traditional jazz. He meets and gradually falls in love with a black American schoolteacher named Connie who is vacationing in Paris. Even though Eddie has been living happily in Paris for several years and appreciates its tolerance for blacks, at the end of the novel he decides to go back to the States to be with Connie. The novel also introduces a trumpet player named Wild Man Moore who is very much like Louis Armstrong. While in Paris, Moore offers Eddie a job that he first refuses, but when Eddie decides to follow Connie, he knows that he can work with Wild Man after he returns. The film takes all of this material directly from the novel.

Of course, Eddie Jones, the black saxophonist, is not the only main character in the movie. The film of *Paris Blues* has greatly expanded the novel's character of Benny, a Jewish pianist in his fifties who is a member of Eddie's band. In the novel, when Connie arrives in Paris with a large

35. Ram Bowen (Paul Newman) and Eddie Cook (Sidney Poitier) contemplate "Paris Blues" in *Paris Blues* (1961, United Artists). Museum of Modern Art Film Stills Archive.

group of tourists, she rooms with Lillian, a middle-aged, white, unmarried schoolteacher. When Lillian insists on accompanying Connie to hear Eddie perform at his club, Benny does Eddie a favor by latching on to Lillian so that Eddie can devote all of his attention to Connie. A little drunk and filled with the desire to *épater le bourgeois,* Benny shows the wilder side of Paris to Lillian. He even takes her to an all-night nudist swimming club where she is titillated almost as much as she is offended. Although Benny later says that he regrets his crude treatment of Lillian and that he wants to apologize, nothing comes of the relationship. Lillian goes back to the States alone.

Benny, the minor character in the novel, becomes Ram Bowen the handsome young (Jewish?) trombonist played by Paul Newman, and Lillian the old maid schoolteacher becomes Lillian the beautiful young divorcée played by Joanne Woodward. Eddie Jones the handsome young black saxophone player and Connie the beautiful young schoolteacher make the transition from the novel relatively unscathed; in the film they are played by Sidney Poitier (as Eddie *Cook*) and Diahann Carroll. The adaptation of the novel by Lulla Adler and the screenplay by Jack Sher, Irene Kamp, and Walter Bernstein also include the significant addition of Ram Bowen's desire to become a "serious" composer. Although Bowen has enlisted Eddie as his arranger, it is also clear that Bowen is the leader of the group and much more of an "artist" than Eddie.

Ellington probably did not know about these aspects of the script when he signed on to do the music. He also was under the impression that the film would dramatically depart from the novel by romantically pairing Paul Newman with Diahann Carroll. The vestiges of this romance are still present in an early scene when Ram seems much more interested in Connie than in Lillian. Even earlier, during the opening credits, the film seems to be preparing audiences for interracial romance by repeatedly showing nontraditional couples in the Paris nightclub where Ram Bowen's band performs. We see male and female homosexuals, interracial couples, and a young man with a much older woman. Intentionally or not, this multiply integrated scene was also an idealized reflection of the milieu actually inhabited by Billy Strayhorn. As the progress of the film's script should make clear, however, the Hollywood of 1961 was not prepared to accept so much tolerance for nontraditional romantic pairings. In another scene in the club that takes place twenty minutes into the film, the camera again pans the customers' faces, but absolutely no interracial or same-sex couples are shown. Not even any older people appear. This sequence was undoubtedly shot after the decision had been made to dispense with the interracial love affair.

According to Mercer Ellington (1978), Duke Ellington agreed to cancel a number of appearances and fly to Paris to do the film's music largely because he liked the idea of a story about romance between the races. For similar reasons he later agreed to write music for *A Change of Mind* about a black man who has the brain of a white person inserted into his skull. Ellington was upset when executives at United Artists lost their nerve and demanded that the couples be color-coded according to more conventional standards (M. Ellington 1978, 183). Billy Strayhorn may have been disappointed for similar reasons, including the transformation of the nightclub from a tolerant, heterogeneous space into something much more conventional.

I also suspect that Ellington and Strayhorn were upset by the film's treatment of jazz. The final print of the film preserves the opening credits sequence with its daring mix of couples, but in the larger context of the film's conservatism the club in this early scene might just as well represent a degraded space that the trombonist hero hopes to escape by becoming a serious composer. The dedication of Ram Bowen (Rimbaud?) (Ram [a trom]Bone?) to art—and Eddie Cook's lack of interest in "serious" music—is established in the first scene after the credits. As the club owner Marie Séoul (Barbara Laage) descends into the club after an early morning trip to the market, Ram is playing a melodic phrase that will later be established as the "Paris Blues" theme. With Eddie, Ram has been working all night on this composition. Asserting that the melody is too heavy, Eddie says that he will score it for an oboe. Ram protests what he considers a criticism of his music and insists that Eddie tell him whether or not he really likes the composition. Eddie seems more interested in calling it a night. In an intriguing reference to this exchange, Ellington and Strayhorn prominently score the "Paris Blues" theme for an oboe when it appears extradiegetically later in the film.

Not until almost thirty minutes into the film is this particular stretch of extradiegetic music first heard by the audience. Lasting approximately six minutes, the music quickly reveals how successfully Ellington and Strayhorn had learned the craft of composing for films after their mixed success with *Anatomy of a Murder.* Like all good background music, the softly soothing version of the "Paris Blues" theme creates the right moods, even before the audience knows exactly what to feel. As Kalinak (1992) has observed, film composers have always struggled to find the right moment to introduce a segment of extradiegetic music (99).[15] Often a composer will "sneak" the music in softly where the audience is unlikely to notice its appearance. This is exactly what Ellington and Strayhorn accomplish with the early stirrings of romance between Ram Bowen and Lillian. The same music continues as the camera picks up the romance between Eddie Cook and Connie and climaxes when we see Lillian the next morning in Ram's apartment wearing his dressing gown. Each of the transitions between the two sets of couples is clearly marked by the music. Ellington and Strayhorn even have written somewhat funkier music for the black couple—Ray Nance can be heard making growling, "jungle" sounds as soon as Poitier and Carroll appear in front of Notre Dame de Paris. Documents in the Smithsonian show that Ellington and Strayhorn knew exactly where each moment of their music would fit in the final film. Several pages from the shooting script are carefully marked with timings, suggesting that someone (the handwriting is not Ellington's) had stopwatched parts of the film so that the music could be precisely correlated with the action. At one point, when Connie is telling Ram about her affection for Eddie, Ellington has written next to her line, "Pretty," a concise description of what happens in the extradiegetic score during her speech.

The choice of an oboe for the "Paris Blues" theme is significant in a score so closely tailored to the dialogue and action. Ellington and Strayhorn had not used an oboe since 1946 when they wrote the score for *Beggar's Holiday,* a musical adaptation of John Gay's *The Beggar's Opera.* The show opened in New York at the Broadway Theater on December 26, 1946, to mixed reviews and closed after fourteen weeks and 108 performances (Hasse 1993, 293). (Walter van de Leur [1994] has pointed out that the section of the score for oboe, strings, French horn, and harp is entirely in Strayhorn's hand.) The oboe solo in the score for *Paris Blues* is played by Harry Smiles, one of about nine musicians added to the Ellington orchestra for a recording session held in New York on May 1, 1961 (Stratemann 1992, 434). The connection between a line of dialogue about an oboe and the presence of the instrument in the extradiegetic version of the same music suggests that Ellington and Strayhorn were blurring the distinction between the diegetic and extradiegetic scores. In the script, Ram Bowen is writing a composition called "Paris Blues" that he wants to see performed as a concert piece. About two-thirds of the way through the film Bowen puts on a record of his "Paris Blues." He is in his apartment with Lillian, who has asked to hear something that he has written. We then hear the same theme by Ellington and Strayhorn that has been extradiegetically featured throughout the film. The music that Ram is playing on the record was written and recorded *after* the scenes with Newman and Woodward had been shot and edited.

On the one hand, the matching of diegetic and extradiegetic music is completely consistent with classical Hollywood practice; it is common in the many biopics about composers, and films often introduce a theme diegetically before it becomes a part of the extradiegetic score. For example, in *Casablanca,* Max Steiner repeatedly uses phrases from "As Time Goes By" after the song has been sung on camera by Dooley Wilson. On the other hand, Ellington and Strayhorn could be using an oboe to wink at those in the audience who recall that Eddie Cook, the black musician, had suggested an oboe as a way of correcting the heaviness of a theme that a white musician had played on his trombone. According to *Paris Blues's* producer Sam Shaw (1994), director Martin Ritt made few demands on Ellington, but he specifically requested that Ram Bowen's trombone have a smooth sound with a strong vibrato in the tradition of Tommy Dorsey. The white trombonist Murray McEachern, who later became a member of the Ellington orchestra, was brought in early to play the first solos that Paul Newman mimes. Billy Byers, who is also white, probably dubbed in solos during location shooting in Paris while he was working as the film's "musical adviser" (Stratemann 1992, 433). I do not wish to emphasize the whiteness of these trombone players, real and fictional; I would rather point out that the film's dichotomous view of jazz and classical music is embodied in the character of Ram Bowen. Because Ellington and Strayhorn would have rejected the kinds of distinctions between jazz and classical music that are central to the ideology of *Paris Blues,* they may have adopted the introduction of an oboe into their score because it is recommended by a musician who has no pretensions about "art." They accepted a musical choice spoken on screen by Sidney Poitier even though it was effectively made by the screenwriters.

The film's discourse on jazz and art is articulated explicitly and with great authority by René Bernard (André Luguet), whom the film identifies as a grand old man of French classical music. Ram Bowen seeks an audience with Bernard through Wild Man Moore, played by Louis Armstrong. The film implies that Moore has a special relationship with Bernard, perhaps because of the kinds of interactions Armstrong had during his European travels in the 1930s when he regularly mixed with the conservatory-trained musicians who recognized his talents. In an early scene, Wild Man Moore arrives at the train station in Paris to a group of cheering fans. Ram Bowen is also there to greet him. After exchanging the obligatory pleasantries, he asks Moore to take his music, "Paris Blues," to the impresario Bernard. Toward the end of the film Ram Bowen actually gets an audience with René Bernard in hopes that the Frenchman can place his music in a concert setting. Although Bernard says that he has long admired Bowen's work as a jazz trombonist, he is only guarded in his praise of the written score that Moore had delivered to him. The ensuing conversation is worth quoting at length.

Bernard: You have a good melodic feel.
Bowen: Mr. Bernard, I want to develop that theme into a piece to be played in concert. Now, what's the possibility?
Bernard: Mr. Bowen, you are a creative musician. Every time you put a horn to your mouth, you are composing. Your improvisations are

highly personal. They give you a stamp as a musician. *But there is a great deal of difference between that and an important piece of serious music.*

Bowen: In other words, you're trying to tell me that I'm just sort of a lightweight.

Bernard: I don't know what you are yet, Mr. Bowen. And neither do you. I'm only saying that you haven't yet given yourself a chance to find out.

Bowen: I've worked with musicians all my life. I know everything I can do.

Bernard: Perhaps you need to do something else now. *Paris is a great city for an artist to work and study composition, harmony, theory, counterpoint.* Perhaps you need to change your life for a couple of years in order to give yourself a chance to do what you wish.

Bowen: Well, in other words, it's no good.

Bernard: On the contrary. I like it.

Bowen: But it's not good enough to be played.

Bernard: Oh, I'm certain, [pause] a record company . . .

Bowen: But nothing more than that.

Bernard: It is what it is. *A jazz piece of a certain charm and [pause] melody.* (Emphasis added.)

The scene ends with Bernard giving Bowen some small encouragement that he might one day become "a serious composer."

In *Paris Blues,* jazz cannot be an art form even if it has been written by Duke Ellington and Billy Strayhorn. Many in the classical music community of Paris in 1961 would probably have agreed with Bernard—jazz can be charming and melodic but not truly serious.[16] If we are to accept the film's message, then Ellington and Strayhorn simply have a "gift for melody." In *Paris Blues,* that melody is the one the audience has been hearing all along, the "Paris Blues" theme, both diegetically from Ram Bowen and extradiegetically on the soundtrack.

Thoroughly discouraged by his conversation with Bernard, Bowen arrives at Lillian's hotel to tell her he is prepared to return with her to the United States immediately. In the States he will simply play his horn and abandon his dream of becoming a great composer. Eddie independently arrives at the decision that he too will return and join Connie a few weeks after she leaves Paris. Later, at a party with his musician friends, Ram tells Eddie what René Bernard has said about his music. In a moment that is, at least for the purposes of this chapter, charged with significance, Ram brushes aside Eddie's attempts to question Bernard's authority. The logical argument that the old Frenchman has used an inappropriate aesthetic to judge jazz in general and Ram's "Paris Blues" in particular is only raised to be rejected. With a noticeable lack of conviction, Eddie says, "He's longhair, and he doesn't always know what he's talking about." Ram replies definitively, "He knows."

On the one hand, the chickens have come home to roost for the view that Ellington belongs within the European musical tradition where some critics—beginning in the 1930s with R. D. Darrell and Constant Lambert—have sought to place him. As Scott DeVeaux (1991) has written in his discussion of *Paris Blues,* the particular art discourse for jazz that had emerged in the 1950s could succeed only if jazz was ultimately regarded as "an immature and imperfectly realized junior partner to European music" (547). A more Afrocentric view of jazz, such as Amiri Baraka would forcefully present two years later in his *Blues People* (1963), was not yet widely available. At least it did not seem to be known to the writers of *Paris Blues.* On the other hand, as we have seen, Ellington never saw himself as part of the European tradition and gently ridiculed those who claimed he was. Almost the entire Ellington discography stands as a refutation of everything that René Bernard has said.

In the final scene of *Paris Blues,* Lillian is waiting for Ram at the train station along with Eddie and Connie. When Ram arrives shortly before the train is due to depart, Lillian can tell from his face that he has decided not to leave with her. Directly behind them workmen are papering over the poster with the laughing face of Louis Armstrong as Wild Man Moore. As Johnny Hodges and the Ellington orchestra play "Paris Blues" beneath his words, Ram explains that he has decided to follow the advice of Bernard and remain in Paris to study. "Lillian, I got to follow through with the music. I got to find out how far I can go. And I guess that means alone." After an emotional farewell speech, Lillian rushes to her train. The solo statement of the theme is now taken over by the trombone of Murray McEachern, whose sound has been associated throughout with the character of Ram Bowen. The music swells as Eddie bids farewell to both Lillian and Connie. Then a new theme emerges, played by the entire band and layered over the trombone solo. The new theme recalls the various train songs written by Ellington and Strayhorn, including "Lightnin'" (1932), "Daybreak Express" (1933), and "Happy-Go-Lucky Local" (1946). Unlike the more lyrical, almost mournful "Paris Blues" melody, the new theme is fast, dissonant, and dominated by percussion. Soon the new theme has overpowered the old one, only occasionally allowing McEachern's trombone to be heard as it continues to play the melody of "Paris Blues." This juxtaposition continues for about sixty seconds as the train departs and Eddie and Ram leave the station. In the final shot of the film, the poster with Armstrong's face has been almost entirely papered over with a new billboard.

I would suggest a number of interpretations for this final scene. First, the closing music can be imagined as emanating from the screen, "oozing from the images we see" (Gorbman 1987, 75), as an expression of the conflicting emotions of the characters. The "Paris Blues" theme might represent the feelings that the lovers have for each other, while the train theme looks toward the future and the need for the characters to get on with their lives. The end music could also be what Ram Bowen is hearing in his head as he plans a more elaborate version of his composition that is made possible by his emotional experiences with Lillian and by his imminent study of "composition, harmony, theory, counterpoint" as recommended by René Bernard. This interpretation combines a rationalist belief in conservatory training with the romantic myth of suffering as the key to artistic creation. Bowen will, according to this reading, write music that will in a sense cover over the "charming" but "lightweight" jazz exemplified by Wild Man Moore/Louis Armstrong, whose image is erased as Bowen sets off to become a "serious" artist. Appropriately, the new billboard that is covering over the face of Armstrong is an advertisement for the Librarie Larousse, the leading French publisher of canonical literature. The script for the film seems to imply that jazz will be replaced by something more established and more literate.

I strongly suspect, however, that Ellington and Strayhorn wrote the music that ends *Paris Blues* as an answer to the statements of René Bernard. Remember that Bernard had said he liked the melody of "Paris Blues" but little else. So Ellington and Strayhorn give us the melody in all its glory as played by the white trombonist, but they audaciously cover it over with another entire piece. The pretensions of the musician who wants to rise above jazz is overwhelmed with rousing African American rhythms and harmonies. (Significantly, Ellington's several subsequent recordings of "Paris Blues" omit the train theme with the trombone solo. The combination is unique to the film.) Even though Ellington and Strayhorn had no say in writing the script, they may be registering their response to René Bernard's pronouncements on jazz by demonstrating that, although their music may not be "serious," it can still be extremely moving and complex. This was a statement worth making. Four years after the release of *Paris Blues*, Ellington would be denied the Pulitzer Prize by the American equivalents of René Bernard. Ellington's famous response was typical. As he said in his autobiography, "Fate is being very kind to me; fate doesn't want me to be too famous too young" (Ellington

1973, 286). He was sixty-six at the time. Similarly, in *Paris Blues,* Ellington and Strayhorn expressed themselves politely but sharply. By pulling out all the stops at the end of *Paris Blues,* Ellington and Strayhorn surely made the filmmakers happy at the same time that they subtly destroyed the film's dichotomies of jazz and art.[17]

When *Paris Blues* was released in November 1961 the critics were mostly dismissive. John Tynan (1961) wrote in *Down Beat,* for example, that it was "dramatic nonsense" (16). As has always been the case with the film scores credited to Ellington, critics have chosen to write only about the music for *Paris Blues* as separate from the film. With this one film score, however, the real achievement of Ellington and Strayhorn can be appreciated only within the film's specific context. Ellington was capable of sending out ambiguous messages, inviting the hip members of his audience to decode in ways that were unavailable to the rest. I would argue that his achievement in *Paris Blues* was foreshadowed by the effect he created with "Goin' Up," the composition he wrote especially for *Cabin in the Sky.* One could cite numerous if less flamboyant examples of Ellington's irony and his subtle habit of "signifying" on those who would hold him to standards other than his own. His droll deflections of Constant Lambert's praises in 1935 is an early example. His conventionalized assurance to his audiences that he and "all the kids in the band love you madly" is another example, as is the ironic "finger-snapping, earlobe-tilting bit" with which he often closed his concerts in his last decades.[18] In June 1960, just after they had begun work on *Paris Blues,* Ellington and Strayhorn recorded brilliant reworkings of music by Tchaikovsky and Grieg that stand on their own as jazz performances at the same time that they signify on the classical repertoire.[19]

When the thirty-year-old Ellington made his film debut in *Black and Tan,* he had already been cast as a devoted composer, even if an art discourse for jazz was not yet in place to characterize him as a full-scale artist. Thirty-two years later, in his most challenging assignment during his career in films, the ideology of *Paris Blues* still did not grant him the stature of a serious artist. There is no other career, however, that so thoroughly casts doubt on the conventional, Eurocentric notions of what constitutes an artist.

"Actor and Musician"

Louis Armstrong and His Films

ouis Armstrong may have been as complex as the discourse that surrounded him. By contrast, Duke Ellington established a persona in his youth that filmmakers and the media could accept throughout his career, even if he had to endure regular affronts to his dignity. Although Ellington drifted in and out of critical favor with various constituencies, most of the public was aware of a single Duke Ellington, an urbane but earthy composer-musician-bandleader with a *faux* British accent. But Louis Armstrong was many things to many people. His mugging and laughing had little to do with the inner life of someone who could be brooding, stubborn, and outspoken. While the biographers may disagree about Armstrong's psychology, the disputes about his performance career have been even more dramatic. For some, the trumpeter achieved greatness with his 1920s recordings and then spent the rest of his life squandering his prodigious talent and thriving on show biz lite. For others, he was a consummate artist who played and sang with wit and intelligence throughout his life. Still other critics have called into question the distinction between artist and entertainer, arguing that Armstrong's life and work stand as a strong counterargument to the empowering of serious "art" over mere "entertainment." Joshua Berrett (1992) has made this case especially well in his analysis of how Armstrong assimilated the opera arias that he quoted in his recorded solos during the 1920s and 1930s.

Regardless of how critics assess Armstrong's achievements, the issue has almost always been argued in terms of his trumpet solos and vocals. Virtually all of Hugues Panassié's (1971) book on Armstrong, for example, is given over to analysis of the recordings. In the first pages of the chapter on Armstrong in his *The Swing Era,* Gunther Schuller discusses the problems surrounding Armstrong's stardom; he then adds in a footnote, "While on the one hand, in the face of Armstrong's uniqueness, it may be futile to pass judgment on his post–1920s' career, on the other hand—precisely because of his preeminent role in jazz—one must eventually come to grips with the *totality* of his life and work. This can only be done in a dispassionate way, which also takes into account Louis's personality and temperament, and the social-economic conditions within which he labored" (Schuller 1989, 160). After these words, however, Schuller devotes the rest of the essay to close readings of the trumpet solos, just as he had done earlier in the Armstrong chapter of his *Early Jazz* (1968).

Although many critics have followed Schuller in paying lip service to the nonmusical aspects of Armstrong's career, few have paid much attention to his roles in twenty-three American feature films.[1] Especially today when jazz canonizers have defined Armstrong as a revolutionary artist, his films are probably ignored to sidestep troubling questions about stage mannerisms that are invisible on the fetishized recordings. Better to remember him as the genius who improvised the stirring choruses of "Potato Head Blues" and "Weather Bird" than as the servile clown grinning at second-rate white actors. At least since the 1930s, however, audiences have probably known Armstrong best for his television and film appearances, including numerous shorts and soundies as well as the feature films. Even when Armstrong did not appear in person, his image graced cartoons such as "Old Mill Pond" (1936), "Clean Pastures" (1937), and "Swing Wedding" (1937), the latter a songfest for frogs who bear striking resemblances to Armstrong, Cab Calloway, Fats Waller, and Stepin Fetchit. In Max Fleischer's Betty Boop cartoon of 1932, "I'll Be Glad When You're Dead You Rascal You," Armstrong appears first in a filmed performance with his band, then as a cartoon cannibal, and finally as a disembodied head singing the title song to Bimbo and Koko as they flee across an African plain.[2]

Although Armstrong did not begin appearing regularly in Hollywood films until 1936, he listed his occupation as "actor and musician" on a passport application in anticipation of his first European tour in 1932 (Giddins 1988, 41). At that time his filmography consisted only of appearances in the nine-minute short *Rhapsody in Black and Blue* (1932), the lost low-budget American film *Ex-Flame* (1931), and the 1932 Betty Boop cartoon. But this listing of "actor" before "musician" may have reflected Armstrong's conviction that he was a *performer* rather than a mere maker of music, indeed a performer who had just broken into cartoons as well as into Hollywood films. Armstrong's words on a passport application can also be regarded as another example of how simple dichotomies break down when his entire career is considered. The actor and the musician were inseparable when Armstrong worked in front of an audience or a camera. His trumpet was never far when he acted in a film, and sooner or later it was at his lips. He was almost always called Satchmo or Louis Armstrong in his films, and later when he played Wild Man Moore in *Paris Blues* (1961) and Sweet Daddy Willie Ferguson in *A Man Called Adam* (1966), these were merely pseudonyms for Louis Armstrong. Many of the most important debates about Armstrong are played out as strikingly in his films as they are in any other aspect of his career.

Reading the Critics

Any study of the reception of Armstrong over the past seventy years invites the methods of what is now known as cultural studies, a collection of approaches that characterize novels, paintings, operas, comic strips, and other forms of cultural production *not* as stable objects into which artists have inscribed meaning but rather as sites where audiences create their own meanings (Grossberg et al. 1992). A film of Armstrong grinning and mugging has radically diverse meanings to audiences of different ages, races, and cultural values at different moments in history. In his several reviews of films with Armstrong during the 1950s, Bosley Crowther inevitably singled him out for praise, especially in films that Crowther otherwise held in contempt. For example, concerning *Glory Alley* (1952), Crowther wrote, "Every now and then, Louis Armstrong sticks his broad, beaming face into the frame and sings or blasts a bit on his trumpet. That makes the only sense in the whole film" (*New York Times* July 30, 1952). And here is Crowther on *High Society* (1956): "Mr. Armstrong beams as brazenly as ever and lets the hot licks fall where they may" (*New York Times* August 10, 1956). But looking at the same films thirty years later, Donald Bogle, writing in *Toms, Coons, Mulattoes, Mammies, and Bucks,* saw "a coon and a tom all rolled into one" and placed his essay on Armstrong in a section called "Stepin's Step-Chillun" (Bogle 1992, 71–75).[3]

These kinds of judgments tell us more about the critics than they do about Armstrong himself. Indeed, if we disregard most of the commentaries on the trumpeter's recorded solos, a number of concerns regularly surface in the critical literature. In this chapter I concentrate on three themes that I find especially important to an understanding of Armstrong's films: (1) attempts to place Armstrong somewhere on either side of (or above) the debate about art versus entertainment; (2) his sexuality and how it may or not have been expressed in his performances; and (3) "role model" arguments relating to his deportment on stage and the larger questions about his significance for African Americans. Often these issues become intertwined in the critical debates. For example, Theodor Adorno combines (1) and (2) by arguing syllogistically that popular music—unlike true art—is castrating; Armstrong played popular music; therefore, Armstrong is castrated. Critics who find evidence that Armstrong is "signifying" (regardless of whether or not they use that word) suggest that he was both (1) transcending the distinction between art and entertainment, and (3) becoming a hero to black people by showing them how to overcome demeaning conditions imposed upon them by the white power structure.

ARTIST OR ENTERTAINER?

Critics began bestowing lavish praise on Armstrong as early as 1928 (Collier 1988, 55). For most jazz writers, the trouble began in the late 1930s when Armstrong regularly worked with a conventional swing band and ventured beyond the vague boundaries of jazz by recording with the Mills Brothers, a gospel choir, and even with a group called the Polynesians. Although some critics today express pleasure in records such as "To You, Sweetheart, Aloha" (1936) and "On a Little Bamboo Bridge" (1937), jazz purists of the 1930s and 1940s felt betrayed. By the mid–1940s, Armstrong was held in contempt by many of the young be-boppers as well as by the New Orleans revivalists who canonized his recordings of the 1920s but rejected most of what followed. Rudi Blesh (1976), for example, wrote in 1946 that Armstrong had abandoned "hot music," or true jazz, for the sensationalism and the easy popularity of "swing," a hybrid, bastardized form of jazz that Armstrong embraced as he moved away from the Hot Fives and Sevens to form a big band. As was often the case in Blesh's writings, the argument was phrased in apocalyptic tones:

> Had Armstrong understood his responsibility as clearly as he perceived his own growing artistic power—had his individual genius been deeply integrated with that of the music, and thus ultimately with the destiny, of his race—designated leadership would have been just. . . . Around Louis clustered growing public cognizance of hot music and those commercial forces, equally strong and more persistent, which utilize the musical communications system of the phonograph record, the then new radio and talking motion picture, and the printed sheets of the Tin Pan Alley tunesmiths. And behind this new symbolic figure was aligned the overwhelming and immemorial need of his own race to find a Moses to lead it out of Egypt. (Blesh 1958, 257–58)

Writing in 1948, the Marxist critic Sidney Finkelstein also took a dim view of Armstrong's move toward swing, but he was more forgiving than Blesh. Finkelstein associated the simultaneously improvising New Orleans ensembles with a utopian, leaderless society; the cult of the soloist in front of a big band was for Finkelstein a symptom of capitalism and the commercialization of art. He conceded the following, however: "Had a genuine, musical culture existed in America, one capable of cherishing its talents and giving them a chance to properly learn and grow, instead of destroying them, Armstrong might have been encouraged to produce a great American music. There was no such opportunity, however; instead, [there was] continual pressure to produce novelties, to plug new songs, or the same songs under new names" (Finkelstein 1988, 106).

James Baldwin dramatized the disdain toward Armstrong among beboppers in his 1957 story "Sonny's Blues" (Albert 1990), in which a black World War II veteran working as a schoolteacher confronts the desire of his younger brother to become a jazz musician. When his brother has trouble explaining the kind of musician he wants to become, the older man intervenes:

> I suggested helpfully: "You mean—like Louis Armstrong?"
> His face closed as though I'd struck him. "No. I'm not talking about none of that old-time, down home crap." (Albert 1990, 189)

The younger brother eventually names Charlie Parker as a musician he aspires to imitate. In Baldwin's story the chasm between Armstrong and Parker becomes a metaphor for the cultural gap separating the brothers as well as for the revolution taking place among young African Americans during the postwar years.

A few years after Baldwin's story, Amiri Baraka took a different view of Armstrong in his *Blues People* of 1963, regarding Armstrong not as the played-out representative of an obsolete music but rather as the "honored priest of his culture." Baraka distinguished Armstrong from Bix Beiderbecke, who was "an instinctual intellectual" with an emotional life "based on his conscious or unconscious disapproval of most of the sacraments of his culture." Armstrong, by contrast, "was not *rebelling* against anything with his music. In fact, his music was one of the most beautiful refinements of Afro-American musical tradition, and it was immediately recognized as such by those Negroes who were not busy trying to pretend that they had issued from Beiderbecke's culture" (Baraka 1963, 154).

In recent decades, critics have made increasingly extravagant claims in favor of Armstrong's music. The view that he was in decline after the 1920s has been rejected by some of the most eminent jazz critics. Dan Morgenstern (1972), for example, wrote that "Armstrong's mastery of his instrument *and* musical imagination continued to grow, far beyond the threshold of the 30s." Even more recently, Stanley Dance (1993) has stated that Armstrong surpassed some of his classic recordings when he rerecorded them for the *Autobiography in Jazz* LPs in the 1950s. In an effort to recuperate *all* of Armstrong's career, Gary Giddins (1988) even defends the 1968 recordings of Disney songs, suggesting that Armstrong is having fun with his material in side remarks such as "Oh, the buckskin buccaneer" in his version of "The Ballad of Davy Crockett" (203).

James Lincoln Collier (1983) tends to agree with the earlier appraisal of writers such as Blesh, identifying 1929 as the year in which Armstrong chose to become a popular entertainer and reach a larger audience beyond African Americans. In his Armstrong biography, Collier attempts to psychoanalyze the trumpeter, presenting him as a tragic figure whose desire to please was completely inconsistent with romantic notions of the artist.

> Armstrong was clearly a man afflicted with deep and well-entrenched insecurity, a sense of his own worthlessness so thoroughly fixed that he was never to shake it off, even after he had become one of the most famous men in the world. But he could quench that relentless, sickening, interior assault on his self-respect, at least temporarily, by performing, standing up there before those dozens or thousands or millions of people and playing and singing and smiling and mugging and soaking up the healing applause, which for a moment pushed away the feeling that nobody liked him, that he was basically no good. And when he was offered the chance to earn ever larger doses of that healing balm, he could hardly have turned it down. (Collier 1983, 202–3)

Collier argues that the distinction between artist and entertainer—the dominant trope in recent discourse around Armstrong—would have been incomprehensible to a man who sought only to quench his desperate thirst for adulation.

At least for Collier, then, Armstrong would seem to be an unlikely character to appear in films where questions of jazz and art are debated. And yet he was cast in film after film where these issues were central to the plot. In *New Orleans* in the 1940s, *High Society* in the 1950s, and both *Paris Blues* and *A Man Called Adam* in the 1960s, Armstrong plays a crucial role in the film's debate about jazz as opposed to classical music or about the value of older jazz as opposed to newer jazz. My guess is that Armstrong held so much appeal for the mass audience that he made these kinds of discussions palatable. No one had to think too long about the issues when Armstrong himself was never making any pompous claims about being an artist. And if he was in fact an artist, he surely did not make anyone feel uncomfortable about so obsequious a fellow assuming that lofty position. Imagine Miles Davis, Thelonious Monk, or virtually any other modernist black jazz musician being extolled for his artistry, and then imagine how much differently white audiences might have reacted to the assertion.

PHALLIC OR CASTRATED?

In *The Story of Jazz,* Marshall Stearns retells an anecdote about Armstrong that is especially relevant to his appearances in American films. In emphasizing the immediacy of communication between jazz artist and audience, Stearns wrote, "There is a legend that, during the late 'thirties when Louis Armstrong recorded a series of wonderful performances, he was starting on his fourth honeymoon" (Stearns 1956, 280). This may be one of the first explicit attempts to associate Armstrong's music and persona with his sexuality. As I argued in chapter 4, the jazz trumpet has always been an especially powerful means for expressing male sexuality, and Armstrong more than anyone else is responsible for perfecting the codes of that expression. Similarly, Gary Giddins (1988) has argued for Armstrong's ability to communicate sexuality in *Rhapsody in Black and Blue* (1932). In this early film appearance Armstrong is part of a fantasy dreamed up by an impoverished black man who imagines himself the "King of Jazzmania." By royal decree, Armstrong and his band perform for the king who sits on a throne in hypermilitary royal garb. Standing on a bizarre set covered with soap bubbles and dressed in leopard skins, Armstrong mugs his way through vocal choruses of "Shine" and "I'll Be

Glad When You're Dead," but when he puts his trumpet to his lips, he becomes a different man. "He transcends the racist trappings by his indifference to every sling and arrow. . . . He's doing it not only with the magnificence of his music, but with his physical muscularity, his carriage, his boding sexuality ('comedian + danger'), the look in his eye" (Giddins 1988, 36).

Only a few years after the release of *Rhapsody in Black and Blue*, Virgil Thomson (1981) had kind words for Armstrong in a 1936 review of Hugues Panassié's *Le Jazz Hot*. Thomson wrote, "[Armstrong's] style of improvisation would seem to have combined the highest reaches of instrumental virtuosity with the most tensely disciplined melodic structure and the most spontaneous emotional expression, all of which in one man you must admit to be pretty rare" (Thomson 1981, 31). But Thomson added a curious historical comparison, suggesting that Armstrong resembled "the great *castrati* of the eighteenth century." Theodor Adorno, in one of his several attacks on jazz and popular music, translated Thomson's remark to support his own claim that jazz brings about the castration of the listener, who ought to be listening to the more manly music of someone like Arnold Schoenberg (Adorno 1981, 130). For Adorno, the obsequious buffoon with the trumpet was anything but phallic.

The American film industry made a variety of attempts to contain Armstrong's sexuality in the 1930s and 1940s. Seldom was he able to assert himself as unequivocally as he had in *Rhapsody in Black and Blue*, if only because of the inevitable toll that aging took on his youthful vigor. Even more importantly, he does not seem to have updated the techniques he learned as a young man for expressing masculinity *without* threatening certain white men in his audiences. If, in fact, black audiences in the 1930s saw sexual power alongside the minstrel foolishness, few would recognize it in later decades when the media's images of black masculinity began to change.

UNCLE TOM OR TRICKSTER?

Indeed, Armstrong's stage mannerisms lost their appeal for many when the civil rights movement made the old minstrel stereotypes untenable. Gerald Early (1989) argues that Armstrong had been a hero in the black community for several decades but that he lost a large portion of this audience when he played the King of the Zulus in New Orleans in 1949. When pictures of the trumpeter in blackface and a grass skirt were widely published, according to Early, many African Americans felt that Armstrong was "holding the entire race up to scorn" (1989, 296). Albert Murray (1976) has defended Armstrong against those who attacked him for appearing as King of the Zulus. Murray suggested that critics outside of New Orleans confused Mardi Gras blackface with minstrelsy and that the specific ritual function of the King of the Zulus was "to ridicule the whole idea of Mardi Gras and the lenten season" (Murray 1976, 190). For Murray, Armstrong was simply playing the trickster once again.

Nevertheless, Armstrong continued to sing his theme song, "When It's Sleepy Time Down South," with its references to "darkies" and "mammies falling on their knees," right up until the end of his life, in spite of pleas from civil rights groups. Barney Bigard (1986) tells of a revealing incident that took place during the shooting of a film with Bing Crosby. Armstrong was told to substitute the word "folks" for "darkies" in his performance of "When It's Sleepy Time."[4] Unwilling to change a lyric he had been performing nightly for decades, Armstrong left the set before the new words could be recorded. When he returned the next day, Bigard quotes him as saying to Crosby, "What do you want me to call those black sons-of-bitches this morning?" (Bigard 1986, 123–24).[5]

Even Armstrong's widely publicized denunciations of President Dwight D. Eisenhower and Arkansas governor Orval Faubus during the struggle to integrate Little Rock's public schools in 1957 did not entirely change his image, in spite of later attempts to give special significance to these statements. (Ralph J. Gleason, for example, begins a 1973 essay on Armstrong with the story of the Little Rock incident to make this the central, redeeming episode in a revised Armstrong biography [Gleason 1975, 33–35].) Shortly after Armstrong said that the American government could "go to hell" and that Eisenhower had "no guts," he was attacked by Sammy Davis, Jr., for appearing before segregated audiences (Collier 1983, 318). And in a notorious column following the fracas, Jim Bishop suggested that Armstrong's subsequent apology to Eisenhower may have been the result of a drop in ticket sales and "some empty tables at the Copacabana" (Bishop, *New York Journal-American* January 2, 1958:17). Bishop did not acknowledge, however, that Armstrong only apologized *after* Eisenhower took action by sending federal troops to Little Rock to enforce court-ordered integration. Although Charles Mingus gave Orval Faubus a permanent role in jazz history with his 1959 composition "Fables of Faubus," Mingus was one of many boppers and post-boppers who did not bother to stand beside Armstrong when he publicly denounced official racism.

There is no question that Armstrong had a reverse influence on the black jazz musicians who were born during the Harlem Renaissance and came of age in the late 1930s and early 1940s. Thinking of themselves as artists rather than entertainers, some of the boppers adopted the aloof stage presence of the classical musician and of more restrained jazz artists such as Teddy Wilson. Even when Dizzy Gillespie danced and performed pelvic thrusts before audiences, his repertoire of stage business overlapped in no way with Armstrong's: his bowing and mugging had an element of fun but not servility.[6] But for most of the boppers and for almost every jazz artist who has come of age since, a poker face has been obligatory. In his autobiography, however, Gillespie wrote, "If anybody asked me about a certain public image of him, handkerchief over his head, grinning in the face of white racism, I never hesitated to say I didn't like it. I didn't want the white man to expect me to allow the same things Louis did. Hell, I had my own way of 'Tomming'. . . . Later on, I began to recognize what I had considered Pops's grinning in the face of racism as his absolute refusal to let anything, even anger about racism, steal the joy from his life and erase his fantastic smile. Coming from a younger generation, I misjudged him" (Gillespie 1979, 295–96). Miles Davis (1989) expressed a similar ambivalence in his autobiography when he included a photograph of Armstrong alongside pictures of Beulah, Buckwheat, and Rochester, all characters who can be associated with demeaning stereotypes of African Americans. The caption reads, "Some of the images of black people that I would fight against throughout my career. I loved Satchmo, but I couldn't stand all that grinning he did." The opinion of an older trumpeter, the articulate Rex Stewart (1972), is also worth quoting in this context:

> Some musicians consciously resent Louis' antebellum Uncle Tomism. The youngsters object to his ever-present grin, which they interpret as Tomming. This I feel is a misunderstanding. No matter where Louis had been brought up, his natural ebullience and warmth would have emerged just as creative and strong. This is not to say that even today, in an unguarded moment, a trace of the old environment, a fleeting lapse into the jargon of his youth will make some people cringe with embarrassment. (42–43)

Acknowledging that Armstrong recorded inferior or highly commercial material at many moments throughout his career, Stearns (1956) argues that he was consistently able to rise above it with irony. Stearns singles out the 1931 recording of "All of Me" in which Armstrong parodies a British accent with the line, "I can't get on, *dee-ah*, without you!" On the one hand, according to Stearns, Armstrong is too embarrassed by the lame lyrics to sing them straight. "At the same time, by changes in the melody and by unusual accents in the rhythm, he makes the listener suddenly realize that he, Armstrong, is in full, double-edged control of the musical situation, embroidering beautifully on the stereotyped mask, and enjoying the whole affair hugely. In a word: he is the master—not of just the music but also of a complex and ironic attitude, a rare, honest way of looking at life" (Stearns 1956, 318–19). Stearns anticipates the comments of Ralph Ellison (1964), who placed Armstrong in the tradition of the trickster: "Armstrong's clownish license and intoxicating powers are almost Elizabethan; he takes liberties with kings, queens and presidents; emphasizes the physicality of his music with sweat, spittle and facial contortions; he performs the magical feat of making romantic melody issue from a throat of gravel; and some few years ago was recommending to all and sundry his personal physic, 'Pluto Water,' as a purging way to health, happiness and international peace" (Ellison 1964, 67). Both Stearns and Ellison look forward to the more extensive discussion of African and African American tricksters in Henry Louis Gates, Jr.'s *Signifying Monkey: A Theory of Afro-American Literary Criticism* (1988). Gates mentions Armstrong only in passing, but he observes that "there are so many examples of Signifyin(g) in jazz that one could write a formal history of its development on this basis alone" (Gates 1988, 63).

In his scrupulous reading of Armstrong's several autobiographical statements, William Kenney (1991) has found evidence of signifying and even protest. Perhaps the most convincing example of how Armstrong "carefully orchestrated his story, creating edited versions of himself" (38), is the account of his feelings for Bix Beiderbecke that appears in his second autobiography, *Satchmo: My Life in New Orleans* (1954). After pledging his immense admiration for Beiderbecke, even calling him godlike, Armstrong adds, "Whenever we saw him our faces shone with joy and happiness, but long periods would pass when we did not see him at all" (209). For Kenney, this passage shows Armstrong slipping his own message past the ghostwriters and editors who controlled texts such as *Satchmo: My Life in New Orleans*. "He keeps his distance by offering a vaudeville stereotype of 'our' greetings to a third-party observer. At the same time, he indicates that while in Beiderbecke's physical presence, 'we' treated him respectfully, but, not 'seeing' him for long periods of time, 'we' were not obliged to pay him respect" (Kenney 1991, 51). Kenney also finds reasons for Armstrong's decision to reach out to popular audiences rather than to the small but discriminating coterie of jazz aficionados. For one thing, Armstrong had begun to worry as far back as 1928 that he would not be able to endure the physical hardships of playing the trumpet every day of his life at a virtuoso level. Lip problems would plague him throughout his life. Armstrong also recalled the fate of his mentor King Oliver, an excellent musical technician and a savvy businessman, but in no way an entertainer who played to the crowd. Oliver died in poverty. As a result, Kenney reasons, Armstrong consciously chose to become the showman who would dance, sing, joke, mug, and perform the popular hits of the day. In 1936 he began a lifelong association with Joe Glaser, the manager to whom he entrusted almost every aspect of his career. At least since the 1920s, Glaser had been urging the trumpeter to rely on showmanship rather than musical proficiency (Kenney 1991, 54). The changes brought on by Glaser may explain why the Armstrong in photographs from the 1920s with King Oliver and Fletcher Henderson seems so unfamiliar. As Stanley Crouch (1979) has written, "There we see an arrogant, surly young man who seemed to think himself handsome and was not to be fucked with" (45).

Reading the Films

In most of the Hollywood films in which Armstrong appeared, he is a marginal figure. In films such as *Artists & Models* (1937), *Jam Session* (1944), *Here Comes the Groom* (1951), *The Beat Generation* (1959), and *Hello, Dolly!* (1969), he is set off from the plot in a single musical number so that he has virtually no interaction with the principal characters. In the Mae West vehicle, *Every Day's a Holiday* (1938), his character does not even have a name; he is simply a street cleaner who wordlessly enlists in the campaign of a political figure supported by West and who then leads a parade performing Hoagy Carmichael's "Jubilee." Sometimes he even appears to be outside the film. Throughout *High Society* (1956) and at the conclusion of *When the Boys Meet the Girls* (1966), he narrates the story with direct address to the audience. When he does play a role within a film's narrative, he is invariably cast as a trumpet player, even if it means awkwardly adjusting the nature of his role. In *Glory Alley* (1952) he is "Shadow," the trainer for the boxer hero Socks Barbarrosa and also the guide for the boxer's blind antagonist, "The Judge." Somehow, the film makes trumpet playing relate to both of these occupations. In *Cabin in the Sky* (1943), Armstrong is the only musician in a group of six devils in the Hotel Hades, none of whom has any comparable distinguishing characteristics (with perhaps the exception of one devil played by Willie Best who sleeps through most of the sequence). It is also safe to say that the racial imagery in these films has not aged well. Joe Glaser seized any opportunity to find work for Armstrong, and if Glaser made no effort to ask if the movies were good for the Negro people, neither did Armstrong.

In his second full-length film,[7] Armstrong has a speaking part in *Pennies from Heaven* (1936) as Henry, a musician hired to play in the "Haunted House Cafe." Henry and his men are invited to perform by Larry Poole (Bing Crosby), a self-styled "wandering minstrel" with no cash but with hopes of earning some by selling shares in his restaurant before it has opened. Larry has no personal need for money in this depression era fantasy, but he is determined to make a home for a young girl whom he has effectively adopted along with her grandfather. When Larry tells Henry that the musicians can have a 10 percent share in the restaurant, the trumpeter responds that there seven men are in the group, and "none of us know how to divide up ten percent by seven, so if you could just only make it seven percent." When Larry says, "Henry, you've got yourself a deal," Armstrong responds, "Thank you, Mr. Poole. I told them cats you'd do the right thing."[8] In the following scene, however, the film does not persist in caricaturing Armstrong as stupid. "Gramps" has hopes of selling chicken dinners at the Haunted House Cafe by raising the birds in the backyard. To his chagrin, the two chickens in his yard have not multiplied. It is Henry/Armstrong who points out that neither of the two birds is a rooster. Knowing that his job is dependent on the success of Gramps's meal plan, Henry then arranges for his musicians to supply Gramps with chickens.

Armstrong's big moment in *Pennies from Heaven* is his performance of "The Skeleton in the Closet," which he sings and plays with the usual gusto. Although the camera regularly shows the trumpeter in erect poses, even emphasizing his phallicism with high-contrast shadows of the trumpet pointed up at stark angles, the scene can be accused of activating racist stereotypes of the timorous black, easily terrified by graveyard images. When a dancer in a skeleton costume appears on stage, Armstrong's eyes bulge as he strikes a pose of trepidation. Those critics looking for signifying in this scene might note that Armstrong's reaction seems underplayed in comparison to the usual medley of exaggerated expressions that cross his face. They might also observe that his reactions have an aura of parody, perhaps allowing him some distance from the racist material. This first major appearance in a Hollywood film shows that Armstrong's mannerisms were already suited to anyone wishing to argue that he was working against the grain. It is possible that Bing Crosby, with whom Armstrong had already established a relationship, may have encouraged or at least tolerated the trumpeter's attempts to take liberties with the scripted material.

The end of Armstrong's sequence, however, is less ambiguous in its evocation of racist stereotypes. Shortly after "The Skeleton in the Closet," a sheriff enters the restaurant accompanied by three farmers. One of them points at the band and shouts, "There's the guys that stole our chickens." Armstrong jumps headfirst out a window, saying, "Look out! The law, gentlemen." The extent to which Armstrong signifies in *Pennies from Heaven* is very much in the eye of the beholder and is hopelessly complicated by backward glances through the distorting lens of history. And as Stanley Crouch (1995) points out, Armstrong's humor is only problematic when contemporary racial sensibilities are invoked without regard to other contexts.

> I am not blind to racist stereotypes nor do I misapprehend the limits of Hollywood conventions, but it is also important in discussions of this sort not to remove Armstrong from the context of styles of humor which Negroes laughed at and which they *still* laugh at (that is, if you are aware of the remarkable similarities between the images in the world of classic minstrelsy—lazy, shiftless, dumb, buffoon, easily conned, roughneck, and so on—and those of black-written and black-directed music video satire). It is also essential—once we acknowledge the influence of Negroes on the conventions of American humor—to remember that the eye-rolling, hustling, and conning of Groucho Marx would play very differently to contemporary audiences if he had been a black comedian, as would the pomposity and imbecility of Laurel and Hardy, the drunkenness and determination not to work on the part of W. C. Fields, and so on. In short, much of what we consider "clean" white humor would be seen as demeaning and derogatory if the performers weren't white. (2)

Artists & Models was directed by Raoul Walsh and released in 1937, but the one production number with Armstrong was directed by a young Vincente Minnelli, six years before he would direct Armstrong again in *Cabin in the Sky*. Most of the number is dominated by Martha Raye in dusky body makeup designed to give her a look more consistent with the stylized Harlem set populated by a large group of black actors and dancers. The sequence begins with a group of white "G-Men" arriving with machine guns in search of "Public Melody Number One," who is eventually revealed to be Armstrong. In this typically Hollywoodian conflation of violence and music, the "corrupting" aspects of jazz culture are playfully compared to the activities of gangsters. More importantly, the phallicism of Armstrong's trumpet is uniquely emphasized through its associ-

36. Louis Armstrong with a blacked-up Martha Raye in *Artists and Models*
(1937, Paramount). Museum of Modern Art Film Stills Archive.

ation with a gangster's gun. In Martha Raye's lyrics, the Armstrong figure
is explicitly compared to famous gangsters: "Al Capone's a bundle of joy /
Dillinger's a teacher's pet / Gattling's gun is only a toy / Compared to a
note shot from a hot cornet."[9] This acknowledgment and exaggeration
of Armstrong's phallicism was daring in its time and probably could not
have been filmed after race became more of a hot-button issue during
the 1940s.

After Raye has compared him to Dillinger and Capone, Armstrong
slowly emerges from the wings preceded auspiciously by his shadow.
When he finally appears, he is attired in Hollywood's image of the overdressed gangster with a double-breasted suit and a bowler hat. With a
stylized look of menace on his face, he shouts to the crowd, "Get under
cover, you rhythm rascals, and run!" To the white men with their machine guns he sings, "Now look here, Mr. Hoover and your G-Men." Although he smiles and sings at other moments in the number, his dominant style of self-presentation is the mock-gangster pose. Meanwhile,
Raye's body language is especially suggestive in the sequence, her dark
skin presumably giving her license to engage in trucking, pecking, and

other exaggerated gestures from black vernacular dance. As she moves and dances, her legs are almost always spread as widely as her tight skirt allows. According to Thomas Cripps, southern distributors raised objections to the interactions of Raye and Armstrong—although there is seldom even eye contact between the two, their proximity may have been too much for those devoted to racial segregation (Cripps 10). Undoubtedly, the fear of a sexual rapport between Raye and Armstrong was increased by the trumpeter's threatening posture, no matter how ironically the gangster/musician analogy was meant to be taken. A few months later, in *Every Day's a Holiday,* Armstrong was also able to inject a certain amount of sexual expression into his scene with some deft dancing in front of a parade.

In *Going Places* (1938), Armstrong was stripped of all sexual menace whatsoever. He did, however, have one of his largest acting roles as Gabriel, the groom for a racehorse named Jeepers Creepers, to which he sings the song of the same name. Rather than discharging his sexual energies in the proximity of a white woman, Armstrong is here asked to play and sing the title song to the horse. Jeepers Creepers the horse is known for his speed as well as for his hostility to riders. The plot, based on the Broadway show *The Hottentot,* revolves around the idea that the horse becomes so fond of Armstrong's rendition of "Jeepers Creepers" that he will submit to a jockey only when he hears the music. At the finale, Dick Powell, playing a romantic hero with no experience as a jockey, rides the horse to victory while the trumpeter and his entire band drive along the course of the steeplechase playing the horse's favorite song. In one of the more inexplicable musical numbers in the film, Gabriel/Armstrong leads an orchestra and sings "Mutiny in the Nursery," eventually joined by vocalist Maxine Sullivan and a host of black singers and dancers. Although Dick Powell and his costar Anita Louise later join in the singing, the film offers no explanation for a song about nursery rhymes, except perhaps to associate children's ditties with the infantilized black characters. The concept of an obstreperous horse fond of music was probably inspired by Howard Hawks's *Bringing Up Baby* (1938), in which a leopard called Baby responds positively to the song, "I Can't Give You Anything But Love, Baby." Similarly, the combination of African American music and horse racing was undoubtedly motivated by the success in 1937 of *A Day at the Races,* in which a horse responded to another trickster figure, Harpo Marx. In the earlier films, however, no black character was ever referred to as "Uncle Tom," the name that the film's two unsavory characters (Allen Jenkins and Harold Huber) use to address Gabriel.

Although he receives fourth billing in the opening credits, Armstrong appears for less than six minutes in director Vincente Minnelli's *Cabin in the Sky* (1943).[10] This is the only film in which Duke Ellington and Armstrong both performed, although they are never in the same frame together. While Ellington appears as "Duke Ellington," the leader of a famous orchestra, Armstrong plays one of several devils in a scene at the "Idea Department" in the "Hotel Hades." Along with other black actors with small horns in their coiffures, he contemplates strategies for winning the soul of Little Joe, whose soul "The Lord" and "Lucifer, Jr." are competing to win. The sequence begins with Armstrong playing an unaccompanied solo on his trumpet until Lucifer, Jr. (Rex Ingram) bursts in and shouts, "Stop that noise!" Putting their heads together, the devils decide on a plan ultimately devised by "The Trumpeter," as Armstrong is called in the credits. The Trumpeter also insists that it was his idea to offer the apple to Eve in the Garden of Eden. After the brief sequence in hell, Armstrong is seen no more. In addition to his trumpet, Armstrong is distinguished from Lucifer, Jr. and the other four devils by his jive talk. Unlike the others, Armstrong uses phrases like "Well, all reet," and ends sentences with the vocative "man."

In his article on *Cabin in the Sky*, Naremore (1992) makes an intriguing connection with the work of James Agee, who gave the film a negative notice when he wrote the unsigned review in *Time*. Basically, Agee objected to the demeaning of distinguished Negro actors, treated by the studio as "Sambo-style entertainers." The next year Agee would publish an article, "Pseudo-Folk," in the *Partisan Review* in which he denounced swing as a corruption of the true jazz produced by Negroes, "our richest contemporary source of folk art, and our best people en bloc." Like Rudi Blesh and many in the revivalist camp of the 1940s, Agee specifically cited the declining quality of Armstrong's work, but he also found evidence of the corruption of pure black folk art in Duke Ellington's slick compositions for big band, the "pseudo-savage" dancing of Katherine Dunham's troupe, and Paul Robeson's performance of Earl Robinson and John Latouche's "esthetically execrable 'Ballad for Americans.'" Naremore observes, "Although he never mentioned *Cabin in the Sky*, he [Agee] could hardly have come closer to describing it. Both Armstrong and Ellington were featured in the movie, and . . . both Dunham and Latouche had contributed to the original Broadway show" (Naremore 1992, 105). For Agee, as well as for many inside and outside the revivalist camp, Armstrong's participation in Hollywood's pseudo-folklore was consistent with his embrace of industrialized popular music. But like Ellington, who was able to overcome the naive and racist dichotomies in *Cabin in the Sky* (although not in the opinion of Agee), Armstrong's exuberance and humor consistently place him outside the film's folklorist projects.

In 1944 and 1945 Armstrong appeared in three films, always in short performance sequences that could easily be excised in communities where sexualized black faces were not welcome on movie screens. In all three, *Atlantic City, Jam Session,* and *Pillow to Post,* his sexuality was explicit in ways that it had never been in earlier films. In *Jam Session* he plays a singing, trumpet-playing bartender who performs "I Can't Give You Anything But Love" to a line of elegantly dressed young black women. There is no question that his character would like to do exactly what the song says. In *Atlantic City* he performs with the lithe, picture-perfect Dorothy Dandridge, who is unrestrained in her erotic body language just before Armstrong enters the stage show at the Apollo Theater. As was not the case in his interactions with Martha Raye in *Artists & Models,* Armstrong appears fully cognizant of Dandridge's sexual presence; even as he holds his horn out straight, he cocks his eyes to watch Dandridge as she dances to his left. When Armstrong sings "Ain't Misbehavin,'" he addresses Dandridge directly with lines like "Your kisses are worth waiting for." The film also allows Armstrong to dip into his bag of tricksterisms; at one point during his trumpet solo, his eyes bulging with impertinence, he stoops down to blow his horn directly into a camera that seems to be placed at the level of his ankles. For a few moments the bell of his horn fills the screen.

In *Pillow to Post,* Armstrong again performs with Dandridge, this time at a roadhouse where she sings "Whatcha Say?" The number is staged so that Dandridge addresses the trumpeter with lyrics such as "Do I get that little kiss? Must you let me down like this?" Armstrong mimes shyness as the singer saunters closer, finally answering her questions by shouting his trademark expression, "Well, all reet!" Dandridge then sighs, "Oh, baby," and moves even closer. Armstrong feigns innocence and indignantly snorts, "Look out here, girl, don't you start that stuff here." He then smiles broadly before he blows the final high notes that end the number. At this time Hollywood was working much harder to contain black male sexuality than black female sexuality. In 1943, for example, the beautiful young Lena Horne was paired with Eddie "Rochester" Anderson (*Cabin in the Sky*) and Bill "Bojangles" Robinson (*Stormy Weather*), both of them long past the age when they could compete with her as leading men. But if *Pillow to Post* is any indication, the effort to repress black male sexuality was not as extreme as it had been just a few years earlier. What makes Armstrong's brief appearance in *Pillow to Post* especially interesting in this context is the presence of Willie Best, a black comedian busy during the 1930s and 1940s, who was probably responsible for the phrase, "to get the willies" (Crouch 1995, 2). Best is featured in *Pillow to Post* as "Lucille," the porter at the motel complex where the action takes place. Like Stepin Fetchit, Best played the most extreme stereotype of the shiftless, shuffling, slow-talking Negro. Although he makes a passing reference to "me and my girlfriend," we never see him in the company of a woman. His feminization is so overdetermined that at one point he even says that his two brothers also have female names. Compared to Willie Best's Lucille, the Armstrong of *Pillow to Post* is a strutting satyr. Although Armstrong and Lucille are never in the same scene, the film does implicitly pair the two black performers when Lucille plays reveille on a bugle. On the one hand, it is possible that Armstrong's familiarity to the mass audience made him less threatening and less in need of the drastic desexualization inflicted upon the black porter Lucille. On the other hand, the filmmakers may have regarded Armstrong's phallicism as problematic after all and consequently chose to pair him with an absurdly unthreatening black male. A similar choice may have been made three years earlier when Best danced ineffectually in two of the three-minute "soundies" that Armstrong filmed in 1942. Best was also paired with Armstrong in the Hotel Hades sequence in *Cabin in the Sky*—again, some racial logic in the minds of filmmakers must have required that the semisomnolent Best should balance out the exuberant Armstrong. Best defuses the phallicism of the trumpeter's erect image by appearing ineffectual, flaccid, often horizontal. Thus, it is Best, not Armstrong, who in the three-minute "Shine" gazes at the row of well-dressed, light-skinned black women, designated as desirable with both class and racial markers. The possibility that Armstrong's trumpet may symbolize something besides a trumpet is in a sense concealed by the antics of Best.

In the brief period that separated *Pillow to Post* (1945) from *New Orleans* (1947) and *A Song Is Born* (1948), the discourse of jazz changed drastically. As I argued in chapter 3, Armstrong suddenly became useful when filmmakers began to accept arguments floated in the jazz press about the music being art. By casting a certified genius from jazz history, both *New Orleans* and *A Song Is Born* achieved their goal of glorifying the white swing musicians that Americans had already embraced. Armstrong is applauded by royalty in *New Orleans* and associated with the generation of innovators who "took a reet jungle beat and brought it to Basin

Street" in *A Song Is Born*. But as the representative of an earlier stage of the art form called jazz, his presence validates the primacy of Woody Herman, Tommy Dorsey, and Benny Goodman, musicians from a more "advanced" stage of the art.

Shortly after *New Orleans,* jazz and swing experienced a large decline in popularity. Following a brief moment as an artist in the movies, Armstrong was no longer needed to affirm that Americans were listening to the right music when popular taste embraced styles with fewer jazz inflections. In *The Strip* (1951), Armstrong's next film, no grandiose claims are made for the trumpeter in particular or for jazz in general as had been the case in his two earlier films. In fact, Armstrong and a band of canonized jazz greats are taken for granted and frequently ignored throughout the movie. *The Strip* is a film noir, complete with a flashback structure and the kind of generic jazz score that was becoming typical for the genre.[11] Armstrong performs several times as the leader of the house band at "Fluff's Dixieland," a posh club with a spacious bandstand and dancing waiters. The film stars a 31-year-old Mickey Rooney in one of his early attempts to transcend the eternal juvenile who played opposite Judy Garland. As Stan, Rooney plays a drummer who takes a job with Armstrong's band, but not because he wants to play with Armstrong, Earl Hines, Jack Teagarden, and Barney Bigard, all of whom appear in the film; rather, he is interested in getting closer to a young woman who works as a dancer at the club. After the brief moment in the late 1940s when jazz was given a history, an aesthetics, and some degree of legitimacy, *The Strip* returns to a culture where the music is strictly for good times, providing at best a little solace now and then. Armstrong, who had been working with a New Orleans–style sextet for the past five years, was now a fixture in the revivalist camp, at least as far as the film is concerned—Fluff (William Demarest) refers to him as "Mr. Dixieland himself." Although he is frequently on camera as the plot develops, Armstrong and his band are confined within the musical numbers. Neither he, Teagarden, Hines, nor Bigard have any lines. Otherwise, this Armstrong is much like the one we know except that he has no control over who plays in his group. Stan is retained by Fluff, with no sign that he has consulted Armstrong (or his manager). At the end, Stan's would-be girlfriend dies, but the drummer finds solace in music, beating the drums with increasing conviction as the music of Armstrong and the band swells under the closing titles.

In *Glory Alley,* Armstrong is also a dispenser of solace for white protagonists, playing another of the strange hybrid roles that combined his

37. Mickey Rooney sits in with Jack Teagarden, Louis Armstrong, Barney Bigard, and Earl Hines in *The Strip* (1951, MGM). Jerry Ohlinger's Movie Material Store, Inc.

public persona with a diegetic character. In this case, he plays Shadow, "the best trainer in the business," according to boxer Socks Barbarrosa (Ralph Meeker). Why the boxer's trainer plays a trumpet is never explained. Nor is the nature of Armstrong's second job as the apparent servant and guide for the Judge (Kurt Kasznar), a cantankerous blind man who is the father of Socks's love interest, a cabaret dancer played by Leslie Caron. Armstrong smiles a good deal as he escorts the Judge, and he is almost invariably given demeaning lines:

> **Judge:** She could have been a great ballerina. You know what a ballerina is, Shadow?
> **Shadow:** More or less, Judge.

Armstrong's first musical number takes place in the awkward space of a barroom frequented by the main characters, who smile benignly as the trumpeter walks among them singing the title song. When Armstrong switches to trumpet, the protagonist wanders to the other side of the bar and his voice-over obscures most of the trumpet solo. The film offers little space for the phallic Armstrong or the trickster Armstrong.

Although his scenes are brief, Armstrong was endowed with real phallic power when he appeared in two biopics, *The Glenn Miller Story* (1954) and *The Five Pennies* (1959). In both he is confined once again to night-club sequences, largely isolated from the films' plots. In *The Glenn Miller Story* the hero interacts just this once with a black artist, as if Armstrong were preparing him for the sexual initiation of his wedding night. No longer identified with art, Armstrong is now brought in for his sexuality, however veiled this signification may be. As I pointed out in chapter 2, Armstrong appears in a surprisingly similar scene in the Red Nichols biopic, *The Five Pennies*. Once again the hero and his girlfriend go up to Harlem to hear Armstrong, and once again the white musician gains sexual maturity after he plays with the black master. Armstrong's brazen treatment of Nichols in the subsequent scene is especially remarkable in light of his 1957 attacks on Eisenhower and Faubus. It is as if his outspoken political statements had spilled over into *The Five Pennies,* the first film he made after his highly publicized remarks on integration.

Later in *The Five Pennies,* Armstrong appears in another nightclub sequence, this time after Nichols has become established as a jazzman and has brought his young daughter to the club. Much in the spirit of the television variety programs in which both Armstrong and Kaye were at that time regulars, the two entertainers sing an elaborate version of "When the Saints Go Marching In" that associates jazz with classical music much more playfully than had been the case in the earnest *New Orleans.*

> Nichols: Do ya dig Rachmaninoff?
> Armstrong: On and off.
> Nichols: Rimsky?
> Armstrong: Of course a-koff!
> Nichols: Ravel and Gustav Mahler?
> Armstrong: Yeah, but don't forget Fats Waller.

The mid-1940s' discourses of jazz as art have been replaced by the more familiar tradition of jazzing the classics, though here it seems more facetious than conciliatory.

In *The Five Pennies,* Armstrong functions primarily to validate Nichols's importance as a jazz artist. More importantly, he is on hand as evidence of the white protagonist's tolerant attitude toward blacks. At least since Jim in *Huckleberry Finn* (1885), a black companion indicates that the white hero has an independent spirit and a capacity to look beyond a person's color in spite of what society might think. These are the typical qualities of the independent hero of American myth who was and still is a staple of American entertainment (Ray 1985, 107).

38. Barrett Deems, Billy Kyle, Louis Armstrong, Edmond Hall, Trummy Young, and Arvell Shaw perform for Bing Crosby's pleasure in *High Society* (1956, MGM). Museum of Modern Art Film Stills Archive.

Much the same can be said of Bing Crosby, who befriended Armstrong at least as early as 1930 when Crosby was in Hollywood filming *The King of Jazz* and making regular trips to Culver City, California, to hear Armstrong perform at Frank Sebastian's New Cotton Club. Although by all accounts the men shared a genuine friendship, the conventions of the film industry invariably placed Armstrong in the inferior position as the servile Negro in need of a white patron. Certainly this is what was dramatized in *Pennies from Heaven* and two decades later in *High Society,* when Dexter (Crosby) brings Armstrong and his group to Newport for a jazz festival staged by Dexter (not by George Wein). Dexter is also in Newport for the wedding of his former wife Samantha (Grace Kelly) to the social-climbing George (John Lund), but Dexter will be remarried to her at the finale just as in *The Philadelphia Story* (1940) on which the film is based.

High Society revives some of the discourse of jazz as art, but not, as in *New Orleans* and *A Song is Born,* to bring white big bands in through the back door. Jazz was no longer a popular music in 1956, but it was developing the elite following that it retains today. The jazz festival at Newport that allows Armstrong entry into the film had begun in 1954 and was a

39. Danny Kaye with Armstrong and Danny Barcelona in *The Five Pennies* (1959, Paramount). Jerry Ohlinger's Movie Material Store, Inc.

popular affair by the time *High Society* was released. The Newport Jazz Festival was one of many signs that a more affluent audience was taking the music seriously as an alternative to the increasingly infantilized music of the popular mainstream. At the same time, the jazz lover could be portrayed as more down-to-earth than those snobs who declared their preference for classical music. (Elvis Presley's denunciation of pretentious intellectual jazz fans in *Jailhouse Rock* was still a year away.) Dexter/ Crosby is clearly on the winning side of this argument when his ex-wife tells him why she left him: "You could have become a serious composer or a diplomat or anything you wanted to be. And what have you become? A jukebox hero!" When Armstrong and Crosby together perform "Now You Has Jazz," their easy grace and humor reveal that Dexter has become something much more than a "jukebox hero."

At least for the white audiences of 1956, Dexter's proximity to Armstrong probably indicated that the white protagonist had *character*, a trait that jazz has been loaning out to American movie heroes in much more recent years, for example, to Clint Eastwood as the Secret Service agent in *In the Line of Fire* (1993), who relaxes by listening to Miles Davis records and playing jazz piano. Jazz has been the emblem of a special sensibility for equally unlikely characters, including Gene Hackman in *The Conversation* (1974), Warren Beatty in *Heaven Can Wait* (1978), and Dennis Hopper in *Backtrack* (1989), all of whom play jazz on a saxophone to express their inner feelings. In *The Fabulous Baker Boys* (1989), we know that Jeff Bridges is the more sensitive brother, at least in part because he has a picture of John Coltrane on his wall and because he plays jazz in a cellar with black musicians. In several of his films, Woody Allen has specifically used Louis Armstrong's music to bring depth to his characters. At the climax of *Manhattan* (1979), for example, the Allen protagonist lists Armstrong's recording of "Potato Head Blues" as one of the things that makes life worth living. Similarly, in 1994 no less than three Hollywood films used photographs of canonical beboppers to reveal a character's sensibilities. In *Renaissance Man* (1994), Danny DeVito has a photograph of Dizzy Gillespie on his wall; in *Wolf* (1994), a picture of Bud Powell sits on Jack Nicholson's desk; and in *Disclosure* (1994), the camera scans past an early photograph of Dexter Gordon on a wall in Michael Douglas's home. The audience is thus informed that all three men are sensitive and unconventional, even though there are no other references to jazz in any of these films. In *High Society*, Bing Crosby was one of the first of many slightly offbeat American film heroes to use jazz in general and Armstrong in particular as evidence of the subtleties in their souls.

Questions of art and jazz return with a vengeance in director Martin Ritt's *Paris Blues* (1961). If, as I argued in chapter 5, Duke Ellington and Billy Strayhorn were able to transform the film with the music they wrote for its final moments, then Armstrong becomes an even more problematic figure than he had been for jazz critics of the previous decades. In *Paris Blues*, Armstrong receives fourth billing for a part that is rather small but that carries much symbolic importance. The action of the film effectively begins with his arrival in Paris and ends with his departure. As Wild Man Moore, Armstrong's face is first seen on a poster in a train station in Paris where wildly cheering crowds have come to greet him. Also in the crowd is Ram Bowen (Paul Newman), the American jazz trombonist living in Paris who has come to show the trumpeter some music he has written. Moore/Armstrong tells Bowen/Newman that he looks good and suggests that Paris must agree with him, "What is it, the chicks or the wine?" He also says that he has heard good things about Bowen's performances in Paris and that some day he will drop by and "blow ya outta the joint." Not since *New Orleans* had an American feature film acknowledged the adoration that Armstrong had long been receiving in Europe, and in no previous film had another musician asked for his expert opinion. Armstrong appears comfortable in what was for him an unusual role—he brings good humor as well as authority to his scenes with Newman. It is also important, as the audience later learns, that Moore has agreed to take Bowen's music to René Bernard, apparently a grand old man of classical music in France.

Later on, when Wild Man Moore brings his orchestra to Bowen's club to challenge the trombonist and his sidemen, Armstrong stages a series of cutting contests with each member of the band. Although jazz enthusiasts are well aware of this ritual, it has seldom been dramatized in a fiction film. Without suppressing the phallic/aggressive aspect of the cutting contest, Armstrong brings a spirit of generosity to the practice, consistently registering joy as he engages each musician. Nevertheless, the script for *Paris Blues* is profoundly suspicious of any serious claims for

40. Paul Newman with Armstrong in *Paris Blues* (1961, United Artists). Jerry Ohlinger's Movie Material Store, Inc.

jazz. As I suggested in chapter 5, the film evokes arguments about jazz and classical music, but it articulates them rather incoherently: a "serious" European composer (Bernard) is held up as the final arbiter of music written by a modernist jazz artist; the modernist jazz artist (Bowen) writes in the most advanced style of Duke Ellington but usually performs 1930s songs such as "Mood Indigo" and "Sophisticated Lady" that were seldom programmed by younger jazz artists in the early 1960s (as opposed to what younger artists have played in the 1980s and 1990s); to meet with the "serious" European composer, the modernist jazz artist must seek the help of an older jazz artist who plays in a decidedly premodern style; and as the modernist artist steels himself for a life of total devotion to art, the face of the older artist is covered over as if to symbolize the eclipse of "jazz" behind the forthcoming work of a composer who will stay in Paris to study theory, harmony, and counterpoint and presumably write something other than jazz. At worst, the film's idealization of a white hero alongside its denigration of Ellington and Armstrong is an especially insidious form of Hollywood racism. On the other hand, the idea that the white artist is the inheritor and resuscitator of a used-up tradition associated with Louis Armstrong is simply a more contemporary version of the same story that was implied in *New Orleans* and *A Song Is Born*.

Except for a brief appearance with Barbra Streisand in *Hello, Dolly!* (1969), Armstrong's last film was *A Man Called Adam* (1966). Sammy Davis, Jr., plays the trumpeter/singer Adam Johnson. As "Sweet Daddy" Willie Ferguson, an elderly trumpeter/singer very much like himself, Armstrong receives second billing in the credits, the highest listing he ever received in a fiction film. Unable to afford a hotel room, Ferguson has been temporarily moved into Adam's apartment by Nelson (Ossie Davis), the owner of a jazz club where Ferguson is performing. When Adam returns home drunk after petulantly and prematurely canceling a tour of club dates, he is outraged to find Ferguson there. Without acknowledging that he even knows who Ferguson is, Adam unceremoniously jettisons him into the hallway. The old man is rescued by the arrival of Nelson and Claudia (Cicely Tyson), a young, black, socially conscious woman, who is also Ferguson's granddaughter. The next morning Adam apologizes to the older trumpeter and assures him that he knows who he is. Accepting the apology, Ferguson makes a pitiful attempt at small talk, asking if Adam has ever heard of "Tree Top Jones." Adam replies, "Oh, of course. I play his 78s every morning before breakfast." Not catching the irony, Ferguson comments, "Yeah, he's a killer." When Adam's agent enters the apartment a few moments later, Adam accompanies him from the room while Ferguson is in midsentence.

Much of the old vocabulary of the war between the ancients and the moderns of the 1940s returns in several sequences, including one in which Adam sarcastically associates Armstrong with "true jazz." Finding Ferguson sitting alone by himself at a party, Adam strikes up a conversation. The old trumpeter says that he feels uncomfortable among a youthful crowd, adding "seems like the people don't know what to say to me." Adam tells him, "Maybe it's just that they don't know what to say to a genius." Almost immediately after this encounter, Adam attacks Nelson for booking the Armstrong character: "What are you doing to that old man over there, huh? You know what you're going to do? You're going to break his heart, you and your 'true jazz.' You know what's going to happen, Nelson? He's going to play a while. He's going to be in. Then the novelty's going to wear off. The oddity's going to be gone. He won't be able to go back home again in the rice fields, and that sweet, nice old man's gonna be bumming drinks at bars up in Harlem."

Although Armstrong's character is given a degree of self-consciousness in *A Man Called Adam,* the trickster Armstrong never emerges except when he is performing on the bandstand. In his performance of "Back o' Town Blues," Ferguson/Armstrong exchanges mock insults with his trombonist, Tyree Glenn. When the trumpeter sings, "I had a woman," Glenn exclaims, "So what! I had five!" Then, after Armstrong sings the line, "She had to run around," he adds as an aside to Glenn, "Like your daddy." This playful, confident performer is barely compatible with the tragic figure we later see sitting alone at a party feeling sorry for himself. Neither Armstrong the trickster nor Armstrong the artist have any place in a film that portrays the "true" black artist as introverted and self-destructive rather than ribald and outgoing. The film uses Willie Ferguson primarily for pathos—a slightly ridiculous old man whose smiling and clowning are transparently obsequious. The bitter, "tell-it-like-it-is" dialogue written for Adam becomes all the more topical thanks to Ferguson's pitiful attempts at humor and reconciliation. Nevertheless, Armstrong shows previously untapped resources as an actor in *A Man Called Adam.* The quality of Armstrong's performance adds an extra dimension to the pathos of the film and, like *Paris Blues,* shows Armstrong's ability to play the kind of serious role that never would have been offered to him in his youth.

41. The tragic Armstrong with Sammy Davis, Jr., in *A Man Called Adam* (1966, Embassy). Jerry Ohlinger's Movie Material Store, Inc.

"How 'Critical' Is It?"

The received wisdom about Armstrong was probably best expressed by Clive James in his *Fame in the Twentieth Century,* a series of BBC programs that were widely shown in the United States on PBS in 1993. Over scenes from *Rhapsody in Black and Blue* and the soundie, "When It's Sleepy Time Down South," James makes the following judgments:

> Louis Armstrong's brilliant trumpet solos were works of art from a sweat-shop. The works of art were preserved on classic records, but white men controlled the record business and stole the money. To stay solvent, the artist had to become an entertainer. Louis Armstrong the revolutionary modern musician turned into Satchmo the showman. . . . Armstrong de-tested the jungle bunny outfits. He didn't like playing Uncle Tom either. But it was the price of fame, and fame was the road to freedom.

It could just as easily be argued that Armstrong never thought of himself as an artist. As early as 1924, the trumpeter was singing and clowning with Fletcher Henderson's band in New York. (Because Henderson did not like his singing style, however, Armstrong's vocal breaks can be briefly heard at the end of one of the two surviving takes of "Everybody

42. The trickster Armstrong with Tyree Glenn and John Benjamin Brown in *A Man Called Adam*. Jerry Ohlinger's Movie Material Store, Inc.

Loves My Baby" [1924] but nowhere else in his recorded output with Henderson.) Crowd-pleasing shenanigans also are abundant on records by the Hot Five and Hot Seven that are now canonized as serious "art" by most jazz writers. The argument that Armstrong "sold out" at some given historical moment is usually based on the automatic canonization of some earlier, edenic moment that can be fetishized but not examined.

Clive James has likewise misread Armstrong's racial politics. On the one hand, Armstrong did not detest wearing "jungle bunny outfits." When he dressed up in a grass skirt and blackface to be King of the Zulus in New Orleans at Mardi Gras in 1949, many black Americans may well have been scandalized, but Armstrong never apologized, insisting that it was an honor to be King of the Zulus. In this case, he liked the jungle bunny outfit, if that is what we wish to call it. On the other hand, Armstrong probably never thought of himself as an Uncle Tom either. By the early 1930s he was touring Europe and encountering a hero's reception, and he continued to be one of the two or three best-known Americans in the world until his death in 1971. He was right to pride himself on passing through doors that had always been closed to blacks. More revealingly, James has evoked the old art/entertainment distinction without acknowledging how easily it can be deconstructed. The duplicitous use that Hollywood has found for the discourse of art should tell us a great deal about the power relations actually at stake when arguments pro and con are made by critics. For a long time the BBC and PBS have invested deeply in keeping myths about "art" alive. James's series is typical of the BBC/PBS product that invites audiences to side with Armstrong the artist rather than with Armstrong the entertainer at the same time that audiences are invited to gaze at the "entertainer" in his "jungle bunny outfits."

More so than with most performers who retained their prominence through several decades, reactions to Armstrong have changed radically over the years. There are younger hipsters, both black and white, who first regarded him as a smiling buffoon with a white handkerchief, but who later came to admire him as a brilliant and original trumpet soloist. As a young man, my view of Armstrong changed from contempt to admiration when I began paying attention to the words of older jazz enthusiasts. Conversely, some of the same black fans who mobbed Armstrong as a hero when he passed through Harlem in the 1930s probably found him something of an embarrassment in the 1950s. Today, his mannerisms are offensive to some young African Americans. After showing footage of Armstrong in the 1930s to a large introductory class in film history, I experienced something similar to the reactions described by bell hooks (1991) at showings of films depicting erotic love between black men.

> When I had Oberlin College show *Passion of Remembrance* to all the incoming freshpeople, during the scene where the two black men kissed in that film, a lot of the black males in the audience put their heads down. And when I went to the screening of *Young Soul Rebels,* when there were tender scenes of lovemaking and eroticism between black men, I remember the Rastas in the audience who were saying "Stop it, man, stop it!" That initially registers as a homophobic response, but it's also a response to seeing the public exposure of a certain kind of black male desire that is vulnerable. (177)

Although there was never anything explicitly homoerotic in Armstrong's self-presentation, his zeal to please surely suggested a similar vulnerability that today makes many young black people uncomfortable. In a culture that regularly castrates black men, many of them are unnerved by the sight of an African American male who appears to accept his castration so readily. If Gary Giddins is correct—that black Americans in the 1930s lionized Armstrong because he communicated his sexuality in code while turning an obsequious face toward his white handlers—then it also must be true that Armstrong did not update his codes. Many in the black audience after the civil rights era ceased to recognize Armstrong's obsolete phallic codings and saw only what the white power structure was meant to see. I would not be surprised if first-time viewers find no evidence of Armstrong's sexuality in *Pillow to Post* or *The Glenn Miller Story,* although I hope that I have made the case that his sexuality is an issue in these films.

Can a case also be made that Armstrong was able to rise above the demeaning material he was regularly asked to perform? When he let his eyes bulge out or when he broke into an absurdly wide grin, was he over-playing to hide his real feelings? Was he saying to those whites in the audience who were uncomfortable with a black man's sexuality, "You may think this is me, but you'll never find the real thing underneath this mask"? Undoubtedly, the answers to these questions will continue to change as the discourses of black and white America continue to change. While Armstrong may have overcome the soap bubbles and leopard skins of *Rhapsody in Black and Blue* (1932) simply with his carriage and the magnificence of his music, it is much more difficult to make this kind of argument for the out-of-place figure who wanders through *Glory Alley* in 1952. We can only speculate about how much of Armstrong's success was related to the reassurances he gave to white audiences who wanted to believe that his grinning visage was more typical of black people than were the menacing faces of young African Americans that regularly showed up on the nightly news. Different constituencies at different historical moments have vacillated between seeing Armstrong as a trickster or as a Tom, just as Armstrong himself reacted differently to these discourses at different moments in his career.

Nevertheless, I would like to expand the comparison that Ralph Ellison (1964) makes between Armstrong and the witty jester of Elizabethan drama. In commenting on Stanley Edgar Hyman's lecture on trickster figures in American literature, Ellison charges Hyman with blurring distinctions between the various types of tricksters in order to group them all within the same archetypal structures. In the large literature on tricksters, most of it by folklorists and comparative anthropologists, a consensus has been reached that tricksters are liminal figures, identified with creative powers and the violation of taboos, especially sexual ones. As Enid Welsford (1966) has written, the fool "as a dramatic character stands apart from the main action of the play, having a tendency not to focus but dissolve events. . . . He does not confine his activities to the theatre but makes everyday life comic on the spot" (xii). Barbara Babcock-Abrahams (1975), in an attempt to synthesize the various trickster traditions, wrote:

The tale of the trickster, picaro, or rogue is one of the oldest and most persistent cultural patterns of negation and one of the oldest of narrative forms. For centuries he has, in his various incarnations, run, flown, galloped, and most recently motorcycled through the literary imagination. Examples are legion. Hermes, Prometheus, Ture, Maui, Eshu-Elegba, Anansi, Wakdjunkaga, raven, rabbit, spider, and coyote are but a few from ancient and native mythology and folktale. And, in Western literature, one could cite Lazarillo de Tormes, El Buscon, Gil Blas, Felix Krull, Augie March, and of late the Butch Cassidys and Easy Riders of film. (158)

As Ellison suggests, little of this really sounds like Louis Armstrong. Babcock-Abrahams does, however, make a distinction between volitional and nonvolitional liminality (151). Obviously, Armstrong as a black American growing up in the early years of the twentieth century had his marginality forced upon him. Part of what makes him so interesting is how he coded his sexuality, surrounding it with highly unthreatening display in his singing and mugging. In this sense, he is most like the trickster whose extreme, hyperphallic behavior is balanced by conduct that tends to deny sexuality.

When Ellison implicitly compares Armstrong to Touchstone in *As You Like It*, or the Fool in *Lear*, he is, of course, invoking fictional characters to define a real one. Ellison may have based this comparison on an Armstrong who in many ways took on a life of his own *as* a fictional character. We see this trickster Armstrong most prominently when he parodies the potent gangsters in the "Public Melody Number One" sequence in *Artists & Models*. He was also claimed as a trickster in the remarkable "Swing Wedding," a cartoon produced by Hugh Harman and Rudolf Ising for MGM in 1937. Armstrong is one of several black performers who are faithfully—almost lovingly—portrayed as animated frogs. Although this cartoon feature is unquestionably dominated by racist stereotypes, the black entertainers are in some ways *honored* by the attention that has been lavished upon reproducing their images and habits of movement. As in "Public Melody Number One," Armstrong is *narrativized* here as a trickster figure. At least at the outset, "Swing Wedding" is about a marriage scheduled to take place between the female frog known as Minnie the Moocher and a male frog Smokey Joe, whose behavior is modeled closely on Stepin Fetchit. Because the groom is too slow to arrive at the wedding on time, a frog bearing a resemblance to Cab Calloway romances the female with his singing and dancing and eventually takes her to the altar himself. (Minnie and Smokey Joe are both characters in the lyrics of Calloway's theme song, "Minnie the Moocher," first recorded in

1931.) Frogs resembling Fats Waller and Bill "Bojangles" Robinson provide wedding entertainment.

The frog resembling Armstrong first appears playing his trumpet off
to one side of the screen and speaking in the unmistakable Satchmo
voice. Then, in praise of weddings, he sings one of his trademark songs
from the 1930s, "Sweethearts on Parade." After Minnie has exchanged
vows with the Calloway frog, the Armstrong frog encounters Smokey Joe
as he is still making his way to the ceremony. Even though it is too late,
the Armstrong character provokes Smokey Joe to compete with the Calloway frog by dancing for Minnie. Perhaps inspired by Smokey Joe's
dance, the Calloway frog spins across the pond to lead his orchestra in a
rendition of "Runnin' Wild." The Armstrong frog has effectively started
a wild party that soon turns into chaos. The Waller frog smashes his
piano, while the bassist in Calloway's band uses his instrument as a pogo
stick. One of the musicians can even be glimpsed injecting himself with
a hypodermic needle. At the cartoon's conclusion the Armstrong frog
takes in so much breath for his trumpet playing that he puffs up to enormous size and floats into the pond. The last shot of the film is a close-up
of his face as he utters, "Ah, swing." Like the Elizabethan fool, Armstrong
disrupts from the sidelines, dissolving the action rather than focusing it.
Armstrong was much too complex a man to be catalogued simply as a
trickster or as an Uncle Tom, but his image was readily available, as here,
when a trickster was needed for a *fictional* text, just as he was available
three decades later when James Baldwin needed a symbol of obsolete
black traditions for his story "Sonny's Blues."

Michele Wallace (1990) has written of Armstrong in a somewhat different but relevant context in an article about Michael Jackson.

> My mother, who is a total fan of Jackson's, says he makes up words. But
> isn't that what black singers have always done? Ella Fitzgerald and Louis
> Armstrong simply made "scatting" official. Henry Louis Gates calls this
> aspect of black culture "critical signification." It is a process in which black
> culture "signifies" on white culture through imitating and then reversing
> its formal strategies and preconditions, thus formulating a masked and
> surreptitious critique. The perfect example is the relationship of "jazz" to
> white mainstream music. But what I'm beginning to wonder is: how "criti-
> cal" is it? (86)

For many young black people in the United States today, the answer is
"not much." Wallace makes a much stronger case for the "cultural signification" achieved by Michael Jackson. But Jackson was born into an en-

tertainment industry that resembled Armstrong's as much as a player piano today resembles a synthesizer.

Wallace is right that Armstrong's critiques of dominant culture may seem a little too "masked and surreptitious" today. Still, Armstrong ought to be read outside narrow notions of what constitutes a positive role model.[12] In much of his self-presentation Armstrong plays on traditions of American humor that are not so easily separated into strictly white and black strands. Nor are these traditions so easily classified as demeaning or resisting. There are, however, legitimate questions about how Armstrong functioned within discourses of race and sexuality, and all of these issues are richly available for interpretation in his films. If we are to understand Louis Armstrong's significance in American culture as well as understanding the culture's impact on him, his films may actually be as valuable a resource as his recordings.

The American Feature Films of Louis Armstrong

Ex-Flame		1931 (Lost)
Pennies from Heaven	Dir. Norman Z. McLeod	1936
Artists & Models	Dir. Raoul Walsh	1937
Every Day's a Holiday	Dir. A. Edward Sutherland	1938
Going Places	Dir. Ray Enright	1938
Birth of the Blues	Dir. Victor Schertzinger	1941
Cabin in the Sky	Dir. Vincente Minnelli	1943
Jam Session	Dir. Charles Barton	1944
Atlantic City	Dir. Ray McCarey	1944
Pillow to Post	Dir. Vincent Sherman	1945
New Orleans	Dir. Arthur Lubin	1947
A Song Is Born	Dir. Howard Hawks	1948
The Strip	Dir. Leslie Kardos	1951
Here Comes the Groom	Dir. Frank Capra	1951
Glory Alley	Dir. Raoul Walsh	1952
The Glenn Miller Story	Dir. Anthony Mann	1954
High Society	Dir. Charles Walters	1956
The Five Pennies	Dir. Melville Shavelson	1959
The Beat Generation	Dir. Charles Haas	1959
Paris Blues	Dir. Martin Ritt	1961
When the Boys Meet the Girls	Dir. Alvin Ganzer	1966
A Man Called Adam	Dir. Leo Penn	1966
Hello, Dolly!	Dir. Gene Kelly	1969

Nat King Cole, Hoagy Carmichael, and the Fate of the Jazz Actor

D uke Ellington and Louis Armstrong both had a profound impact on jazz at the same time that they had important if not prominent presences in the American cinema. I have tried to place them within several discourses and to identify the extent to which they could and could not change the nature of the mostly pedestrian films in which they appeared. In this chapter I look at two jazz performers who were of much less consequence to the history of jazz but who had careers in the movies that were more substantial, if not major. Because both of these artists more willingly surrendered to the wishes of filmmakers, it is more difficult to argue that they transformed their films. Nat King Cole starred in *St. Louis Blues* (1958), had speaking parts in several other films from the 1950s, and appeared in his own weekly television series in 1956 and 1957. Hoagy Carmichael worked frequently in films from 1937 until 1955, hosted the television program *Saturday Night Revue* for a season in 1953, and was a series regular on *Laramie* during the 1959–60 season (McNeil 1980, 395 and 613). As jazz musicians, neither performer was ever totally distanced from the music, almost always playing a "musical" character of one kind or another. Unlike more ambitious performers, such as Frank Sinatra and Bette Midler, who started out in music, Cole and Carmichael were never able to play completely nonmusical roles. The two men's jazz associations undoubtedly determined the kinds of roles they could and could not play. But because the music was still bound up with conflicted American attitudes about race and masculinity during their film careers, the movie industry consistently sought to deny them certain kinds of subjectivity. As I have pointed out, Nat Cole in *St. Louis Blues* became one of the few black actors who functioned essentially as a white hero. But in achieving this dubious distinction, Cole had to surrender a good deal of his masculine presence and sex appeal, while at the same time being required to bear many of the negative qualities that whites conventionally attributed to blacks. In spite of his color, Carmichael suffered a similar fate—his association with African American musicians left a mark on his screen persona that never went away, no matter how little his films addressed racial matters. In effect, Carmichael ended up playing parts that could just as easily have been played by blacks.

"Straighten Up and Fly Right"

Purely for heuristic purposes, Nat King Cole's career can be inelegantly divided into five stages, the last four of which involved ever-new makeovers to satisfy his ever-expanding audience. Sexuality even more than race was a central though seldom acknowledged element in these transformations. In the first phase of his career, from approximately 1935 until 1938, Cole was a working jazz pianist who occasionally sang. The second stage began in 1938 with the first recordings on which he sang ballads and pop tunes with his trio but maintained a jazz pianist's identity. In his third stage, Cole achieved great crossover success into both the rhythm and blues *and* the white record market when he recorded "Straighten Up and Fly Right" for Capitol in 1944. The hugely successful 1946 recording of "The Christmas Song" ("Chestnuts roasting on an open fire . . . ") began the fourth stage of Cole's career and made him an even greater musical presence in white households. His starring role in his own TV series in 1956 marked the beginning of a fifth and culminating stage.

As a black jazz pianist in the 1930s, Cole was, like most of his peers, largely ignored except by a small segment of the culture industry that made no attempt to alter his sexual presence. This is not to say that jazz pianists did not develop sexual personae on their own or that Cole's physical height and exotic appearance did not give him an appeal that few others among his peers enjoyed. But he was primarily a piano player and, in the opinion of most jazz critics, a good one. Even before he made his first vocal recordings in 1938, however, Cole had been singing with his trio for several years, but he was not widely known as a singer until he signed with Capitol Records in 1944 and almost immediately became a prominent vocalist with the success of "Straighten Up and Fly Right." Nevertheless, Cole himself encouraged the legend that he began singing because a drunken customer insisted that he provide the vocal on a version of "Sweet Lorraine."

This apocryphal story became part of an eighteen-minute feature that was filmed in CinemaScope in 1955. Directed by Will Cowan and narrated by Jeff Chandler, *The Nat "King" Cole Musical Story* begins with Cole playing himself as a nightclub pianist. A drunken customer repeatedly demands that he sing, even calling him "boy," striking him on the back, and pounding on the piano. The drunk seems to be setting himself up for a punch in the jaw or at least a shouting match with the reluctant pianist. Recall that in *Blues in the Night* in 1941 the character Jigger (Richard Whorf) finds himself in a similar predicament. Refusing to compromise by playing anyone's music but his own, Jigger punches the drunken customer and eventually the bar's owner. But *Blues in the Night's* pugnacious piano player was white. In *The Nat "King" Cole Musical Story* a black pianist in the mid-1950s can only protest politely that he does not sing. The club's owner is also spared Cole's wrath, even after he tells the pianist that the drunk is a big spender and that Cole should accede to his wishes. Cole protests, "But, you see, I just can't sing." The manager, whose demeanor suggests an underworld character, warns him, "Well then you better learn how fast. Sing!" When Cole does in fact sing "Sweet Lorraine," much to the pleasure of the drunk and the manager, the short film tells us that a theatrical manager happens to be in the audience, and a new career has begun.

Most Americans did not hear Cole sing until "Straighten Up and Fly Right" became one of the nation's ten best-selling records for seven weeks, beginning in April 1944. Eventually, it sold a half-million copies. At least some of the song's success might be attributed to the suggestiveness of its lyrics:

Straighten Up and Fly Right

A buzzard took a monkey for a ride in the air,
The monkey thought that everything was on the square.
The buzzard tried to throw the monkey off his back,
But the monkey grabbed his neck and said, "Now listen, Jack.

Straighten up and fly right
Straighten up and fly right

Straighten up and fly right
Cool down, papa, don't you blow your top.

Ain't no use in divin'.
What's the use of jivin'?
Straighten up and fly right
Cool down, papa, don't you blow your top.

The buzzard told the monkey "You are choking me.
Release your hold and I will set you free."
The monkey looked the buzzard right dead in the eye and said,
"You're story's so touching, but it sounded like a lie.

Straighten up and fly right,
Straighten up and stay right
Straighten up and fly right
Cool down, papa, don't you blow your top."

(Words and music by Nat King Cole
and Irving Mills)

According to one of Cole's biographers, Leslie Gourse (1991), Cole was invited to perform "Straighten Up and Fly Right" in an unnamed film that Lucille Ball was making at MGM. When Ball heard Cole perform the song, she declared, "That's the filthiest song I ever heard in my life" and refused to allow it in the film (63). Gourse writes that Cole was surprised by Ball's reaction because he had taken the line from his father, a Baptist minister from Alabama. Although Ball apparently assumed that the monkey was urging the buzzard to get an erection, Gourse says that Cole's father actually used a version of the story in his sermons.

> Don't give up, was the message, even though it's a cold, cruel world and the buzzard doesn't care whether you survive. Nat always regarded his strict, devoutly religious father with awe. "Whatever sincerity I have," he told an interviewer, "I get from him." "Straighten up and fly right," his father used to call out in a rich voice in his sermon, urging people to cling to their Christian beliefs no matter how precarious their lives were. (25)

A case can be made that Gourse and Ball have both misread the song and Cole's explication of it.[1] On the one hand, Gourse makes an artificial distinction between narratives of Christian fortitude and the traditions of black vernacular when one overlaps the other, certainly in the black folk preacher's discourse. In fact, the musical careers of several eminent black composers were built along what might appear to be split lines. W. C. Handy composed church hymns as well as vernacular songs about loose women and hard-drinking men. Thomas Andrew Dorsey, known as "the Father of Gospel Music" for writing such famous anthems of the black church as "Precious Lord," was also capable of writing the bawdy gem of sexual double entendre "It's Tight Like That," even after his "second conversion" to Christianity (Harris 1994). There is no denying the sexual suggestiveness in Cole's lyric about one animal mounting another from behind, in terms like "divin,'" and "jivin,'" and, as Lucille Ball noticed, "straighten up." The song also features ejaculatory imagery like "blow your top," not to mention echoes of drug culture slang with the image of a monkey on the back.

On the other hand, Ball assumed that the primate was asking the bird to get an erection, even though the monkey was behind the buzzard. And Ball may be reading too much into a song whose narrative is basically a vernacular version of an Aesopian fable or a medieval exemplum. Certainly a Baptist preacher could use the story, its suggestiveness unchanged, in the same way that priests in the Middle Ages would have used it, to argue that we must work together if we are to survive. In many ways the dispute over the lyrics to "Straighten Up and Fly Right" is emblematic of the tensions that dominated Cole's career. While some might find Cole guilty of vulgarity and a reluctance to observe the niceties of sexual restraint, others feel impelled to whitewash the singer, portraying him as an almost asexual naïf. Various strategies were deployed throughout Cole's career to convince listeners like Lucille Ball that Cole was more like the benign character in Leslie Gourse's biography.

In fairness to Ball, Cole did present a playful, often sexually piquant character in many of his early film appearances. She may have been responding to this persona as much as to the song when she refused to allow Cole in her movie. There are several three-minute glimpses of Cole in the "soundies" that he made from 1943 until 1946. In such of these as "I'm a Shy Guy" (1943) and "Come to Baby Do" (1946), Cole is very much the trickster, smiling slyly and ogling the attractive black women who adorn the sets. Cole fits right in when one of the soundies turns self-referential. "Frim Fram Sauce," released in 1945 and directed by William Forest Crouch, casts Cole as an indigent musician sitting at a table in a restaurant, singing about how he cannot afford to buy anything. When he motions to a waitress, she ignores him. The restaurant has a machine in one corner that is playing a soundie in which Cole and his trio are featured. The Cole in the soundie within the soundie looks out at the diegetic Cole and raises his eyebrows in recognition. The music the trio plays on the machine is carefully synched so that it fits seamlessly with the song that Cole sings in the restaurant. The song, "Frim Fram Sauce," which was already a hit record on its own, features a collection of nonsense syllables that an impoverished man concocts so that he can sit in a restaurant without ordering anything that a waiter can bring: "I want the frim fram sauce with the aussen fay with chafafa on the side." At the end of the three-minute short, when a waiter arrives at his table, Cole speaks the final trickster line of this trickster soundie, "Now if you don't have it, just bring me a check for the water."

Even after he had won over a white audience with "The Christmas Song," Cole continued to inject a great deal of sexual innuendo into his performances. For example, in *Killer Diller,* a race film directed by Josh Binney in 1948, Cole wears a pencil mustache and smiles suggestively throughout his performance of "Oo Kick-a-Rooney." At one point, he pats the underside of the piano keyboard as if it were a woman's backside. The character we see here is entirely capable of using double entendres in a fable about animals, regardless of the source.

But few whites knew the Cole of *Killer Diller.* The larger, whiter audience that sought out "The Christmas Song" saw and heard a much different Cole. For the first time in his career, he stood up from the piano and sang without playing. Logistically, this makes impossible the seated trickster image of *Killer Diller* and the soundies. Gone is the impish figure with the mustache who bends over the piano and sings with casual mastery of both music and lyrics. As a singing pianist, Cole was very much in the tradition of Fats Waller, Putney Dandridge, Harry "The Hipster" Gibson, and even Jimmy Durante, all of whom knew how to balance singing with playing so that one seemed to be a series of commentaries on the other. Fats Waller's performance of "Ain't Misbehavin'" in the film *Stormy Weather* (1943) provides an example of the trickster at work that is as amusing as it is remarkable; singing, playing, and feverishly exercising his lips and eyebrows, Waller proves that he can do several things at once while seeming to be involved with none. Everything seems to be an ironic aside about something else, including the solos of his drummer. Sometimes his lyrics even become a commentary on other lyrics. Throughout the film Waller maintains this trickster quality, never actually advancing the plot, always commenting from the side.

More importantly, Cole's voice on the 1946 record of "The Christmas Song" for the first time was supported by a string orchestra. Whatever sexual threat may have remained in the Cole persona was sugared over with violins and cellos. And, of course, Cole was encouraged to emphasize the mellower inflections in his delivery, perhaps made possible by a more comfortable singing posture. A few years later, when he was filmed singing another of his crossover hits, "Nature Boy," Cole wore heavy white makeup that completely hid his blackness.[2]

As Cole's popularity grew through the 1950s, he became one of the few black male singers who could find regular work in television and the Hollywood film industry. Although Cole had been appearing in these media for several years, he was inevitably confined to short films and brief guest appearances in movies and on other people's TV shows. On November 5, 1956, however, he became an entirely new figure with the premiere of *The Nat King Cole Show*. He obviously created problems for an industry that was squeamish about presenting audiences with a sexually attractive black male whose singing voice had already been the source of fantasy for many of his listeners. For most of the show's run, NBC paid the bills because no sponsor could be found. The show was moved around to different time slots for most of its run, and although it was at one point expanded from fifteen minutes to a half-hour, it was eventually canceled on December 17, 1957, after a little more than a year of weekly broadcasts. Two months before its cancellation, the show did find a few regional sponsors (Rheingold Beer bankrolled the program in the New York City area), but a few stations in the South and in the East still refused to run the show because it starred a black man. It was not until 1966 that a black performer, Sammy Davis, Jr., would again host a regular network TV show (McNeil 1980, 502).

Nat Cole was the fourth black performer to have his own television series. Bob Howard, Hazel Scott, and Billy Daniels starred in their own shows in the early years of television, but all of them were substantially different from Cole. Howard, billed as "The Jive Bomber," was a jazz singer with some panache who had recorded with esteemed figures such as Teddy Wilson, Benny Carter, Ben Webster, and Rex Stewart in the 1930s. The portly Howard occupied a tiny studio in which he sang and mugged at a grand piano. Franklin Heller (1986), one of the program's original producers, referred to Howard as a "road company Fats Waller." Hazel Scott was well-known as the female jazz pianist with classical training who regularly began different numbers by displaying great virtuosity with a showpiece from the nineteenth-century European piano repertoire before breaking into jazz tempo. Billy Daniels, whose biggest hit was "That Old Black Magic," had played leading men in race films such as *Sepia Cinderella* (1946), but he was so light-skinned that some viewers of his television program may have assumed that he was white. In his acting roles Daniels seemed to be working hard at projecting a boyish quality of freshness and enthusiasm. By the time he appeared on television, however, he was a highly mannered performer who seemed to impersonate sex appeal rather than project it. In other words, none of the African American performers who preceded Cole as TV series regulars had any of his masculine sexual intensity.

Perhaps the only other well-known black male singer from the 1940s and 1950s who projected strong male sexuality was Billy Eckstine. His career in films and television, however, was extremely limited. Even when Eckstine appeared in the race film *Rhythm in a Riff* (1946), his hypermasculine crooning was undercut substantially by his boyishness and timorous self-presentation. The plot of *Rhythm in a Riff* had him struggling to find a job for his band, hardly the image of manly self-confidence that he was capable of projecting. Although Eckstine and Cole were the only two black male singers of the late 1940s and early 1950s whose recordings of romantic ballads were regularly consumed by white audiences, Eckstine was never able to become a *visual* presence beyond a black audience. Cole was able to make that transition, but in the process he was substantially transformed.[3]

Throughout the run of his program, Cole was surrounded by white performers playing "white" music, most notably vocal groups such as the Boateneers and the Cheerleaders and an orchestra led by Nelson Riddle. And on many episodes he was surrounded by groups of all-white dancers and singers. Cole did present black performers now and then, even jazz performers. On one memorable occasion he welcomed the canonical performers from Norman Granz's "Jazz at the Philharmonic" tour and joined them at the piano. Cole himself, however, was always presented as detached and restrained, never the trickster. The producers had numerous strategies for containing his sexuality, at some points playing up his status as a family man; in one episode, he sings "I've Grown Accustomed to Her Face" while the camera cuts to family photos of his young children. More often than not, Cole was photographed from the waist up in much the same way that Elvis Presley's lower body was concealed when he appeared on the *Ed Sullivan Show,* an event that took place during the run of Cole's own television show. Although, in a sense, Cole was the inverse of Presley—a restrained black man acting "white" rather than a shameless white man acting "black"—NBC felt a need to conceal his hips in the same way that CBS attempted to censor Presley.

A tendency to neutralize Cole also occurred in his movie appearances. In several films, including *The Adventures of Hajji Baba* (1954), *Autumn Leaves* (1956), and *Raintree County* (1957), Cole is literally invisible, only his voice being heard over the opening credits. Of the nine feature films in which he appeared after 1950, Cole is confined to a single musical number in three of them (*The Blue Gardenia* [1953], *Small Town Girl* [1953], and *The Scarlet Hour* [1956]). In *Istanbul* (1957) his two musical performances are followed by brief conversations with the protagonist played by Errol Flynn. In both scenes Flynn's infatuation with the heroine reminds Cole of his girlfriend back in New York. When he sees the two lovers in action, Cole is overcome with the desire to call his own lover, but he complains about the expense of phoning New York from Istanbul. After he has left the table to return to his piano, Flynn calls him "a nice guy, first-class." In the second scene, when Cole hears that Flynn is about to be married, the camera follows the pianist to the bar where he nods purposefully at the bartender who nods back and hands him the telephone. "Long distance, please. New York." Although Cole is hardly demasculinized in *Istanbul*, the sexual presence of a man who mellifluously croons his way through "When I Fall in Love" is at least somewhat contained when he turns out to be completely smitten with a woman on the other side of the world. In his last film appearance, *Cat Ballou* (1965), Cole and Stubby Kaye operate extradiegetically as strolling minstrels who strum on small stringed instruments while they sing the narration that unites various scenes in the heroine's life. Cole and Kaye here function in much the same way as Louis Armstrong, who was outside the narrative in much of both *High Society* and *When the Boys Meet the Girls*. Significantly, Hoagy Carmichael has a similar extradiegetic function in both *Young Man with a Horn* and *The Las Vegas Story*.

Nat King Cole's brief appearance in *The Blue Gardenia* (1953) is especially interesting in terms of how his performed song is echoed in the extradiegetic score. Director Fritz Lang was always sensitive to the possibilities of film sound, as in his early aural experiments in *M* (1931). During his Hollywood years, Lang used sound, music, and imagery to evoke guilt and fear rather than the bourgeois optimism perfected by many of his peers. Although the plots of Lang's films usually stay firmly within the boundaries of classical Hollywood, their discursive aspects frequently border on the experimental, as in the Brechtian excursions of *You and Me* (1938). E. Ann Kaplan (1978) has shown how *Blue Gardenia* strongly undermines the patriarchal conventions of film noir before reasserting them at the end (89). In some ways, the film's music complements these subversive strategies, but it also does a good deal more.

The female lead in *The Blue Gardenia* is a telephone operator named Norah Larkin (Anne Baxter). On the same evening that she has been rejected by her fiancé, she recklessly accepts a dinner invitation from Harry Prebble (Raymond Burr), a notorious womanizer who plies her with liquor as a prelude to seduction. At the restaurant where Norah meets Prebble, the title song is performed on camera by Cole, interrupting the progress of the story much longer than moviegoers would expect in a nonmusical film but about as long as they would expect when the singer is a major star. Through the rest of the film the song ("The Blue Gardenia") is deeply inscribed into both the diegetic and extradiegetic score. When Prebble plays the music on his phonograph after he lures Norah back to his apartment, the love song becomes what Michel Chion calls "anempathic" (Gorbman 1987, 151–61), and the film appears to be indifferent to Prebble's progressively more heavy-handed seduction maneuvers. When Norah attempts to protect herself by striking Prebble with a fireplace poker, however, a more dramatic version of "The Blue Gardenia," cued to the violence of the story, overwhelms the diegetic version on the record player.

Later, the Nat Cole recording of the song reappears in the diegesis when Norah is in a seedy café with the male protagonist, Casey Mayo, a newspaper columnist played by Richard Conte. Intimations of romance emerge as the record plays on the jukebox. Throughout the film, however, motives from the song are associated extradiegetically with Norah as she attempts to avoid capture after becoming mistakenly convinced that she killed Prebble with the poker. She is even more strongly linked to the song when the newspapers begin referring to the murderess as "The Blue Gardenia" after the flower that was found in the dead man's apartment. The song's romantic resonance eventually disappears as it comes more and more to signify Norah's status as a fugitive and a fallen woman. The song was introduced in the context of Norah's seduction by the oleaginous Prebble, and even when it plays on the jukebox during her meeting with Mayo, the scene unfolds in the place where she is about to be betrayed to the police.

In this sense, the choice of a black jazz artist to introduce the title song is ideologically appropriate. In spite of Cole's popular success, and in spite of the syrupy, nonjazz arrangement of "The Blue Gardenia" (scored for the film by Nelson Riddle), Cole's presence carried associations with black jazz artists, linked in the popular imagination with loose sexuality and drug abuse. Otherness is encoded into the music from the beginning. Thus, the song "Blue Gardenia" becomes a sliding signifier, eventually moving toward connotations of murder and attempted rape, but never really uncontaminated either in the performance by Cole or in the subsequent diegesis. The tune is last heard when Norah is arrested in the same café where she and Mayo had earlier listened to the record on the jukebox. After she has been led out of the frame, the arresting police officer thanks the sleazy counterman for informing the authorities of Norah's whereabouts. A motif from the song appears as a brief tag to the background score when the counterman acknowledges the policeman's gratitude. Even though an orchestral version of "The Blue Gardenia" had played over the opening credits, the melody does not reappear at the film's conclusion, as was often the case in classical Hollywood; David Raksin's love theme for *Laura,* for example, is heard at the end as well as at the opening of the film. In *The Blue Gardenia,* once Norah has been found innocent and recuperated as a love object for the hero, the song's codes no longer apply to her or to the film. The "Blue Gardenia" theme is not, as we might expect, a leitmotif for Norah; its apposition to the counterman's complicity with the police reveals that the song is anchored more to Norah's supposed guilt than to Norah herself. The last minutes of the film feature a grab bag of musical signifiers: the triumphant march that anchors the justice insignia on the floor of the courthouse; the fluid melody that connotes the easy camaraderie among the women; the music of big city bustle that accompanies Mayo's return to the center after the women leave the frame; the chromatic descending tones that follow Casey's address book as it flies into the hands of his photographer; the wolf-whistle effects that parallel the photographer's reactions to the addresses; and the heroic flourishes that play behind the end credits.[4]

If Cole's sexuality and racial difference are both acknowledged and denied in most of his films, his otherness is most excessively contained in Samuel Fuller's *China Gate* (1957), one of the first American films about the war in Vietnam. Shot three years after Vietnamese forces defeated French colonial troops at Dien Bien Phu in 1954, the film presented most of the excuses for the subsequent American invasion of Vietnam that five presidents articulated over the next twenty years. Bearing the woman's name "Goldie" in the film, Cole first appears in soldier of fortune garb singing to the child with whom he will eventually return to the United States. Significantly, the audience hears Cole's voice before his face is revealed, as if they must be soothed into the full experience of his body. The audience may also have experienced him, at least initially, as outside the narrative when they hear his unmistakable voice accompanied by an off-screen orchestra. Cole is more fully assimilated into the narrative later when he explains his presence among a detachment of French soldiers by saying that he did not finish the job he started in

Korea. "There's still a lot of live commies around." Goldie is part of a band of French-led guerrillas on a mission to blow up a cache of Chinese weapons. Also on the mission are Brock (Gene Barry) and Lucky Legs (Angie Dickinson). Brock had married Lucky Legs five years earlier, even though he knew that one of her parents was Chinese. (To look mildly Asian, Dickinson wears a wig and a little more eye makeup than usual.) When their child was born looking *unmistakably* Chinese, Brock abandoned his wife and child, only to reappear years later at the beginning of the film to lead the guerrilla force that must blow up the ammunition dump. In two of the film's more bizarre plot elements, the beautiful, feminine Lucky is the only person who can lead the group through the Vietnamese jungles, and she accepts the mission on the condition that her son be taken to the United States where she believes he will be the target of less bigotry than in Vietnam.

On the mission, Brock and Lucky have moments of reconciliation, but Brock still refuses to accept his child. Goldie, not expressing his angry disapproval of Brock's behavior, watches all of this silently until he steps on a huge nail set as a booby trap. The camera focuses tightly on Goldie's foot as the spike emerges from the top of his boot and then again as he painfully raises his foot to extricate himself. Significantly, he must stifle his feelings—if he cries out, the enemy soldiers will hear him. After he has been patched up, however, Goldie lets go of some of his pain and scolds Brock for abandoning his son.

> I always wanted a kid, Brock. When my wife was told we couldn't have one, we put in papers to adopt one. Then my wife got sick, eaten up inside, not being able to have one. Just eaten up. I watched her go down to seventy-five pounds. She died, feeling sorry for me. That's how much she knew I wanted a kid. When I learned you walked out on yours. . . . Let me tell you something, Brock. I've belted through two wars, and I'm coming out of this one. You know why? 'Cause I got a reason. I'll get my release when they know why I want out. I'll tell you one thing. Lucky Legs is going through hell for your son. And if something happens to her on this job, he'll still get to the States even if I have to crawl all the way back with him on my back. I always wanted a son, Brock. Especially a five-year-old one.

Goldie's life as a soldier of fortune seems to be an attempt to escape the unfulfilled life he led as a childless husband back in the States. In essence, moments after Goldie is symbolically castrated by the nail in his foot, he admits to his own impotence. Nevertheless, Cole has been loaded down with weapons from the beginning, and he is one of two characters who survives the mission. In *China Gate,* Cole is alternately manned and unmanned, but his sexuality is contained by his complete devotion to the child he appears ready to adopt at the conclusion.

Cole's race is also contained through several narrative ploys in *China Gate.* Goldie's plea to Brock that he accept his child is cast entirely in terms of the family with no suggestion that Brock may be a racial bigot. This is a common strategy in Hollywood's dealings with racial prejudice; a black character represents or expresses a white view that denies the importance of race. In *Home of the Brave* (1949), for example, a black soldier accepts a psychiatrist's explanation that his problems are within himself and that he is actually "just like everybody else" (Sayre 1982). Judith Mayne (1993) has observed how *Field of Dreams* (1989) used the black actor James Earl Jones to cast baseball as a "pure" activity that transcends racial division. Although Jones mentions the trials that Jackie Robinson endured when he integrated major league baseball, "*Field of Dreams* quickly puts explicit acknowledgement of race aside in the pursuit of a white fantasy of a mythic world where blacks articulate the myths that exclude them" (Mayne 1993, 150). Appropriately, *Field of Dreams* ends with the Jones character disappearing so that the protago-

43. The phallic Nat King Cole is paired with a child in *China Gate* (1957, 20th Century Fox). Museum of Modern Art Film Stills Archive.

nist can be reunited with his dead reactionary father. In *China Gate,* Cole erases Brock's racial bigotry at the same time that he angrily criticizes his lack of fatherly feeling.

By far the most interesting film in which Cole appeared is *Night of the Quarter Moon* (1959). John Drew Barrymore plays Chuck, a shell-shocked veteran of the Korean War who is fortunate enough to have a wealthy family to subsidize his recovery on a tropical island. There he meets Ginny, played by Julie London in a black wig and body paint designed to show that she has one black grandparent (hence the unfortunate reference to the quarter moon in the title). The plot involves the couple's love affair and marriage and the subsequent attempts by Chuck's mother (Agnes Moorehead) to have the marriage annulled. Although Chuck eventually fends off the attempts to separate him from his wife, he has some uncomfortable moments when he meets Ginny's family. Having settled in San Francisco, the couple goes to a nightclub owned by Cy, played by Cole. At the club, Ginny and Chuck are greeted first by Ginny's cousin, who is a few shades darker than Ginny. We later learn that the cousin has *two* black grandparents. This scene is shot from Chuck's point of view as he sees himself as one end of a chain that leads directly to much greater blackness than he had bargained for. First, we have Ginny, then Ginny's cousin. Finally, the camera reveals the cousin's husband, Cy. When Cole enters the frame and Chuck sees him, extradiegetic tympani make booming sounds, and whining saxophones slur into a dissonant chord. For Chuck, a relationship with one dusky female has led to the vertiginous feeling that he is about to be swallowed up by the blackness symbolized and embodied by Cole. Although Chuck eventually comes to accept Ginny in spite of her color, he does not immediately prevent his mother from keeping him in a drugged, semiconscious state while she undertakes legal proceedings to dissolve the marriage.

In *Night of the Quarter Moon* the important scene for Cole takes place when Ginny comes to ask Cy for his help in winning back her husband. Cy is at first sinister and dismissive, assuming that Ginny has married Chuck with the hopes of a quick annulment and a large financial settlement. When Cy discovers that Ginny really loves her husband, he becomes more sympathetic. After they understand one another, Ginny asks Cy how he tolerates the bigotry from which she herself has until recently been protected. (She had grown up on an island with her white father.) After expressing real anger, Cy says that sometimes he just shrugs it off; at other times he "takes it out in the music." Cole then sits down at the piano and improvises a piece that begins angrily but slowly becomes

44. Although he is smiling in this publicity shot, Chuck (John Drew Barrymore) is not entirely pleased to be part of a chain that leads from his quadroon wife (Julie London) to her mulatto cousin to Nat King Cole in *The Night of the Quarter Moon* (1959, MGM). Museum of Modern Art Film Stills Archive.

bluesy and soothing. As when he takes a spike through the foot in *China Gate,* Cole is asked to play a scene in which he represses his pain. And once again he is on the side of a woman who is supposedly of mixed racial background but who is in fact played by a white actress.

My description of *Night of the Quarter Moon* is much too charitable to a film that was primarily designed to sensationalize the issue of intermarriage. In the climactic courtroom scene Ginny is ordered by the judge to disrobe in order to establish her racial identity. When an attorney strips off her dress in a courtroom flourish, only her back is exposed, but the scene is played for maximum titillation. According to Thomas Cripps (1993), the film quickly ended up in "exploitation grind houses" after its initial release (283).

Cole's performance in *Night of the Quarter Moon* is especially moving, however, when considered in the context of his own unpleasant experiences at the hands of white bigots. Among the more publicized of such events were the vandalism committed against his house when he moved into a WASP neighborhood in Los Angeles in 1948. Cole's daughter re-

45. W. C. Handy (Nat King Cole) with his Aunt Hagar (Pearl Bailey) in *St. Louis Blues* (1958, Paramount). Jerry Ohlinger's Movie Material Store, Inc.

calls another incident after her family moved in: "Someone came in the night and on the front lawn they burned in the word 'Nigger.' This was an isolated incident, but it was so powerful—burned in the lawn. I think I went out that morning to wait for the school bus, and here was this word. And it seemed to take the longest time for the grass to grow in. The shadow of that word was always there" (Haskins 1990, 81). In 1949, Cole was gratuitously harassed by the Internal Revenue Service, and in 1956 he was actually attacked on stage by members of a racist organization who rushed him during a performance. To add insult to injury, the attack took place in his hometown of Birmingham, Alabama.

On the one hand, Cole's scene at the piano in *Night of the Quarter*

Moon can be considered another attempt to reassure white audiences by suggesting that any anger a black man might feel can be quickly dissipated into harmless music. On the other hand, we can read Cole's performance as one of several moments in the American cinema when a black actor communicates in spite of the script, direction, and merchandising. Playing in character on a musical instrument that he himself had long used for self-expression, Cole produces, as James Baldwin (1976) has written, "hints of reality, smuggled like contraband into a maudlin tale, and with enough force, if unleashed, to shatter the tale to fragments" (100). Of course, after Cole's scene at the piano, *Night of the Quarter Moon* remains intact. By the end, no blow has been struck for racial equality except that a happy ending has been handed to a couple played by a pair of white actors. (To add an extra level of irony to the conclusion, the attorney who engineers the reconciliation and who rejoices in victory is black.) But when Cole first attacks the piano to dramatize his response to racism, audiences witnessed one of those rare occasions when a black performer was able to express himself eloquently within a narrative designed to stifle that eloquence. Like Duke Ellington in *Paris Blues* and Louis Armstrong in *Rhapsody in Black and Blue,* Cole found a means of self-expression that could easily be overlooked by filmmakers and audiences who were not sensitive to the realities of black experience in America.

"Though I Dream in Vain"

Although he was neither black nor denied the opportunity for self-expression, Hoagy Carmichael was also a marginal figure in his many film roles. No doubt this had much to do with his long face and his slight build. After all, Franklin Pangborn and Ned Sparks never became leading men either. But the particular kind of marginalization that Carmichael experienced also may have been related to how he appropriated black American music into his own unique musical world.

Born in 1899, the same year as Duke Ellington, Carmichael grew up mostly in Bloomington, Indiana, where he was faced with a choice between comfortable bourgeois stability and the exciting lure of hot music. Although he went so far as to earn an undergraduate degree in law at Indiana University, he eventually chose jazz. By the mid-1930s he was well-known to most Americans as the composer of "Stardust," "Lazy River," "Rockin' Chair," "Georgia on My Mind," and a number of other songs with complex harmonies but melodies so "natural" that they appeared to exist before anyone had written them down. Even "Skylark," with what Gary Giddins (1992) has called "one of the most ethereal, jazz-inspired middle parts in all pop music" (25), does not sound contrived, even today. Carmichael first appeared in a Hollywood film in *Topper* (1937)—he plays the piano and sings a trio with Cary Grant and Constance Bennett on the night before the pair become ghosts. Carmichael appears after a montage shows the couple partaking of nightlife in a variety of clubs. After a long evening on the town, the moment with Carmichael is a quiet nightcap in which three sleepy people sing the songwriter's "Old Man Moon." The audience knows that the hour is late because the café owner, anxious to close, demands that the festivities end. Bidding farewell to the pianist—Grant calls him "Hoagy"—the couple make their auspicious departure. Carmichael is last seen sipping a large mug of beer.

By the mid-1940s, Carmichael had become a well-known songwriter, singer, and radio personality who also maintained a steady presence in films. Seven years after *Topper,* he began a string of featured roles in Hollywood films, including *To Have and Have Not* (1944), *Johnny Angel*

46. Cary Grant and Constance Bennett close a restaurant with Hoagy Carmichael in *Topper* (1937, MGM). Museum of Modern Art Film Stills Archive.

(1945), *The Best Years of Our Lives* (1946), *Canyon Passage* (1946), *Night Song* (1947), *Johnny Holiday* (1949), *Young Man with a Horn* (1950), *The Las Vegas Story* (1952), *Belles on Their Toes* (1952), and *Timberjack* (1954). In his second autobiography, Carmichael describes the movie roles he was regularly offered: "It was usually the part of the hound-dog-faced old musical philosopher noodling on the honky-tonk piano, saying to a tart with a heart of gold, 'He'll come back, honey. He's all man'" (Carmichael 1965, 269). This description is only partially accurate. Although a case can be made for Jane Russell's tartishness in *The Las Vegas Story*, Carmichael was more often associated with children than with loose women. In all of his films, his precise role in American music had a great effect on the kinds of roles he was offered.

Carmichael's relationship to blacks and their music is the subject of a 1983 essay by Roger Hewitt, who charges Carmichael with "the cultural reproduction of racism" in spite of "his own anti-racist personal opinions and the practices of his private life" (34). Several songs that Carmichael wrote or cowrote invoke the mythical South where older darkies long for release from their troubles, while younger ones spend the day sleeping under trees. Hewitt cites several examples of lyrics that perpetuate the casual racism of America in the 1920s. The most egregious is probably "Lazybones," which includes lines such as "Lazybones, sleepin' in the sun / How you gonna get your day's work done?" and "Long as there is chicken gravy on your rice, everything is nice / Long as there's a watermelon on the vine, everything is fine." Strictly speaking, these lines were written by Johnny Mercer, although Carmichael certainly did not disown them. In the lyrics that Carmichael himself wrote for "Snowball," also criticized by Hewitt, a black male persona sings to his son: "You're my only sweetheart, little chocolate bar / I'll eat you up some day." Hewitt further suggests that the lines in Carmichael's "Rockin' Chair"—"My dear old Aunt Harriet / In Heaven she be / Send me sweet chariot / For the end of the trouble I see"—strongly recall the minstrel stereotypes set down by Stephen Foster in "Old Black Joe" (Hewitt 1983, 44–46).

Carmichael's interactions with black musicians began early and went well beyond voyeurism. He holds an important place among jazz artists for being one of the few white performers to appear on a "race" record, specifically a 1929 session by a band called "Blind Willie Dunn's Gin Bottle Four." The band consisted of three black musicians—King Oliver (trumpet), J. C. Johnson (piano), and Lonnie Johnson (guitar)—along with Carmichael on drums and the white guitarist Eddie Lang. Anticipating the mixed groups assembled by John Hammond in the 1930s, the

Oliver/Carmichael band was strictly a recording unit and never played in public. Hewitt credits the heady financial climate of pre-depression 1929 for making this collaboration possible. After the stock market crash, he points out, the possibilities for musicians quickly dwindled, and it was not whites who suffered most. "Seven years later, when Carmichael was moving to Hollywood and great personal wealth, Oliver was working as a janitor in a pool room and soon after died in obscurity" (Hewitt 1983, 47). Hewitt does not mention that Carmichael himself tells Oliver's story with even greater pathos in his own writings (1965, 124–25).

In both of his autobiographies Carmichael observes that jazz has always been the fortuitous result of mixing white and black cultures. Especially in rural Indiana before the arrival of the first jazz records from New Orleans, the early sounds of jazz were absorbed by the local black culture in ways that already recalled certain kinds of "white" folk music.

> There was a white strain of popular music that was close to the roots of jazz. I had heard it came from the poverty of white people, from the life of the hillmen and the shanty and shack boatmen of the rivers and bayous. It came from the meetings and the turkey shoots and it was as real and true to the people who made it as the Negro music of the same time. The two streams weren't pure, weren't kept apart, and each took from the other what was liked or needed. (Carmichael 1965, 26)

As I have suggested, questions about the early history of jazz cannot be resolved with appeals to jazz "purity," just as the sensitive issue of who "owns" jazz cannot be resolved by giving too much credit to any one culture. Without question, early accounts of jazz ignored the contributions of black artists, while white musicians have reaped the rewards of the deplorable power imbalance between the two cultures. And white writers have almost always "colonized" jazz (Meltzer 1993), whether they are extolling the contributions of Paul Whiteman, Jelly Roll Morton, or Ornette Coleman. A white artist like Hoagy Carmichael cannot be held responsible for all of this. In fact, Carmichael may represent one of the more intriguing meetings of black and white culture.

Eric Lott (1993) is surely correct that young white males continued to emulate aspects of black male display long after the grotesque (mis)representations of black masculinity in the minstrel shows. The case of Carmichael shows how this tradition could be played out in less obvious ways along the curiously sanctioned paths of musical interaction. Carmichael's writings suggest that he was not interested in the physical and sexual prowess of black men as much as he was fascinated by the more subtle musical skills of the black musicians he encountered in his youth. In both autobiographies, Carmichael writes with real admiration for Reggie DuValle, the black pianist in Indianapolis from whom he first heard improvised music and ragtime sometime around 1916.[5] Carmichael (1965) reports that DuValle once told him, "Never play anything that ain't *right*. You may not make any money, but you'll never get mad at yourself" (33) A few years later, Carmichael heard a traveling band from Louisville, Kentucky, led by Louie Jordan (not to be confused with the singer/saxophonist popular in the 1940s). Hearing this black band probably inspired Carmichael to begin working with his own musical group, which ultimately led to his meeting Bix Beiderbecke. Carmichael also reports the overwhelming experience of hearing King Oliver and Louis Armstrong for the first time in 1923 when he accompanied Beiderbecke and Bob Gillette to the Lincoln Gardens in Chicago.

> I dropped my cigarette and gulped my drink. Bix was on his feet, his eyes popping. For taking the first chorus was that second trumpeter, Louis Armstrong. Louis taking it fast. Gillette slid off his chair and under the table. He was excitable that way.
> "Why," I moaned, "why isn't everyone in the world here to hear this?" (Carmichael 1946, 53).

Carmichael then claims that, high on liquor and marijuana, he rushed to the bandstand and took the place of the pianist so that he could join the band in a performance of "Royal Garden Blues." The regular pianist with the Oliver band at that time was Lil Hardin, soon to become Louis Armstrong's second wife. I would not argue that Carmichael was feminized by this decision to take the place of a woman at the moment of his first exposure to what was surely the most "advanced" jazz of the day. What is more significant, I believe, is that Carmichael was sufficiently secure about his own masculinity to feel neither fear nor shame at taking the place of a woman. In addition, Carmichael's desire to sit in a woman's chair suggests that his interactions with blacks had more to do with a genuine interest in the music than with a desire to appropriate black masculinity.

In chapter 4, I argued that Bix Beiderbecke, whose musical upbringing was in some ways similar to Carmichael's, eventually chose the phallic cornet as his instrument even if he perfected what might be called a post-phallic style. Like Beiderbecke, Carmichael was raised in a musical household in the Midwest and discovered jazz at a crucial moment in his development. Although Beiderbecke was younger than Carmichael, he was apparently further along in developing a musical voice. So great was Beiderbecke's impact on him that Carmichael named his first son Hoagy

Bix. In two of his most respected compositions, "Stardust" and "Skylark," Carmichael has clearly introduced the delicate lyricism of Beiderbecke's improvisations into the songs' melodies. Both men appropriated the music as something other than the dramatic, urban sounds that can be made to signify a swaggering masculinity. For Carmichael, jazz came to mean lilting melodies and life in the country, where an old woman grabs at flies buzzing around her rocking chair, the sky resembles buttermilk, and the nightingale sings a fairy tale. Even after he had spent much of the early 1930s living in New York City and making regular trips to Harlem, Carmichael personified the center of the city's black population not as an African native playing jungle music or as an uninhibited dancer, but as "Old Man Harlem."

Unlike Beiderbecke, Carmichael did not grow up in a family that was financially secure. His father drifted from job to job, and his mother had to pick up the slack by playing piano in the local movie theater. Although the Carmichaels did not suffer from the grinding poverty that the young Hoagy witnessed when he visited the small black community in Bloomington known as "Bucktown," he surely found some points of identification with poor blacks. Long after he had begun earning a small fortune in royalties from his songs, Carmichael's melodies—as well as his own understated performance practice—transcended the false nostalgia of Stephen Foster and the many others who invoked the old plantation stereotypes. Here is how Gary Giddins (1992) has summed up Carmichael's art: "It is high tribute to their melodic craftsmanship, to the closely observed images in their lyrics, and the guileless nature of their art that the minstrel echoes can be put to rest, while the songs retain their charm. If a phrase or performance is a bit patronizing, malice is utterly absent" (26). Louis Armstrong paid a sustained tribute to Carmichael by recording more than a dozen of his compositions. This tradition was extended when Wynton Marsalis played "Stardust" at a memorial service for Ralph Ellison in 1994. Marsalis was honoring Armstrong's great 1931 recording of the song that was a personal favorite of Ellison's, but he was also at least indirectly paying tribute to Carmichael.

Just as Hollywood filmmakers were unable or unwilling to represent the alternative forms of masculinity represented by the post-phallic trumpeters, neither were they able to accommodate the version of maleness that Carmichael forged from his interactions with black music in Indiana. He usually played a kind of asexual trickster figure who commented on the action from the outside. The names of his characters reveal a great deal about his film persona. Just as Nat Cole bore the feminized name Goldie in *China Gate*, Carmichael is called Cricket (*To Have and Have Not*), Celestial (*Johnny Angel*), Chick (*Night Song*), Happy (*The Las Vegas Story*), and Jingles (*Timberjack*). In an ironic switch from his usual androgynous appellations, he is called Butch in *The Best Years of Our Lives*. He is never involved romantically with a woman in any of his films, although he often sings about romance and is occasionally surrounded by adoring women while he performs at the piano. In *Night Song*, however, he plays gin rummy with grandmotherly Ethel Barrymore while Dana Andrews is pursued by Merle Oberon. Let me reiterate that Carmichael was not at all effeminate in his films and certainly not in his public appearances. This was clear as late as the 1970s when he was still vigorous and dynamic in a series of interviews filmed for a documentary on Bix Beiderbecke.[6] Carmichael's feminized image in films reflects Hollywood's codes of masculinity rather than his own self-presentation.

Probably the most inspired use of Carmichael took place the first time he had a sizable role in a film, when Howard Hawks cast him as a piano-playing expatriate in *To Have and Have Not*. Although Hawks usually presented himself as a tough-talking, no-nonsense craftsman, he was one of the few directors of classical Hollywood to allow men and women some latitude in how they played out their gender roles.[7] In addition to the many "Hawksian women" who could hold their own with men, the director created numerous situations in which men must survive without some portion of their usual privileges—Cary Grant's scenes in drag in both *Bringing Up Baby* (1938) and *I Was a Male War Bride* (1949) are only two of the most obvious examples. In *To Have and Have Not*, a young Lauren Bacall as Slim proves that she is in many ways as resilient as the character played by Humphrey Bogart. The film was a success at the box office at least in part because audiences could see the romantic sparks flying between Bogart and Bacall, who met and fell in love on the set of the film. Carmichael, too, was given a rare opportunity, and he seized it to show several sides of his personality.

In *To Have and Have Not*, Carmichael sits at the piano in the same trickster posture as the early Nat King Cole. Flanked by two black musicians, he sings "Am I Blue" in his nasal tenor voice while dangling a match from his mouth. Carmichael later wrote that the match was his own contribution—something to chew on to settle his nerves. The match stick turned out to be an ingenious way of underlining the character's insouciant, devil-may-care attitude, a quality that comes through most strongly after the death of the man (Walter Sande) who had tried to cheat Bogart of his earnings. When Bogart turns the man over and

47. Cricket (Hoagy Carmichael) and Slim (Lauren Bacall) with a mixed band in *To Have and Have Not* (1944, Warner Bros.). Jerry Ohlinger's Movie Material Store, Inc.

declares him dead, Cricket/Carmichael plays a few bars of Gustav Lange's "The Flower Song," a highly familiar musical signifier of strained melodrama. Later in the film, Carmichael is surrounded by beautiful, well-dressed women as he sings one of his most tricksteresque songs, "Hong Kong Blues," about the "very unfortunate colored man" who is arrested in Hong Kong for "kicking old Buddha's gong around."

Hawks, who had first seen Carmichael in action at a party, knew that the songwriter could play other roles besides the trickster. The author of "Hong Kong Blues" could also write in a deeply romantic mode, and Hawks saw to it that Lauren Bacall sang Carmichael's "How Little We Know" in her husky, Hawksian voice. Later, Carmichael noodles romantically at the piano while the lovers engage in a tête à tête. And in one of the more memorable finales to a Hollywood love story, Bacall does a coyly erotic rhumba into the arms of Bogart while Carmichael supplies an up-tempo version of "How Little We Know" (Mast 1982, 267).

Carmichael's role in *To Have and Have Not* as trickster/musician, always at the sidelines and often commenting ironically, set the tone for most of his subsequent appearances, although his trickster quality was usually translated into less disruptive characteristics. As with Hollywood's efforts to tame Harpo Marx, the polymorphously playful aspects of Carmichael's persona were often trivialized and even infantilized. Just as Marx went from the skirt-chasing, all-consuming anarchist of the Paramount period to the harmless clown surrounded by children in the MGM films, Carmichael developed into a character more often associated with children than with elegant women leaning over his piano. In this sense he resembled Nat Cole's character in *China Gate,* who first appears singing to a child and later declares his intention to bring the boy home with him to the States. In *Johnny Angel,* playing a taxi driver in the service of George Raft, Carmichael entertains a black child with a small propeller on a stick. In *The Best Years of Our Lives* he teaches a group of children how to sing "Here Comes the Bride" just before the wedding that ends the film. At a party in the frontier western *Canyon Passage,* when everyone else in the community is paired heterosexually, Carmichael dances with Andy Devine. In *Belles on Their Toes,* the sequel to *Cheaper by the Dozen* (1950), he is the asexual, mildly irresponsible house servant for Myrna Loy and her twelve children.

In fact, the role that Carmichael plays in *Belles on Their Toes* might have gone to a black actor. Much the same could be said of most of the roles he played, especially in his capacity as a kind of male nursemaid for a variety of protagonists. I have written of the therapeutic function that Carmichael performs for Kirk Douglas in *Young Man with a Horn,* perhaps in a belated, displaced attempt to undo the death of Bix Beiderbecke on whom Douglas's character was loosely based. In *The Best Years of Our Lives,* Carmichael runs the saloon where the damaged veterans of World War II turn up for what is literally, at least in one scene, music therapy: Butch/Carmichael teaches Homer (Harold Russell) how to play "Chop Sticks" on the piano with the metal prostheses that have replaced the hands he lost in the war. In *Night Song,* Chick/Carmichael appears to abandon his life as a bandleader in order to be a constant source of support for Dana Andrews as he regains his sight and ascends to the status of serious composer. Although he works for the large Gilbreth family in *Belles on Their Toes,* Tom/Carmichael is more of a family mascot. At one point in the film, after Myrna Loy has assigned the oldest daughter to look after the female children and the oldest son to take care of the boys, she adds, "And we'll all take care of Tom."

In *Belles on Their Toes,* Tom secretly makes beer in the basement but without much success. When the household is disrupted by exploding

48. Chick (Hoagy Carmichael) tends to the emotional and professional needs of Dan (Dana Andrews) in *Night Song* (1947, RKO). Museum of Modern Art Film Stills Archive.

bottles, the matriarch is determined to fire him. The children, however, intercede and beg for him to be spared. Apart from playing inappropriate death music in *To Have and Have Not,* surreptitiously brewing beer may be the most daring act that Carmichael performs in any of his films. In general, he has a single-minded devotion to an employer or a close friend, very much like Hollywood's numerous black servants and companions such as Dooley Wilson in *Casablanca* (1942), Louis Armstrong in *Glory Alley* (1952), Woody Strode in *The Man Who Shot Liberty Valance* (1962), and Morgan Freeman in *Robin Hood: Prince of Thieves* (1991).

No doubt, Hoagy Carmichael's history of performing with and writing about blacks affected Hollywood's practice of casting him in roles that made him interchangeable with African Americans. Unlike Nat Cole and to a large extent Louis Armstrong, both of whom possessed a trickster masculinity that was not amenable to Hollywood's racial codes, Carmichael *was* able to assume a trickster persona. But only by default. With few exceptions, the cinema could not accommodate other aspects of his persona. Even when he played the trickster, he was allowed to do so only in the most anemic fashion. As David Bordwell has pointed out, Hollywood has long produced "an excessively obvious cinema" (Bordwell et al. 1985, 3). The many faces of the trickster, and the many fronts on which even a single one of his statements must be negotiated, do not always fit Hollywood's penchant for clarity, at least not the kind of clarity that has been constructed to conform to American mythology. In spite of the immense appeal that Hoagy Carmichael held for Middle America, his roots were in an experience that few Americans had bothered to acquire, especially those who believed that the races should be kept separate. By the time the civil rights movement had broken down some of the barriers between black and white cultures, the jazz that had inspired Carmichael's unique sensibilities was a thing of the past.[8] Even when Hollywood tried to tell the story of Beiderbecke and Carmichael, even when they prevailed upon Carmichael for assistance, the result was *Young Man with a Horn*. The Carmichael who wrote "Riverboat Shuffle," "Baltimore Oriole," and "Hong Kong Blues" *as well as* "Lazy River" was not a natural subject for the movies.

New York, New York and *Short Cuts*

[Sonny Stitt] played for an hour maybe, did everything that could be done on a saxophone, everything you could play, as much as Charlie Parker could have played if he'd been there. Then he stopped. And he looked at me. Gave me one of those looks, "All right, suckah, your turn." And it's *my* job; it's *my* gig. I was strung out. I was hooked. I was drunk. I was having a hassle with my wife, Diane, who'd threatened to kill herself in our hotel room next door. I had marks on my arm. I thought there were narcs in the club, and I all of a sudden realized that it was *me*. He'd done all those things, and now I had to put up or shut up or get off or forget or quit or kill myself or *something*.

I forgot everything, and everything came out. I played way over my head. I played completely different than he did. I searched and found my own way, and what I said reached the people. I played myself, and I knew I was right, and the people loved it, and they felt it. I blew and I blew, and when I finally finished I was shaking all over; my heart was pounding; I was soaked in sweat, and the people were screaming; the people were clapping, and I looked at Sonny, but I just kind of nodded, and he went, "All *right*." And that was it. That's what it's all about.

—Art Pepper, *Straight Life* (1979, 476)

ost of this book has been devoted to American films released before 1970 if only because jazz has seldom played more than a marginal role in the films of the last few decades. More often than not, jazz appears because an earlier era is being evoked (*Pretty Baby* [1978], *1941* [1979], *The Cotton Club* [1984], *Swing Shift* [1984]), or because characters in the present have a nostalgia for the music of an earlier era (*All of Me* [1984], *The Gig* [1985], *Mr. & Mrs. Bridge* [1990]).[1] A few other films have brought canonical jazz musicians on screen simply for a quick laugh. A panning camera in *Blazing Saddles* (1973), for example, shows that the seemingly extradiegetic music of the Count Basie orchestra is in fact the band itself playing in the desert; and when Miles Davis, David Sanborn,

Larry Carlton, and Paul Shaffer appear as street corner musicians playing for loose change in a brief scene in *Scrooged* (1988), Bill Murray chides them with remarks such as, "Great. Rip off the hicks, why doncha? Didja learn that song yesterday?"

An unlikely pair of actor/directors have regularly featured jazz musicians and jazz performances in their work. Both Woody Allen in *Sleeper* (1973), *Stardust Memories* (1980), *September* (1987), *Alice* (1990), and *Bullets Over Broadway* (1994), and Clint Eastwood in *Play Misty for Me* (1971), *The Gauntlet* (1977), *Bird* (1988), and *In the Line of Fire* (1993) have enough control over their films to be able to satisfy their own passions for jazz in spite of audiences that are mostly indifferent to the music. If there are other American filmmakers with similar tastes, they have been more interested in catering to market forces than in making jazz part of their work.

Robert Altman and Martin Scorsese have long possessed reputations as Hollywood outsiders answering to their own unique visions rather than to the marketplace. Although neither director seems to share the jazzophilia of Eastwood or Allen, both have been sensitive to music's ability to transform a film. Scorsese included a fascinating variety of musical effects in *Raging Bull* (1980), including the lyrical intermezzo from *Cavalleria rusticana* as background to the film's most brutal boxing footage. In *Goodfellas* (1990) the director placed each scene in time by constantly updating the steady stream of popular songs on the soundtrack. Altman built an entire film around the music industry with *Nashville* (1975), and he carefully chose a number of popular tunes from the 1930s, including Jimmie Lunceford's "Organ Grinder's Swing," to play on radios throughout *Thieves Like Us* (1974). For *The Long Goodbye* (1973), Altman played an elaborate game of hide-and-seek with a title theme by the pre-*Star Wars* John Williams. Never played in its entirety, the song is first heard in two different vocal versions on car radios as the camera cuts back and forth between two automobiles. Moments later, the song becomes the Muzak in a grocery store. Before the film is over, the tune has been played almost everywhere by almost everything, including doorbell chimes and a passing mariachi band.

The different ways that Altman and Scorsese have used jazz illustrate the changing attitudes toward the music in American films since 1970. In *New York, New York* (1977) Scorsese has written a brief history of popular music that begins with the declining popularity of jazz immediately after World War II. As the male hero played by Robert De Niro becomes more devoted to bebop and other post-swing manifestations of the music, he surrounds himself with black artists and neglects his wife (Liza Minnelli) and their child. Ultimately, the film, released at a moment when the fortunes of jazz were close to the nadir, seems to lose interest in the music while celebrating the spectacle of Liza Minnelli in performance. In Altman's *Short Cuts* (1993) the stories of Raymond Carver are united by the diegetic and extradiegetic music of a jazz group led by singer Annie Ross. The group's musical selections are part of what Robert T. Self (1995) has called the film's "hypertext," a series of shared nuances in a collection of narratives about unextraordinary people who are, in the words of Ross's first song, "Prisoners of Life." *Short Cuts* appeared at a moment in the mid–1990s when Americans were becoming more sympathetic toward jazz. Although the music was working its way up the cultural ladder and even competing with opera and the symphony in some hierarchies, this is not at all what *Short Cuts* invokes. A better comparison would be the television commercials and movie soundtracks mentioned in chapter 3, many of which suggest that jazz can stand comparison with classical music as the subliminal signifier of affluence, pleasure, and real feeling. In Scorsese's film, by contrast, emotional expression is mostly the property of Liza Minnelli.

New York, New York may be the most ambitious if not the most disappointing of all the films with jazz content released since 1970. The film speaks to many of the issues that have been central to this study. Like *Bird* and *Sweet Smell of Success* (1957), it evokes the art versus commerce dichotomy that has been essential to jazz talk since the 1940s; as in *Mo' Better Blues* (1990) and *Lady Sings the Blues* (1972), jazz is central to the performance of gender roles; like *The Benny Goodman Story* (1956) and *A Man Called Adam* (1966), it involves the problematic interactions between white and black musicians; and like John Cassavetes's *Shadows* (1960) and very few films since, *New York, New York* adopts a jazz aesthetic to tell a story about jazz musicians. In fact, Scorsese has cited Cassavetes's improvisatory style of filmmaking as an early influence on his own work: he prominently mentions *Shadows* and *Faces* (1968) as the inspiration for his films *Who's That Knocking at My Door?* (1968), *Mean Streets* (1973), and much of *New York, New York*.[2]

With his exhaustive knowledge of film history, Scorsese has compiled a long list of films and directors that also helped determine the shape of *New York, New York*. Scorsese has said that he wanted to write a "love note" to the great musicals of classical Hollywood at the same time that he wanted to critique the genre. The most prominent and most obvious inspiration for this project is the 1954 remake of *A Star Is Born*, a "revisionist musical" directed by George Cukor and featuring Liza Minnelli's mother, Judy Garland. In both Scorsese's film and in Cukor's *A Star Is Born*, a husband sees his wife surpass him in her career. Cukor's film marries the well-established conventions of the musical to film noir, a match made in heaven for Scorsese, whose *Mean Streets* and *Taxi Driver* (1976) showed his ability to both master and transcend noir conventions.

But Scorsese is perceptive enough as a cinema historian to find the beginnings of the revisionist musical before 1954. He has found revisionist tendencies in earlier, more traditional musicals such as *Blue Skies* (1946) and *My Dream Is Yours* (1949) that anticipate generic changes of the 1950s and later. Both films feature characters who do not precisely fit the mold of the musical romantic hero. Like Jimmy Doyle (Robert De Niro) in *New York, New York*, Bing Crosby plays what Scorsese calls a "lovable heel" in *Blue Skies*; in *My Dream Is Yours*, Doris Day is a singer with a career on the ascendant who falls for Lee Bowman, a petty, self-centered singer whose career is in decline. For Scorsese, both of these films have noir elements lurking beneath their bright, colorful surfaces. Although it was shot in black and white, *The Man I Love* (1946) is also cited by Scorsese among the films that influenced *New York, New York* because it is effectively a film noir with musical characters. Ida Lupino is a singer enamored with a jazz musician (Bruce Bennett), and even though the film treats their love affair as genuine, they walk off in different directions at the end, just like the protagonists in *New York, New York*.

In addition to rethinking the conventions of the classical Hollywood musical, Scorsese was intent on combining the styles of several different directors and schools of filmmaking. *New York, New York* was only the fourth film that Scorsese made for a major studio, and in spite of the relatively huge budget at his disposal, he was still committed to his early, Cassavetean ideal of a low-budget cinema built around improvisations in which actors seem to be "behaving" rather than acting. Scorsese also mentions the films of Elia Kazan, presumably *On the Waterfront* (1954) and *East of Eden* (1955), in which a sense of realism was achieved through the shrugging, often improvised performances of James Dean and Marlon Brando. At the same time, however, Scorsese says that he was enchanted by the "seamless" camera and editing techniques of John Ford as well as by the "self-conscious filmmaking" of Orson Welles. Scorsese also mentions the art cinema of Godard, Fellini, Kurosawa, and Mizoguchi as inspirations. And he studied the "Girl Hunt Ballet" in Vincente Minnelli's *The Band Wagon* (1953), a fascinating moment when film noir is blended with the classical traditions of the musical and embodied in the person of Fred Astaire.[3]

Finally, Scorsese has said that he chose *New York, New York* (producer Irwin Winkler had bought the rights to the script a few years earlier) because of his early affection for the records that his father and uncles used to play when he was growing up in the 1940s. He says that the older members of his family schooled him carefully in the differences among the bands of Tommy and Jimmy Dorsey, Benny Goodman, Artie Shaw, Gene Krupa, "even down to Kyser." (Like most commentators on the big bands today, Scorsese utters the dominant view that Kay Kyser was "a little interesting for the time—that's all you can say.") One of Scorsese's stated goals in making *New York, New York* was to faithfully re-create the music of the late 1940s as well as the *look* of the period, something that was inevitably lacking in films of the 1960s and 1970s that were set in the 1940s. Scorsese even tried to shoot the film in the same aspect ratio and three-strip Technicolor that characterized films of the 1940s. In addition, he hired the production designer Boris Leven who had created the spare, almost expressionistic sets for films such as *Alexander's Ragtime*

49. Jimmy Doyle (Robert De Niro) with jazz musicians in *New York, New York* (1977, United Artists). Jerry Ohlinger's Movie Material Store, Inc.

Band (1938), *The Silver Chalice* (1954), *Giant* (1956), and *West Side Story* (1961).

With Scorsese's endless list of influences and revisionist intentions, it is no wonder that *New York, New York* seems stylistically incoherent. As many critics pointed out, Scorsese's top-heavy agenda yielded a film that puzzled audiences: highly "realistic" performances by De Niro and Minnelli took place in front of obviously "unrealistic" stage settings. Scorsese himself ultimately said that *New York, New York* "was a mess, and it's a

50. Francine Evans (Liza Minnelli) poses in *Happy Endings,* the film within a film in *New York, New York.* Jerry Ohlinger's Movie Material Store, Inc.

miracle that the film makes any kind of sense" (Thompson and Christie 1989, 72). As a tradition of filmmaking, the musical may simply be too artificial to accommodate Scorsese's ambitious attempts at revision. Certainly the film's heavy reliance on improvisation makes for too many scenes in which actors simply repeat themselves, and on occasion, break down into screaming fits. Scorsese has effectively written off *New York, New York* as a preparation for the much more successful use of improvised performances in *Raging Bull*. At least in terms of De Niro's performances, *Raging Bull* is a devastating portrait of a possessed man; by contrast, the Jimmy Doyle of *New York, New York* is simply obnoxious.

Although moments occur when the interactions between De Niro and Liza Minnelli are successful—Scorsese singles out the scene where they clash over who should "kick off" the band in rehearsal—the film ceases to be a revisionist musical whenever Minnelli plunges into her highly mannered style of singing. Some attempt at parody takes place in *Happy Endings*, the film within the film, but at virtually every other moment when Minnelli performs, the audience is asked to regard her as a great entertainer. If the film presented her excesses with some degree of irony, it might have succeeded as a more thorough critique of a familiar genre. Scorsese might have achieved what Dennis Potter, Steve Martin, and Herbert Ross accomplished a few years later with *Pennies from Heaven* (1981), a "Brechtian" take on the musical and its myths (Feuer 1993, 126). But then *Pennies from Heaven* was an even bigger box-office failure than *New York, New York*. Scorsese was taken with Minnelli during their collaboration, and he stated that he found her to be a major talent. Shortly after *New York, New York* was completed, he even continued working with her, directing her onstage in a play called *The Act*. Scorsese quickly realized, however, that he was out of his element directing for the stage, and he soon was replaced by Gower Champion (Thompson and Christie 1989, 74–76).

New York, New York's lavish attention to Minnelli's performances is often at the expense of the film's representation of jazz artists. Even so, the director tried in a few ways to give jazz its due. He began the project with a script by Earl Mac Rauch and Mardik Martin that, at least in its first draft, took jazz history seriously.[4] For example, during the cab ride in which Jimmy brings Francine along for his audition at the Palm Club in Brooklyn, the shooting script has him talking about "the giants of jazz": "Ellington, the Count, Mundy, Sampson, Sy Oliver—and the new guys—have you heard what's been happening? Gillespie and Charlie Parker. Now, Parker I admire the cat a great deal, but I got to admit there's something about his style I don't agree with. That don't mean he's not important, understand?" Later, when Jimmy and Francine celebrate their success after the audition, Francine lists her favorite vocalists: "Ella Fitzgerald, Bessie Smith, Billie Holiday, and Helen Forrest, Jo Stafford, Peggy Lee—I like them, too." The early script also has Jimmy speaking the argot of the bop era, referring to money as "bread" and condemning a club owner with the phrase, "this egg here don't like my groove." Writing several years before bebop became the sanctioned style of a new generation of young, well-dressed jazz musicians, the authors of the original screenplay for *New York, New York* were also scrupulous about the details of bebop history. In the hiring hall scene in which Jimmy first encounters the black trumpeter Cecil Powell, Jimmy is told that he ought to go uptown to Minton's Playhouse. Jimmy then refers to the club as the "birthplace of bop."

Although the final film follows most of the structure of the original script, including the painful path the lovers take toward their eventual separation, the endings of the first and last versions are significantly different. In Rauch and Martin's screenplay, Jimmy slowly moves away from jazz and eventually becomes a producer of rock and roll records. By the end, he and Francine have both become successful, and, as in the film, Jimmy sees Francine backstage after her performance at the Starlight Terrace. After Jimmy invites Francine to join him, the two walk out together, chatting comfortably. Rejecting the advice of director George Lucas, whose wife Marcia edited *New York, New York,* Scorsese ends his film with the two principals independently deciding not to meet. Lucas told Scorsese that the originally scripted ending would have added $10 million to the box-office receipts (Thompson and Christie 1989, 69). This was significant advice from a director whose film *Star Wars* (1977) opened at roughly the same time as *New York, New York* and ushered in an age of filmmaking in which Scorsese's revisionism was even less likely to win support.

In Scorsese's hands, *New York, New York* does not retain all of the attention to the jazz life that was present in the original screenplay. The naming of specific jazz artists—whether Duke Ellington and Billie Holiday or Charlie Parker and Dizzy Gillespie—has disappeared. Nor does Jimmy speak the patois of the hipster. Neither Minton's nor any other historic location of forties' jazz is mentioned. Instead, the black artists perform in a spacious dance hall called the "Harlem Club" that is akin to nightspots of the 1920s such as the Cotton Club. Still, the Jimmy Doyle of Scorsese's film perseveres as a jazz artist, and the film associates his drive toward self-realization with his need to pursue the jazz life. Even the musical selections show a sophisticated awareness of the codes of jazz. When Jimmy sits in with the black musicians at the Harlem Club, for example, he quotes from Ben Webster's solo on Duke Ellington's "Cottontail," a recording from 1940 that anticipated some of the elements of more "modern" jazz. Earlier, when Jimmy performs at the Palm Club anticipating the arrival of Francine the day after their romantic night on the town, the film winks at the insiders when Jimmy plays "Fit as a Fiddle (and Ready for Love)."

Furthermore, Scorsese has been extremely faithful to swing music and the 1940s. In spite of his stated intentions, he has delivered a more ardent love note to the big bands than to the classical Hollywood musical. When the film opens with a fastidious re-creation of the look and sound of Tommy Dorsey's orchestra, the details are in place: the repertoire of "I'm Getting Sentimental Over You," "Song of India," and "Opus No. 1" is exactly what the band was playing at the end of World War II. In addition to casting an actor who both looks like Tommy Dorsey and accurately mimes his trombone gestures, the film features musicians who resemble the drummer Buddy Rich and the black trumpeter Charlie Shavers, both of them key members of TD's band in the mid–1940s. Even the patter between the radio announcer and Dorsey is true to the banalities commonly heard on broadcasts of the period. In spite of his genuine affection for the big bands, Scorsese has been just as careful in representing the end of the era when dancing audiences dwindled and more attention was being paid to singers.

As many critics have pointed out, De Niro learned his lessons well when Georgie Auld taught him how to comport himself as a jazz saxophone player. At this point in his career with Scorsese, De Niro was carefully establishing himself as the consummate actor prepared to pay any price for his art. For his role as Jake LaMotta in *Raging Bull,* De Niro devoted himself daily to learning how to box; he also gained fifty-five pounds in order to resemble the older LaMotta (Thompson and Christie 1989, 93). Later, when Scorsese directed him in *The King of Comedy* (1983), De Niro faithfully learned the mannerisms of second-rate stand-up comedians. In *New York, New York,* Scorsese deserves credit for aspects of De Niro's performance, if only because he made the intelligent choice of hiring Auld to play the part of bandleader Frankie Harte and to tutor De Niro on the tenor saxophone. Scorsese has said that Auld possessed "a little bit of menace along with the sweetness" and was an inspiration for the character of Jimmy Doyle. Auld reveals much of himself in the scene on the band bus when he tells Francine that he is about to give up his band; the audience briefly glimpses the diamond-in-the-rough qualities of a man who had directed his own big band during the same era when the fictional Frankie Harte was in the business. In fact, in 1945 Auld hired many young musicians like Jimmy Doyle for a big band that was in the vanguard of the bop revolution. Auld employed white modernists such as Gerry Mulligan, Serge Chaloff, and Al Cohn but also black artists such as Dizzy Gillespie, Freddie Webster, Shadow Wilson, Tadd Dameron, and Sarah Vaughan. In both his playing and in the film image he presents, Auld personifies the artist as tough guy, undoubtedly a role he developed from close attention to black tenor saxophonists such as Ben Webster and Coleman Hawkins.

Auld's self-presentation can probably be understood in terms of Eric Lott's paradigm (1993) of the white working-class male who bases his masculine image on the comportment of black men. In *New York, New York* Jimmy Doyle is also attracted to the world of black jazz musicians. The film shows him joining them in the highly suggestive locus of a closed restroom stall where they share a marijuana cigarette; he also comes on to a black female singer in one crucial scene. Although he makes no mention of the erotic appeal of black culture, Scorsese is explicit about Jimmy's attitude toward African Americans. He says that Jimmy seeks the "pure jazz expression" of great black musicians, but that this goal is "impossible to obtain" and that Jimmy has to find his own means of expression. In Scorsese's reading of Jimmy's character, the saxophonist "punishes" himself because he cannot live up to the standards he has set for himself.

Scorsese says that Jimmy's struggles as an artist are complicated when he falls in love with someone who exemplifies a completely different view of music. Since most of *New York, New York* is structured on this clash of styles, it is tempting to read the conflict embodied by Jimmy and Francine as central to critics' and audiences' difficulties with the film. The same conflict also may characterize Scorsese's own dilemma as an artist throughout his career. Scorsese is as fascinated by Vincente Minnelli and John Ford as he is by John Cassavetes and Jean-Luc Godard. He wants to be an artist of the cinema, but he is extremely eclectic about the meaning of art. For Scorsese, the graceful, invisible camera of Vincente Minnelli is as artistically valid as the jarringly self-referential camera of Godard. Each of Scorsese's films represents a different solution to the problem of how a mainstream Hollywood film can absorb influences from the art cinemas of Europe and the American avant-garde. *Taxi*

Driver, for example, takes its plot from John Ford's *The Searchers* (1956), but specific moments in the film were inspired by Godard. A scene in which the camera slowly zooms in on the bubbles in Travis Bickle's glass of Alka-Seltzer, for example, recalls a similar shot in Godard's *Two or Three Things I Know about Her* (1966).[5] Even Scorsese's *The Age of Innocence* (1993), with its multiple resemblances to the British cycle of "Laura Ashley movies" such as *A Room with a View* (1985), *Enchanted April* (1991), and *The Remains of the Day* (1993), audaciously adopts a camera style that frequently turns away from smooth narrative to zoom in on the diegetically irrelevant objects that make up the world of the characters.

Nevertheless, Scorsese is firmly committed to a commercially viable cinema. His films invariably tilt toward the certifiably reliable conventions of mainstream entertainment. In spite of its avant-garde artiness, *New York, New York* reveals again and again that Scorsese's real sympathies lie with the more accessible art of Liza Minnelli, not to mention the work of her mother and father. Unlike jazz musicians and the actors in a Cassavetes film, Liza Minnelli does not improvise. The tightly choreographed production numbers of the classical Hollywood musical are incompatible with a Cassavetean or a jazz aesthetic, even though many directors have perfected the art of making musical numbers *appear* spontaneous and "natural"; Judy Garland's cakewalking duet with Margaret O'Brien in Vincente Minnelli's *Meet Me in St. Louis* (1944) is a convincing example. The narrative of *New York, New York* is in fact saturated with the incompatibility between two aesthetics. Jimmy Doyle is a jazz musician for whom improvisation is essential, even when music is not involved. When he first meets Francine at the Starlight Terrace, he performs multiple riffs on the pickup line. Later, when he is trying to avoid paying for his room at the hotel, he improvises speeches on the theme of society's debt to its war veterans. In what may be Jimmy's most memorable improvisation, he proposes marriage to Francine with the phrase, "Put your coat on. Let's go." In the subsequent scene at the home of the justice of the peace, Doyle/De Niro accidentally breaks a pane of glass while knocking on the door. Scorsese says that the incident was not planned but that he let De Niro incorporate it into his interactions with the justice of the peace.

But if Robert De Niro and Jimmy Doyle are improvisers, Liza Minnelli and Francine Evans are not. In the wedding scene, Francine demands the more conventional script of courtship, which Jimmy then gives her in another improvisation, lying behind the wheels of their taxi and commanding the driver to back up. The contrast in styles between the two characters and the actors playing them is evident from the first moment they perform together. When Jimmy auditions in Brooklyn with Francine standing by as a reluctant observer, the saxophonist ad-libs several bars of jazz while De Niro creates a medley of body movements in which he "performs" his masculinity. When Francine breaks in with the Maurice Chevalier song that the club owner has requested, she too acts out a gender display, but one that is much more familiar, including the coy, gently remonstrative finger-wagging with which she answers his demand that she show her legs. But while Jimmy improvises an obbligato behind her song, Francine sings scripted lyrics. Even her dance steps seem highly conventionalized. The scene is prophetic because Jimmy feels contempt for the music that Francine sings, even though supporting that music is essential to his landing the job. *His* success is entirely the result of her mastery of a popular, accessible idiom, but in no way does her subsequent success depend on his abilities as an improviser.

The musical styles of the two artists—as well as the film's own preferences—are clearly expressed in two rhymed scenes where each actor performs under a spotlight. On the day after the audition in Brooklyn, when he receives the "billet doux" from Francine and is contemplating following her, Jimmy plays his tenor saxophone a cappella beneath a streetlight. Scorsese says that the look of the scene was inspired by the "Girl Hunt Ballet" in *The Band Wagon* and that the light was literally painted onto the floor. During the few seconds that Jimmy improvises a bluesy solo, he stands in a stark, highly artificial set. Later on, after Francine has been abandoned by Jimmy and has begun her own career, she stands alone in a studio under a spotlight and sings "The World Goes Round," one of the boffo songs like the title tune that were written by John Kander and Fred Ebb before the film went into production. Scorsese has been generous in praising the songwriters, insisting that he had to build Francine's character around their showstopping music.

Jimmy's brief solo is appropriately paired with the scene in which Francine belts out Kander and Ebb's song. Like Jimmy, she is alone on camera, but she is hardly unaccompanied—a full orchestra plays behind her, presumably on a tape with which she has been rehearsing. Only a few abandoned musical instruments are evident in the background. At first, Francine is strongly framed while she stands in front of the microphone. Unlike singers who actually record over taped accompaniment, she wears no headphones to inhibit her movements or distract from her flamboyant appearance. After several minutes, the lights on the instruments in the background dim and then come up again in expressionist patterns. Finally, all the lights go off accept for a pencil spot on her face. Francine's highly dramatic performance is surely meant to indicate her ability to draw upon and transcend the experience of being abandoned by Jimmy on the day their child was born. Here the film invokes the myth, most commonly associated with singers such as Billie Holiday, that heartfelt musical performances are made possible by emotional suffering. As I suggested in the discussion of *Lady Sings the Blues* in chapter 2, this myth suggests that a singer who has had her heart broken can, transparently and without artifice, express her feelings in a musical performance. In fact, the singing style that the Francine Evans of *New York, New York* has previously practiced—pop tunes sung in front of a live band for dancers—has been replaced in "The World Goes Round" sequence by a meticulously planned performance in which her body and voice completely dominate the screen. Presented in one long take, the scene allows Minnelli to build her climaxes carefully while the elaborate lighting effects enhance the stylized emotion in her delivery.

If Francine is the decided winner over Jimmy in the matched scenes under spotlights, she is never even given a chance to compete with him in an earlier scene at the Harlem Club. Here Scorsese's fascination with jazz—especially as it is performed by African Americans—seems to undercut the film's more obvious project of celebrating the talents of Liza Minnelli. Diahnne Abbott's performance of "Honeysuckle Rose" provides a strong contrast to Minnelli's "The World Goes Round." Abbott, who was De Niro's wife during the making of *New York, New York*, would later costar with him in Scorsese's *King of Comedy* (1983) as well as in a film directed by Cassavetes, *Love Streams* (1984). Playing a character who is not identified by name in *New York, New York*, Abbott first appears walking down the steps at the Harlem Club en route to the bandstand. When she passes Jimmy Doyle, she pauses briefly and asks wryly, "Family night?" in reference to Francine, her manager (Lionel Stander), and a record producer (Leonard Gaines), the only other white faces in the club. Then, as she walks to the bandstand, Doyle reaches for her and says, "Come here." Avoiding his grasp, she continues on her way without breaking stride. Abbott plays a woman who, unlike Francine, does not submit to Jimmy. Whether or not she has in the past is never established. We do know that Jimmy has cheated on his wife by sleeping with Bernice Bennett (Mary Kay Place), the singer who took Francine's place after she left Jimmy's band. If, in her handling of Jimmy, the Abbott character appears to be much tougher than Francine, she exhibits a certain softness when she actually sings. Without dwelling on Diahnne Abbott's strengths or weaknesses as a jazz singer, I would observe only that she sings with a great deal of understatement. Her performance of female sexuality is less hysterical but substantially more direct than Francine's. Abbott avoids the histrionic combination of vulnerability and assertiveness that Liza Minnelli (and Judy Garland) practice, engaging instead in eroticized play with the other musicians on the bandstand, including Jimmy's friend, the robustly handsome trumpeter Cecil Powell (Clarence Clemons). If Francine exemplifies the art of a soloist performing in a narcissistic cocoon, Abbott is the collaborative artist submerging a measure of her self into the group effort and obviously enjoying it.

Throughout Abbott's song, however, the camera is much less attentive to the vocalist than it was during Francine's "The World Goes Round." Several cutaways are made to Jimmy, who appears to be miming a conversation on the telephone to justify his absence from the table where Francine is being assured of imminent success by her two male companions. After Abbott has completed her first vocal chorus and the Harlem Club trombonist has begun his solo, the camera focuses on a motionless Jimmy for a full thirty seconds. In a pensive mood, he looks down with a half-smile, perhaps contemplating Francine's success and his own enticing but ambiguous place in a room filled with blacks. He may also be assessing what he can and cannot have. While Francine is being courted by an executive from Decca Records, Jimmy is realizing that he cannot really achieve the place among black artists to which he aspires. Because of his personality and his color, he knows he can never fully participate in the seemingly effortless interaction the audience has just witnessed. Certainly he was never able to sustain it for long with Francine.

Moments after Abbott has sung "Honeysuckle Rose," Jimmy returns to the bandstand to play "Just You, Just Me" with Cecil Powell and the house band. This is the same song that Francine had earlier performed with the big band when Jimmy was the leader. In a rare moment of joyous interaction with Jimmy, she had injected a good deal of what appeared to be jazz feeling into her presentation of the song. Immediately after this earlier performance of "Just You, Just Me," however, Francine had left the stage and fainted from the early effects of her pregnancy. It would be her last performance with the band. Now at the Harlem Club, Francine begins to act on her recent decision to bring her marriage with Jimmy to a crisis. In the one and only tight close-up in the film, Francine had looked at herself in the mirror while she was alone in her apartment listening to a 1938 recording of "Billet Doux" by the Quintet of the Hot Club of France. Scorsese says that the song, which features the Gypsy guitarist Django Reinhardt, was his favorite among the records that he heard when he was growing up. He has also said that he spent a great deal of time listening to it while he was alone (Holdenfield 1977, 41). Although the scene in which Francine gazes darkly into her mirror while "Billet Doux" played in the background was temporarily cut from the film, Scorsese says that he still considers it to be a crucial moment in *New York, New York,* the occasion when Francine decides to bring her tangled marriage to a head.

At the Harlem Club, realizing that she is taking a substantial risk, Francine walks through a crowd of dancers so that she can sing "Just You, Just Me" with Jimmy. Watching her every step, Jimmy waits until she is a few feet from the microphone and then suddenly changes tempo, beginning a new performance of "Jumpin' with Symphony Sid." Written for the jazz disc jockey Sid Torin and known as Lester Young's theme song in his later years, the tune had no lyrics at that time. Even if the riff-style phrase did come with words, Jimmy has set a tempo that is inhospitable to vocalists. He thus sadistically prevents Francine from assuming any place in a domain where her style of performance is out of place. How she might have fared on the bandstand with black jazz artists is an issue the film cannot address because it conceals the extent to which Minnelli's effectiveness as a performer depends on the star treatment that Scorsese grants her when she sings "The World Goes Round" and "New York, New York." We are not allowed to find out whether she can work with the house band in any of the ways that the Diahnne Abbott character does. In preventing this interaction, Jimmy is further setting himself off from the black musicians—by jumping into "Jumpin' with Symphony Sid," he is not so much playing *with* the black artists as he is playing *without* his wife.

At the end of the film, the musical worlds of Jimmy and Francine are again juxtaposed, this time with their separate performances of Kander and Ebb's "New York, New York." Now a successful performing artist and owner of the spacious nightclub the Major Chord, Jimmy stands in front of a quartet playing a slow, breathy version of the tune's principal motif while the pianist repeatedly hits a minor, not a major chord. The music lasts for only a few seconds. Then, in a fascinating image of the film's racial dynamics, Jimmy introduces Cecil Powell and his group as they appear on a revolving, circular stage. The black musicians emerge into the club while Jimmy's group rotates into the shadows. Powell's group is literally the dark side of Jimmy's music. And in fact Powell and his sidemen play a music that is nothing like anything previously heard in the film: after a brief introductory figure, both the trumpeter and the saxophonist improvise simultaneously without key signature or melodic structure; after Jimmy Doyle's languid playing, the Powell group's music sounds mysterious and chaotic. The chronology of the film has not been clearly established, but Scorsese says that the scene in the Major Chord takes place in 1957. Very few jazz groups were playing this kind of "outside" music at such an early date.[6] The filmmakers clearly have been much less attentive to the jazz of 1957 than they were to the jazz of 1945. Clarence Clemons, who plays Cecil Powell, is himself a tenor saxophonist best known for his long tenure with the white rocker Bruce Springsteen. When he appears on the revolving stage, Powell is wearing dark glasses and playing the trumpet with his arms tight against his sides and his shoulders hunched. Striking an uncomfortable pose for a trumpet player, his body has an almost pinched look. The band has played only a few seconds before the camera cuts away and follows Doyle as he flirts with two well-dressed, unaccompanied young women at the bar. A black bouncer then approaches him to inquire about a customer's credit. Declaring that the customer is not a good risk and that the bouncer can use the bill with the man's signature "for wallpaper," Doyle walks into his office and picks up the telephone to make a reservation for one at the Starlight Terrace.

Unlike the racially mixed group of hipsters and socialites at the Major Chord, the audience at the Starlight Terrace is large, undifferentiated, and wildly enthusiastic. This is of course the same ballroom where Jimmy and Francine had first met, and Jimmy sits at the same table where he saw Francine at the beginning of the film. Francine's scrupulously choreographed and photographed performance of "New York, New York" is completely unlike the downbeat version that Jimmy had played only minutes earlier. If nothing else, the audience watches and hears a complete reading of the song, unlike the brief tastes of music presented at the Major Chord amid a variety of distractions. Francine's expansive, ostentatious body language and intense singing style provide a release from the cramped, inaccessible jazz of Cecil Powell and his group. The film suggests that if a crowd-pleasing, infectious performance style is what made the jazz musicians of the big band era popular, then they ceded it in the 1950s to popular entertainers like Francine.

Scorsese has made no apologies for writing a "love note" to the classical Hollywood musical. He knows that audiences leave the theater humming memorable tunes rather than improvised solos by jazz musicians. Still, Scorsese has passed up an opportunity to give the same kind of attention to jazz that he has lavished on the posturings of Liza Minnelli. Why is there nothing in *New York, New York* like the passage from Art Pepper's autobiography that begins this chapter? Scorsese has said that the film deals with the same themes that he has faced throughout his career—the dilemma of an artist in a commercial world. Specifically, Scorsese says that he has had to keep the box office in mind while asking himself, "How much can I get away with?" In addition, Scorsese has said that Jimmy Doyle must ask himself the same question: what kind of compromises does the artist have to make in order to survive? But if the director identifies with the Doyle character, why has he made a film that portrays his artistic world as ultimately uninteresting in contrast to the unproblematic domain of entertainment inhabited by Francine? And why must the uncompromising artist be presented as so thoroughly unlikable, while the popular entertainer never lets success go to her head?

New York, New York is very much a film about jazz as an art form, and it has been directed by a cinephile who understands as well as anyone all the ways in which a movie can be artistic. We might expect *New York, New York* to posit equivalences between, on the one hand, jazz and the art cinema and, on the other, popular music and the mainstream commercial cinema. Jimmy Doyle might be a metaphor for the art cinema and Francine Evans for popular movies. This is what the film reviewer Carrie Rickey suggests in her oral commentary on the 1993 laser disc reissue of the film:

> [*New York, New York's*] conflict was that of a mainstream artist versus a vanguard artist, a struggle perilously close to the filmmaker's own dilemma. [It] is a movie in which Scorsese asks himself whether he should make art that was popular and readily understood or art that was difficult and challenging. Without taking sides against one of his principal characters, Scorsese chooses the latter. His film, like the best art, is honest and challenging, and it leaves us thinking that sometimes an unhappy ending is not only the most honest one but perhaps can lead to the greater happiness.

I would disagree with Rickey's statement that Scorsese has not taken sides with either character and that he has made a film that is "difficult and challenging." The story may end on a downbeat, but Scorsese has in effect handed his film to Liza Minnelli and asked audiences to lose themselves in her seamless presentations of the Kander and Ebb songs. Although serious students of jazz, swing, and the Hollywood musical can go on hunting expeditions to track down the intertextual references in *New York, New York*, Scorsese has basically made a film in which viewers are asked to accept the pathos of two talented people who realize that they cannot live as a couple in dissimilar artistic and emotional worlds. Audiences are much more likely to remember the triumphant performances of Minnelli, not to mention the happy endings of *Happy Endings*, as Scorsese himself has pointed out.

Critics have long struggled to claim the status of art for jazz. On some levels, jazz devotees have reason to celebrate now that this goal has been achieved. But as we look over the music's representation in much of the American cinema, the victory may seem hollow. In many ways, *New York, New York* answers the question of why Hollywood has for so long appeared uninterested in exploring the range of possibilities offered by jazz. Rightly or wrongly, jazz has been configured as the refutation of the ideology of entertainment on which the American cinema has thrived. Even in films such as *Bird* and *Round Midnight* (1986), where the interactions of jazz musicians ought to be celebrated, there is little of what Richard Dyer (1981) has called the "utopian" spirit that Hollywood has kept alive in its all-singing, all-dancing musicals.[7] In chapter 5, I argued that Vincente Minnelli and Duke Ellington created a utopian moment in 1943 when Ellington and a troupe of black dancers perform at Jim Henry's Paradise in *Cabin in the Sky*. Three decades later, Scorsese built his utopian vision around Minnelli's daughter rather than around the jazz artists and dancers at the Harlem Club. Even in the films of the 1980s and early 1990s, when the traditions of the classical Hollywood musical were effectively abandoned, utopias were still evoked in nostalgic returns to the 1940s (*A League of Their Own* [1992]) or the early 1960s (*Dirty Dancing* [1987]). In these films, pop music and premodern jazz loudly accompany scenes of joyous communal dancing. Consider, by contrast, the dark and brooding performances of modern jazz in *Bird* and *New York, New York*. And compare Spike Lee's utopian vision of black youths of the 1940s lindy-hopping to Lionel Hampton's "Flying Home" in *Malcolm X* (1992) with Lee's depiction of Shadow Henderson and Bleek Gilliam bitterly contesting over musical/sexual terrain in *Mo' Better Blues*.

I make no claims for a utopian vision of contemporary jazz in *Short Cuts*.[8] When Tess Trainer (Annie Ross) and the band perform diegetically at the Low Note Club, patrons are inevitably talking, often in loud and obnoxious tones. At home with her daughter, Tess searches for a "roach" while complaining about the unruly audiences, even entertaining the possibility of following the large group of American jazz artists who spend large portions of their careers in Europe. "I hate L.A. All they do is talk and snort coke. . . . Think I'll get a job in Amsterdam. They really know how to treat a jazz person there." In two separate scenes, Tess tells the story of Chick Trainer, her late husband and the father of Zoe (Lori Singer), her cello-playing daughter. She tells Zoe that her father "exploded" when Zoe was six years old. When asked for more details, Tess is concise: "He was a prick. That's the long and the short of it." Later, she is equally candid with the audience at the Low Note Club, telling the customers that Chick made her pregnant in Miami and then "blew his brains out." Tess's unabashed, gratuitous pronouncements about her marriage resemble what she sings, much of it extending her self-presentation as a tough and ironic but still vulnerable survivor. Her songs have titles such as "To Hell with Love," "I Don't Want to Cry Anymore," and "Punishing Kiss." Another song, "Conversations on a Bar Stool," contains lyrics with phrases such as "I can't breathe in the air in this city tonight. . . . I just want to get out of here. But I won't be sorry if you won't be, and I don't want your pity or your sympathy."

Zoe shares a house with her mother but little else. Lori Singer, who is in actual fact an accomplished cellist, plays Zoe as a woman who would lose herself in her music. (Altman rhymes Tess's reception in the club with Zoe's performance in a concert hall where spectators talk among themselves, although the decibel level is lower than at the Low Note Club.) While Tess lounges about the house drinking Bloody Marys and reminiscing about her dead husband, Zoe seldom speaks, preferring to

51. Annie Ross with Lori Singer in *Short Cuts* (1993, Fine Line). Jerry Ohlinger's Movie Material Store, Inc.

play basketball with the young men who join her for a game on her driveway court. Zoe also takes an interest in her next-door neighbors, the Finnigans, whose son is hospitalized after being injured when struck by a car. Late in the film, when Ann Finnigan (Andie MacDowell) tells Zoe that the boy has died, Zoe is overwhelmed with grief. She drives to the Low Note Club to tell the news to her mother. Ironically, Tess is in the act of giving one of her most emotionally charged musical performances with "I Don't Want to Cry Anymore," a song recorded in 1955 by Billie Holiday. Tess, however, appears unaffected by the news of the Finnigans' loss. Even more devastated by Tess's insensitivity, Zoe drives home, pulls her car into the garage, closes the door, and plays her cello while the car belches forth exhaust fumes. As the film come to an end, Tess sits alone in her house, drinking and singing a blues for her dead daughter.

Before the film has concluded, however, Ross's voice appears extradiegetically in a reprise of "Prisoner of Life," the song she sang at the beginning of the film. Then, as the final credits roll, she sings an uptempo version of "I'm Gonna Go Fishin,'" a tune originally written by Duke Ellington for *Anatomy of a Murder* (1959), to which Peggy Lee later added lyrics. Ross's final reading of both these songs carries none of the grief that Tess Trainer had experienced moments before in the diegesis. Annie Ross's simultaneously diegetic and extradiegetic presence in *Short Cuts* is not unusual for a jazz artist in a Hollywood film. The same dual role was played by Louis Armstrong in *High Society* and by Hoagy Carmichael in both *Young Man with a Horn* and *The Las Vegas Story.* Altman was involved with a similar effect when he produced Alan Rudolph's *Welcome to L.A.* (1977) in which Richard Baskin plays a character in the film who also sings on the soundtrack. Although Altman has given a limited role to jazz within the several narratives in *Short Cuts,* he has made extensive use of a jazz-inflected score that slips in and out of the diegesis.

Altman and screenwriter Frank Barhydt have in fact given a strong jazz ambience to *Short Cuts* by adding Tess and Zoe to the various characters found in the nine Raymond Carver stories on which the script is based. Although most of the characters in the 1993 film are profoundly unlike Carver's original creations, almost every character can be traced back to a Carver story. A major exception is Paul Finnigan (Jack Lemmon), the grandfather of the dying child, who has been added to the plot of Carver's story, "A Small, Good Thing" (Carver 1993, 93–121). Tess and Zoe, however, are unique in constituting a separate narrative thread that cannot be attributed to a specific story by Carver.

Altman has said that he added the two characters because he wanted "a reason for the music. I didn't want the music to come from a sound studio outside and amplify the emotions. And yet I know that music does that. . . . I just didn't want to *apply* music" (Stewart 1993, 42; italics in original). Although Tess Trainer is not an entirely sympathetic character, Altman has apparently named her after Tess Gallagher, the poet who is Carver's widow and who worked closely with Altman in the genesis of the film. Gallagher appears to have been pleased with the tribute, calling Tess Trainer "a real gift to me," and saying that she could "recognize some of the widowhood things" from her own life in the singer's behavior (Stewart 1993, 42). I would even speculate that the world-weary but fragile quality of Ross's singing recalls the tone of many of Gallagher's poems: the matter-of-factness in Ross's delivery and in Gallagher's poetry stops their sentiments from becoming maudlin or melodramatic. Much the same can be said for the effect of Ross and her group on the film itself.

Few jazz enthusiasts would question Annie Ross's credentials as an important jazz vocalist. She left an indelible mark on the history of jazz singing when she set words to a 1949 improvisation by Wardell Gray and produced "Twisted" (1952). The song was subsequently recorded by Joni Mitchell, Bette Midler, and Mark Murphy. Ross spent four years with Lambert, Hendricks and Ross (1958–62), one of the most important vocal groups in jazz history. The group's popularity with jazz audiences may be surpassed only by that of the Boswell Sisters in the 1930s (Grant 1995, 289). Critics have regularly praised Ross for the extraordinarily broad range of her voice as well as for her ability to communicate emotion. When she left LH&R in 1962 because of illness, she returned for a while to her native England. The years with LH&R took a toll on her voice, and she lost much of the flexibility and purity of her original sound (Cooper 1979, 9). Since the 1970s, Ross has moved back and forth between England the United States, working as both a singer and an actress, appearing in mainstream films such as *Yanks* (1979), *Superman III* (1983), and *Pump Up the Volume* (1990) as well as in low-budget cult items such as *Witchery* (1989), *Basket Case 2* (1990), and *Basket Case 3* (1992). Ross shows her age in *Short Cuts*, but as is often the case with jazz singers, including Billie Holiday, Sarah Vaughan, and Frank Sinatra, much is gained from the "authenticity effect," which becomes more pronounced only with the fading of youth's technical prowess.

If Ross possesses an undisputed pedigree as a jazz singer, the same cannot necessarily be said for the Low Note Quintet with which she performs throughout. The band was assembled solely for *Short Cuts* by Hal Willner, a producer who has long practiced the kind of musical eclecticism at which the film hints. Willner is best-known for producing music to back up sketches during thirteen seasons of *Saturday Night Live* and for the twenty-eight episodes of *Night Music,* a late-night program of jazz and sophisticated pop that ran on NBC in 1989 and 1990. Willner also put together a handful of albums on which a variety of performers recorded compositions associated with a single individual. Although Willner built albums around the music of Nino Rota and the films of Walt Disney, he has also paid tribute to Thelonious Monk and Charles Mingus, recording their compositions with performers as diverse as Carla Bley, Joe Jackson, Steve Lacy, Keith Richards, Elvis Costello, Chuck D, Sun Ra, and Henry Threadgill. For *Short Cuts,* he assembled a group of players who have seldom devoted themselves entirely to jazz, even though Willner hoped to re-create the sounds of some classic ensembles.

> I based the sound of this band on the mid–50s Miles Davis band with Milt Jackson and Thelonious Monk. But other than the vibes player [Gene Estes], none of the musicians in Tess' band are "jazz" musicians. Terry Adams plays rock 'n' roll piano with NRBQ, Greg Cohen plays bass with Tom Waits. The drummer Bobby Previte is pretty successful playing and composing new music. The trombone player Bruce Fowler worked with Zappa and Captain Beefheart for years. (Mandel 1994, 11)

Willner may have exaggerated the nonjazz background of some of these performers. Bobby Previte has recorded frequently with downtown New York jazz musicians such as John Zorn, Marty Ehrlich, Tim Berne, and Wayne Horvitz. Bruce Fowler has been involved with the West Coast avant-garde, playing with the Ed Mann Group and on sessions for Vinny Golia's Nine Winds label. Greg Cohen has played with Woody Allen's New York Jazz Ensemble, and Terry Adams has recorded with Carla Bley. The songs in Tess Trainer's repertoire, however, do tend to originate somewhere beyond the established borders of the jazz canon. "Conversations on a Bar Stool," for example, was originally written for Marianne Faithfull by Bono and the Edge, both members of the rock group U2.[9] "To Hell with Love," "I Don't Know You," and "Prisoner of Life" were all written by Doc Pomus and Dr. John. Before his death in 1988, Pomus had flourished as the composer of rhythm and blues lyrics such as "Save the Last Dance for Me" and "Little Sister." Dr. John, who put out some eclectic blues-rock piano and vocal recordings under his real name, Mac Rebennack, in the 1980s and early 1990s, also made some mildly psyche-delic, commercially successful recordings using New Orleans voodoo references in the late 1960s. "Punishing Kiss" was written especially for the film by Elvis Costello and Cait O'Riordan. These unlikely vehicles for

Annie Ross cause her to reach beyond her usual singing practice, but they mesh surprisingly well with songs by canonical jazz composers such as Duke Ellington, Horace Silver, and Jon Hendricks, as well as "I Don't Want to Cry Anymore," written by Victor Schertzinger for the 1940 film *Rhythm on the River* and recorded engagingly by Holiday.

Regardless of whether or not jazz purists will celebrate the film's music, the band maintains a rapport with Ross that was strong enough to survive several sessions of live filming. Unlike the vast majority of Hollywood films, *Short Cuts* presents its musical numbers "in the moment" rather than showing artists as they mime or lip-synch to prerecorded sounds. Compare the easy interactions among Ross and the Low Note Quintet with the stiff performance of "Body and Soul" by Herbie Hancock, John McLaughlin, Pierre Michelot, Billy Higgins, and an ailing Dexter Gordon in Bertrand Tavernier's *Round Midnight,* a film that also presented its musicians in a "live" setting. *Short Cuts* also offers a unique opportunity to watch an artist performing simultaneously as an actor *and* as a jazz musician. In preparing Ross to sing as Tess Trainer, Hal Willner told her to use the bottom part of her register to help represent the "darkness" of her life (Mandel 1994, 11). (Although Ross does in fact sing the low notes to great effect, she is the same singer who once made brilliant use of her upper register in re-creating the trumpet parts on LH&R's vocalizations of recordings by the Count Basie orchestra.) In performance, singers try to project personae unlike themselves, if only because no singer spends his or her entire life singing. In this sense, virtually every singer is an actor. But when singers play roles in films, and when they sing "in character," they seldom seem much different from the characters they play off screen. Liza Minnelli in *New York, New York* is as good an example as any. Annie Ross's performance in *Short Cuts* is especially unusual because she is an accomplished jazz singer playing a jazz singer who is unlike herself.[10] By adjusting her vocal range and delivery, Ross is creating a character whose singing is consistent with her nonmusical behavior. Her acting may be most apparent when she adopts a gruff aspect to interpret "Conversations on a Bar Stool." Seldom has a jazz musician of such stature gone to such lengths to accommodate a filmmaker's vision.

As Self (1995) has suggested, the Tess/Zoe contrast may provide one means of pulling together all nine of the Carver stories that were originally devised independently. Unlike most American films, *Short Cuts* has no single plot strain that makes each character's actions comprehensible. Throughout its three hours, audiences must keep track of several discrete plot lines that are almost completely unrelated and that seem to come to an end only because of the climax supplied by a California earthquake. Perhaps to give coherence to the multiple, barely related narratives, Altman has suggested that Carver's stories, and presumably *Short Cuts,* can be united by a dark "view of the world" that he shares with the writer: "Somebody wins the lottery. The same day, that person's sister gets killed by a brick falling off a building in Seattle. Those are both the same thing. The lottery was won both ways. The odds of either happening are very much against you and yet they both happened. One got killed and the other got rich; it's the same action" (Altman 1993, 9). The addition of Zoe and Tess seems to respond to this reading of Carver's stories—one survives while the other doesn't, even though no strong reason determines why this has to be the case.

On a somewhat different level, Altman and Barhydt may have seen Carver's characters falling into two large groups: those who wear their emotions on their sleeves and those who repress their feelings until, like Tess's husband whose story presages Zoe's suicide, they "explode." As Altman has said in the film's production notes, "The cello that Lori Singer plays represents inner feeling—it's more internal and secret—and Annie Ross's jazz is what we express outwardly." In this sense, Tess and Zoe represent the extreme ends of a continuum with virtually all the other characters in between; while the mother eternally rolls with the punches and seldom stifles her emotions, the daughter quietly suffers until she kills herself. Among the many characters at Zoe's end of the spectrum is Jerry Kaiser (Chris Penn), who listens affectlessly while his wife, Lois (Jennifer Jason Leigh), earns money in the phone sex industry at the same time that she tends to their small children. It may be significant that Jerry watches silently as Zoe, whom he resembles in many ways, jumps nude into her swimming pool and mimes death. At the conclusion of the film, Jerry erupts and kills a young woman who has aroused him sexually. Casey, the Finnigan child who dies after being hit by a car, is especially interesting in terms of this character type. At first he seems oblivious to his injuries and manages to walk home unassisted after the accident. He never seems to acknowledge the fatal blow he has received. Also consider Stormy Weathers (Peter Gallagher), who seems to tolerate the affairs of his estranged wife, Betty (Frances McDormand), until he reaches his limit and gleefully destroys every scrap of furniture and clothing in her house. Similarly, Marian Wyman (Julianne Moore) patiently endures her husband's needling until she loudly confesses to a long-past, drunken infidelity. These repressed but explosive characters are contrasted with people such as Lois Kaiser, Sherri Shepard (Madeleine Stowe), Claire Kane (Anne Archer), Doreen Piggot (Lily Tomlin), Ralph Wyman (Matthew Modine), and, of course, Tess Trainer, who are more consistently expressive and less likely to experience emotional extremes.

Zoe and Tess may provide another paradigm for reading *Short Cuts,* one that resembles the relationship between the central couple in *New York, New York.* As in Scorsese's film, some characters in *Short Cuts* are improvisers, while others seem to need a script. Because both Altman and Scorsese have encouraged their actors to improvise, it is tempting to understand the characters in both directors' films in terms of this practice. For Altman in particular, questions of performance style have been central to his work, from *Nashville* to *The Player* (1992). Altman has been able to continue working despite numerous failures, in large part because so many actors enjoy the freedom to create that he offers on the set. It is no surprise that Altman should be interested in jazz or that he should call attention to the distinction between improvisers and performers who need a script. No doubt he knows the distinction well, having regularly faced actors with varying degrees of tolerance for his improvisational approach to filmmaking. Compare, for example, Elliott Gould, who flourished with Altman in *The Long Goodbye* and *California Split* (1974), to Paul Newman, who could not disguise his discomfort with Altman's style in *Buffalo Bill and the Indians* (1976) and *Quintet* (1979).

In *Short Cuts,* Tess expresses herself in the moment through jazz, while Zoe re-creates the music of Dvořák, Bach, and Stravinsky. The three weekend fishermen (Fred Ward, Buck Henry, and Huey Lewis) seek the predictable script of a fishing vacation away from civilization, refusing to alter it even to report a dead body in the water nearby. Claire Kane, who is married to one of the fishermen, Stuart Kane (Ward), is devastated when she hears what happened and carefully enacts the conventional script of mourning for the dead woman. Howard Finnigan (Bruce Davison), who reads his televised editorials from written copy, must cope with the baker (Lyle Lovett), who elaborately improvises his anger over a forgotten cake in a series of telephone calls to the Finnigans. Marian Wyman is a painter, an improvising artist, married to Ralph, a doctor who demands that she play from the script of the traditional faithful wife. Honey Bush (Lili Taylor) tries to abide by the rules of housesitting handed to her by the couple setting off on vacation, while her husband Bill (Robert Downey, Jr.) wants to explore the apartment and violate his neighbors' privacy. Stormy Weathers improvises the destruction of Betty's possessions, while she enacts the script of romance with at least two different lovers. Gene Shepard, the policeman played by Tim Robbins, improvises throughout the film: first he finds a means of dispensing with the obnoxious family dog; then, like Jimmy Doyle in *New York, New York,* he creates a seduction scenario on the spot by stopping Claire to give her a ticket; and when his wife finds Claire's phone number in his pocket, he throws together an implausible story about a police investigation. Finally, there is Paul Finnigan (Jack Lemmon), a man who probably adhered closely to the script of family, home, and work, but who suffered devastating consequences on the one occasion when his wife's sister offered him a unique opportunity for extramarital improvisation.

Following Barthes (1975), Self (1995) would regard these efforts at aligning the characters in *Short Cuts* as the function of a "writerly" text, a film that leaves much unsaid and thus invites the reader to supply what is missing. Barthes was referring to literature when he distinguished between readerly and writerly texts, but as Fredric Jameson (1990) has observed, images and musical sounds offer much greater pleasure to those who would add their "writing" to what they experience aesthetically (2–4). By leaving the text open on several levels, Altman has invited his audiences to provide connections among scenes that float loosely about each other at the same time that he has benefited immensely from the intelligent choices made by the film's editor, Geraldine Peroni.

Altman has also been extremely sensitive to the allusive possibilities of music. Although Tess and Zoe spend no more time on-screen than the other twenty principal characters in *Short Cuts,* their music is present on the extradiegetic score throughout most of the film. Ross's songs frequently continue into scenes with other characters, and the Low Note Quintet regularly performs instrumental versions of the same songs to accompany the characters' actions. Like all background music in Hollywood films, the extradiegetic jazz in *Short Cuts* provides continuity, unity, and narrative cuing. But by constantly showing the musicians on camera and allowing their performances to drift in and out of the diegesis, Altman has shown little reverence for the standard Hollywood practice of making the music "invisible" and "inaudible" (Gorbman 1987, 73). And even when the music does provide continuity, it does not always seem appropriate as when a playful instrumental performance of "I'm Gonna Go Fishin'" begins behind Stormy's bizarre encounter with a vacuum cleaner salesman but then continues as Claire Kane grimly drives off to the funeral of the young woman discovered by her husband. Sometimes the music unites scenes in ways that make sense, as when Zoe's suicide is accompanied by the band's introduction to "I Don't Know You," which then continues while Tess sings the song in the Low Note Club. Similarly, an instrumental version of "To Hell with Love" is regularly played behind scenes in which Gene the policeman moves awkwardly among the various women with whom he is trying to maintain or initiate extramarital relations.

The songs of Annie Ross and her accompanists are not, however, the film's only extradiegetic music. Mark Isham—who has written music for numerous films including *The Moderns* (1988), *Everybody Wins* (1990), *Reversal of Fortune* (1990), *Little Man Tate* (1991), *Billy Bathgate* (1991), *A River Runs through It* (1992), *Of Mice and Men* (1992), *Romeo Is Bleeding* (1994), and *Quiz Show* (1994), as well as the theme for the CBS television series *Chicago Hope*—has composed an abstract, often brooding score for the film that sometimes alternates with performances by the Low Note Quintet. Isham began his career playing trumpet in symphony orchestras before recording and touring with Van Morrison, Bruce Springsteen, Charles Lloyd, Willie Nelson, the Rolling Stones, and Lyle Lovett. He has recorded a number of CDs under his own name, including at least two for Windham Hill, a label that specializes in the moody, often mantra-like music called "New Age." His score for *Short Cuts* occasionally mixes the "classical" sound of a cello with more conventional jazz instruments such as saxophone and vibraphone, suggesting that Altman's addition of the carefully differentiated characters of Tess and Zoe to Carver's fictions may have required a unification at the "inaudible" level of the background score. Unlike the music of Annie Ross and her group, Isham's score is much more typical of Hollywood practice, even if his compositions seem to bring together a jazz and classical ambience uniquely appropriate to *Short Cuts*. Isham's music is frequently played in scenes involving the Finnigans, beginning shortly after the child is hit by a car, when a cello accompanies his walk past Zoe and the basketball players. The same music returns later when Casey's parents are waiting at the hospital for word on the child's progress, and when Stuart tells Claire about the dead body. When Casey dies, Isham's music continues seamlessly as the scene changes to Claire at the funeral of the young woman.

In one fascinating sequence, music becomes an essential element in the interactions between Tess, Zoe, and characters in the scenes that follow. Coming home early in the morning from the jazz club, Tess enters her daughter's room while she is playing a passage from Stravinsky's *The Firebird*. Tess does almost all of the talking, at one point even humming along with Zoe's music. The mother begins reminiscing about her late husband, eventually singing a bit of Jon Hendricks' "Blue" as she dozes off. The Low Note Quintet plays a few extradiegetic notes just as Tess is about to begin singing. The instrumentalists then continue without the singer as the camera cuts to a tense scene between Stuart and Claire and then to an emotionally charged confrontation between Doreen Piggot and her husband Earl (Tom Waits). Thanks to the musical "glue," the emotional energy in the two subsequent family scenes seems to grow out of the interactions between Zoe and Tess.

Regardless of how we wish to interpret the presence of Tess and Zoe in *Short Cuts,* without question jazz is a crucial ingredient. And yet this is not the jazz of canonical black male jazz artists. Annie Ross is not even from the United States; although she speaks with a solid general American accent in *Short Cuts,* she was born in England and has spent a substantial amount of time in that country, at one point operating a nightclub in London (Cooper 1979, 10). Furthermore, all of the musicians in Ross's quintet are white, a fact that Altman seems to observe ironically by making the audience in the Low Note Club almost entirely black. Like Scorsese's film, *Short Cuts* is not concerned with the transformative qualities of jazz so vividly described in Art Pepper's autobiography. But Altman has also turned away from Hollywood's conventional script of the jazz artist by avoiding direct reference to obsessions about race, gender, and art, at least in terms of how they effect Tess Trainer. Although Tess, like any entertainer, "performs" her gender, there is no problematization of her performances as in the several films in which jazz trumpeters fail to hit the high note while an important woman is present. And unlike *New York, New York, Short Cuts* does not have a black female singer to provide a destabilizing contrast to Tess. The director seems much more interested in the affective potential of jazz, bringing the music directly into his stories only in the scenes with Tess and Zoe, but using a large measure of the music to pull together the film's diegetic and extradiegetic scores as well as the multiple plot elements.

In a brief sequence in *Short Cuts,* Bill Bush (Robert Downey, Jr.) and Jerry Kaiser (Chris Penn) stand on the balcony of the apartment where the Bushes are blithely abusing their privileges as housesitters. Bill and Jerry are smoking pot and drinking beer as they listen to the Low Note Quintet's recording of "Evil California (These Blues)." Jerry says that he likes the music. In a speech that was probably improvised, Bill characterizes the music with the following words: "Yeah, this is good, huh? It's like, it's not . . . I don't know, it's different, it's kind of dry . . . it's like dry humping . . . some wet . . . pussy. . . . I don't know." Bill's groping attempt to describe the music is one of the few moments in which jazz is actually discussed by someone other than Tess. Clearly, the music is not something the characters can easily classify, although Bill Bush has no difficulty associating it with sex. Later, when the Bushes and the Kaisers walk into the Low Note Club, the hostess tells them to sit by Art Blakey. As the audience sees a photographic blowup on the wall of the late bop drummer in action, Bill says, "Who's Art Blakey?" In spite of their ignorance of jazz history and aesthetics, the two couples do make the music part of their social activities.

It is significant that no one besides Tess uses the term "jazz" in *Short Cuts*. Today, the word has much more significance within an institutional context that, on the one hand, valorizes a few artists who play in clubs or in concert halls and that, on the other, allows for the colonization of the music. For better or worse, this colonization is most apparent in the rise of the academic discipline called "jazz studies." But like Bill Bush, many people respond to the music outside the discourses that became attached to jazz as it began to develop an elite audience. As for Art Blakey, he himself had no illusions about the audience for jazz. Once, when a French reporter asked him what the American people thought of Charlie Parker, Blakey is rumored to have said, "They never heard of him." Just as most Americans have never heard of Charlie Parker or Art Blakey, they probably know little about Clint Eastwood's box office failure, *Bird*. Today, the moviegoing audience does "know," however, that jazz musicians take drugs, that their music is difficult if not unlistenable, that many jazz musicians like to ignore the audience, and that some of them play in concert halls wearing suits. Nevertheless, many of these same nonfans are likely to experience the music and even enjoy it when jazz is presented without elevated discourses, as is the case, for example, in *Short Cuts*.

Both the music and its reception have gone through drastic changes during the twentieth century. The public was given a strange but abiding image of jazz when *The Jazz Singer* was a major attraction in 1927. A jazz musician was a white man who put on black face to achieve success that might otherwise have eluded him. Although the jazz singer loved his mother, he was capable of flamboyantly sexual body language and a certain amount of innuendo. The large audience for a film such as *The Jazz Singer* may not have been explicitly aware that the white artist drew upon the supposedly sexual and transgressive inclinations of black Americans, but this practice became paradigmatic as the movies continued to appropriate the music. As for blacks themselves, jazz films were no different from the rest of what Hollywood produced; with few exceptions that have been duly noted, the artists who played jazz in the movies were docile, eager to please, and maybe even a little ridiculous. By the 1950s they were also likely to congratulate white musicians on their superiority. During that same decade, jazz fans were often portrayed as pretentious and out of touch, while real-life jazz enthusiasts were making claims for jazz as a valid art form. Hollywood effectively lost interest in the music after the 1950s, and jazz made it into the movies only if the budgets were small or the filmmakers were true believers. Even when the jazz life was dramatized in independent and ambitious films such as *Sweet Love Bitter,* *A Man Called Adam,* and *Mo' Better Blues,* the music often seemed irrelevant in plots about race, sexuality, and the struggles of driven individuals. Especially when a major studio and a major director took on the subject, as in *New York, New York, Bird,* or *The Cotton Club,* the filmmakers seemed to fear that too much attention to the music would drive away audiences. In spite of the attempts to make crises of sexuality and masculinity the subjects of these films, audiences still stayed away.

If a film such as *New York, New York* suggests that jazz cannot comfortably occupy the center of a Hollywood film, something like *Short Cuts* is evidence that the music can transform a movie when it plays about the edges. This was certainly true in European films such as *Sait-on jamais?* (*No Sun in Venice,* 1957), *Ascenseur pour l'échafaud* (*Elevator to the Gallows,* 1957), and *À bout de Souffle* (*Breathless,* 1959). It was also true in a handful of films that involved remarkable individuals such as Duke Ellington and Louis Armstrong. More recently, it has been true in American films as diverse as *Quiz Show* (1994) and *Vanya on 42nd Street* (1994). At least in recent decades, jazz films may be most vital when the artists are *jamming at the margins.*

Introduction

1. For the most sophisticated critiques of the trope of jazz as autonomous art, see Tomlinson (1991) and DeVeaux (1991). Also see my introduction and the essays in the anthology *Jazz among the Discourses* (Gabbard 1995a).

2. I reference Mulvey here because she is essential to Corbett's important argument. In spite of the extraordinary influence of Mulvey's original essay, "Visual Pleasure and Narrative Cinema" (1975), virtually every aspect of her theory has been questioned by film theorists. Mulvey herself has revised her thesis on several occasions (1989). For compelling studies that can be read at least in part as responses to Mulvey's work, see Modleski (1988), Studlar (1988), L. Williams (1989), and Clover (1992).

3. See, for example, the analysis by Steven B. Elworth (1995) of the sexual persona projected by drummer Cindy Blackman (74).

4. The denial of blackness in *King of Jazz* must have been even more ironic when it was shown in some theaters on the same bill with *Black and Tan* (1929), Dudley Murphy's black-cast film that featured Duke Ellington and his orchestra. For more about Ellington's films, see chapter 5.

5. The false binarism—original/copy—is an essential part of Jacques Derrida's project. See his "Plato's Pharmacy" (1981). In addition, see Andrew Ross's discussion of the tendency to associate a discourse of race with a discourse of commercialization: "it is often assumed that the two are necessarily aligned; that commercialized music = whitened music, that the black performance of uncommercialized and therefore undiluted black music constitutes the only truly genuine form of protest or resistance against the white culture industry and its controlling interests, and that black music which submits to that industry

automatically loses its autonomous power. To subscribe to this equation is to imagine a very mechanical process indeed, whereby a music, which is authentically black, constitutes an initial raw material which is then appropriated and reduced in cultural force and meaning by contact with a white industry. Accordingly, music is never 'made,' and only ever exploited, in this process of industrialization" (Ross 1989, 69–70).

6. For sources on Kyser's career, I have relied on Bogue (1989), Simon (1981, 312–17), the introductory pages of Garrod and Korst's discography (1990), and the essays included with two CDs, *The Best of Kay Kyser* (Columbia) and *Kay Kyser and His Orchestra: I'll Be Seeing You* (Vintage Jazz Classics).

7. Because I was born in 1948, I discovered Kyser only because of cable television's American Movie Classics, a remarkable source of information about those portions of American entertainment that have not been preserved in popular and academic canons. Some day an important article will be written on how AMC has revolutionized film study in the United States.

8. The two currently available CDs of the Kyser band offer both sides of the band's repertoire: the vocal hits on the Columbia release such as "(I've Got Spurs That) Jingle Jangle Jingle" (1942), "Praise the Lord and Pass the Ammunition" (1942), and "The Old Lamplighter" (1946) were the band's meal ticket, but the music on the VJC disc consists of World War II–era broadcasts that show off the band's technical polish and the imagination of its soloists and arrangers.

9. For somewhat different theories of a heterogeneous, resisting audience, see de Certeau (1984) and Stuart Hall (1981). For case studies of audiences radically remaking the products of popular culture according to their own needs, see Hebdige (1979 and 1987) and Jenkins (1992a).

10. The inconsistencies between what Schuller says on p. 199 and what he says on p. 661 probably result from his own changing attitudes during the twenty years that he worked on *The Swing Era*. Lewis Porter (1991, 183–200) is especially attentive to these kinds of inconsistencies in his review of Schuller's book.

11. Perhaps the single best application of Louis Althusser's theories of ideology to the cinema is still Robert B. Ray, *A Certain Tendency of the Hollywood Cinema* (1985).

Chapter One

1. The part of Jack Robin's father was first offered to Rosenblatt with the promise of a salary as high as $100,000. According to Rosenblatt's biographer, the cantor refused because of his religious convictions but eventually agreed to appear in one scene as himself only after laying down strict conditions, including a ban on makeup (Rosenblatt 1954, 289). I thank Lewis Porter for calling this text to my attention.

2. For a more rigorous approach to the semantics of films such as *The Jazz Singer*, I recommend the much more detailed "coding sheet" with no less than twenty-seven categories that George Custen (1992, 237–39) developed for his work on biopics.

3. In his book on Yiddish cinema (1991b), Hoberman discusses *Der Vilner Balebesl* and several related films in greater detail. For studies that contextualize

The Jazz Singer with other American films about Jews, see Erens (1984) and Friedman (1982).

4. Lewis, who owns exclusive rights to his 1959 *Jazz Singer,* has expressed dissatisfaction with the program and has made it unavailable for public viewing. I have obtained most of my information on Jerry Lewis's *Jazz Singer* in conversation with Scott Bukatman, an ardent student of Lewis's work, who was given access to the film by Lewis himself.

5. I can only speculate that Warner Bros. decided early on to omit blackface scenes from the 1952 *Jazz Singer* after receiving complaints about Doris Day's blackface imitation of Al Jolson in *I'll See You in My Dreams,* released one year earlier. Like the 1952 *Jazz Singer, I'll See You in My Dreams* was directed for Warner Bros. by Michael Curtiz and starred Danny Thomas. This was not the end of blackface in the cinema, however. In 1953, Joan Crawford performed under cork in *Torch Song.* As far as I can tell, the tradition does not reappear until it reaches a socially conscious stage with *Black Like Me* (1964). Elliott Gould does a brief parody of blackface and Jolson in *The Long Goodbye* (1973), and there is a sentimental but vaguely sinister revision of the practice in *Soul Man* (1986).

6. Jolson's real father passed away when Jolson was a child (Goldman 1988). *The Jolson Story* also erases Jolson's first two wives as well as the name of his third wife, Ruby Keeler, whose marriage to Jolson was well-known in the 1930s. In the film, Jolson marries a dancer/actress named Julie Benson (Evelyn Keyes), whose name appears above the title of several films in which Keeler starred, including *42nd Street* (1933), *Dames* (1934), and even *Go into Your Dance* (1935), the one film in which Jolson and Keeler appeared together. When *The Jolson Story* was filmed, Keeler had divorced Jolson and remarried. She also refused to allow her name to appear in the film. "I don't want my children to grow up someday and maybe see the picture and know I was married to a man like that. Hear 'Ruby Keeler' from the screen and Jolson singing love songs to her. Making love speeches to her. Saying, 'Baby, everything you want you'll have. This is Jolie talking to you.' I want none of that" (McClelland 1987, 44).

7. When Goodman performed at Carnegie Hall in 1938, Alice Hammond was living in London with her first husband, a British aristocrat, and their three children, none of whom are mentioned in the film. Alice's romance with Goodman did not begin until after 1940. More importantly, Alice Hammond was probably not wooed by performances of Mozart's clarinet concerto. Like her brother John Hammond, she had developed a taste for jazz and blues long before her romance with Benny. She was also a much more down-to-earth character than the film suggests, probably attracted to the rough-hewn Goodman and his milieu as a refreshing contrast to the stiflingly proper world of her first husband (Collier 1989; Firestone 1993).

Chapter Two

1. For an excellent discussion of Vodery's career, see Berger et al. 1982, I:26–29.

2. Ferguson (1982) is a collection of all of his jazz writings, including several essays on Beiderbecke.

3. C. James Klett (1988) writes that he and friends in the early 1940s frequently ended notes to one another with "Bix lives!"

4. The terms diegetic and extradiegetic have become essential to the discussion of narrative and sound in films. Plato used the term *diegesis* in *The Republic* to describe a story or narration, as in "all mythology and poetry is a *diegesis* of events, either past, present, or to come" (392D). In the *Poetics,* Aristotle distinguished between two modes of poetic *mimesis:* a story told in narration, *diegesis,* and one that is acted out in front of spectators, *drama* (1448a). Literary theorists such as Gérard Genette (1982) appropriated the term diegesis to describe the narrating of events that take place "within the world of the characters" as opposed to those portions of a novel or story in which the narrator might philosophize or recall some history. In film study, diegetic sound refers to what the characters might actually hear, while extradiegetic sound is something taking place elsewhere, for example, in the voice-over narration by an unseen character. Diegetic music, then, can emerge from the radio in a character's room or from an orchestra in a concert hall. Extradiegetic music is usually the "background" score that the characters do not hear. Although we might speak of a radio playing music "in the background," this is still diegetic sound if it is being played in the world of the characters. Unfortunately, these terms are not always adequate; in many cases the music in a film does not perfectly fit either category. What do we say, for example, about the song that a young man associates with his long-lost sweetheart and that plays on the soundtrack whenever he is thinking about her? The music is not in the room with him, but since he can be understood as hearing the song in his head, it can also be understood as "within the world of the characters." Gorbman (1987) has coined the term "metadiegetic" to describe this kind of music (22–23), and François Jost (1987) has developed an elaborate chart labeled "Classification narratologique des combinaisons audio-visuelles" that creates even more categories for distinguishing among the varieties of hearing in a fiction film (57). Nevertheless, because the terms diegetic and extradiegetic have entered the basic language of film scholarship, I will use them throughout this study.

5. The actual impact of Armstrong's playing on Beiderbecke's is impossible to assess, if only because Beiderbecke had been exposed to a wide variety of influences, white and black, before his first recordings in 1924. Some commentators have argued that a white, unrecorded trumpeter from New Orleans named Emmett Hardy was a major factor in Beiderbecke's development, but the argument is convincingly dismissed by Sudhalter et al. (1974, 49–51).

6. Wilbur de Paris, however, gives the names of several black trumpeters from the early 1920s who were performing primarily in the Midwest and who played, according to de Paris, in a style much like that eventually developed by Beiderbecke (Feather 1959, 21).

7. In both the film and the novel, Rick Martin's parents die early, leaving him to be raised by a mostly absent sister. The historical Beiderbecke was outlived by both of his staid, Victorian parents.

8. For a history of psychiatry and psychoanalysis in American film, see Gabbard and Gabbard (1987). For a more recent, feminist view of the subject, see Walker (1993).

9. It is also possible that Carmichael is recalling a version of the script for *Young Man with a Horn* that did in fact end with Rick's death. A publicity release in the Film Study Division of the Museum of Modern Art dated September 14, 1949, gives a plot synopsis that ends with Rick dying after he is hit by a taxi. For the debates among Curtiz, the producers, the scriptwriters, and the actors over how *YMWH* should end, see Robertson (1993, 103).

10. For an excellent overview of film documentaries of jazz artists, see the forthcoming work of Christopher Harlos.

11. Webb's tough-guy trumpeter has more to do with the actor/director's own psychology than with any revisionist tendencies in the film. See Webb's *The D.I.* (1957) for a representation of masculinity at its most hysterical.

12. It can even be argued that *The Benny Goodman Story* overstates the importance of black artists in Goodman's career by showing Teddy Wilson as the big band's regular pianist, even though Wilson's actual role was confined entirely to the small groups with which Goodman performed when the full band was not on stage. In the film, Wilson is even seen with the band during the performance of "Sing, Sing, Sing" at the 1938 Carnegie Hall concert when it was the white pianist Jess Stacy who played the critically acclaimed piano solo on that number.

13. After opening at the Cannes Film Festival in 1991, *Bix: An Interpretation of a Legend* played in few American theaters. It is now available on videocassette from Rhapsody Films.

14. For an exhaustive history of birds in general and nightingales in particular as phallic symbols, see Vasvari (1994).

15. I thank Kevin Whitehead for these readings of what he calls "The Jolson Effect" in *Adventures in Babysitting* and *Back to the Future.*

16. In fairness to Gershwin and to *Rhapsody in Blue,* the film does show that the composer used African American singers in a subsequent performance of *Porgy and Bess.* For a brief history of how Warner Bros. removed black influences from Gershwin's story, see Cripps (1993, 96–97).

17. Jeff Smith (1995) has written an essential history of the music industry's efforts to market soundtrack albums for Hollywood films.

18. According to Stanley Crouch (1994), it is even possible that Rodney fabricated the story that he toured the Deep South with Parker as "Albino Red," the blues singer. In writing his biography of Parker, Crouch has not found any witnesses to confirm that the tour took place.

19. Similarly, in Bertolucci's *The Last Emperor* (1987) much of the action at the Royal Chinese court is incomprehensible until Peter O'Toole arrives to present the Western audience with normative reactions to the court's strange behavior.

20. A similar scene occurs in John Cassavetes's film, *Too Late Blues* (1961), in which the jazz pianist hero (Bobby Darin) is powerless to stop an aggressive drunk in a restaurant. Although the hero never achieves financial success, his real decline begins when he cannot summon the courage to protect his girlfriend (Stella Stevens).

21. *Sweet Love Bitter* is one of the few films in which a saxophone is used to signify a character's impotence. Usually the instrument is the trumpet. See chapter 4.

22. *Sweet Love Bitter* might have been even more interesting if it had not been shortened and completely reedited by the producers. The cut of the film delivered by director Herbert Danska took liberties with the structure of the narrative, and the producers feared that audiences would be confused. Ultimately, the film "bypassed proper theatrical release and went straight to drive-in and grind houses under the mildly salacious title *It Won't Rub Off, Baby*" (Davis 1992a, D19).

23. Throughout his study of minstrelsy, Lott (1993) is especially attentive to the white male's erotic fascination with black men. See, for example, pages 120–22.

24. According to Clarke (1994), Legrand was brought in to write the score for *Lady Sings the Blues* after Oliver Nelson abandoned the project because, Nelson said, the script "wasn't really about Billie Holiday" (451).

25. The rehearsal session took place on August 22, 1955. It has been issued in the 10-CD box set, *The Complete Billie Holiday on Verve, 1945–1959* (Verve), which was lavishly and meticulously produced by Phil Schaap. Portions of this tape were previously issued on LP on the Paramount and Different Drummer labels.

26. For an excellent discussion of the blaxploitation cycle, see Guerrero (1993).

27. The early life of Nat King Cole has major similarities to what is dramatized in the life of Handy (Whitehead 1992). Both men grew up in the rural South with ministers for fathers, and both broke away to perform for popular audiences. Interestingly, Handy's father in *St. Louis Blues* is played by Juano Hernandez, the same actor who earlier played Kirk Douglas's trumpet mentor in *Young Man with a Horn*.

28. *Sid and Nancy* (1986), the film about the scrupulously self-destructive white rock star Sid Vicious, is an English film. By contrast, the various American television movies about Elvis Presley—as well as the many films such as *Honeymoon in Vegas* (1992) and *True Romance* (1993) that evoke his memory—have *not* emphasized his drug abuse and the pathological behavior of his final years.

Chapter Three

1. An Italian book on Duke Ellington, for example, has sections entitled "Il periodo arcaico," "Il periodo della consacrazione," and "Il periodo del declino" (Berini 1994).

2. See also the attacks on modern jazz by Philip Larkin, Albert Goldman, and others (Meltzer 1993), all of whom write with style and wit but still hate canonical jazz musicians such as Charlie Parker, Sonny Rollins, Bud Powell, and Miles Davis.

3. The critics who embraced bebop saw it as the future of jazz, a natural outgrowth of all that was good in the history of the music. But the public's response to bebop was so feeble that "jazz" suddenly began to seem a dead end. At least partially as a result of jazz and bop becoming synonymous, *Down Beat* ran a contest in 1949 to find a new name for a music that could include swing and its aftermath but not necessarily bop ("New Word" 1949). The winning entry was "Crewcut music" ("Crewcut Contest's $" 1949). For a detailed study of the

reception of bebop in the 1940s, see Gendron (1994). See also the essay by El-worth (1995) that links the first boppers with the bop revivalism of the 1980s.

4. For a wide variety of views on jazz that resist the claims of autonomy, see the articles in my two anthologies, *Jazz among the Discourses* (Gabbard 1994a) and *Representing Jazz* (Gabbard 1994b).

5. Among the countless works that can be cited in support of this argument, I recommend McDowell (1980), Barbara Herrnstein Smith (1988), Levine (1988), Gates (1989), Guillory (1990), McClary (1991), and Brett (1994). For an attempt to connect these arguments with the view of jazz as art, see my essay, "The Jazz Canon and Its Consequences" (Gabbard 1995a).

6. For an excellent survey of American jazz criticism in the 1930s, see Wel-burn (1989).

7. The appearance of Lewis in Goodman's jazz history lesson can be ex-plained, at least in part, by his immense popularity in the 1920s and early 1930s, but also by the young Goodman's presence at several recording sessions with Lewis in 1931 and 1932.

8. I have relied heavily in these two paragraphs on the excellent discussion of *Jammin' the Blues* by Arthur Knight (1995).

9. Whiteman's big buildup at the end of *Birth of the Blues* was among his final bows as a central figure in American popular music, at least in terms of how he would appear in the movies. He would be ridiculed by pseudonym in *Young Man with a Horn* (1950). In 1940, however, he was still taken seriously in *Strike Up the Band;* virtually canonized at that moment in American popular music history, Whiteman stiffly pontificates about the importance of music to an adoring Mickey Rooney. But he makes no appeals to art in his speech—he speaks of "rhythm" in moral and biological terms, suggesting that a man who plays a musi-cal instrument is less likely to turn to crime and that the first and last thing we have in life is the rhythm of our heartbeat.

10. The brief shots of jazz musicians at the end of *Birth of the Blues* were collected from preexisting films. The footage of Ellington, for example, is taken from *Murder at the Vanities* (1934). The Whiteman footage was first seen in *Strike Up the Band* (1940).

11. Adler had actually requested Ellington over Lombardo, but the studio chose not to identify the black musicians.

12. Much the same can be said of *Hollywood Hotel* (1937). When Benny Goodman's big band and quartet appear in one sequence, all of the musicians, including the black Teddy Wilson and Lionel Hampton, are dressed in studiedly casual uniforms. But the dignified Wilson and the exuberant Hampton must be contrasted with the plantation stereotypes in an earlier scene in which a num-ber of black actors in antebellum slave costumes appear on a movie set where a pre–*Gone with the Wind* epic is being made.

13. In fact, the genesis of *New Orleans* was even more auspicious. The script for the film is credited to Elliott Paul, who had been enlisted in 1941 by Orson Welles to write the story of jazz for the aborted film *It's All True* (Stowe 1994, 139). The project was also to have involved Duke Ellington, whose participation in the musical revue *Jump for Joy* had convinced Welles that he ought to include

the bandleader/composer in his next project. Because of Welles's falling out with RKO, *It's All True* was never completed. Although footage was shot for three of the four projected segments of the film, and although portions of one segment were edited, scored, and shown in theaters in 1993 (as *It's All True*), the projected segment on jazz never got off the ground. Ellington did, however, undertake some research for the project, at least some of which became part of his "A Drum Is a Woman," a fantasy on the origins of jazz that was presented on CBS television in 1957. For a thorough account of Ellington's involvement with Welles's project, see Stratemann (1992, 193–95).

14. Benny Goodman has a rare appearance as an actor in *A Song Is Born*, playing one of the unworldly professors working on the encyclopedia of music. He even wears his hair in a fashion that would have been anathema to all white hipsters in 1947. In a scene that anticipates the young Benny learning to play jazz in *The Benny Goodman Story* (1955), Goodman's character immediately becomes an accomplished jazz improviser after reading a few pages of Sargeant's *Jazz, Hot and Hybrid*.

15. Of course, Hampton did not remain a "pure" jazz artist throughout the entire decade of the 1950s. He often played what might be called big band rhythm and blues. The "narration" that he sings at the beginning of *Mr. Rock and Roll* is an intriguing contrast to the organic jazz history that has been so carefully constructed by jazz writers. Hampton sings, "First there was Mr. Blues. Then Mr. Dixieland. Then came Mr. Jazz with his swinging band. The music they play, they felt deep down in their soul. But they had to make way for Mr. Rock and Roll." Notice the use of the past tense.

16. In spite of his long association with big bands and jazz artists, Frank Sinatra has no real connection with jazz in *Kings Go Forth*. Unlike many black musicians who started out in jazz, Sinatra was able to redefine himself as much more than a jazz singer. Also intriguing is the constant rewriting of Sinatra's maleness. In *Kings Go Forth*, as in many of his films, his masculinity and sexuality are often on the verge of crisis. As Keir Keightley (1994) has written, "Sinatra's persona is continuously being masculinized in order to be re-feminized, and feminized in order to be re-masculinized" (2).

17. The jazz-drenched bohemian subculture of the 1950s was important to Hollywood in several films, if only for a brief period. *The Subterraneans, Bell, Book, and Candle* (1958), *Visit to a Small Planet* (1959), and *The Beat Generation* (1959) all feature jazz performances in exotic nightclubs that exploit the public's fascination with the Beats. Perhaps the most memorable of these scenes takes place in *Visit to a Small Planet* when Jerry Lewis, as Creton the being from another world, fits right in at a Beatnik club called The Hungry Brain. When a singer warbles the canonical bop syllables "Oo be doo be, ool ya koo, mop mop," Lewis bursts into tears. Having understood all of the words, he announces that it's a very sad song.

18. For excellent single-volume introductions to jazz fiction, see Albert (1990) and Parker (1986).

19. For a fuller discussion of the exact function of music for films, see chapter 5.

20. "Max Steiner's grandfather owned the Theater an der Wien, one of Vien-

na's operatic showplaces, and by the age of sixteen Steiner himself had written an operetta which ran for a year. Korngold was a child prodigy (Mahler pronounced him a genius at age ten) and by the age of seventeen had written two operas widely performed throughout Europe. Dimitri Tiomkin, Franz Waxman, Bronislau Kaper, and Miklós Rózsa were all emigrés who brought with them a musical predilection for the nineteenth century. In fact, with the exception of American-born Alfred Newman, the development of the classical Hollywood film score in the crucial decade of the thirties was dominated by a group of composers displaced from the musical idiom in which they had been trained" (Kalinak 1992, 100).

21. Mingus wrote and recorded music for *Shadows*, only a fraction of which found its way into the final cut of the film. Seven-and-a-half minutes of extraordinary but rejected music for *Shadows* has been released on *Charles Mingus: The Complete Debut Recordings* (Debut). According to Brian Priestley (1982), Mingus was not able to compose all of the music in time to meet the film's production schedule, so Mingus's tenor saxophonist Shafi Hadi simply improvised behind the several scenes that still needed music (91).

22. Although some of what happens in *Shadows* was improvised at an early stage, virtually everything that the actors say on screen was ultimately written down by Cassavetes after he pulled the original release print of the film from distribution and reshot and reedited most of it. See Carney (1985, 20–62 and 1994, 27–73) for a history of the film's development. Carney's books also examine the ways in which the actors in Cassavetes's films can be said to be "improvising," even when every scene has been written out and rehearsed.

23. Wexman (1993) specifically discusses the improvisational techniques used by stars such as Marlon Brando in *On the Waterfront* (1954) and James Dean in *Rebel without a Cause* (1955) (170–79).

Chapter Four

1. According to Ulrich Schönherr (1991), Adorno wrote his jazz criticism "in almost complete ignorance of the subject" (87).

2. For the application of Gates's Signifyin(g) aesthetic to jazz, see Tomlinson (1991) and Gabbard (1991).

3. But see Gendron (1986) for a practical application of Adorno's work to popular musics along with a critique of its limitations.

4. I thank Steven Elworth for coining the term "post-phallic."

5. The penis as physical organ is distinguished from the more symbolic phallus in several discourses. For the extraordinarily influential work of Jacques Lacan on the phallus as the signifier par excellence, see Silverman (1983). Rancour-Laferriere draws upon sociobiology and semiotics as well as psychoanalysis to make a more interdisciplinary but complementary argument in "Some Semiotic Aspects of the Human Penis" (1979).

6. See Silverman (1988). DiPiero (1991) makes the important distinction between castration as "bodily mutilation restricted to males" and the "psychic alienation all subjects undergo upon access to the symbolic order," pointing out that a great deal of psychoanalytic writing has conflated the two (113).

7. Of course, the combination of blowing and fingering associated with tubu-

lar instruments has been sexualized at least since the Renaissance. See, for example, the entries for "pipe," "bugle," and "horn" in Partridge (1968).

8. For a revealing record of Gillespie's performance persona, see the videocassette *Jivin' in Be-Bop.*

9. For a sophisticated analysis of gender codings in Western music, see McClary (1991).

10. This kind of competition is captured in the 1958 musical battle between Buck Clayton and Charlie Shavers through a series of chase choruses on "This Can't Be Love," anthologized on the videocassette *Trumpet Kings.*

11. Davis poses with his wardrobe in a photograph included in *Miles: The Autobiography* (1989), plate 88.

12. Hear Davis's famous fluff on the 1964 recording of "My Funny Valentine." By not editing this portion of the performance, the producers at Columbia Records were promoting the image of Davis as the profound but fragile genius. I would also cite this recording as an excellent example of how Davis alternated strongly phallic elements of his playing with moments of post-phallic vulnerability. For a brilliant analysis of Davis's 1964 "My Funny Valentine," see Walser (1995).

13. For a concise account, see Giddins (1985).

14. To be sure, Ray Nance, Sonny Berman, and Rex Stewart all played in "ironic" styles in the 1930s and 1940s. A case can also be made that the underrecorded Freddie Webster, an early influence on Miles Davis, was the first post-phallic trumpeter. Furthermore, aggressive trumpeters, black and white, did *not* cease to exist after the 1950s. Lee Morgan, a virtuoso player who was strongly influenced by Gillespie and Clifford Brown, died in 1972. The technically proficient, often flamboyant Freddie Hubbard is still active, as are young phallic trumpeters such as Jon Faddis, Brian Lynch, Philip Harper, and Roy Hargrove.

15. The picture is on the cover of Miles Davis, *Tune Up.* Released as a double LP in 1977, this album collects Davis's Prestige recordings from 1953 and 1954.

16. A video record of a 1982 Farmer performance is included in the "Jazz at the Smithsonian" series.

17. When he appeared on the cover of *Time* (October 22, 1990), Marsalis was declared by the magazine to be a "full-fledged superstar." The cover article placed his gross income in the seven-figure range (71). Marsalis's ability to reach a large audience of serious and casual jazz fans surely owes a great deal to the considerable cachet he gained by regular performances of both jazz *and* classical music. I should also point out that Marsalis moved away from the Miles Davis legacy around 1990 and began exploring other modes, such as the growling, blues-based style of Cootie Williams.

18. It could even be argued that the tenor saxophone replaced the trumpet as the most phallic jazz instrument sometime in the 1950s. While Miles Davis was turning inward, John Coltrane was aggressively opening up new modes of expression on the tenor. Today, the most phallic and most adventurous hornmen may be tenor saxophonists Sonny Rollins, David Murray, and, until his untimely death, George Adams. For Rollins, see *Saxophone Colossus;* for Murray, see *David Murray Quartet Live at the Village Vanguard;* Adams appears in *Charles Mingus's Epitaph.*

19. The relationship between Gillespie and Faddis was clearly evident at the Wolf Trap performance. For an example of Faddis's self-assured Signifyin(g) on the music of earlier trumpet masters, hear his album *Legacy*.

20. When Davis was asked to talk about *Miles Smiles,* his 1966 LP that epitomizes the style imitated by players such as Marsalis, Blanchard, and Wallace Roney, Davis responded, "I can't remember it" (Ephland 1988, 18). Davis had an especially confrontational relationship with Wynton Marsalis. After criticizing one another in the press for several months, Marsalis walked on stage one night in 1986 in hopes of playing with Davis when both musicians were in Vancouver at a jazz festival. Miles wrote in his autobiography that he told Marsalis, "Man, get the fuck off the stage" and then stopped his band until Marsalis left. See Davis (1989, 374). Marsalis has responded to these remarks in Helland (1990, 16). To my knowledge, Davis never appeared on the same stage with Terence Blanchard, but at the Montreux Jazz and Blues Festival of July 1991—just two months before he died—Davis participated in a highly unusual revival of his early work with Gil Evans and traded solos with Wallace Roney.

21. In *A League of Their Own* (1992), even female teams function according to the well-established paradigm of Hollywood's baseball films; at its conclusion, the film powerfully reinscribes mainstream sex and gender roles after superficially interrogating them throughout.

22. When asked by Henry Louis Gates, Jr. (1991), why he put a "fairy-tale ending" on *Mo' Better Blues,* Spike Lee responded, "I don't know why it's unrealistic for a couple, a black couple, to be happily married and have a child at the end of a movie. We suppose to end up broke and OD-ing in some little funky hotel in the lower east side?" (197).

23. Spike Lee may also have been working through ambivalence about his father's life in *Jungle Fever,* which addresses the romance between a black man and a white woman. Bill Lee married a white woman after the death of Spike's mother, and Spike has candidly told interviewers that he does not get along well with his stepmother. See Richolson (1991). In the overtly autobiographical *Crooklyn* (1994), the director offers a more detailed portrait of his father as a failed artist whose solo concert is attended only by a small group of friends and family. Most significantly, the child in the film who represents the young Spike deeply resents being forced to attend his father's concert on a night when he would have preferred watching the New York Knicks compete for the NBA championship.

24. Adorno makes this connection explicitly in "On the Fetish-Character in Music and the Regression of Listening": "These smart chaps can be found everywhere and are able to do everything themselves: the advanced student who in every gathering is ready to play jazz with machinelike precision for dancing and entertainment; the gas station attendant who hums his syncopation ingenuously while filling up the tank; the listening expert who can identify every band and immerses himself in the history of jazz as if it were Holy Writ. He is nearest to the sportsman: if not to the football player himself, then to the swaggering fellow who dominates the stands" (Adorno 1978, 291).

25. Modleski (1986) is sensitive to the positive association of men with production and the negative association of women with consumption.

26. "Likewise, when Adorno remarks that 'the extent to which jazz has anything at all to do with genuine black music is highly questionable,' he is referring to the popular, commercially produced hits that were accessible to any European civil servant on the radio, and not to what now would be recognized as authentically *black* jazz, a jazz of which few white Europeans in the 1930s would have been aware" (Daniel 1989–90, 41).

Chapter Five

1. All the comparisons to Ellington during this period show his singularity. The black bandleader Chick Webb performed in the 1929 short film *After Seben* but without his name appearing anywhere in the credits or in the dialogue. Although the nine-minute *Yamekraw* (1930) was built around an ambitious composition by James P. Johnson, no musicians appeared on screen. In the early 1930s, Louis Armstrong, Don Redman, and Cab Calloway were seen in Max Fleischer's various Betty Boop cartoons, but only as exotics: Armstrong, for example, is compared to an African cannibal, while Calloway is caricatured as a singing walrus.

2. The CDs, *The Brunswick Era (1926–1929)* (Decca) and *Early Ellington, 1927–1934* (RCA Bluebird), contain the first recordings of Miley soloing on "Black and Tan Fantasy."

3. Cripps (1977, 232) reproduces a photograph of Ellington shaking hands with Van Vechten and looking over his shoulder at Dudley Murphy. The meeting takes place on the nightclub set for *Black and Tan*, complete with the prostrate body of Fredi Washington at their feet.

4. In this sense, Murphy's fascination for blacks resembled the French Negrophilia of the day, which found a universal *âme nègre* in "an expansive category that included North American jazz, Brazilian rhythms, African, Oceanean, and Alaskan carvings, ritual 'poetry' from south of the Sahara and from the Australian outback, the literature from the Harlem Renaissance, and René Maran's *Batouala* (subtitled 'véritable roman nègre') which won the Prix Goncourt" (Clifford 1989, 901).

5. The piece "Black and Tan Fantasy" itself, with its "twisted beauty" (Darrell 1932, 153), exemplifies many of these unresolved ambiguities. The first theme composed by Miley is much darker than the more florid second theme probably contributed by Ellington; in addition to flavors of both "jungle music" and sedate ragtime, there is the ironic quotation from Chopin. For more extensive analyses of "Black and Tan Fantasy," see Schuller (1968, 329–31) and Tucker (1991, 242–48).

6. Ellington was not the only jazz composer to have fun with Liszt's well-known rhapsody. According to Gunther Schuller (1989), during the swing era there was "hardly a band that did not quote or steal from its famous themes" (66). I should also add that this practice of jazzing up the classics bears little relation to the heartfelt claim that jazz is art. To quote Schuller again, the many jazz records of the 1930s that poached on the classical repertoire were devoted to "the 'daring' notion among swing fans that 'classical music really might not be that bad'" (1989, 25).

7. In an article published later in *Orchestra World*, Ellington retracted most of what he is quoted as saying in the *New Theatre* piece. In his introductory note

to the reprinted versions of the two articles, however, Tucker argues convincingly that Ellington had been caught off guard by the reporter but that the sentiments he expressed in the first article were probably genuine (Tucker 1993, 117–18).

8. Tucker (1991) has argued that *Symphony in Black* and *Black, Brown, and Beige* both recall a 1911 musical production called *The Evolution of the Negro in Picture, Song, and Story.* Presented at a black theater in Washington, D.C., the performance included a glee club conducted by Henry Lee Grant, an especially important figure for the young Ellington. The structure of the presentation strongly resembled the program for *Symphony in Black* and *BBB*:

Overture
Night of Slavery—Sorrow Songs
Dawn of Freedom
Day of Opportunity.

As Tucker observes, "The man who devoted so much of his career to championing the achievements of his race through his music and words grew up amidst people whose art could express the same ideals" (1991, 12–13).

9. Stratemann (1992) provides a thorough history of the soundies and of Ellington's participation in their production.

10. For an excellent discussion of Whitey's Lindy Hoppers and of their participation in the Ellington soundie, see Crease (1995).

11. Like Kay Kyser, Lena Horne is at the boundaries of this study. Although purists have excluded her from the elite circle of jazz musicians, Horne has always had multiple associations with many important artists from the jazz canon. And unlike virtually every other black female singer who worked in films in the 1940s, Horne was able to present a strong sexual presence that appealed to a multiracial audience. This quality has been especially important to Shari Roberts's (1995) excellent work on Horne's career.

12. In a letter to Marshall Stearns, the journalist Frank M. Davis describes a cutting contest in the mid-1920s between Bubber Miley and Johnny Dunn in which Miley, appearing with the Ellington orchestra, actually dressed as a preacher and played a "sermon" with his plunger-muted trumpet (Tucker 1991, 248). When Ellington rerecorded "Black and Tan Fantasy" in 1938, Cootie Williams took an especially preacherly role in the call-and-response section of his solo. For an even more explicit combination of the sacred and the profane, hear Louis Armstrong's mock sermon on his 1931 Columbia recording of "The Lonesome Road." The tradition can be traced back to Bert Williams and, undoubtedly, to earlier figures in African American humor.

13. While working on the score for *Anatomy,* both in Ishpeming, Michigan, and in Hollywood, Ellington was probably away from his orchestra for the longest time in its history (Stratemann 1992, 402).

14. Several of these reworkings, including a return to "Creole Rhapsody" called "Neo-Creole," have been issued on *Up in Duke's Workshop* (Pablo).

15. Kalinak (1992) quotes a contemporary of Erich Wolfgang Korngold, Herbert Stothart: "If an audience is conscious of music where it should be conscious only of drama, then the musician has gone wrong" (99).

16. When George Gershwin met Maurice Ravel in 1928 and asked if he could

study with him, Ravel refused, adding, "You might lose your *melodic* spontaneity and write bad Ravel" (Seroff 1953, 248, emphasis added). Nevertheless, Ravel shared an enthusiasm for jazz with composers such as Milhaud and Stravinsky, just as Ansermet had expressed delight at a performance of Sidney Bechet as early as 1919. Members of the conservatory, however, such as the fictional René Bernard, were more likely to police the confines of what is and is not "serious art."

17. The "stylistic excess" of the Ellington/Strayhorn composition that ends *Paris Blues* can be understood in terms of an argument that Caryl Flinn makes in her discussion of music in film noir and melodrama: "Stylistic excesses and unconventional formal practices have often been identified as the purported means by which cinematic content (e.g., story lines) can be politicized and rendered subversive" (Flinn 1992, 116). Accordingly, the critique of *Paris Blues* that I hear in the film's final music depends on the "excesses" of a music that completely overwhelms ever other aspect of the film, including the "Paris Blues" theme itself.

18. A good example of this routine has been preserved on a CD of a November 26, 1969 concert in Manchester, England, on the Sequel Jazz label. Ellington was by no means the only jazz artist to engage in some version of signifying. Jed Rasula has written: "Because Ellington was perceived as debonair, his (much noted) strategies of verbal evasion were regarded as displays of inscrutable charm, where corresponding strategies on the part of other musicians tended to be seen as dissimulation, insolence, capriciousness, or a simple inability to speak standard English (or, as in the case of Lester Young, symptomatic of some alleged mental fatigue). It would be more accurate to see Ellington as the norm rather than the exception here, practicing a strategically contrapuntal speech intended to glance off and otherwise evade the dominant code" (Rasula 1995, 155).

19. Ellington and Strayhorn's adaptations of Tchaikovsky's *The Nutcracker Suite* and Grieg's *The Peer Gynt Suite* have been released on CD as *Three Suites* (Columbia). (The third suite is *Suite Thursday*, inspired by John Steinbeck's novella *Sweet Thursday*.)

Chapter Six

1. The filmography at the end of this chapter includes only full-length narrative films in which Armstrong appeared. It does not include television, documentary, and other performance films such as *Satchmo the Great* (1957), *Jazz on a Summer's Day* (1960), and *Jazz, the Intimate Art* (1968); nor does it include European films such as *Kφbenhavn Kalundborg* (Denmark, 1933), *La Botta e Riposta* (Italy, 1949), *La Route du bonheur* (France, 1952), *Kaerlighedens Melodi* (Denmark, 1959), and *Die Nacht vor der Premiere* (Germany, 1959), as well as the widely anthologized three-minute soundies "Sleepy Time Down South" (1941), "Shine" (1942), "I'll Be Glad When You're Dead You Rascal You" (1942), and "Swingin' on Nothin'" (1942).

2. I have also excluded the several films that do not feature Armstrong but that prominently feature his music on the soundtrack. A few noteworthy examples are *On Her Majesty's Secret Service* (1969), *Minnie and Moskowitz* (1971), *The Man Who Fell to Earth* (1976), *Rambling Rose* (1991), and *Corinna Corinna*

(1994). In Peter Bogdanovich's *Saint Jack* (1979), Armstrong's performance of "Someday You'll Be Sorry" is a favorite record of the eponymous hero. The song is not heard throughout the film's middle sections when the protagonist gives into a government official who would make him complicit in the American invasion of Vietnam. When Jack is managing a brothel for American servicemen— virtually all of whom are portrayed unsympathetically—country music regularly plays on the diegetic soundtrack. At the end, when Jack definitively renounces the official who would involve him in further sleazy dealings, the Armstrong recording is heard once again, this time as the first extradiegetic music in the film. Woody Allen's *Stardust Memories* (1980) takes its title from Armstrong's 1931 recording of "Stardust" and uses the song as the background for the one moment in which Allen's hero is most in love with the manic-depressive Dorrie (Charlotte Rampling). Perhaps the most striking appropriation of an Armstrong recording takes place in Barry Levinson's *Good Morning, Vietnam* (1987): Armstrong's 1967 recording of "What a Wonderful World" functions as what Michel Chion (Gorbman 1987, 151–61) would call the "anempathic" background for scenes of soldiers fighting and dying in Vietnam. The film's success lifted the recording onto the pop charts, sixty-one years after Armstrong first scored a hit with his "Muskrat Ramble" in 1926 (Giddins 1988, 32).

3. The increase in cultural capital that jazz gained in the 1990s may explain the dramatic change in Bogle's view of Armstrong. In an essay on Armstrong's films written several years after the first publication of *Toms, Coons, Mulattoes, Mammies, and Bucks,* Bogle wrote, "his movie and television image is an all-grinning, all-mugging, ever-cheerful minstrellike figure who with unabashed glee performs corny, knuckle-headed routines." Then he adds that Armstrong possessed "an almost mythic power and resonance" (Bogle 1994, 148).

4. It is possible that Bigard's memory was faulty and that the filming was for a television program, not a movie. In his Armstrong discography, Hans Westerberg (1981) has an entry for a November 28, 1951, session in which Armstrong recorded "When It's Sleepy Time Down South" with the Gordon Jenkins orchestra: "Two versions have been issued of this title. They are otherwise identical except that the word 'darkies' in the lyric has been replaced by the word 'people' in the second version" (Westerberg 1981, 119).

5. Ironically, "When It's Sleepy Time Down South" was written by Clarence Muse and the René brothers, all of them black. For an extraordinary transformation of the song, hear Betty Carter's reading on her 1992 album, *It's Not about the Melody* (Verve).

6. According to Stanley Crouch (1995), however, many younger jazz musicians in the late 1950s and early 1960s considered Gillespie a Tom because he danced, laughed, and joked on the bandstand.

7. Armstrong's first appearance in a feature film is probably lost. After exhaustive searches, no Armstrong collector has been able to locate a copy of the 1931 film *Ex-Flame.* Jack Bradley, who has contacted film collectors worldwide in search of a print of *Ex-Flame,* has seen a lobby card for the film.

8. Armstrong does not appear to have found this kind of material problematic. In an undated audiotape from the 1950s in the Louis Armstrong Archive at Queens College, Armstrong repeats the dialogue from the scene in *Pennies from*

Heaven in which he asks for 7 instead of 10 percent. After laughing at the punch line, he pronounces the scene "a gassuh."

9. The sexual discourse of this song is definitely enhanced by the mention of Dillinger, a phallic character of legendary proportions. When I was in high school, it was common knowledge that Dillinger's penis was preserved at the Smithsonian Institution. Anecdotal evidence has since suggested that Dillinger used to keep a sawed-off shotgun down his trouser leg and that it was mistaken for his penis, but no one has ever explained to me how the Smithsonian Institution became part of the oral tradition.

10. According to David Meeker (1981), Armstrong filmed a musical number for *Cabin in the Sky* that was cut from the release print of the film. Similarly, all footage of Armstrong was excised from the Bing Crosby vehicle *Dr. Rhythm* (1938).

11. Pete Rugolo, who was Stan Kenton's arranger-in-chief in the mid- to late 1940s, is credited with some of the orchestrations for *The Strip*. The film was in fact his first assignment during the thirty years he worked in Hollywood. His second job was *Glory Alley* (Woolley 1995, 10).

12. For an excellent introduction to the problems faced by anyone looking for "positive role models" in minority or Third World cultures, see Stam and Spence (1985).

Chapter Seven

1. A case can also be made that the story is apocryphal. In the late 1940s, Lucille Ball was a modestly successful contract player at MGM. It is highly unlikely that she would have had sufficient power to deny someone a part in a film.

2. A tape of the "Nature Boy" performance is part of the video *Unforgettable: Nat "King" Cole* (MPI).

3. Although *Rhythm in a Riff* undermined the phallic masculinity of Billy Eckstine, the industry at roughly the same time allowed Cab Calloway to play a conventional hard-boiled detective in *Hi De Ho* (1945). In fact, black actors regularly played tough guys and dashing romantic leads in race films. It seems, however, that Calloway and Herb Jeffries ("The Bronze Buckaroo") were the only such actors who also had careers in music, and neither performer had a large following among white audiences. Cole, Eckstine, and the rest might also be compared with Johnny Mathis, an extremely popular black singer whose sexual presentation was much more ambiguous.

4. *The Blue Gardenia* is also remarkable for its use of the Prelude and Liebestod theme from Wagner's *Tristan und Isolde*. As with the title song, the music slips in and out of the diegesis but in much more complex patterns. Just as "The Blue Gardenia" (song) is tied to Norah as supposed murderer, Wagner's music is tied to the actual murderer, Rose, who was rejected by Prebble. The music twice begins diegetically, on a phonograph and as piped-in music at an airport restaurant, and then shifts to the extradiegetic score; in another case, it begins as background music and is subsequently assimilated as the diegetic sound of a record. At one point, it seamlessly moves between two diegetic sources, from the airport speakers to the record player in Prebble's apartment. During a four-minute period toward the end of *The Blue Gardenia*, each moment of Wagner's music is cued to

specific emotions, indicating first Rose's dawning sense of resignation as the police close in and then, in a flashback, the pain of her unrequited love for Prebble. Casey's unrequited love for Norah finds its *ancrage* in the same sounds a few moments later, just after the music has provided a melancholy tone as Rose confesses to Prebble's murder after a suicide attempt. At one point, the music even "Mickey-Mouses" Rose's attack with the fireplace poker on Prebble.

5. Carmichael spells the black pianist's name "Duval." In the carefully researched booklet that accompanies a series of recordings of Carmichael's songs (Smithsonian Collection), John Edward Hasse reproduces a photograph of the black pianist and spells his name "Reginald DuValle."

6. The documentary was released on a videocassette in 1994 as *Bix: "Ain't None of Them Play Like Him Yet"* (Playboy Home Video).

7. Robin Wood (1968) is especially sensitive to gender roles in the films of Hawks.

8. But hear the surprisingly successful recording that Carmichael made with serious jazz artists such as Harry Edison, Jimmy Rowles, and Art Pepper in 1956 (Pacific Jazz).

Conclusion

1. This book went to press before the appearance of two important films with jazz content, Robert Altman's *Kansas City* and Clint Eastwood's *The Bridges of Madison County.*

Save the Tiger (1973) may be the most unsettling of the various films in which jazz functions as a character's anchor in a forgotten era. Featuring tunes like "Stomping at the Savoy," "Air Mail Special," and "Flying Home" on both the diegetic and extradiegetic soundtracks, the film stars Jack Lemmon as an unscrupulous businessman who tries to keep his idealized youth separate from the fallen world in which he manages to function with some degree of success. At the film's ironic conclusion, after he has carefully set in motion a highly illegal and potentially deadly moneymaking scheme, the Lemmon character achieves a moment of peace contemplating the past while Bunny Berigan gives his utopian performance of "I Can't Get Started" on the soundtrack.

2. Unless otherwise noted, all statements attributed to Martin Scorsese in this chapter are from his audio commentary on the "Deluxe Collector's Edition" of *New York, New York,* issued on laser disc in 1993 by MGM/UA Home Video. Scorsese also discusses the influences on *New York, New York* in his "Guilty Pleasures" essay in *Film Comment* (Scorsese 1978).

3. Cohan (1993) sees the hard-boiled detective of film noir and Astaire's "feminized" song-and-dance man as two major types of performative masculinity in the 1950s. He also points out how ingeniously they have been combined in the "Girl Hunt Ballet."

4. The original shooting script for *New York, New York* is also available on the laser disc issued by MGM/UA.

5. As Robert B. Ray (1985) points out, however, the camera-in-the-glass scene in *Taxi Driver* is clearly meant to reflect Travis Bickle's state of mind, while the corresponding scene in Godard's film is less conventionally motivated and substantially more alienating (349–51).

6. In 1957 some avant-garde jazz artists were experimenting, but their music was much less extreme. Compare the music of "Cecil Powell" with, for example, Charles's Mingus's *The Clown* (Atlantic) from 1957. Even Ornette Coleman's first recordings from 1958 (Contemporary) and Cecil Taylor's 1959 quintet recordings (United Artists) are not as "outside" as the music at the Major Chord.

7. Fredric Jameson (1990) is also sensitive to the "utopian" or transcendent functions of Hollywood films, especially as those functions support the purely ideological aspect of movies (30). His analysis of *Jaws* and the *Godfather* films in "Reification and Utopia in Mass Culture" is especially useful for clarifying how a film's "meanings" play off its more pleasurable qualities (9–34).

8. Nor do I deny that there are numerous utopian moments in the many jazz documentaries and performance programs that are outside the scope of this book. Nevertheless, I recommend *The Sound of Jazz* (1957), *Jazz on a Summer's Day* (1960), *Memories of Duke* (1984), *A Brother with Perfect Timing* (1986), *Thelonious Monk: Straight No Chaser* (1988), and, of course, *Jammin' the Blues* (1945). Then, again, must jazz necessarily always be utopian? Might not the music's incompatibility with certain utopias—particularly those manufactured for ideological purposes in Hollywood—carry with it a heroic element? In this sense, *New York, New York* may be more of a tribute to jazz than I have allowed in my dismay at its lavish attention to Liza Minnelli.

9. Much of this information about the songs in *Short Cuts* can be found in the liner notes for the soundtrack album (Imago).

10. If nothing else, the real Annie Ross plays to more attentive audiences. When I saw her at Reno Sweeney's in New York in 1979 and at the Village Vanguard in 1986, the audiences were under her spell, including those who knew her only as the writer of a Joni Mitchell song. Ross has also had a more elaborate love life than what appears to be the case with Tess Trainer. In the late 1940s Ross bore a child to the canonical bop drummer Kenny Clarke while they were both living in Paris; she has had long-lasting affairs with Lenny Bruce and Tony Bennett; and she was married to the Irish actor Sean Lynch for twelve years (Gourse 1984, 283–92).

Adorno. Theodor. [1936] 1989–90. "On Jazz." Trans. Jamie Owen Daniel. *Discourse* 12, no. 1:45–69.

———. 1973. *Philosophy of Modern Music.* Trans. Anne G. Mitchell and Wesley V. Blomster. New York: Seabury Press.

———. 1978. "On the Fetish-Character in Music and the Regression of Listening." In *The Essential Frankfurt School Reader,* ed. Andrew Arato and Eike Gebhardt. New York: Urizen Books.

———. 1981. "Perennial Fashion—Jazz." In *Prisms.* Trans. Samuel and Shierry Weber. Cambridge, Mass.: MIT Press.

Albert, Richard N., ed. 1990. *From Blues to Bop.* Baton Rouge: Louisiana State University Press.

Allen, Walter C. 1973. *Hendersonia: The Music of Fletcher Henderson and His Musicians.* Jazz Monographs 4. Highland Park, Ill.: Walter C. Allen.

Altman, Rick. 1986. "A Semantic/Syntactic Approach to Film Genre." In *Film Genre Reader,* ed. Barry Keith Grant, 26–40. Austin: University of Texas Press.

———. 1989. *The American Film Musical.* Bloomington: Indiana University Press.

Altman, Robert. 1993. "Introduction." In *Short Cuts: Selected Stories by Raymond Carver.* New York: Vintage.

Althusser, Louis. 1977. *For Marx.* Trans. Ben Brewster. London: New Left Books.

Anderson, Edmund. 1993. "Personal Reminiscences of Duke." Unpublished paper delivered at the International Duke Ellington Conference, New York, August.

Anderson, Jervis. 1994. "The Public Intellectual." *New Yorker* January 17:39–48.

Arato, Andrew, and Eike Gebhardt, eds. 1978. *The Essential Frankfurt School Reader.* New York: Urizen Books.

Armstrong, Louis. [1936] 1993. *Swing That Music.* New York: Da Capo.

———. 1955. Letter to Joe Glaser dated August 2. Library of Congress, Washington, D.C.

———. 1954. *Satchmo: My Life in New Orleans.* New York: Prentice-Hall.

Babcock-Abrahams, Barbara. 1975. "'A Tolerated Margin of Mess': The Trickster and His Tales Reconsidered." *Journal of the Folklore Institute* 11:147–86.

Baker, Dorothy. 1938. *Young Man with a Horn.* Boston: Houghton Mifflin.

Baker, Houston A., Jr. 1984. *Blues, Ideology, and Afro-American Literature: A Vernacular Theory.* Chicago: University of Chicago Press.

———. 1991. "Spike Lee and Popular Culture." Unpublished paper delivered at the Humanities Institute, State University of New York at Stony Brook, April.

Baldwin, James. 1976. *The Devil Finds Work.* New York: Dial.

———. [1957] 1990. "Sonny's Blues." In Albert 1990, 174–206.

Baraka, Amiri (as LeRoi Jones). 1963. *Blues People: Negro Music in White America.* New York: Morrow.

———. (as LeRoi Jones). 1967. *Black Music.* New York: Morrow.

Barthes, Roland. 1972. *Mythologies.* Trans. Annette Lavers. New York: Hill and Wang.

———. 1975. *The Pleasures of the Text.* Trans. Richard Miller. New York: Hill and Wang.

———. 1977. "Introduction to the Structural Analysis of Narratives." In *Image—Music—Text,* trans. Stephen Heath, 79–124. New York: Hill and Wang.

Bechet, Sidney. [1960] 1978. *Treat It Gentle.* New York: Da Capo.

Bellour, Raymond. 1979. "Alternation, Segmentation, Hypnosis: Interview with Janet Bergstrom." *Camera Obscura* 3–4:93.

Benjamin, Walter. 1969. "The Work of Art in the Age of Mechanical Reproduction." In *Illuminations,* ed. Hannah Arendt, trans. Harry Zohn, 217–52. New York: Schocken.

Berg, Charles Merrell. 1978. "Cinema Sings the Blues." *Cinema Journal* 17, no. 2:1–12.

Berger, Morroe, Edward Berger, and James Patrick. 1982. *Benny Carter: A Life in American Music.* 2 vols. Metuchen, N. J.: Scarecrow Press and the Institute of Jazz Studies, Rutgers University

Berini, Antonio, and Giovanni M. Volonté. 1994. *Duke Ellington, un genio, un mito.* Florence: Ponte alle Grazie.

Berrett, Joshua. 1992. "Louis Armstrong and Opera." *Musical Quarterly* 76, no. 2:216–41.

Bigard, Barney. 1986. *With Louis and the Duke,* ed. Barry Martyn. New York: Oxford University Press.

Bingham, Dennis. 1994. *Acting Male: Masculinities in the Films of James Stewart, Jack Nicholson, and Clint Eastwood.* New Brunswick, N. J.: Rutgers University Press.

Blesh, Rudi. [1958] 1976. *Shining Trumpets: A History of Jazz.* 2d ed. New York: Da Capo.

Bloom, Harold. 1973. *The Anxiety of Influence.* New York: Oxford University Press.

Bogle, Donald. 1992. *Toms, Coons, Mulattoes, Mammies, and Bucks: An Interpretive History of Blacks in American Films.* New ed. New York: Ungar.

———. 1994. "Louis Armstrong: The Films." In *Louis Armstrong: A Cultural Legacy,* ed. Marc H. Miller, 147–79. Seattle: University of Washington Press.

Bogue, Merwyn, with Gladys Bogue Reilly. 1989. *Ish Kabibble: The Autobiography of Merwyn Bogue.* Baton Rouge: Louisiana State University Press.

Bordwell, David. 1985. *Narration in the Fiction Film.* Madison: University of Wisconsin Press.

Bordwell, David, Janet Staiger, and Kristin Thompson. 1985. *The Classical Hollywood Cinema: Film Style and Mode of Production to 1960.* New York: Columbia University Press.

Bourjaily, Vance. 1987. "In and Out of Storyville: Jazz and Fiction." *New York Times Book Review* December 13:1, 44–45.

Brett, Philip, Elizabeth Wood, and Gary C. Thomas, eds. 1994. *Queering the Pitch: The New Gay and Lesbian Musicology.* New York: Routledge.

Bukatman, Scott. 1991. "Paralysis in Motion: Jerry Lewis's Life as a Man." In *Comedy/Cinema/Theory,* ed. Andrew S. Horton, 188–205. Berkeley: University of California Press.

Carmichael, Hoagy. 1946. *The Stardust Road.* New York: Rinehart.

Carmichael, Hoagy, and Stephen Longstreet. 1965. *Sometimes I Wonder: The Story of Hoagy Carmichael.* New York: Farrar, Straus.

Carney, Raymond. 1985. *American Dreaming: The Films of John Cassavetes and the American Experience.* Berkeley: University of California Press.

———. 1994. *The Films of John Cassavetes: Pragmatism, Modernism, and the Movies.* Cambridge Film Classics. Cambridge: Cambridge University Press.

Carringer, Robert L., ed. 1979. *The Jazz Singer.* Wisconsin/Warner Bros. Screenplay Series. Madison: University of Wisconsin Press.

Carver, Raymond. 1993. *Short Cuts: Selected Stories by Raymond Carver.* New York: Vintage.

Chapman, Robert L. 1986. *The New Dictionary of American Slang.* New York: Harper and Row.

Chatman, Seymour. 1978. *Story and Discourse: Narrative Structure in Fiction and Film.* Ithaca: Cornell University Press.

———. 1981. "What Novels Can Do That Films Can't (and Vice Versa)." In Mitchell 1981, 117–36.

Chilton, John. 1975. *Billie's Blues: The Billie Holiday Story, 1933–1959.* New York: Stein and Day.

Clarke, Donald. 1994. *Wishing on the Moon: The Life and Times of Billie Holiday.* New York: Viking.

Clifford, James. 1989. "1933, February: Negrophilia." In *A New History of French Literature,* ed. Denis Hollier, 901–8. Cambridge, Mass.: Harvard University Press.

Clover, Carol. 1992. *Men, Women and Chainsaws*. Princeton, N. J.: Princeton University Press.

Cohan, Steven. 1993. "'Feminizing' the Song-and-Dance Man: Fred Astaire and the Spectacle of Masculinity in the Hollywood Musical." In *Screening the Male: Exploring Masculinities in Hollywood Cinema*, ed. Steven Cohan and Ina Rae Hark, 46–69. New York: Routledge.

Cole, Pat. 1993. "Joshua Redman: So, You Wanna Be a Jazz Star?" *Down Beat* December:17–18.

Collier, James Lincoln. 1978. *The Making of Jazz*. New York: Dell.

———. 1983. *Louis Armstrong: An American Genius*. New York: Oxford University Press.

———. 1987. *Duke Ellington*. New York: Oxford University Press.

———. 1988. *The Reception of Jazz in America: A New View*. Brooklyn: Institute for Studies in American Music.

———. 1989. *Benny Goodman and the Swing Era*. New York: Oxford University Press.

———. 1993. *Jazz: The American Theme Song*. New York: Oxford University Press.

Cooper, Reg. 1979. "The Art of Annie Ross." *Jazz Journal International* 32, no. 7 (July):9–10.

Corbett, John. 1994. *Extended Play: Sounding Off from John Cage to Dr. Funkenstein*. Durham, N. C.: Duke University Press.

Crease, Robert P. 1995. "Divine Frivolity: Hollywood Representations of the Lindy Hop, 1937–1942." In Gabbard 1995b, 207–28.

"Crewcut Contest's $." 1949. *Down Beat* November 4:1.

Cripps, Thomas. 1977. *Slow Fade to Black: The Negro in American Film, 1900–1942*. New York: Oxford University Press.

———. 1993. *Making Movies Black: The Hollywood Message Movie from World War II to the Civil Rights Era*. New York: Oxford University Press.

Crouch, Stanley. 1978. "Laughin' Louis." *Village Voice* August 14:45.

———. 1989. "Bird Land." *The New Republic* February 27:25–31.

———. 1990. *Notes of a Hanging Judge: Essays and Reviews, 1979–1988*. New York: Oxford University Press.

———. 1994. Personal communication. August 21.

———. 1995. Personal communication. January 21.

Custen, George. 1992. *Bio/Pics: How Hollywood Constructed Public History*. New Brunswick, N. J.: Rutgers University Press.

Dance, Stanley. 1967. Liner notes to *The Ellington Era, 1927–1940* (Columbia).

———. 1970. *The World of Duke Ellington*. New York: Scribners.

———. 1993. Review of *The Complete Decca Studio Recordings by Louis Armstrong and the All Stars* (Mosaic). *Jazz Times* November:64.

Daniel, Jamie Owen. 1989–90. "Introduction to Adorno's 'On Jazz.'" *Discourse* 12, no. 1:39–44.

Darrell, R. D. 1932. "Black Beauty." *disques* June:152–61.

Davis, Francis. 1992a. "Dick Gregory's 1st Jazz Film." *Philadelphia Inquirer* June 18:D1, D19.

————. 1992b. "Lester Leaps In: The Difficult Life of the First Jazz Modernist." *TLS* June 12:16.

Davis, Miles, with Quincy Troupe. 1989. *Miles: The Autobiography.* New York: Simon and Schuster.

De Certeau, Michel. 1984. *The Practice of Everyday Life.* Trans. Stephen Rendell. Berkeley: University of California Press.

Derrida, Jacques. 1981. "Plato's Pharmacy." In *Disseminations,* trans. Barbara Johnson. Chicago: University of Chicago Press.

Desser, David. 1991. "The Cinematic Melting Pot: Ethnicity, Jews, and Psychoanalysis." In *Unspeakable Images: Ethnicity and the American Cinema,* ed. Lester D. Friedman, 379–403. Urbana: University of Illinois Press.

DeVeaux, Scott. 1991. "Constructing the Jazz Tradition: Jazz Historiography." *Black American Literature Forum* 25, no. 3: 525–60.

DiPiero, Thomas. 1991. "The Patriarch Is Not (Just) a Man." *Camera Obscura* 25–26:101–24.

Doherty, Thomas. 1988. *Teenagers and Teenpics: The Juvenilization of American Movies in the 1950s.* Boston: Unwin Hyman.

Dyer, Richard. 1981. "Entertainment and Utopia." In *Genre: The Musical,* ed. Rick Altman, 179–89. London: Routledge and Kegan Paul.

Early, Gerald. 1989. *Tuxedo Junction: Essays on American Culture.* New York: Ecco Press.

Eisler, Hanns [and Theodor Adorno]. 1947. *Composing for Films.* New York: Oxford University Press.

Ellington, Duke. 1973. *Music Is My Mistress.* Garden City, N. Y.: Doubleday.

Ellington, Mercer, with Stanley Dance. 1978. *Duke Ellington in Person: An Intimate Memoir.* Boston: Houghton Mifflin.

Ellison, Ralph. 1964. "Change the Joke and Slip the Yoke." In *Shadow and Act,* 61–73. New York: Random.

Elworth, Steven B. 1995. "Jazz in Crisis, 1948–1958: Ideology and Representation." In Gabbard 1995a, 57–75.

Ephland, John. 1988. "Miles: The Interview." *Down Beat* 55, no. 10 (December):18.

Erenberg, Lewis A. 1989. "Things to Come: Swing Bands, Bebop, and the Rise of a Postwar Jazz Scene." In *Recasting America: Culture and Politics in the Age of the Cold War,* ed. Lary May, 221–45. Chicago: University of Chicago Press.

Erens, Patricia. 1984. *The Jew in American Cinema.* Bloomington: Indiana University Press.

Fadiman, Clifton. 1943. "Foreword." In *Young Man with a Horn,* by Dorothy Baker. New York: Readers Club.

Feather, Leonard, and Ira Gitler. 1976. *The Encyclopedia of Jazz in the Seventies.* New York: Horizon.

Feather, Leonard. 1959. *The Book of Jazz.* New York: Meridien.

————. 1979. Liner notes to Billie Holiday, *Fine and Mellow* (Commodore).

Ferguson, Otis. 1982. *The Otis Ferguson Reader,* ed. Dorothy Chamberlain and Robert Wilson. Highland Park, Ill.: December Press.

Feuer, Jane. 1993. *The Hollywood Musical.* 2d ed. Bloomington: Indiana University Press.

Finkelstein, Sidney. [1948] 1988. *Jazz: A People's Music.* New York: International Publishers.

Firestone, Ross. 1993. *Swing, Swing, Swing: The Life and Times of Benny Goodman.* New York: Norton.

Flender, Harold. 1957. *Paris Blues.* New York: Dutton.

Flinn, Caryl. 1992. *Strains of Utopia: Gender, Nostalgia, and Hollywood Film Music.* Princeton, N. J.: Princeton University Press.

Foster, Morrison. [1896] 1932. *My Brother Stephen.* Indianapolis, Ind.: Foster Hall.

Foster, Pops, with Tom Stoddard. 1971. *The Autobiography of a New Orleans Jazzman.* Berkeley: University of California Press.

Fredrickson, George M. 1971. "The Negro As Beast." In *The Black Image in the White Mind,* 256–82. New York: Harper.

Friedman, Lester. 1982. *Hollywood's Image of the Jew.* New York: Ungar.

Gabbard, Krin, and Glen O. Gabbard. 1987. *Psychiatry and the Cinema.* Chicago: University of Chicago Press.

Gabbard, Krin. 1991. "The Quoter and His Culture." In *Jazz in Mind: Essays on the History and Meanings of Jazz,* ed. Reginald T. Buckner and Steven Weiland, 92–111. Detroit: Wayne State University Press.

———, ed. 1995a. *Jazz Among the Discourses.* Durham, N. C.: Duke University Press, 1995.

———, ed. 1995b. *Representing Jazz.* Durham, N. C.: Duke University Press.

Gabler, Neal. 1988. *An Empire of Their Own: How the Jews Invented Hollywood.* New York: Crown.

Garber, Frederick. 1995. "Fabulating Jazz." In Gabbard 1995b, 70–103.

Garrod, Charles, and Bill Korst. 1990. *Kay Kyser and His Orchestra.* Zephyrhills, Fla.: Joyce Record Club.

Gates, Henry Louis, Jr. 1988. *The Signifying Monkey: A Theory of Afro-American Literary Criticism.* New York: Oxford University Press.

———. 1989. "Canon-Formation, Literary History, and the Afro-American Tradition: From the Seen to the Told." In *Afro-American Literary Study in the 1990s,* ed. Houston A. Baker, Jr., and Patricia Redmond, 14–39. Chicago: University of Chicago Press.

———. 1991. "Final Cut: Spike Lee and Henry Louis Gates, Jr., Rap on Race, Politics, and Black Cinema." *Transition* 52: 176–204.

Gendron, Bernard. 1986. "Theodor Adorno Meets the Cadillacs." In *Studies in Entertainment: Critical Approaches to Mass Culture,* ed. Tania Modleski, 18–38. Bloomington: Indiana University Press.

———. 1993. "Moldy Figs and Modernists: Jazz at War (1942–1946)." *Discourse* 15, no. 3:130–57. Rpt. in Gabbard 1995a, 31–56.

———. 1994. "A Short Stay in the Sun: The Reception of Bebop (1944–1950)." *Library Chronicle* 24, no. 1–2:137–59.

Gennari, John. 1991. "Jazz Criticism: Its Development and Ideologies." *Black American Literature Forum* 25, no. 3:449–523.

Genette, Gerard. 1982. *Figures of Literary Discourse*. Trans. Alan Sheridan. New York: Columbia University Press.

Giddins, Gary. 1977. "Jazz Is Back on Films, Too." *Village Voice* October 31:53.

————. 1985. "Miles's Wiles." In *Rhythm-a-ning: Jazz Tradition and Innovation in the '80s*, 78–85. New York: Oxford University Press.

————. 1988. *Satchmo*. New York: Doubleday.

————. 1992. *Faces in the Crowd*. New York: Oxford University Press.

Gillespie, Dizzy, with Al Fraser. 1979. *To Be or Not to Bop*. Garden City, N. Y.: Doubleday.

Gioia, Ted. 1988. *The Imperfect Art*. New York: Oxford University Press.

Gleason, Ralph J. 1975. "Louis Armstrong." In *Celebrating the Duke and Louis, Bessie, Billie, Bird, Carmen, Miles, Dizzy and Other Heroes*, 33–61. Boston: Little, Brown.

Goffin, Robert. [1944] 1975. *Jazz: From the Congo to the Metropolitan*. Trans. Walter Schaap and Leonard G. Feather. New York: Da Capo.

Goldberg, Isaac. 1931. *George Gershwin*. New York: Simon and Schuster.

Goldman, Herbert G. 1988. *Jolson: The Legend Comes to Life*. New York: Oxford University Press.

Gorbman, Claudia. 1987. *Unheard Melodies: Narrative Film Music*. Bloomington: Indiana University Press.

Gourse, Leslie. 1984. *Louis' Children: American Jazz Singers*. New York: Quill.

————. 1991. *Unforgettable: The Life and Mystique of Nat King Cole*. New York: St. Martin's Press.

Grant, Barry Keith. 1989. "'Jungle Nights in Harlem': Jazz, Ideology and the Animated Cartoon." *University of Hartford Studies in Literature* 21, no. 3:3–12.

————. 1995. "Purple Passages or Fiestas in Blue?: Notes Toward an Aesthetic of Vocalese." In Gabbard 1995b, 285–303.

Gretton, Viveca. 1990. "You Could Look It Up: Notes Towards a Reading of Baseball, History, and Ideology in the Dominant Cinema." *CineAction* 21–22:70–75.

Grossberg, Lawrence, Cary Nelson, and Paula Treichler, eds. 1992. *Cultural Studies*. New York: Routledge.

Guerrero, Ed. 1993. *Framing Blackness: The African American Image in Film*. Philadelphia: Temple University Press.

Guillory, John. 1990. "Canon." In *Critical Terms for Literary Study*, ed. Frank Lentricchia and Thomas McLaughlin, 233–49. Chicago: University of Chicago Press.

Hajdu, David. 1994. Personal communication. May 11.

————. 1996. *Lush Life: Billy Strayhorn—A Story of Jazz and Cocktails*. New York: Farrar, Straus and Giroux.

Hall, Stuart. 1981. "Notes on Deconstructing 'the Popular.'" In *People's History and Socialist Theory*, ed. Raphael Samuel, 232–45. London: Routledge and Kegan Paul.

Hansen, Miriam. 1981–82. "Introduction to Adorno, 'Transparencies on Film' (1966)." *New German Critique* 24–25 (Fall–Winter):186–98.

Harris, Michael W. 1994. *The Rise of Gospel Blues: The Music of Thomas Andrew Dorsey.* New York: Oxford University Press.

Harris, Tom. 1994. Personal communication. November 10.

Haskins, James, with Kathleen Benson. 1990. *Nat King Cole: A Personal and Professional Biography.* Chelsea, Mich.: Scarborough House.

Hasse, John Edward. 1993. *Beyond Category: The Life and Genius of Duke Ellington.* New York: Simon and Schuster.

Hebdige, Dick. 1979. *Subculture: The Meaning of Style.* New York: Methuen.

———. 1987. *Hiding in the Light.* London: Methuen.

Helland, Dave. 1990. "Wynton: Prophet in Standard Time." *Down Beat* 57, no. 9 (September):16.

Heller, Franklin. 1986. Videotape of interview with Loring Mandel on *Studio One Video History.* Available at Museum of Television and Radio, New York City.

Hewitt, Roger. 1983. "Black Through White: Hoagy Carmichael and the Cultural Reproduction of Racism." *Popular Music* 3:33–50.

Hoberman, J. 1991a. "The Show Biz Messiah." In *Vulgar Modernism: Writing on Movies and Other Media,* 64–68. Philadelphia: Temple University Press.

———. 1991b. *Bridge of Light: Yiddish Film Between Two Worlds.* New York: Museum of Modern Art.

Hodeir, André. 1956. *Jazz: Its Evolution and Essence.* New York: Grove Press.

Holdenfield, Chris. 1977. "*New York, New York:* Martin Scorsese's Back-Lot Sonata." *Rolling Stone* June 16:36–44.

Holiday, Billie, with William T. Dufty. 1956. *Lady Sings the Blues.* Garden City, N. Y.: Doubleday.

Holley, Eugene, Jr. 1990. "The Black Director and the Sinner Jazzman." *Pulse!* September:54.

Holmes, John Clellon. [1958] 1988. *The Horn.* New York: Thunders Mouth.

hooks, bell, and Isaac Julien. 1991. "States of Desire." *Transition* no. 53:168–84.

Huyssen, Andreas. 1986. *After the Great Divide: Modernism, Mass Culture, Postmodernism.* Bloomington: Indiana University Press.

James, David. 1990. "Rock and Roll in Representations of the Invasion of Vietnam." *Representations* 29:78–98.

Jameson, Fredric. 1990. *Signatures of the Visible.* New York: Routledge.

Jarrett, Michael. 1994. Personal communication. September 14.

———. 1995. "The Tenor's Vehicle: Reading *Way Out West.*" In Gabbard 1995b, 260–82.

———. 1996. *Drifting on a Read: Jazzography and Heuretics.* Durham, N. C.: Duke University Press (forthcoming).

Jenkins, Henry. 1992a. *Textual Poachers: Television Fans and Patricipatory Culture.* New York: Routledge.

———. 1992b. *What Made Pistachio Nuts? Early Sound Comedy and the Vaudeville Aesthetic.* New York: Columbia University Press.

Jewell, Derek. 1977. *Duke: A Portrait of Duke Ellington.* New York: Norton.

Jost, François. 1987. *L'Oeil-camera: entre film et roman.* Lyon: Presses universitaires de Lyon.

Kalinak, Kathryn. 1992. *Settling the Score: Music and the Classical Hollywood Cinema.* Madison: University of Wisconsin Press.

Kaplan, E. Ann. 1978. "The Place of Women in Fritz Lang's *The Blue Gardenia*." In *Women in Film Noir,* ed. E. Ann Kaplan. London: British Film Institute.

Keightley, Keir. 1994. "Singing, Suffering, Sinatra: Articulations of Masculinity and Femininity in the Career of Frank Sinatra, 1953–1962." Unpublished paper delivered at the Society for Cinema Studies Conference, Syracuse University, March.

Kenney, William Howland. 1991. "Negotiating the Color Line: Louis Armstrong's Autobiographies." In *Jazz in Mind: Essays on the History and Meanings of Jazz,* ed. Reginald T. Buckner and Steven Weiland, 38–59. Detroit: Wayne State University Press.

Kernfeld, Barry, ed. 1988. *The New Grove Dictionary of Jazz.* 2 vols. London: Macmillan.

Klett, C. James. 1988. Personal communication. January 29.

Knee, Adam. 1995. "Doubling, Music, and Race in *Cabin in the Sky*." In Gabbard 1995b, 193–204.

Knight, Arthur. 1995. "*Jammin' the Blues,* or The Sight of Jazz, 1944." In Gabbard 1995b, 11–53.

"Kyser Draws World Record Dance Crowd." 1943. *Down Beat* August 15:1.

"Kyser's Komplaint." 1943. *Newsweek* March 22:83.

Lambert, Constant. 1934. *Music, Ho!* London: Faber and Faber.

Lee, Spike, with Lisa Jones. 1990. Mo' Better Blues: *The Companion Volume to the Universal Pictures Film.* New York: Fireside.

Leonard, Neil. 1962. *Jazz and the White Americans: The Acceptance of a New Art Form.* Chicago: University of Chicago Press.

Levine, Lawrence W. 1988. *Highbrow/Lowbrow: The Emergence of Cultural Hierarchy in America.* Cambridge, Mass.: Harvard University Press.

López, Ana M. 1991. "Are All Latins from Manhattan? Hollywood, Ethnography, and Cultural Colonialism." In *Unspeakable Images: Ethnicity and the American Cinema,* ed. Lester D. Friedman, 404–24. Urbana: University of Illinois Press.

Lott, Eric. 1993. *Love and Theft: Blackface Minstrelsy and the American Working Class.* New York: Oxford University Press.

McCarthy, Albert. 1968. "Fletcher Henderson." In *Jazz on Record: A Critical Guide to the First 50 Years,* by Albert McCarthy, Alun Morgan, Paul Oliver and Max Harrison, 128–30. London: Hanover Books.

McClary, Susan. 1991. *Feminine Endings: Music, Gender, and Sexuality.* Minneapolis: University of Minnesota Press.

McClelland, Doug. 1987. *Blackface to Blacklist: Al Jolson, Larry Parks, and "The Jolson Story."* Metuchen, N. J.: Scarecrow Press.

McDowell, Deborah E. 1980. "New Directions for Black Feminist Criticism." *Black American Literature Forum* 14, no. 4:153–59.

McNeil, Alex. 1980. *Total Television: A Comprehensive Guide to Programming from 1948 to 1980.* New York: Penguin.

Major, Clarence, ed. 1994. *Juba to Jive: A Dictionary of African-American Slang.* New York: Viking.

Maltin, Leonard. 1976. "A Guide to Available Jazz Films." In *The Encyclopedia of Jazz in the Seventies*, by Leonard Feather and Ira Gitler, 382–86. New York: Horizon.

———. 1994. *Leonard Maltin's Movie and Video Guide, 1995*. New York: Signet.

Mandel, Howard. 1994. "Cutting It." *Sight and Sound* n.s. 4, no. 3 (March):11.

Mast, Gerald. 1982. *Howard Hawks, Storyteller*. New York: Oxford.

Mayne, Judith. 1993. *Cinema and Spectatorship*. New York: Routledge.

Meeker, David. 1981. *Jazz in the Movies*. Enlarged ed. New York: Da Capo.

Meltzer, David, ed. 1993. *Reading Jazz*. San Francisco: Mercury House.

Metz, Christian. 1982. *The Imaginary Signifier: Psychoanalysis and the Cinema*. Trans. Celia Britton et al. Bloomington: Indiana University Press.

Mitchell, W. J. T., ed. 1981. *On Narrative*. Chicago: University of Chicago Press.

Modleski, Tania. 1986. "Femininity as Mas(s)querade: A Feminist Approach to Mass Culture." In *High Theory/Low Culture*, ed. Colin MacCabe, 37–52. New York: St. Martin's.

———. 1988. *The Women Who Knew Too Much: Hitchcock and Feminist Theory*. New York: Methuen.

Morgenstern, Dan. 1972. Liner notes to *Louis Armstrong V. S. O. P.* (Columbia).

Mulvey, Laura. 1975. "Visual Pleasure and Narrative Cinema." *Screen* 16, no. 3:6–18.

———. 1989. *Visual and Other Pleasures*. Bloomington: Indiana University Press.

Munden, Kenneth W., ed. 1971. *The American Film Institute Catalog of Motion Pictures Produced in the United States: Feature Films, 1921–1930*. New York: R. R. Bowker.

Murray, Albert. 1976. *Stomping the Blues*. New York: McGraw-Hill.

Naremore, James. 1992. "Uptown Folk: Blackness and Entertainment in *Cabin in the Sky*." *Arizona Quarterly* 48, no. 4:99–124. Rpt. in Gabbard 1995b, 169–92.

———. 1993. *The Films of Vincente Minnelli*. Cambridge: Cambridge University Press.

"New Word for Jazz Worth $1,000." 1949. *Down Beat* June 15:10.

O'Meally, Robert. 1991. *Lady Day: The Many Faces of Billie Holiday*. Boston: Little, Brown.

Ondaatje, Michael. 1976. *Coming Through Slaughter*. New York: Norton.

Osgood, Henry O. 1926. *So This Is Jazz*. Boston: Little, Brown.

Panassié, Hugues. 1971. *Louis Armstrong*. New York: Scribner's.

Parker, Chris, ed. 1986. *B Flat, Bebop, Scat: Jazz Short Stories and Poems*. London: Quartet Books.

Partridge, Eric. 1968. *Shakespeare's Bawdy: A Literary and Psychological Essay and a Comprehensive Glossary*. Rev. ed. London: Routledge and Kegan Paul.

Pepper, Art, and Laurie Pepper. 1979. *Straight Life: The Story of Art Pepper*. New York: Schirmer.

Piazza, Tom. 1988. "Black and Tan Fantasy." *New Republic* July 11:39.

Porter, Lewis. 1991. Review of *The Swing Era: The Development of Jazz, 1930–1945*, by Gunther Schuller. *Annual Review of Jazz Studies* 5:183–200.

Preminger, Otto. 1977. *Preminger: An Autobiography.* Garden City, N. Y.: Doubleday.

Radano, Ronald M. 1992. Personal communication. January 6.

Rancour-Laferriere, Daniel. 1979. "Some Semiotic Aspects of the Human Penis." *Versus* 24:37–82.

Rasula, Jed. 1995. "The Media of Memory: The Seductive Menace of Records in Jazz History." In Gabbard 1995a, 134–62.

Ray, Robert B. 1985. *A Certain Tendency of the Hollywood Cinema, 1930–1980.* Princeton, N. J.: Princeton University Press.

Reid, Mark A. 1988. "*A Man Called Adam.*" *Black Film Review* 4, no. 2 (Spring):15, 19.

Richolson, Janice Mosier. 1991. "He's Gotta Have It: An Interview with Spike Lee." *Cineaste* 18, no. 4 (December):12–15.

Roberts, Shari. 1995. *Seeing Stars: Feminine Spectacle, Female Spectators, and World War II Hollywood Musicals.* Durham, N. C.: Duke University Press

Robertson, James C. 1993. *The Casablanca Man: The Cinema of Michael Curtiz.* New York: Routledge.

Rogin, Michael. 1992a. "Blackface, White Noise: The Jewish Jazz Singer Finds His Voice." *Critical Inquiry* 18:417–53.

———. 1992b. "Making America Home: Racial Masquerade and Ethnic Assimilation in the Transition to Talking Pictures." *Journal of American History* 79, no. 3:1050–77.

Rosenblatt, Samuel. 1954. *Yoselle Rosenblatt: The Story of His Life as Told By His Son.* New York: Farrar, Straus and Young.

Ross, Andrew. 1989. *No Respect: Intellectuals and Popular Culture.* New York: Routledge.

Rust, Brian. 1978. *Jazz Records: 1897–1942.* 4th ed. New Rochelle, N. Y.: Arlington House.

Sadie, Stanley, and H. Wiley Hitchcock, eds. 1986. *The New Grove Dictionary of American Music.* London: Macmillan.

Sales, Grover. 1984. *Jazz: America's Classical Music.* Englewood Cliffs, N. J.: Prentice-Hall.

Sapoznik, Henry, with Pete Sokolow. 1987. *The Compleat Klezmer.* Cedarhurst, N. Y.: Tara Publications.

Sayre, Nora. 1982. *Running Time: Films of the Cold War.* New York: Dial.

Schönherr, Ulrich. 1991. "Adorno and Jazz: Reflections on a Failed Encounter." *Telos* 87:85–96.

Schuller, Gunther. 1968. *Early Jazz: Its Roots and Musical Development.* New York: Oxford University Press.

———. 1989. *The Swing Era: The Development of Jazz, 1930–1945.* New York: Oxford University Press.

Scorsese, Martin. 1978. "Martin Scorsese's Guilty Pleasures." *Film Comment* 14, no. 5 (September–October):63–66.

———. 1993. Oral commentary on "Deluxe Collector's Edition" of *New York, New York* (laser disc). MGM/UA Home Video.

Self, Robert T. 1995. "Adapting Centers Elsewhere/13 Short Cuts: 'Raymond

Carver' and 'Robert Altman.'" Unpublished paper delivered at the Florida State University Conference on Literature and Film, Tallahassee, January.

Seroff, Victor I. 1953. *Maurice Ravel.* New York: Henry Holt.

Sharma, Shailja. 1996. "Citizens of the Empire: Historiography and the Social Imaginary in *Gandhi.*" *The Velvet Light Trap* (forthcoming).

Shaw, Sam. 1994. Personal communication. August 17.

Silverman, Kaja. 1983. *The Subject of Semiotics.* New York: Oxford University Press.

———. 1988. "Masochism and Male Subjectivity." *Camera Obscura* 17 (May):31–67.

Simon, George T. 1981. *The Big Bands.* 4th ed. New York: Schirmer.

Smith, Barbara Herrnstein. 1981. "Narrative Versions, Narrative Theories." In Mitchell 1981, 209–32.

———. 1988. *Contingencies of Value.* Cambridge, Mass.: Harvard University Press.

Smith, Charles Edward. 1939. "White New Orleans." In *Jazzmen,* ed. Fredric Ramsey, Jr., and Charles Edward Smith, 39–58. New York: Harcourt Brace.

Smith, Ernie. 1988. "Films." In *The New Grove Dictionary of Jazz,* ed. Barry Kernfeld, I:375–86. London: Macmillan.

Smith, Jeff. 1995. "The Sounds of Commerce: Popular Film Music from 1960 to 1973." Ph.D. diss., University of Wisconsin.

Smith, Paul. 1993. *Clint Eastwood: A Cultural Production.* Minneapolis: University of Minnesota Press.

Spence, Kenneth C. 1988. "Jazz Digest." *Film Comment* 24, no. 6 (December):38–43.

Stam, Robert, and Louise Spence. 1985. "Colonialism, Racism, and Representation: An Introduction." In *Movies and Methods, Volume II,* ed. Bill Nichols, 632–49. Berkeley: University of California Press.

Stearns, Marshall W. [1956] 1970. *The Story of Jazz.* New York: Oxford University Press.

Stewart, Rex. 1972. *Jazz Masters of the 30s.* New York: Macmillan.

———. 1991. *Boy Meets Horn,* ed. Claire P. Gordon. Ann Arbor: University of Michigan Press.

Stewart, Robert. 1993. "Reimagining Raymond Carver on Film: A Talk with Robert Altman and Tess Gallagher." *New York Times Book Review* September 12:3, 41–42.

Stowe, David W. 1994. *Swing Changes: Big-Band Jazz in New Deal America.* Cambridge, Mass.: Harvard University Press.

Stratemann, Klaus. 1992. *Duke Ellington Day by Day and Film by Film.* Copenhagen: Jazz Media.

Studlar, Gaylyn. 1988. *In the Realm of Pleasure: Von Sternberg, Dietrich and the Masochistic Aesthetic.* Urbana: University of Illinois Press.

Sudhalter, Richard M., Philip R. Evans, and William Dean Myatt. 1974. *Bix: Man and Legend.* New York: Schirmer.

"Sully Mason Marries for 12th Time." 1942. *Down Beat* February 15:42.

Szwed, John F. 1975. "Race and the Embodiment of Culture." *Ethnicity* 2, no. 1:19–33.

Thomson, Virgil. 1981. "Swing Music." *A Virgil Thomson Reader,* 28–32. New York: Dutton.

Thompson, David, and Ian Christie, eds. 1989. *Scorsese on Scorsese.* London: Faber and Faber.

Tomlinson, Gary. 1991. "Cultural Dialogics and Jazz: A White Historian Signifies." *Black Music Research Journal* 11, no. 2:229–64. Rpt. in *Disciplining Music: Musicology and Its Canons,* ed. Katherine Bergeron and Philip V. Bohlman, 64–94. Chicago: University of Chicago Press, 1992.

Traver, Robert. 1958. *Anatomy of a Murder.* New York: St. Martin's.

Tucker, Mark. 1991. *Ellington: The Early Years.* Urbana: University of Illinois Press.

———, ed. 1993a. *The Duke Ellington Reader.* New York: Oxford University Press.

———. 1993b. "The Renaissance Education of Duke Ellington." In *Black Music in the Harlem Renaissance,* ed. Samuel A. Floyd, Jr., 111–27. Knoxville: University of Tennessee Press.

———. 1993c. "The Genesis of *Black, Brown and Beige.*" *Black Music Research Journal* 13, no. 2:67–86.

Tynan, John. 1961. "Paris Blues." *Down Beat* November 23:16.

Ulanov, Barry. [1946] 1975. *Duke Ellington.* New York: Da Capo.

Van de Leur, Walter. 1994. Personal communication. June 8.

Vasvari, Louise O. 1994. "*L'usignuolio in gabbia:* Popular Tradition and Pornographic Parody in the *Decameron.*" *Forum Italicum* 28, no. 2: 224–51.

Walker, Janet. 1993. *Couching Resistance: Women, Film, and Psychoanalytic Psychiatry.* Minneapolis: University of Minnesota Press.

Wallace, Michele. 1990. "Michael Jackson, Black Modernisms and 'The Ecstasy of Communication.'" In *Invisibility Blues: From Pop to Theory,* 77–90. New York: Verso.

Walser, Robert. 1995. "'Out of Notes': Signification, Interpretation, and the Problem of Miles Davis." In Gabbard 1995a, 165–81.

Welburn, Ron. 1989. "The American Jazz Writer-Critic of the 1930s." *Jazzforschung/Jazz Research* 21:83–94.

Welsford, Enid. [1935] 1966. *The Fool: His Social and Literary History.* Cambridge, Mass.: Harvard University Press.

West, Cornel. 1990. "New Cultural Politics of Difference." *October* 53:93–109.

Westerberg, Hans. 1981. *Boy from New Orleans: Louis "Satchmo" Armstrong on Records, Films, Radio and Television.* Copenhagen: Jazz Media.

Wexman, Virgina Wright. 1993. *Creating the Couple: Love, Marriage, and Hollywood Performance.* Princeton, N. J.: Princeton University Press.

Whitehead, Kevin. 1992. Review of *Unforgettable: The Life and Mystique of Nat King Cole,* by Leslie Gourse. *Cadence* 18, no. 1 (January):24.

Williams, Linda. 1989. *Hard Core: Power, Pleasure, and the "Frenzy of the Visible."* Berkeley: University of California Press.

Williams, Martin. 1983. *The Jazz Tradition.* Rev. ed. Oxford: Oxford University Press.

———. 1985. *Jazz Heritage.* Oxford: Oxford University Press.

Williams, Raymond. 1983. *Keywords: A Vocabulary of Culture and Society.* New York: Oxford University Press.

Willis, Sharon. 1991. Comments on "A World Without Whole Notes: The Intellectual Subtext of Spike Lee's *Blues,*" by Jim Merod. *Boundary 2* 18, no. 2 (Summer):250.

Wiseman, Rich. 1987. *Neil Diamond, Solitary Star.* New York: Dodd, Mead.

Woolley, Stan. 1995. "Pete Rugolo: Reel Jazz." *Jazz Journal International* 48, no. 4 (April):10–11.

Wood, Michael. 1975. *America at the Movies.* New York: Basic Books.

Wood, Robin. 1968. *Howard Hawks.* London: Secker and Warburg.

Ya Salaam, Kalamu. 1990. "*Mo' Better Blues:* The Movie." *Black Film Review* 6, no. 2:12–13.

"Your Automatic Hostess Selects the Most Played Records!" 1942. *Down Beat* September 1:9.

INDEX

Unless otherwise noted, titles in italics refer to films.